Noise, Water, Meat

A History of Sound in the Arts

Douglas Kahn

The MIT Press   Cambridge, Massachusetts   London, England

First MIT Press paperback, 2001
© 1999 Massachusetts Intitute of Technology

This book was set in Janson and Rotis Semi Sans by Graphic Composition, Inc. and was printed and bound in the United States of America.

Library of Congress Cataloging-in-Publication Data

Kahn, Douglas, 1951–
   Noise, water, meat: a history of sound in the arts / Douglas Kahn.
     p. cm.
   Includes bibliographical references and index.
   ISBN 0-262-11243-4 (hc: alk. paper), 0-262-61172-4 (pb)
    1. Sound in art.   2. Arts, Modern—20th century.   I. Title.
NX650.S68K25   1999
700—dc21

98-51886
CIP

To Fran, Aleisha, and Sy.
All at once.

And to the memory
of my dear father.

Contents

Acknowledgments

There are a number of key individuals whom I would like to acknowledge. Some may have thought they were merely engaging in conversation, but they were unwittingly contributing to this text, while others could have had no illusions about wrestling with the manuscript. In chronological order: Alvin Lucier, Ron Kuivila, Mitchell Clark, Mladen Milicevic, Daniel Wolf, Dan Lander, Heidi Grundmann, Margaret Morse, Mel Gordon, Gregory Whitehead, Ken Sitz, Paul DeMarinis, Arthur Sabatini, Laura Kuhn, Christian Marclay, Ellen Zweig, Dick Higgins, Gerald Hartnett, Norie Neumark, Virginia Madsen, Martin Harrison, Adam Lucas, Paul Carter, and Sean Cubitt. I am particularly indebted to Jane Goodall, whose book *Artaud and the Gnostic Drama* (Oxford University Press, 1994) makes a great gift idea and who selflessly fielded my every phone call, and to Helen Grace, my doctoral supervisor, whose special expertise in Russian Revolutionary cinema was icing on the cake to wide-ranging discussions on things art historical. In a different way I am indebted to the tutelage of Charles Amirkhanian's radio programs long ago while he was at KPFA-FM in Berkeley, the organological research of Hugh Davies, and the writings of Michael Nyman, who so deftly worked the art-music nexus. I would also like to acknowledge several individuals at *The Listening Room* of ABC Radio in Sydney, including Roz Cheney, Robin Ravlich, Tony MacGregor, and Andrew McLennan. Special thanks goes to the Faculty of Performance, Fine Arts and Design, University of Western Sydney, Nepean, and to the Faculty of Humanities and Social Sciences, University of Technology, Sydney. My deepest appreciation goes to both Roger Conover at MIT Press for his encouragement over the years and to Christopher Schiff, an inexhaustible font of knowledge and irreverence (who else working at

Shorty's Barbecue was reading hieroglyphics?). Finally, I would like to note my good fortune of meeting not so many years ago one of the few artist-theorists of sound and new media, Frances Dyson, whose background in philosophy has been both a complement and challenge to mine in history. Above all, she is responsible for my greatest good fortune since we are together to this day, with our wonderful children Aleisha and Sy Samuel. Many of the ideas in this book are no doubt hers, although I have lost track. She can have any she wants.

Noise, Water, Meat

Introduction

Listening through History

Sound saturates the arts of this century, and its importance becomes evident if we can hear past the presumption of mute visuality within art history, past the matter of music that excludes references to the world, past the voice that is already its own source of existence, past the phonetic task-mastering of writing, and past what we might see as hearing. None of the arts is entirely mute, many are unusually soundful despite their apparent silence, and the traditionally auditive arts grow to sound quite different when included in an array of auditive practices. The century becomes more mellifluous and raucous through historiographic listening, just that much more animated with the inclusion of the hitherto muffled regions of the sensorium. Yet these sounds do not exist merely to sonorize the historical scene; they are also a means through which to investigate issues of cultural history and theory, including those that have been around for some time, existing behind the peripheral vision and selective audition of established fields of study. Indeed, many issues have not been addressed precisely because they have not been heard. Thus, the dual task here is to listen through history to sound and through sound to history—in particular, the history of sound in artistic modernism, the avant-garde, and experimental and postmodern points beyond, from the latter half of the nineteenth century into the 1960s, shifting from a largely European context to an American one. Reconstituting the auditory dimension can pry open the century to question and, ideally, better attune us to the changing conditions of aurality and artistic possibilities for sound in our own time.

The book concentrates on the *generation* of modernist and postmodernist techniques and tropes among artistic practices and discourses. Some are soundful in themselves; others are contingent on ideas of sound, voice, and aurality.[1] As products of the new possibilities for hearing and as functional constraints for actually doing so, these techniques and tropes pertain to three main practical areas: the early development of sound within and across artistic practices, the response and accommodation of sound within artistic practices, and the use of ideas of sound within the development of important tropes within the arts. It would be a mistake to put too much stock in abstract categories because when they are examined in their historical contexts, techniques, tropes, and practices overlap, mediate and influence one another, and, most important, alternate quickly and exist simultaneously. The main ones discussed here are noise, auditive immersion in spatial and psychological domains, inscription and visual sound, the universalism of *all sound* and panaurality, musicalization of sound, phonographic reproduction and imitation, Cagean silence, nondissipative sounds and voices, fluidity at the nexus of performance and objecthood, William Burroughs's virus, and the bodily utterances of Michael McClure's beast language and Antonin Artaud's screaming.

By *sound* I mean *sounds, voices, and aurality*—all that might fall within or touch on auditive phenomena, whether this involves actual sonic or auditive events or ideas about sound or listening; sounds actually heard or heard in myth, idea, or implication; sounds heard by everyone or imagined by one person alone; or sounds as they fuse with the sensorium as a whole. It should be stated clearly at the outset that this study, although it no doubt stands in contrast to the wealth of recent material on visuality and visual culture, is not constituted in opposition to the visual image. Rudolf Arnheim in his book *Radio* (1936) was excited that "wireless claims the whole attention of the theorist of art because for the first time in the history of mankind it makes practical experiments with an entirely unexplored form of expression in pure sound, namely, blind hearing,"[2] but it would in fact be impossible to discuss sound in this way. Blind hearing, even for the blind, is a difficult proposition to sustain in a society that so thoroughly internalizes vision into every aspect of its being and in other ways integrates aspects of the sensorium with one another. Obviously, the same would apply to deaf seeing.

To hear past the historical insignificance assigned to sounds, we need to hear more than their sonic or phonic content. We need to know where they might touch the ground, momentarily perhaps, even as they dissipate in air. The terms *significant sounds* and *significant noises* are used in the first part of the book—not to differentiate these sounds and noises from insignificant or meaningless ones but to counter long-standing habits of imagining that sounds transcend or escape meaning or that sounds elude sociality despite the fact they are made, heard, imagined, and thought by humans.[3] To understand the sounds of modernism requires closer examination of how phenomena are invoked and muted by amplitude (or lack thereof) and affect. A scream, for instance, is thought to be an irrepressible expression, instantaneously understood through unmediated communication. Indeed, screams in their natural habitat usually demand and receive a direct response. However, the literary, theatrical, musical, or cinematic habitats in which modernist screams reverberated are very different. Does anyone rush to the stage to lend assistance? Art screams bank on emphasis, amplitude, and affect, but they mute significance and deafen us in other ways with their rhetorical force. The same is true for noise, which can interrupt itself as capably as what it ostensibly interrupts, and Cagean silence, which has silenced other things, as it dwells at the problematic edge of audibility and attempts to hear the world of sound without hearing aspects of the world in a sound. In short, the sound and the fury never signify nothing or, rather, just nothing. What such auditive states have proven to drown out are the social in sound—the political, poetical, and ecological— and these are what the present text seeks to reinstate.

Prelude: Modernism

Modernism has been read and looked at in detail but rarely heard. The historiographic interruption of the sound is due in part to technical difficulties. Sound inhabits its own time and dissipates quickly. Its life is too brief and ephemeral to attract much attention, let alone occupy the tangible duration favored by methods of research. Only recently in historical terms have there existed the conceptual and technological techniques available to sustain a full range of sounds outside the unstable environs of their own time. Previous recording techniques of script, musical notation, and print relied on their soundfulness to extraneous readings and performances, while pictures appeared to be most faithful to the exegetical eye. The study of artistic modernism should have an advantage in this respect, since its early days were concurrent with the advent of the phonograph. Like modernism itself the phonograph represented a new day in aurality through its ability to return virtually any sound back again and again into the sensorium and into the historical register. However, as it happened, phonography was busy recording other things besides the auditive output of artistic modernism, and, consequently, the record of recording is thin. Nevertheless, the mere existence of phonography—its ability to hold any one sound in time and keep all sounds in mind—produced a new status for hearing, which was energetically entered into libraries, laboratories, literature, artistic ideas, and philosophies.[4]

Just as the phonograph was not necessary to record its own impact, a new hearing was recorded prior to its invention in 1877. The big bang of modernist aurality might very well have occurred in 1868 with Lautréamont's *Les Chants de Maldoror*, even though the novel did not create a big noise at the time. The pivotal scene of the book, chant II, stanza 8, describes the birth of hearing. The narrator informs us that he had been born deaf and had remained deaf until he confronted a truly horrific scene, one worthy of Dante or Bosch, of an anthropophagic creature sitting on a throne of shit and gold, cloaked in filthy pestilent hospital sheets.[5] The creature was "*that* one who calls himself the Creator!"[6]

In his hand he held the decaying trunk of a man and he lifted it successively from his eyes to his nose and from his nose to his mouth, where one may guess what he did with it. His feet were bathed in a vast morass of boiling blood to the surface of which there suddenly arose like tape-worms in the contents of a chamber-pot, two or three cautious heads which disappeared instantly with the speed of arrows. . . . Like amphibians they swam between two waters in that unclean juice! And when the Creator had nothing left in his hands he would seize another swimmer by the neck with the two first claws of his foot as in a pincers and raise him up out of that ruddy slime (delicious sauce!).[7]

One person after another was pincer-plucked from this steaming paella-from-hell and summarily devoured by the huge creator creature with no regard for their pleas. He was not punishing transgression but was simply taking pleasure in the sight of his own creations' suffering. Although the deaf man's ears heard no crunching or chewing, no gagging and screaming from these fish, the bellows of his body began to wretch in front of the full horror of what he saw:

At last, my heaving bosom being unable to expel the life-giving air speedily enough, my lips opened and I cried out . . . a cry so heart-rending that I myself heard it! The obstacle in my ears snapped abruptly, the eardrum cracked beneath the shock of that mass of noisy air expelled from within me so violently, and a new phenomenon took place within that organ condemned by nature. I had heard a sound! A fifth sense was born in me![8]

The scream created his hearing, as though a cry at parturition had itself given birth. The voice and his hearing were linked for the first time, thereby completing the circularity of utterance and audition that the hearing world takes for granted, and this circuit closed off all others. His scream neither addressed the Creator nor reached the ears of his creations. It merely announced the presence of himself as a subjugated creature: "the expression of my smothered feelings in a sudden shriek, the tone of which was identical with that of my fellow creatures!"[9] He was empathetic to his fellow creatures' plight, but most immediately as a means to constituting his own identity, wherein the power of the scream to create an instantaneous social space was recuperated into a newborn self-consciousness. The circuit of utterance and audition, in other words, was not extended to a social circuit of communication. He had become aware of the presence of his voice, an act most commonly experienced by hearing one's own voice while speaking or rather by subliminally hearing one's own voice, since it is an act naturalized since birth through day-to-day use and goes by unnoticed. Because he had been deaf since birth, the accumulated years of a suppressed selfsame voice accumulated and were released in a scream at the horror of the social under the reign of the Creator, which in turn created the schismatic state of an acute awareness of self-presence.

When one speaks, the act of hearing one's own voice is the most widespread private act performed in public and the most common public act experienced within the comfortable confines of one's own body. Hearing one's own voice almost always passes by unnoticed, but once acknowledged it presents itself as a closed system remaining within the experience of the individual. The immateriality of speech itself ensures that everything will not escape the voracity of time as both voice and moment precipitously disappear. It also ensures that the voice will thus elude unwanted appropriations by others, which might steer it away from its singular ties with individual experience and ultimately result in the type of metaphysical and rhetorical discomfort that Jacques Derrida has described and perpetrated within the ranks of Western philosophy.[10]

In addition, the circuit of utterance and audition has more of a body than the bit of cheek separating the mouth from the ear. While other people hear a person's voice carried through vibrations in the air, the person speaking also hears her or his own voice as it is conducted from the throat and mouth through bone to the inner regions of the ear. Thus, the voice in its production in various regions of the body is propelled through the body, its resonance is sensed intracranially. A fuller sense of presence is experienced as the body becomes attached to thought as much as the generation of speech is attached to thought.[11] Yet at the same time that the speaker hears the voice full with the immediacy of the body, others will hear the speaker's voice infused with a lesser distribution of body because it will be a voice heard without bone conduction: a deboned voice. Where bones once stood, there will be only the air within which the voice's vibrations dissipate.[12] Thus, the presence produced by the voice will always entail a degree of delusion because of a difference in the texture of the sound: the speaker hears one voice, others hear it deboned.

Maldoror's convulsing body—the scream that was the irrepressible voice of the body—remained with Maldoror. Horror had precipitated the scream, but the scream did not return to the scene of the horror; it vanished before being heard by others, before becoming manifest in the social. The scream wrenched him away from the horror as surely as the horror itself had wrenched from his body a scream. Thus the social was lost in the sound of Maldoror's new born self-consciousness on hearing his own voice—in a fascination with the first sound, the first voice, the first word and in the emphatic sound of the scream. This conforms enough to the features of a new social shift within sound to describe modernist aurality at its own birth for, as we shall see in broad outline, the new ability to hear had the effect of attracting classes of sounds that could both invoke (or be invoked by) and silence the social.

If Lautréamont's text seems too fugitive (and it was much more obscure in its own day than it is now) for an emblematic function here, then wait a decade when Edison could be found busily reworking the same set of principles in his phonograph. Whereas Maldoror's scream created hearing in a last-ditch attempt to recuperate presence, the phonograph's discursive gears produced a veritable machine critique of the presence of the voice. No longer was the ability to hear oneself speak restricted to a fleeting moment. It became locked in a materiality that could both stand still and mute and also time travel by taking one's voice far afield from one's own presence. A new loop of utterance and audition was interjected into the existing one, which, in effect, had been stretched and broken. The voice no longer occupied its own space and time. It was removed from the body where, following Derrida, it entered the realm of writing and the realm of the social, where one loses control of the voice because it no longer disappears. From bone to air to writing, permanence outside the subject invites greater mutability, where the primacy and purity of the voice are subjected to the machinations and imaginations of culture and politics.

Because Edison's speaking machine was also a listening machine, it could reverse the loop of utterance and audition. Unlike humans it could not speak and hear simultaneously, but the displacement and delay it introduced could establish a new circularity that enabled a person to hear his or her own voice for the first time without the bones. It was a way to hear one's own voice outside the confines of presence but with a novelty reminiscent of Maldoror. This phonographic birth of hearing not only redressed the balance of utterance and audition but also introduced a new weighting in the balancing of the ear and the eye. Echoes were capable only of returning fragments or the tail-end of speech, and the voice was nearly unrecognizable because it absorbed much of the interceding space. Narcissus possessed better technology than Echo. Humans had always been able to see their own faces, see their own seeing—ever since the moment of species consciousness when some very distant relative looked into a pool. But it was not until the late nineteenth century with the phonograph that people could hear their own voices (or reasonable facsimiles thereof), if not hear their own hearing:

One can look at seeing;
one can't hear hearing.[13]

It was at this time that speech and other human utterances were subjected to forms of delay, storage, and dissemination that had previously been reserved for less ephemeral modes of communication. The singular cries of parturition became the repeated nurturing of a Promethean de-liverance. Writing had silenced the words from one's voice; phonography kept one's voice and words together but wrenched the voice from the throat and out of time. Given that, as the saying goes, you hear other people in your ears, but you hear yourself in the throat, all that had made its home in the presence of the voice was forced to become like writing and fend for itself.

Because phonography did not just hear voices—it heard everything—sounds accumulated across a discursive diapason of *one sound* and *all sound*, from isolation to totalization. It wrenched the voice from its cultural preeminence and inviolable position in the throat and equalized it with all other sounds amid exchange and inscription. With the voice fell other forms of utterance such as music (the shift arose with phonautography, since thinking about sound could rest on visualization and was not reliant on auditive reproduction). Because phonography did not simply produce sounds or ideas about sounds but produced audibility, it heard past physiological constraints to the imaginary realms of conceptual sounds, ancient and future sounds, voices of inner speech and the dead, subatomic vibrations, and so on. While war in particular provided an emphatic model for an all-encompassing *all sound*, apart from a technical promise *all sound* itself was conditioned by the ever-expanding machinations of imperialist exploits, mass culture, global militarism, scientific incursions, ideas of an infinite nature, the other world of spiritism, communications technologies, and the like. Modernism thus entailed more sounds and produced a greater emphasis on listening to things, to different things, and to more of them and on listening differently.

Phonography, therefore, existed discursively and most evidently in the idea of all-sound, even as it abandoned any immediate technological association. In this way, at the minimum, it influenced the arts long before actual technological realization could be entertained. Most notably, it was manifested in the idea of noise and music when in 1913 the Italian Futurist Luigi Russolo celebrated the entire breadth of sounds in the world in his *art of noises*. Historians attempting to explain the genesis of noise have rightly pointed to increased social raucousness of a late-arriving industrialization in Italy and to the correlation of noise with other transgressive tactics within the avant-garde at the time. However, noise also developed because of the unwillingness, inability, and awkwardness within the arts to adequately incorporate these sounds and tactics. In keeping with the conventions of Western art music at that time, Russolo rejected "imitation" and, in the end, simulated worldliness only through an expansion of timbre. What was ostensibly an autonomous art became a rejuvenation of music (quite apart from his marginalization from the musical establishment, then and now). Russolo's noise was returned to extramusical significance as it was embraced by the left-leaning avant-garde, despite the fact that what inspired him most was to be found in the all-sound and transgressiveness of military combat, especially as they aligned with the proto-fascist sensibilities of Italian Futurism.

Some of the most provocative uses of sound occurred during the heyday of the avant-garde, primarily because artists were not hampered by the problems of technological realization. By the latter half of the 1920s, the arts were suddenly better equipped, due to an audiophonic-led revolution in communications technologies involving radio, sound film, microphony, amplification, and phonography. Previously, the mere promise of technology exerted pressure on established artistic practices, but now artists were confronted with actual implementation. Defenses against technological influence became increasingly difficult to maintain as ideas became abundant, tropes were legitimated, and different realizations were developed. What did occur with audiophonic experimentation, however, never grew to the level of consistent practice, primarily because technology was not the only thing experienced during that time. There would also be global economic collapse, the consolidation and expansion of authoritarian regimes, the exile of artists and intellectuals, the Spanish Civil War, genocide, the events leading to World War II, and the war itself. A modicum of artistic life did go on in certain quarters, even in the middle of the war, as we shall see. Still, we can only imagine what would we have today if *musique concrète* had been launched two decades earlier and flourished uninterrupted, if radio art had time to experiment and mature, if an autonomous phonographic art had developed, or if asynchronous sound film in Russia had been supported and not suppressed.

Modernist sound rattled differently through the different auditive arts. Western art music was never fond of working with the imitative sound associated with phonography or, for that matter, of incorporating different classes of technology. Yet if it was to remain the art of sound and the penultimate artistic trope of the time, it would at least simulate the worldliness that modernist sound represented, if not the sound itself, in word and in deed. Once transported as a trope to other practices, it could help extricate them from noise, imitation, and other signs of worldliness, and thereby it could reproduce, disseminate, and protect itself. A fundamental destabilization in practice would have had enormous repercussions if music had lost its distinct value as a trope.

Cinema, on the other hand, was more amenable and less defensive. Not only was film sound a phonographic form, but cinema and phonography shared parentage by Thomas A. Edison. The precedents of cinema were also well rehearsed in mimetic techniques. It had grown from theater and photography, and certain trends of cinematic montage went one better by developing beyond the naturalism of "photographed theater." Cinema also provided an ample model for artistic practices that sought to work within the new world of technology. When the principles of montage were applied within the context of asynchronous sound film, sound—once it was no longer tied directly to visual images, speech, and story—was able to exist in a more complex relationship with them. In turn, once sound was no longer tied to cinema, a radical form of sound and radio art was implied. Sound also became radical once it was tightly tied to cinema in the form of animated cartoons. Not only could sound and image exist in a pronounced one-to-one relationship, but sound came first in the production process instead of being secondary or tertiary to the primacy of visual image and the limited sounds of dialogue. These developments were concurrent with other artistic acts and ideas inhabiting loose disciplinary locations defined by a three-way tension between music, cinema, and an unnamed art of phonography.

After a hiatus of the avant-garde, in the two decades following World War II an abundance of artistic activities incorporated new approaches to sound. Just as artists in the late 1920s confronted changed conditions led by the technical possibilities of audiophonic technologies, artists in the postwar period, given greater ease in access and technological realization, confronted a changed materiality of sound due to the sustained and ubiquitous social fact of these technologies. After all, there may have been a hiatus of the avant-garde, but there was no commensurate interruption of the auditive mass media. By midcentury there had been more than two decades of radio, sound film, and improved phonography, and by the end of the 1950s television and youth-oriented radio and music had insinuated themselves deeply into mass-mediated societies, summoning the din we have today. The redundancies exercised within the media resulted in an increasing accumulation of sounds as they became differentially coded, and a new facility developed for apprehending these sounds at an accelerated pace. Simply put, there were more sounds, and people could hear them more quickly.[14] Whereas many artists today have internalized this state of sound, artists during the postwar years worked between two epochs, regenerating modernist premises in dramatically different communicative conditions.

But the character of sound, voice, and aurality in the postwar years was also transformed by dramatically different social conditions, especially those impinging on the body and the environment. In the United States, the ravages of the war were registered on men's bodies instead of on its cities or countryside. The disciplining energy released by its fire bombing and atomic bombing of civilian populations in Japan echoed across its own domestic landscape in a desperate postwar abandon of affluence, suburban sprawl, and the petroleum economy—in the car culture, the paving of the landscape, electricity generation, petrochemical herbicides and pesticides, oil spills and toxic waste, and global warming. While people remained religiously transfixed, waiting for peril to be punctuated by a spectacular nuclear event, multiple repressions continued to develop under the auspices of the cold war and its "containment culture,"[15] as the earth itself underwent a slow-motion explosion due to accelerated ecological decline. Artists had long related to nature, but in the 1950s an environmentalism arose from what Michael McClure has called a politics of disappearance, evident over the course of a very few years.[16] For William Burroughs the prewar saturation of the atmosphere with Wilhelm Reich's sexualized orgone energy became confused with the fallout of above-ground testing, creating a reproduction *per se* rife with mutation. For John Cage and Jackson Pollock the fluidity they would release among the arts in the 1950s was not merely an eruption of Bachelardian elemental poetics but entailed an agency unsettled by and distinct from a commanding social determination. These factors conditioned sound, were conditioned by sound, and were in turn interdependent with communicative conditions and with the traditions and disciplinary negotiations among the arts themselves. The sounds themselves are best appreciated in close proximity to the complex conditions that gave rise to them and that, in this book, are refracted primarily through the perspective of the artists themselves.

Explanations and Qualifications

The twelve chapters of this book are grouped into five sections. Since each section bears a separate introduction, I will forgo repeating them here. The first two sections are generalist in nature and cover events in Europe and the United States from the late nineteenth century to the mid-twentieth century. They are structured either as pastiche or loose historical trackings, ending with longer treatments of specific areas—Italian Futurist noise and Russian Revolutionary film, respectively. The remaining three sections consist of detailed studies of artists in the United States (Artaud is the exception here, although his influence on American artists is not) in the two decades following midcentury. To a certain extent, the first two sections set the stage for the more in-depth studies to follow and are tied together by numerous continuities, including a cast of characters who grow increasingly familiar as they reappear throughout the book. One character in particular becomes very familiar: John Cage appears throughout the book and is the subject of an entire section. He would occupy a central position within any discussion of sound and art in this century because of the importance and influence across the arts of his music, writings, and ideas about sound throughout his long and prolific career. Moreover, like Artaud he connects the first half with the second half of the century, but unlike Artaud he lived to see the second half, almost all of it.

By ending in the late 1950s and making only scattered forays into the early 1960s, the book produces an imbalance weighted on the side of Euro-American males. The rhetorical uses of women in terms of immersion, noise, noise abatement, and other instances are examined, but the major historical participation of female artists in their own right begins just after the timeframe of the book. While there are still fruitful studies to be made of female artists in the heart of modernism—Esfir Schub or Gertrude Stein come immediately to mind—practicalities of time and resources have prevented me from attending to them.[17] Given that the European-based avant-garde has not often been appreciated for the multicultural dynamics that did exist, the predominance of transmissional themes (as opposed to inscriptive) in the international avant-garde proper, especially in its poetry, places it outside the central themes of this book. Within the American context, the achievements and influences on the rest of the arts of the musics of Charlie Parker, John Coltrane, Albert Ayler, Cecil Taylor, Ornette Coleman, and others and of African-American poetries and linguistic play are necessary for a more complete representation of aurality in the 1950s and 1960s. Within the specific topics of this book, the screaming in the last chapter needs to be joined by a chorus of saxophones. In fact, there is still much work to be done on all the activities that fall squarely within the focus of the book.

Among reasons for concentrating on the artists included here (apart from the fact that many are among the most prominent artists working with sound in the period under investigation) is that many have held the attention of many contemporary artists working with sound. Indeed, Luigi Russolo, the Dadaists, Dziga Vertov, Antonin Artaud, John Cage, William Burroughs and other Beats, the *musique concrète* composers, artists associated with Fluxus, and others in the book all enjoy solid reputations that continue to grow with each passing year. I have offered here reinterpretations and additional information on these artists and proposed others who might rightfully join this list. The history and theory of the arts are regularly used by artists in developing their own work; I have simply attempted to incorporate this fact more directly in the formation of this book. Likewise, by concentrating on the actions and statements of artists within specific conditions, especially in acknowledging the complexities involved and the artistic possibilities that stem from them both then and now, I am attempting to maintain a perspective on art making that might be of use to working and aspiring artists.

The emphasis on technique is also derived from the concerns of working artists. With respect to the many ideas of what *techniques* are, please note that in the present text they are not servants to meanings, content, reception, and social situation but are instead already infused with these very properties as artists finesse the material—conceptual, social, political, aesthetic, and poetical—in the seemingly most insignificant moments wrought within a work. The relationship of techniques to technologies is a little more complicated, since it is clear that technologies can derive from techniques (for example, sound recording from ideas of nondissipative voices) and techniques can derive from technologies (the use of fragmented syntax rationalized through simultaneity of transmissions). While the voice within the arts will always relate to techniques (for example, the mnemotechniques of orature), I would restrict its relation to auditive technologies (architectural, mechanical, electrical) to the times when they are used to modify the sonorous voice or when the voice is clearly understood to function in a technological trope—which means I would never say that the voice is a technology in and of itself. Finally, I would warn against the tendency of subsuming techniques and technologies under technology alone when the two are encountered in the same setting.

I am also responding to the prominence that recorded sound has assumed as artistic raw material since midcentury. While there has been a ready stock of references associated with such work, one of the purposes of this book is to introduce additional historical and theoretical considerations. It would be impossible to write at length about sound in the twentieth century without such an emphasis; both sound and listening have been and continue to be transformed through the cultural elaboration of technology. In fact, I work under the assumption that the history of the arts using auditive technologies, including those in concert with vision, constitute a large, rarely acknowledged portion of the history of the media arts, and while I do not draw out the implications for present-day artistic practice, I believe it would be possible to do so.

It is important to remember that technology has never been manifested in the arts in a simple way. The influence of technologies in early modernism was often registered through mislaid ideas about what actually existed or what they could do, with little regard for the state of technological development, let alone an understanding of the tough realities of institutional access. Yet such presumptions and desires often bore greater insight into the technology and spoke of greater artistic possibilities than the ideas accompanying actual implementation. On the other hand, since the 1920s and especially since midcentury, recording technologies have belonged to a larger *culture of recording* in media-saturated societies, which necessarily intercedes in any technical consideration within artistic production. This not only would pertain to patently auditive phenomena but would extend to the implications of sound within other forms of recording. In this sense, for instance, William Burroughs stands at a cantankerous cusp between older forms of phonographic inscription and those belonging to present-day digital and genetic modes.

Technologically, the book concentrates primarily on ideas of phonography, by which I mean all mechanical, optical, electrical, digital, genetic, psychotechnic, mnemonic, and conceptual means of sound recording as both technological means, empirical fact, and metaphorical incorporation, including nineteenth-century machines prior to the invention of the phonograph. Moreover, I approach phonography primarily in terms of inscription, although inscription is hardly limited to phonography. As I have written elsewhere, among the discourses of sound within the avant-garde arts (yet limited neither to sound nor to the avant-garde) three prevailing figures can be discerned through which technological tropes were directed: vibration, inscription, and transmission.[18] These figures did not originate with actual technologies but existed prior to them and were transformed by their adoption within a technological sphere. The figure of vibration was upheld by the Pythagoreans, refurbished by neo-Platonic and neo-Pythagorean thought centuries later, and invigorated by scientific, Eastern, and spiritist thought in the West in the nineteenth century. The monochord—the technology that underscored the harmonic totality of Pythagorean thought, the vibrating string structuring the cosmos—was so overcoded by the late-nineteenth century locus of vibrations in the synesthetic arts that it was functionally nonexistent, although the connections between acoustics, music, and mathematics, not to mention certain ambitions toward the cosmos, remained strong. The inscriptive attributes of phonography became coterminous with the legacies of writing, universal alphabets, and languages, as well as other inscriptive practices, while the telegraphic, telephonic, and radiophonic attributes of transmission became coterminous with a range of mythological, theological, and literary instances where the communication at a distance produced compensatory and exaggerated relationships among objects and bodies.

The book focuses on inscriptive practices (but is in no way restricted to them), whereas ideas of vibration and transmission occur only intermittently and have not been addressed directly. The book ends with a contrast between the manner in which, with Burroughs's virus, inscription has been sunk from the surface of bodies into each and every cell (a shift that itself should complicate notions about writing or inscribing on bodies), and the energetic configuration and situation of bodies and environments found in Artaud's post-Rodez work and McClure's meat science. Their use of energetic flows, derived from Eastern bodily practices and elsewhere, poses a challenge to techniques and tropes of inscription that have so strongly informed and problematized modernism and suggests that any theorization of contemporary aurality will have to take into account not only the changed status of inscription and the historical background of transmission but also a figure or phenomenon, particle and wave, capable of spatial elaboration and vice versa, which supersedes both.

On a more anecdotal level, the present writing has flowed from work initially undertaken in the mid-1980s at the World Music Program at Wesleyan University, where I studied composition with Alvin Lucier and Ron Kuivila. Wesleyan, because of its association with John Cage, was one of the few places in the United States where one could study music by first asking about the composition *of* sound prior to composition *with* sound, whereas almost everywhere else the nature of sound remained unproblematic, with attention paid instead to how it might be organized. The former admitted the possibility of attention to the sounds of the world, whereas the latter was restricted to a set of analytical and practical conventions. On undertaking an investigation into what the avant-garde meant by sound, I was surprised to find that it was repeatedly recuperated into musical sound. There was an historical unwillingness to allow certain characteristics of sound into compositional practice that contradicted the transgressive rhetoric of noise and the emancipatory claims of an openness to the world of sound, among other positions. The banishment of these characteristics was due primarily to the fact that they *signified.* Through their banishment, they became the new noises; but unlike the old noises, they brought the world with them. A position that considered signification to be the noise of noise was obviously unsatisfactory on a number of counts. It was ill adapted to understanding sound within contemporary arts, mass media, and the culture of recording, and it foreclosed too many artistic possibilities, including those available to music itself. In the course of trying to hear what was muted, the actual abundance of historical moments of sound became evident. Awkwardly situated in their original contexts, once brought into proximity with one another these moments formed a very different story about sound, voice, and aurality.

A number of other people were interested in similar questions during the mid-1980s. Nearly all of them were artists of one type or another who had grown dissatisfied with what historical, theoretical, and critical texts had made of sound and significance. Although the reigning poststructuralist and postmodern theories did little to address the issues concerning sound, they did raise expectations about the possible nature of discussions one could have. Among the intellectual disciplines, there were a number of important texts,[19] but it was left to the film and media studies to provide examples of how sound and signification could be approached.[20] However, the nature of film and television where sound has had secondary if not ancillary status meant that too many matters of concern for artists interested in a more central role for sound were left untreated.

With respect to music, the emergence of sound art in the 1980s was characterized by a problematic attitude toward Western art music—in particular, the avant-garde and experimental work claiming a relationship to sound per se. The idea of the *musicalization of sound* arose as a means to identify and supersede techniques in which sounds and noises were made significant by making them musical.[21] As a tactic to direct attention toward the semiotic complexity of sound and new ways of thinking about sound, it was a way to begin to account for artistic activities already underway and to invite a greater range of artistic possibilities, including those operating within music. It was also a means to examine the status of musical tropes underscoring so many other discourses, including philosophy and contemporary theory, since aerating the bounds of music itself might very well destabilize what the tropes supported.

Over the past decade the growing interest and activity in sound and the arts have been demonstrated by a number of important publications, conferences, exhibitions, and events.[22] My own participation within this area has been concerned, as you might suspect, with the interdisciplinary history and theory of sound within the avant-garde and experimental arts and with the use of sound by contemporary artists. The publication that relates most directly to the present text is the book I coedited and introduced, *Wireless Imagination: Sound, Radio and the Avant-Garde.* While I would refer readers to this book for a more wide-ranging treatment of the general topic, the present text undertakes fundamentally different approaches to some of the same topics (Artaud, Cage, Burroughs) and investigates many areas not covered in the book. It is apparent that innumerable new topics and fundamental revisions are attendant on studies of sound and the arts, more so once they are brought into play with developments in other disciplines, and that the same holds true for innovation and sophistication with artistic practice itself. Indeed, despite the din we are in, it seems like the early days of sound.

Part I

Significant Noises

Flaws and imperfections are part of this total desired look.

Display card on a shirt in a men's clothing store

window, on Sackstrasse, Graz, Austria, 1988.

Wherever they might occur among the arts, noises—interchangeably soundful and figurative, loud, disruptive, confusing, inconsistent, turbulent, chaotic, unwanted, nauseous, injurious—and noises silenced, suppressed, sought after, and celebrated always pertain to a complex of sources, motives, strategies, gestures, grammars, contexts, and so on. As such, they become significant. I concentrate here on noises manifested in some way sonically among the arts, attempting to hear the intricacies of the sounds among the noises and to determine the significance of the sounds that amount to noise. I am interested also in *significant noise* abatement occurring at specific sites known for their noise; in other words, silencing can occur in the midst of a din. The trouble is that noises are never just sounds and the sounds they mask are never just sounds: they are also ideas of noise. Ideas of noise can be tetchy, abusive, transgressive, resistive, hyperbolic, scientistic, generative, and cosmological. Indeed, the specter of noise—that is, the rhetoric of all those raucous associations and figurative expressions that arise once the idea of noise is invoked—can both mimic the complexes of meaning at the empirical roots of significant sounds and make an actual audible event called noise louder than it might already be. Of all the emphatic sounds of modernism, noise is the most common and the most productively counterproductive.

History does not give way to these storms of genesis and autodestruction; it is only what is made of noise, of the history of noise, that must explain itself in the face of the possibility that there is no such thing as noise. Noise in the avant-garde was linked to the sounds of military combat, the specter and incursion of technology and industrialism, the forms of popular culture and public demonstrations, nature and the sounds of other species, religious and occult activities, psychosis and drug-induced experiences, the music and languages of cultures outside reigning cultures of European society, and the sounds of the domestic sphere gendered female in contrast to the male face of the noisy parts of the avant-garde. With so much attendant on noise it quickly becomes evident that noises are too significant to be noises. We know they are noises in the first place because they exist where they shouldn't or they don't make sense when they should. But here too in knowing this we already know too much for noise to exist. But noise does indeed exist, and trying to define it in a unifying manner across the range of contexts will only invite noise on itself. Suppressing noise only contributes to its tenacity and detracts from investigating the complex means through which noise itself is suppressed, while celebrating noise easily becomes a tactic within the suppression of something else.

True, noise has performed admirably. Where better to set the ear loose to hear and feel unexpected licks than on the complexity and unpredictability called noise? Where better to imagine ontological riches in the raw? What better way to test authoritarian tolerance than with a raucous rage or arresting ridicule, and how better to bring attention to things without bringing things to attention? Where better to lose wayward thoughts, attempt to lose thought altogether (if only to give it a rest), and find thoughts where none might have existed? Where better to find damn near anything?

Noise is the forest of everything. The existence of noise implies a mutable world through an unruly intrusion of an other, an other that attracts difference, heterogeneity, and productive confusion; moreover, it implies a genesis of mutability itself. Noise is a world where anything can happen, including and especially itself. In a predictable world noise promises something out of the ordinary, and in a world in frantic pursuit of the extraordinary noise can promise the banal and quotidian. In a predictable world it can generate possibility and then obligingly self-destruct. Yet noise has also been an occasion for hearing loss and loss of hearing, psychic malaise, and psychological warfare. It has been a rehearsal for intolerance, perpetuated adolescence where celebrated, provided rationale for paltry works, steered attention away from seamy acts of complicity, and in the course of dismantling a local relationship of power reinforced a larger one.

The following is not a survey of the use of noise in modernism and its surrounds, although many key moments are taken into account. It is restricted instead to selected instances of significant noises relative to three concerns: acts of interpolation and immersion, other people and other languages, and militarism. Chapter 1, "Immersed in Noise," examines techniques, dispositions, and places where significance has been or could be sought through or within noise; my main task here is to return these noises to sound or imagine them as if they existed aurally. The mimetic impulses in Walter Benjamin's idea of sentience and Surrealist techniques for interpolating noise are steered toward their aural implications, while Jack Kerouac's practice of an interpolation of voices already takes place on the noisy brink of water sound. Then the homophonic culling of voices from speech and writing is examined in Louis Zukovsky and Benjamin to end at the lone figure of the writer writing, surrounded by the dish and din of café clatter. In these techniques and situations there is a supple give and take between the subject and his or her world, where phenomena threatened to take on their own agency, appearing to climb out of chaos like an amoeba finding form and hitting stride, or where attributes of the observer are discovered in a self-consciousness exercised on a hobby horse of noise. These instances are formed predominantly from the perspective of the subject who perceives *other things* apart from what was immediately apparent; however, at all times, even where a perception of nature alone apparently takes place, these other things involve other people and personifications. The social world exists prior to immersion and seems insistent on asserting itself in the most meaningless noise. At a minimum, no matter where the artist may be, wherever there is someone intent on telling, there is always a background dish and din and clatter of gregariousness, even when the other is formed from an estrangement of one's own voice.

The practices of noise discussed in chapter 1 are rarely self-identified as such, but there is no need to steer the bruitism, simultaneism, sound poetry, and noise music toward sound. Chapter 2, "Noises of the Avant-Garde," concentrates instead on how avant-garde noises are rationalized in terms of other people, other languages, and militarism. I do this not as a way to exhaust the possibilities of noise associated with these practices but to listen to what is too often lost in the noise. Where the first chapter concentrated on the supple give and take from which sociality emerges, chapter 2 provides a more immediate factoring of cruder forms of otherness. Also examined are how confusion and disruption of otherness are represented in the polyglot and how the influence of Christianity, with its own tradition of ritual nonsense and noises, made its way into the avant-garde.

The violence inherent in these relationships becomes explicit on the battlefield, particularly in the valorization of the noises of war by the Italian Futurists. Indeed, in the history of avant-garde noise, war is not the continuation of politics through other means; war is the major political source that artistic noise echoes. Militarism rationalized noise within the rhetoric of Luigi Russolo's founding text on noise, *The Art of Noises* manifesto (1913), just as it inaugurated and legitimated a myriad of other noise practices to follow. A violence subtended avant-garde practices of noise, not just the one commonly understood to have fueled its transgressions or even the violence in trading off the suppression of others, but those heard in the pounding reverberations of the killing fields. Modernism prospered on emphatic sounds, and none were as imposing and persuasive as those that announced an encounter of metal and flesh.

IMMERSED IN NOISE

To write badly is to plunge the graphic message into this noise which interferes with reading, which transforms the reader into an epigraphist.

Michel Serres[1]

Sentient Sound

Noise can be understood in one sense to be that constant grating sound generated by the movement between the abstract and empirical. It need not be loud, for it can go unheard even in the most intense communication. Imperfections in script, verbal pauses, and poor phrasing are regularly passed over in the greater purpose of communication, yet they always threaten to break out into an impassable noise and cause real havoc. As a precautionary measure, such local impurities are subsumed under a communication presumed to be successful, even if many important details and larger associations are lost in the process. The process of abstraction itself, what is lost, is thereby involved in the elimination of noise. Noise in this way is the specific, the empirical, even while "at the extreme limits of empiricism, meaning is totally plunged into noise."[2] The interesting problem arises when *noise* itself is being communicated, since it no longer remains inextricably locked into empiricism but is transformed into an abstraction of another noise. With respect to sound, noise is an abstraction of sound, and if the "process of abstraction . . . is involved in the elimination of noise,"[3] then noise is itself a form of noise reduction; it is something done to sound that most often goes unheard. In the following, therefore, the noise brought to bear on noise is the *specifics* of sound.

A silent figure of significant noise exists in handwriting. There exists a basic form of letters intended to be read without any problem whatsoever. It is a form similar to the one in front of you at this very moment, lodged long ago in the institution of printing. Between pure legibility and an entirely illegible scrawl there lies a great deal of variability. Significant noise cannot be disentangled from the specifics of such variability; it is a legibility of an apparent illegibility. What in some cases might be considered either undesirable or extraneous—that is, noise—might also be read as a person's style, the result of physiological (sickness) or environmental forces (writing on a bus), and the like. What one considers to be a scrawl depends on who is doing the considering, when, where, and in what capacity. Where a teacher would be intolerant of scrawl, a graphologist would be excited by its wealth of information, and this would not preclude the teacher who moonlights as a graphologist. Instead of inhibiting communication, where noise exists so too does a greater communication. For those with a large investment in noise, this situation poses difficulties because it means that noise is always subject to operations that render it nonexistent.

Walter Benjamin, a well-known student and teacher of graphology, once wrote legibly enough, "Graphology has taught us to recognize in handwriting images that the unconscious of the writer conceals in it."[4] He found in graphology a propensity for greater communication through pre-semiotic *nonsensuous similarities* and *nonsensuous correspondences* pertaining to what he called the *mimetic faculty* and the *doctrine of the similar*, contemporary manifestations of the ancient task "to read what was never written."[5] As such it provides a basis from which to understand Benjamin's own idea of noise and not merely because it provides a general impetus for reading. It may be no accident that a short statement entitled "Noises" is strikingly similar to a statement in "One Way Street," which is key to the understanding of the mimetic faculty. Because they exist in different perceptual registers, before comparing the two I need to set the stage by proposing how sound might provide an appropriate figure to Benjamin's empathetic idea of mimetic functioning.

The mimetic faculty entails the disintegration of the gulf separating observer and object, a separation usually held in check through representation. In "One Way Street" Benjamin writes, "we sentiently experience a window, a cloud, a tree not in our brains but, rather, in the place where we see it; there we are, in looking at our beloved, too, outside ourselves."[6]

Humans perceive the world while being within the world; they are implicated within it and are not somehow outside looking in or on. The object does not extend itself to the waiting individual: the individual finds it. And if meaning and feeling resides there, it is because the individual finds a piece of himself or herself. The person precedes the perception, making the process an empathetic one: the beloved is already loved, the distance has already been traveled. But what might be the sentient means of getting *outside ourselves?*

To exist to any degree where we perceive seems perceptually awkward with respect to vision because it is not given to an experience of spatial projection. Although light traverses the space between an object and observer just as readily as sound does between an action and listener, the reflection of light is understood not as an action comparable to one that might create a sound but, because of a constancy of action, as the result of a state. As Naum Gabo and Anton Prevsner ask in 1920, "Look at a ray of sun. . . . the stillest of the still forces, it speeds more than 300 kilometers in a second. . . . behold our starry firmament. . . . who hears it?"[7] Terrestrially, sound is not only experienced as occurring *in between* but as surrounding the listener, and the source of the sound is itself surrounded by its own sound. This mutual envelopment of aurality predisposes an exchange among presences. Baudelaire hears the wind in a tree as sighs already endowed with empathy through observation: "First you lend the tree your passions, your desires or your melancholy; its sighs and its oscillations become yours and soon you are the tree."[8] Hashish can hasten the experience: "You are sitting and smoking; you believe that you are sitting in your pipe, and that *your pipe* is smoking *you;* you are exhaling *yourself* in bluish clouds."[9]

Moreover, sounds can be heard coming from outside and behind the range of peripheral vision, and a sound of adequate intensity can be felt on and within the body as a whole, thereby dislocating the frontal and conceptual associations of vision with an all-around corporeality and spatiality. Michel Leiris wonders why the foliage of the Square de Vert-Galant and thereby all of reality "remains separate and remote? . . . This is understandable where sight is concerned, the most abstract of our senses, the one that constructs all things as things belonging to the outside, projected at our far edges, mounted like a stage set. Up to a point this is understandable where hearing is concerned too, even though what strikes our ears is thereby already penetrating us, insinuating itself smoothly or erupting violently deep inside us." [10] Spatial projection here begins to move between the object, action, and observer in both directions, and here the eye is handicapped because there is no visual equivalent to the utterance of the voice. No matter how the idea of visuality might be activated—whether through the early Greek idea of eyes projecting light (Aristotle would ask of Empedocles and Plato of the *Timaeus:* Okay, then why can't we see in the dark?) or the evil eye of the objectifying gaze—there is little experiential sense of how the light of sight might be established beyond the corporeal confines of the individual. Our eyes create parallax across the bridge of the nose but are dependent on light from elsewhere to constitute space, whereas our mouths emit sound that can be heard internally and at a distance and can fill its own space. Moreover, the voice is a good way to project perception into the world because it shares sound with hearing. The sound of the voice returns if not in the voice itself then in the union of utterance and audition, and it creates the constitution and collapse of space required of a sentient *getting outside ourselves*. While the centrifugal trajectory of the voice can return to form the centripetal base for solipsism, the everyday experience of an action at a distance is most palpable in dialogue, where exchanges are formed by statements already framed in anticipation. Through the figure of dialogue, an intimated voice can constitute an acoustic spatiality in which sounds, and by extension their actions and affiliated objects, are imbued with the returning voice of the other. Once this process is mapped on vision, the sentient requirements of mimesis are fulfilled.

Benjamin's comments from "One Way Street" on the sentient experience of objects as the collapse of distance occurring as one gets outside oneself takes on attributes of eros and desire but especially love. Like the mimetic faculty, love always finds a greater communication, an entranced beholding of the *beloved* in what would otherwise be perceived as noise, being here the seemingly extraneous imperfections of "Wrinkles in the face, moles, shabby clothes, and a lopsided walk bind him more lastingly and relentlessly than any beauty." [11] He looked directly at the *noise*, not past it. Flaws and imperfections are part and parcel of this total desiring look:

If the theory is correct that feeling is not located in the head, that we sentiently experience a window, a cloud, a tree not in our brains but, rather, in the place where we see it, there we are, in looking at our beloved, too, outside ourselves.

But in a torment of tension and ravishment. Our feeling, dazzled, flutters like a flock of birds in the woman's radiance. And as birds seek refuge in the leafy recesses of a tree, feelings escape into the shaded wrinkles, the awkward movements and inconspicuous blemishes of the body we love, where they can lie low in safety. And no passer-by would guess that it is just here, in what is defective and censurable, that the fleeting darts of adoration nestle.[12]

His feelings are vision-borne; feelings and sight in flight constitute the means through which he is transported. His gaze silently follows the trajectory of the voice, and she too is silent, without response, as she erotically receives his "fleeting darts of adoration" into her wrinkles. But where is the voice of the beloved? Would it rudely interrupt this docile parade of imperfection and adorable flaws? Would a returning gaze situate him at the point from where he saw? This would be the true test of love, since such agency would break the silence of the beloved, although no word or sound need occur, and she would no longer fall within the sentient experience of objects. It would be possible to test this with Benjamin's life of love and his well-known obsessions and determine what might be required to interrupt his experience, whether the strength of a returned love or just simple agency would introduce too much information into his graphological gaze. But the unfortunate fact remains that sentience predisposes but does not secure love for the empath. Thus, we have competing noises, as similarities in our second passage demonstrate:

Noises. High in the empty streets of the harbor district they are as densely and loosely clustered as butterflies on a hot flower bed. Every step stirs a song, a quarrel, a flapping of wet linen, a rattling of boards, a baby's bawling, a clatter of buckets. Only you have to have strayed up here alone, if you are to pursue them with a net as they flutter away unsteadily into the stillness. For in these deserted corners all sounds and things still have their own silences, just as, at midday in the mountains, there is the silence of hens, of the ax, of the cicadas. But the chase is dangerous, and the net is finally torn when, like a gigantic hornet, a grindstone impales it from behind with its whizzing sting.[13]

His steps, a voice from the feet uttered on the lower jaw of the ground, trigger the sounds that, like feelings and birds and butterflies, become airborne and ephemeral. Likewise, they then come to rest in silence, in wrinkles, or in deserted corners. The silence in no way means that the hens, ax, or cicadas have left but works instead to affirm their presence, just as she, the beloved, is silent. Sounds dissipate through animal behavior, not among an animism of objects. Nevertheless, through sound the mimetic takes on another register, the register of the other. Instead of accepting his darts a noise impales his net, the operative space of his listening from *behind the peripheral plane of vision*, of his presence more fully *outside himself*. Compared to the spatiality of his net, his hearing, a feeling located in the head betrays the visual influence of the text and is only partially remedied as the screen's surface brings on ideas of visual projection. Thus, the actual noise here appears to be what does not appear, what escapes the frontal field of visual control. Benjamin's noise speaks of the implicit dangers of becoming implicated within the world, there is a give-and-take of power, even as it might occur as the absent voice of the beloved suddenly making itself known in another sound.

In contrast, Nietzsche in section 60, book 2, of *The Gay Science* has differentiated his noises by gender, and this has enabled him to know where he stands among them: "Do I still have ears? Am I all ears and nothing else? Here I stand in the flaming surf whose white tongues are licking at my feet; from all sides I hear howling, threats, screaming, roaring coming at me, while the old earth-shaker sings his aria in the lowest depths, deep as a bellowing bull, while pounding such an earth-shaking beat that the hearts of even these weather-beaten rocky monsters are trembling in their bodies."[14] He then sees a sailboat silently gliding just offshore and imagines himself in another place amid the clamor, another attitude within life where he could "move *over* existence."[15] The silence of this sailboat turns out to be "quiet magical beings gliding past"—that is, *women*. Their proximity to "the *Rauschen* of the waves," in Rüdiger Campe's words, acts to rhetorically inaugurate Nietzsche's testy discourse on what he knows best for women for the next fifteen sections of book 2.[16] Nietzsche's women are in fact inverted sirens: he stands on shore while they are on the boat, and it is the call of his own bellowing bull noise that drives him into fantasy while they no longer sing but are silent. He is briefly seduced into thinking that a man's better self might dwell among women, but he quickly grabs hold of his senses, or at least his sense of hearing, to acknowledge that noise is inevitable and that a distinction among noises must be made. This enables him—Nietzsche-man—to avoid drowning in his misdirected dream about life: "Noble enthusiast, even on the most beautiful sailboat there is a lot of noise, and unfortunately much small and petty noise."[17] Among the small and petty noises of these silent sirens are yet another class of female sounds derived from antiquity—rumors—that corrosive speech silent to men because it is kept from them, offshore, as it were. He thus answers one of his initial questions; he is not "all ears and nothing else" since the only one to have been covered to completely with ears (and eyes and tongues) was the female grotesque known as Fame or Rumor, and he keeps his distance from the sailboat, from woman, from the source of petty noises.[18] Indeed, Nietzsche finishes section 60 with this warning: "The magic and the most powerful effect of women is, in philosophical language, action at a distance, *actio in distans;* but this requires first of all and above all—*distance*."[19] Nietzsche destroyed the sound that would destroy the distance when the sirens' song was rendered silent and maintained the distance with the gendered gulf established between the two noises. Therefore, in these two statements, Nietzsche presumes *all women* and professes distance, while Benjamin invokes a beloved and invites dissolution.

Interpolation of Noise

The sense of an immersion in noise is guaranteed by the ease through which so much can be perceived within it. There was a proliferation of acts and techniques within the avant-garde for interpolating noise, most of them related to seeing images within visual noise, as innocently as children see animals and faces within the clouds, just a little more intoxicated. Nowhere was this more pronounced than in Surrealism, where such interpolation became elevated through its psychological, psychic, and psychotic associations. While much of the avant-garde was concerned with processes of abstraction, it was exactly the opposite for Surrealism. The interpolation of noise was a means by which meaning was generated from abstraction and thus corresponded directly to Surrealism's larger project of bringing realms of reality hitherto guarded or unknown into mimetic practice.

Salvador Dalí's paranoiac-critical method, developed in practice from the late 1920s and named as such in his 1933 essay *L'Ane pourri*, sought to reproduce the "delirium of interpretation" characteristic of paranoiacs who would see something else in something and then something else in that: "A representation of an object is also, without the slightest physical or anatomical change, the representation of another entirely different object."[20] Visual noise overlaps with his *method* and comes into play in his paintings as a means to generate imagery—for example, how the rocks of his seaside home at Cadaqués provided the contours for the painting *The Great Masturbator* (1929). Visual noise can be interpolated similarly. The easiest way to think about it is through that well-known optical illusion that switches back and forth between a duck and a rabbit. Dalí established the visual punning in so many of his paintings on the basis of such oscillation—as in *The Metamorphosis of Narcissus* (1937), where the image of Narcissus resting his head on his knee at the edge of a pond becomes a stone hand holding an egg hatching a flower. Instead of presuming a range if not an infinity of possibilities culled from a field of noise, Dalí's paranoiac-critical method limited its attention to one proper oscillation, lodging the unconscious in the atemporality of painting, a frozen moment within an ongoing state of noise and process of interpolation. Both Dalí's seeing and his painting were conditioned by being an immersion in a discrete field of vision, whereas immersion might be better produced through the spatiality associated with aurality.

The images Dalí found in the seaside rocks of Cadaqués, Antonin Artaud found among the rocks and mountains in the land of the indigenous Tarahumara on his 1936 trip to Mexico:

When Nature, by a strange whim, suddenly shows the body of a man being tortured on a rock, one can think at first that this is merely a whim and that this whim signifies nothing. But when in the course of many days on horseback the same intelligent charm is repeated, and *when Nature obstinately manifests the same idea;* when the same pathetic forms recur; when the heads of familiar gods appear on the rocks, and when a theme of death emanates from them, a death whose expense is obstinately borne by man; when the dismembered form of man is answered by the forms, *become less obscure,* more separate from a petrifying matter, of the gods who have always tortured him; when a whole area of the earth develops a philosophy parallel to that of its inhabitants; when one knows that the first men utilized a language of signs, and when one finds this language formidably expanded on the rocks—then surely one cannot continue to think that this is a whim, and that this whim signifies nothing.[21]

Within this land where "Nature *has chosen to speak*" he saw "a naked man leaning out of a large window. His head was nothing but a huge hole, a kind of circular cavity in which the sun and moon appeared by turns, according to the time of day,"[22] and "heard" a Kabalistic "music of Numbers . . . which reduces the chaos of the material world to its principles, explains by a kind of awesome mathematics how Nature is ordered and how she directs the birth of the forms that she pulls out of chaos. And everything I saw seemed to correspond to a number. . . . The broken-off busts of women numbered 8; the phallic tooth . . . had three stones and four holes; the forms that became volatile numbered 12, etc."[23] He had walked into hills where the frothing noise of the rocks had been frozen into Herder's Book of Nature. Artaud read this book and wrote into another one, whereas Dalí could observe figures in the visual noise and then reproduce them in painting, replete with noise.

Max Ernst also drew images out of visual noise, unlike Dalí and Artaud, who culled from a preexisting field of noise, his technique of *frottage* generated the noise in the first place. His discovery of this technique was nevertheless dependent on a preexisting noise. As the legend goes, while at an inn on a rainy day by the seaside, he looked down on the floor and was reminded of his childhood and how a piece of imitation mahogany produced, as he prepared to fall asleep, a repertoire of images. He took a rubbing of the floorboards and found within the scratches, pits, and grain all manner of images. These images recommended themselves because they were wrenched from an "irritated" mind far from the complacent crowd of "Renoir's three apples, Manet's four sticks of asparagus, Derain's little chocolate women, and the Cubists' tobacco-packet."[24] Just as Artaud was required to travel across the Atlantic to read nature in the noise, Ernst used noise to remove himself from genteel Europe. Nevertheless, amid his self-generated nature the image of Ernst's Loplop was often divulged phoenix-like from the noise, a creature with an uncanny resemblance to Ernst's own bird-like countenance.[25] As with so many techniques of interpolation, nature refracts.

Surrealism did little to shift from a visual to an auditory mode for perceiving the world, despite its roots in the chattering unconscious of automatism. There was, after all, a certain prohibition against the auditive supported through the Surrealist antipathy toward music. André Breton wrote that "Auditive images . . . are inferior to visual images not only in clearness but also in strictness, and with all due respect to a few melomaniacs, they hardly seem intended to strengthen in any way the idea of human greatness."[26] He, of course, was speaking of Western art music, if not all "musical expression, the most deeply confusing of all!"[27] As he continued, "So may night continue to fall upon the orchestra, and may I, who am still searching for something in this world, may I be left with open or closed eyes, in broad daylight, to my silent contemplation."[28] Breton would have found his antipathy toward Western art music confirmed by the scene in Buñuel and Dalí's film *Un Chien andalou* where the protagonist's frustrated desire is represented in his attempt to return to the woman, pulling a contraption consisting of ropes over each shoulder towing two bound priests and grand pianos with dead donkeys draped across the strings, their heads spilling out over the keyboard. Dalí, who placed music at the low point in the hierarchy of the arts, cut back the lips of the donkeys to stress the visual pun between their teeth and the keys of the piano.

Breton did celebrate films that were innovative in their use of sound, such as Luis Buñuel's *L'Age d'or*, in which mad love is accompanied by the sound of cowbells. Back home after having been separated by the crowd from her lover Don X, the daughter of the bourgeois walks into her room to find a large bovine on her bed. Sternly instructing it to leave, the cow bell lingers long after the creature has toppled off the bed and sauntered out of the room. As the woman reflects in front of the vanity mirror on Don X being led down the street by two officials, the dog barking at him mixes with the sound of the bell. then both sounds join gently effusive music combined with the sound of the wind as the woman, her hair blowing back, looks into the mirror filled with sky.

Breton seems to have associated the auditive too closely with the musical and thereby restricted the possibilities for techniques for interpolating auditive noise. Such techniques were, nevertheless, just one small step away from Surrealism, give or take a few centuries. Ernst found precedent for his noise-generating techniques in Leonardo da Vinci's *Treatise on Painting*, in which he proposed throwing a sponge soaked in different colors up against a wall and finding landscapes in the blotch of paint. Where Ernst remained within a visual register, Leonardo himself related this technique to how one could hear a multitude of voices in chiming bells. Under the sectional title *What to augment and stimulate the mind toward various discoveries*, Leonardo wrote:

I shall not fail to include among these precepts a new discovery, an aid to reflection, which, although it seems a small thing and almost laughable, nevertheless is very useful in stimulating the mind to various discoveries. This is: look at walls splashed with a number of stains or stones of various mixed colors. If you have to invent some scene, you can see there resemblances to a number of landscapes, adorned in various ways with mountains, rivers, rocks, trees, great plains, valleys and hills. Moreover, you can see various battles, and rapid actions of figures, strange expressions on faces, costumes, and an infinite number of things, which you can reduce to good, integrated form. This happens thus on walls and varicolored stones, as in the sound of bells, in whose pealing you can find every name and word you can imagine.[29]

The exceedingly complex and ever-changing acoustical patterns within the sound of bells set up a field of auditory noise out of which Leonardo heard voices. Although he mentions voices in the most dispassionate, technical manner, a passionate person like Joan of Arc could hear angelic voices.[30] The fact that angels filled bells is in itself significant, for in these emblems of the church one person might hear hosannas while another might hear the rustling straps before a flogging. The call to community can be for the purposes of a stoning, just as rough music could celebrate a wedding or punish a sexual transgression.[31]

By 1944 Breton began to revise his position. When asked by Virgil Thomson to assess his position on music for publication in *Modern Music*, he took the opportunity to reassess it. In his essay "Silence Is Golden," he proposes an auditive practice that, in its fusion of music and poetry, would *"unify, re-unify hearing* to the same extent that we must determine to *unify, re-unify sight."* [32] This does not mean a "closer collaboration between musician and poet" because that would be only more examples of poems set to music, and they are almost as pathetic as the "silly nonsense of opera librettos." [33] Instead, he celebrated the way surrealist writers have already discovered the *tonal* value of words, not in their external auditive characteristics but at the point of their psychological generation where "the 'inner word' is absolutely inseparable from 'inner music'" and where "inner thinking is free to tune itself to the 'inner music' *which never leaves it.*[34] Thus, he writes, "Great poets have been *auditives,* not visionaries." However, musical practice is still awaiting its commensurate fusion with the poetics of "inner words," and Breton, lacking the vocabulary to speak with musicians, is unable to point them in the direction of "the virgin soil of sound."[35]

Protean Noise

Interpolating significance from a field of noise can be a private affair, perhaps communicable only through debased means if at all, its techniques breaking down along lines of perception and media. Cadaqués is immediately perceptible in Dalí's *The Great Masturbator,* but we must take Artaud's word for his vision in Mexico. Hearing voices or sounds within auditory noise becomes another matter altogether. Breton might compare Apollinaire's laugh to "the same noise as a first burst of hailstones on a window pane," but hundreds of bursts of hailstones on hundreds of window panes would never pry it from metaphor.[36] Nevertheless, when it comes to hearing voices in water, the experience is so common that the manner in which the call and response takes place within the white noise is significant in itself. Away from the sustained noises of waves, the human voice dominates the social enclaves of the arts; once the voice engages the sea, it declares its designs on the nature of utterance and audition. The full conceit of the human utterance was demonstrated in F. T. Marinetti's early poetry, where the loudness of the sea was a test of Demosthenean oratorical power and the sea's sustained sound stretching over the horizon an expanse given over to one's dominance and immortality. But when it comes to listening, so many things are heard in the noise of the sea and waters that it is no coincidence that Proteus, the quick-change artist, is also the old man of the sea. While in the New Testament the voices of the multitudes are to be heard in the turbulent waters, Vicente Huidobro listened to sea sounds in *Altazor* and heard the voice commanding all multitudes speaking, casually:

Then I heard the Creator speak, nameless, just a simple hole in space, as beautiful as a navel:

"I made a great noise and this noise made the ocean and the ocean's waves.

"This noise will be tied to the sea's waves forever and the sea's waves will forever be tied to it, like stamps to a postcard."[37]

A little later the Creator "drank a little cognac (for the hydrography)."[38] It was this creator who sat down with Jack Kerouac, ample sweet wine in hand, for a conversation in wavespeak in his autobiographical novel *Big Sur* (1962). Kerouac, former merchant marine and close reader of Melville, was already an alcohol-sodden victim of fame when Lawrence Ferlinghetti, fellow Beat and editor of City Lights Books, invited him to stay in his cabin in Big Sur, just south of San Francisco, to dry up and find his bearings in the midst of nature. But Kerouac would become as uncomfortable with isolation as he was with fame, finding voices of the multitude where there were none. The more benign voices arose from the most powerful source, the ocean waves crashing on the rocks and shore, just a short walk down from the cabin:

I'd go to . . . my corner by the cliff not far from one of the caves and sit there like an idiot in the dark writing down the sound of the waves in the notebook page (secretarial notebook). . . . —One night I got scared anyway so sat on top of 10-foot cliff at the foot of the big cliff and the waves are going "Rare, he rammed the gate rare"—"Raw roo roar"—"Crowsh"—the way waves sound especially at night—The sea not speaking in sentences so much as in short lines: "Which one? . . . the one ploshed? . . . the same ah Boom." . . . Writing down these fantastic inanities actually but yet I felt I had to do it because James Joyce wasn't about to do it now he was dead.[39]

His onomatopoetic record of this interpolative immersion melding his "noisy brains" with the voices of the waves was formed into the poem "'Sea': Sounds of the Pacific Ocean at Bug Sur," of which the following is an excerpt:

Reach, reach, some leaves
havent hastened near
enuf—Roll, roll, purl
the sand shark floor
a greeny pali andarva
—Ah back—Ah forth—
As shish—Boom, away,
doom, a day—Vein we
firm—The sea is We—

Parle, parle, boom the
earth—Aree—Shaw,
Sho, Shoosh, flut,
ravad, tapavada pow,
coof, look, roof,—
No, no, no, no, no, no—
Oh ya, ya, ya, yo, yair—
Shhh-[40]

The other source of water was from a creek that ran by the cabin. At first
Kerouac would sit and listen contemplatively, much like Gochiku, whom
he had no doubt come across in Allan Watts's *The Way of Zen:*

The long night;
The sound of the water
Says what I think.[41]

But the little sounds and voices of the creek would eventually taunt him as
he moved closer to a nervous breakdown:

The creek gurgles and thumps outside—A creek having so many voices it's
amazing, from the kettledrum basin deep bumpbumps to the little gurgly feminine crickles over shallow rocks, sudden choruses of other singers and voices
from the log dam, dibble dabble all night long and all day long the voices of
the creek amusing me so much at first but in the later horror of that madness
night becoming the babble and rave of evil angels in my head.[42]

He had intended to dry up amid the natural environs of Big Sur, but a
steady diet of sweet wine and little food—one friend reprimanded him for
being the only Frenchman without a taste for dry wine—would prevent
him from transforming into one of Alfred Jarry's dreaded "dipsomaniacs
of aquatism"[43] and fuel his paranoid hallucinations. Just as weeks before,
during an alcohol stupor in a San Francisco fleabag hotel, he was unable
to distinguish between the moaning of the other drunks on the floor and
his own, the sounds of the creek became a menacing stream of consciousness, as though the sounds met and melted in his liver in an embodiment
of Platonic acoustics:[44] "And now a babble in the creek has somehow en-

tered my head and with all the rhythm of the sea waves going 'Kettle blomp you're up, you rop and dop, ligger lagger ligger' I grab my head but it keeps babbling."[45] Because "everything is over—everything is swarming all over me," the babble becomes an enlightened harbinger of death, an auditory Doppelgänger, begging Kerouac to cut it out of his forehead with the same lobotomy that had been performed on Allen Ginsberg's mother (Ginsberg silenced his own voices through chanting).[46] Unlike the loud, dazzling sound of crashing waves, the creek babble was too soft to drown out his noisy brains ("my mind is just a series of explosions that get louder and louder and more 'multiply' broken in pieces some of them big orchestral and then rainbow explosions of sound and sight mixed")[47] and too pathetic to be recuperated into poetry ("Ah the keselamaroyot you rot").[48] He was immersed in water voices on his own level, and as he degenerated, so did they. Like Nietzsche knee deep in the *Rauschen* of the waves, Kerouac could answer the threats of the old earth shaker but was overrun by gentleness and silence.

Kerouac is best known for having listened to jive and jazz and incorporating them into his writing style. He is less known for listening to the deep bass and hiss of pounding seas, the slurred sibilants of the waves, the vicious babble of other waters. Nevertheless, the "voice" associated with his style may have been close to immersion in the sound of waters all along. Allen Ginsberg said that Kerouac's most important attribute was "a reason founded on sounds rather than a reason founded on conceptual associations," an auditory "modality of consciousness" that occurred at the point of transformation when "he was suddenly aware of the sound of language, and got swimming in the seas of sound, got lost swimming in the seas of sound, and guided his intellect on sound rather than on dictionary associations with the meanings of the sounds."[49] Indeed, in his own "Essentials of Spontaneous Prose" Kerouac modeled his consciousness on the sea: "Not 'selectivity' of expression but following free deviation (association) of mind into limitless blow-on-subject seas of thought, swimming in sea of English."[50]

Oscillator Noise

Kerouac's consciousness may have developed through swimming in a sea of English. His technique of interpolation nevertheless took place in a sea of sea sounds. Yet what happens when such privatized audition occurs within a sea of language as incomprehensible as the noise of the sea? People with hearing difficulties live with processes of significant noise on a daily basis. Where the graphologist might find greater communication in noise, for individuals who are hard of hearing it is often difficult to determine the first line of meaning. Partial deafness and noise breed and feed on homophony, a device that almost always operates unconsciously as a salvaging maneuver but that can also be used more deliberately as a source of enjoyment. While resourcefully weaving phonemes and vocables through anticipation and recursion, generating options and making choices of what may be appropriate or at least plausible in the context, the range of communications can be an arena for play and for entertaining difference toward whatever ends. A similar thing happens when one encounters a foreign language. Although at times a person may listen very intently and yet go away with few tangible rewards, it nevertheless demonstrates that the urge against all odds to continuously make meaning from linguistic noise is very strong.

The most sustained exercise within English of interpolating significant linguistic noise is to be found in Louis Zukovsky's homophonic translations, or transliterations, of the Book of Job in his poem *A-15* (1964) and, with his wife Celia Zukovsky, *Catullus* (1958–1969). Working with the original Hebrew and Latin he misconstrued the sound of the language with the dual purpose of supplying a certain synopsis in English of the original (translation of sorts) and simultaneously fulfilling his own poetic agenda. In the preface to *Catullus* the Zukovskys wrote: "This translation of Catullus follows the sound, rhythm, and syntax of his Latin—tries, as is said, to breathe the 'literal' meaning with him."[51] And among these, according to Robert Creeley, "his first and abiding purchase on the text is its sound—much as if one were trying to enter the physical place of language, making sounds like 'they' do, trying to inhabit the gestures, pace, and density of those ('objective') words."[52] Zukovsky himself, in reference to Catullus, once characterized the process more roughly, and not coincidentally in the dual figure of deafness and a tourist hailing from an officially monoglottal country, when he told a college audience, "I'm trying to read the old passionate guy's lips like an ignorant American."[53]

Sometimes a familiar language can degenerate into linguistic noise, and the experience may not be a comfortable or productive one. It may instead reject the listener, driving the person back into a private realm, perhaps retreating into a more serious threat. Under the influence of hashish in a bar filled with a din of voices, Walter Benjamin heard perfectly good French slip over into a new dialect. He related this to a statement by Karl Kraus that pertained to the visual process of reading: "The more closely you look at a word the more distantly it looks back."[54] This is an obstinate orthography repulsing every graphological attempt to find meaning. The increased unintelligibility encountered by Benjamin may not have been an alienation resulting from a hashish-clouded comprehension but could have resulted from the drug's enticement to listen, an attunement to the noises of café banter. Foreignness could have been created as the language spoken by an individual was atomized by a spatialized din of combined voices, spreading quickly as a dialect back through the room.[55] Whatever the case may be, the transformation of speech into linguistic noise under the influence of hashish was mild when compared to the threat facing René Daumal under the influence of carbon tetrachloride. What could be more frightening than to finally realize that the noisy speech he heard was emanating from his own voice, that the voice that was meant to give him the comfort of presence was either unwanted magic or hopeless babbling? Only the proper cadence of an incantation sounding his being in a battle of attunement and alienation could ward off the truly remote from breaking through past the infinitely close:

And all space was endlessly divided thus into circles and triangles inscribed one within another, combining and moving in harmony, and changing into one another in a geometrically inconceivable manner that could not be reproduced in ordinary reality. A sound accompanied this luminous movement, and I suddenly realized it was I who was making it. In fact I virtually *was* that sound; I sustained my existence by emitting it. The sound consisted of a chant or formula, which I had to repeat faster and faster in order to "follow the movement." The formula (I give the facts with no attempt to disguise their absurdity) ran something like this: "Tem gwef tem gwef dr rr rr," with an accent on the second "gwef" and with the last syllable blending back into the first; it gave an unceasing pulse to the rhythm, which was, as I have said, that of my very being. I knew that as soon as it began going too fast for me to follow, the unnamable and frightful thing would occur. In fact it was always *infinitely close* to happening, and infinitely remote . . . that is all I can say.[56]

The experience resembles certain types of aphasia, the hell of language where one's own meaningless speech is propelled along an irrepressible urge to communicate. If a meaning might manifest itself fleetingly here or there, it is only in the form of one or two frustrating words that are one's coded appeal to what might make sense out of life; this equals an attempt at a pathetic magic. Everyone else follows the rules of communication—syntactical progressions and inflectional trajectories—but their speech too is totally incomprehensible, even though they are your closest friends. They suddenly speak another language. Your home has become a foreign country, however hospitable.[57] For Daumal, what was close was the assurance of the voice per se, asserting itself through his being as it corporeally produced the repetitive and pulsing meaninglessness, holding unknown consequences in check. What was remote and frightening was to be driven by communication and totally incapable of it and not to know whether each attempt was taking you further away or closer to an unfettered psychosis on the other side of noise.

When one's own speech is not implicated, the noise returns to more peaceable settings. Walter Benjamin recommends that writers at certain phases within the production of a work seek out complex sounds: "In your working conditions avoid everyday mediocrity. Semirelaxation, to a background of insipid sounds, is degrading. On the other hand, accompaniment by an *étude* or a cacophony of voices can become as significant for work as the perceptible silence of the night. If the latter sharpens the inner ear, the former acts as touchstone for a diction ample enough to bury even the most wayward thought."[58] Jean Cocteau, on the other hand, pleads with an American audience not to read his letter to them "while your radio is broadcasting a programme of music with the title 'Music to Read By.'"[59] The speech of the raucousness of cafés and other such haunts produces in itself a figure of the social where poets and writers in midst of the craft need not feel so alone. The dish and din can provide a peaceful home for the overriding conflict within the very act of writing—the gregarious motive of communication versus the solitude of its execution—by providing a chatty noise within which a collectively discursive interlocutor can be divined, a nascent public imagined. Café noise also models the supple field of exchange between inner speech-sounds and those of the world and, thus, situates the writer. Similarly it is commonplace for even the most dedicated musical aesthete to listen at times more concertedly to the psyche than to the concert as he or she prefigures a particular passage with an expectation about how it should or has sounded in the past, associates a passage with another work or with matters of the world adjusts breathing to take in an emotive rendering or suppresses a cough—all those apperceptual processes that constitute listening. Baudelaire's experience on hashish was but an amplification of an infinite number of conditions and settings where the same takes place: "I will not try to tell you that I *listened* to the players; you know that's quite impossible; now and then, my stream of thought would seize on some sentence fragment, and, like an able dancer, would use it as a trampoline, to spring to distant dreams."[60]

Oscillating between stage and seat, constantly interrupting or melding in a mix that is, ironically, the means through which an idea of unity is negotiated. Again, Baudelaire confirms this as he continues his description: "You might suppose that a play heard in this way would lack logic and connection; allow me to enlighten you; I found a very subtle meaning in the drama spun by my distracted state of mind. Nothing fazed me."[61] There is a constant state of interruption, shattering the continuity of the music because the "stage" is always oscillating from one location to the other, at times entirely masking one or ephemerally fusing the two. Moreover, this *mix* is the very process through which some idea of a unity is brought to bear on the actual profusion and disparity of phenomena. In other words, it is through interruption that the semblance of a continuous integrity is established; it is only through noise that the famed ephemerality of music is secured as ephemeral. In the café where the sound is not the object of thought, the mix is exteriorized and thus brings unity to an inaudible intellectual life by providing an atmospheric dispensary for tangents as a stand-in for sociality.

Elsewhere, Benjamin mentions this occurring outside the café: "When Dickens went traveling, he repeatedly complained about the lack of street noises and activities which were indispensable to him for his production. 'I cannot express how much I want these [the streets],' he wrote in 1846 from Lausanne while he was working on *Dombey and Son*. 'It seems as if they supplied something to my brain, which it cannot bear, when busy, to lose.'"[62] Benjamin then cites George Simmel in noting a silence and a silencing of the social operating through the modern city's predilection for visuality:

Someone who sees without hearing is much more uneasy than someone who hears without seeing. In this there is something characteristic of the sociology of the big city. Interpersonal relationships in big cities are distinguished by a marked preponderance of the activity of the eye over the activity of the ear. The main reason for this is the public means of transportation. Before the development of buses, railroads, and trams in the nineteenth century, people had never been in a position of having to look at one another for long minutes or even hours without speaking to one another.[63]

Ostensibly, the reduced social products of a preponderance of sight would give way to the gregarious texts written alone among the sounds of bohemian hubbub. Fields of significant sound constituted by café speech may indeed suffice, as may the less homogenous sounds of big city streets, because they invoke the phenomenal depths articulated by language, as opposed to the surfaces of visual imagery, signage included. But they only go so far. They only offer better aid than none since, as Leonardo says, "those stains give you inventions, they will not teach you to finish any detail."[64]

NOISES OF THE AVANT-GARDE

Bruitism

Earlier this century in Europe when men, mostly, got together in cafés and made noise as art, noise became very significant. One café in particular, the Cabaret Voltaire of Zurich dada, left a legacy of artistic revolution. This noise was made significant in part by making others—primarily women and non-Europeans—insignificant in a context of war and religion. Situated in the middle of World War I both geographically (Switzerland) and chronologically (1916), Cabaret Voltaire was filled with people who were lucky enough to have escaped by stealth or wealth the horrors gripping the rest of Europe. Noise music, noise making, and even sound poetry and simultaneous poetry in Dada fell under the term *bruitism*, and although bruitism was varied and used any number of noise-making devices, its emblem at the Cabaret Voltaire was Richard Huelsenbeck banging on the big drum. As Huelsenbeck himself would have it, all of Dada itself "beats a drum, wails, sneers and lashes out."[1] Tristan Tzara described it this way in his "Zurich Chronicle": "the big drum is brought in, Huelsenbeck against 200, Trou-serfly accentuated by the very big drum and little bells on his left foot—the people protest shout smash windowpanes kill each other demolish fight here come the police interruption."[2] *Trouserfly* refers to Huelsenbeck's bruitist poem "Plane," a mix of nonsense words and letters, "behold the way the placenta creams in the high school boys' butterfly nets/sokobauno sokobauno/the vicar closeth his trou-serfly rataplan rataplan his trou-serfly and his hair juts ou-out of his ears/the buckcatapult the buckcatapult fa-alls from the sky and the grandmother hoiks up her breasts."[3]

The Italian Futurists, who had been involved in the traffic of noise since 1913, proved to be an inspiration for Dada noise, as Huelsenbeck

wrote in 1920: "[Dadaism] disseminated the BRUITIST music of the futurists (whose purely Italian concerns it has no desire to generalize)."[4] He
was actually relying on reports, and not very accurate ones, about Italian
Futurist noise. He credited F. T. Marinetti with inventing the *art of noises*
(a common mistake), thought that Russolo's noise music was imitative, and
thought that it was performed on a ragtag assortment of instruments instead of on noise-intoning instruments designed by Russolo and Ugo Piatti
specifically for the purpose:

From Marinetti we also borrowed "bruitism," or noise music, *le concert bruitiste*,
which, of blessed memory, had created such a stir at the first appearance of
the Futurists in Milan, where they had regaled the audience with *le reveil de la
capitale*. I spoke on the significance of bruitism at a number of open Dada
gatherings.

"*Le bruit*," noise with imitative effects, was introduced into art (in this connection we can hardly speak of individual arts, music or literature) by Marinetti, who used a chorus of typewriters, kettledrums, rattles and pot-covers to
suggest the "awakening of the capital"; at first it was intended as nothing more
than a rather violent reminder of the colourfulness of life.[5] ·

Huelsenbeck thought that the Italian Futurists were to be commended for
being on the side of noises and other nonabstract *things:* "tables, houses,
frying-pans, urinals, women, etc." Huelsenbeck's endorsement of this list
was telling, for it included the things known as women in close proximity
to urinals, no less. Furthermore, everything on the list was a domestic item,
or when they were public, they were kept for the use of men out of sight.
He went on to state that things took on an independent life of their own,
left their unexceptional habitat of domestic space, to march off into the
exceptional event and public province of men—war: "The highest expression of the conflict of things, as a spontaneous eruption of possibilities, as
movement, as a simultaneous poem, as a symphony of cries, shots, com-
mands, embodying an attempted solution of the problem of life in motion. . . . Every movement naturally produces noise."[6] War as the highest
expression of *things*, their vitality exposed by the dynamics of combat and
voiced in their movement as noise. Even though Huelsenbeck was not an
advocate of war, in his acclimation of Italian Futurist noise, which as see

below arose from war, he became rhetorically associated with it. The new art favored noise made from actual things; war simply did it better.

Like other aspects of the avant-garde and modernist arts, the Dadaists found a source for bruitism in primitivism. Prior to coming to Zurich, Huelsenbeck had recited some "Negro poems" at an expressionist evening in Berlin. The first evening he entered the Cabaret Voltaire, he met the owner of the building, the former seaman Jan Ephraim, and recited for him "some Negro poems that I had made up myself":[7]

"They sound very good," he said, "but unfortunately they're not Negro poems. I spent a good part of my life among Negroes, and the songs they sing are very different from the ones you just recited." He was one of those people who take things literally, and retain them verbatim. My Negro poems all ended with the refrain "Umba, umba," which I roared and spouted over and over again into the audience.[8]

Ephraim later brought him poems ostensibly written in a "Negro language" from either Africa or the South Seas, which Huelsenbeck went on to recite in front of an audience—that is, with the addition of *umba umba*, which "no force on earth could have gotten me to leave out."[9] Perhaps this was the germ of an enduring interest for Huelsenbeck for he would set sail to Africa during the mid-1920s, similar to Tristan Tzara's own study of African languages and culture, but during the days of the Cabaret Voltaire his Negro poems were clearly part of the trivializing appropriation of other cultures that Europeans found necessary to vitalize their own.

Thus, the grinding sound of power relations are heard here in the way noises *contain* the other, in both senses of the word. Noises are informed by the sounds, languages, and social position of others. It is only because certain types of people are outside any representation of social harmony that their speech and other sounds associated with them are considered to be noise. In the process of appropriation these others are subjected to forms of containment they have already known in other less semiotic exercises. Because they were bohemian or antimilitarist, the male artists making most of the noise were themselves on the margins of society. When they sought the source of noise from others even further outside the main, it was not because they experienced any sense of camaraderie of mutual exclusion but because they still had a base in the norms of their culture from which these others signified noise. This admixture meant that when they marshaled the noise of others to transgress or attack aspects of different dominant cultures, they reinforced other aspects of domination. Avantgarde noise, in other words, both marshals and mutes the noise of the other: power is attacked at the expense of the less powerful, and society itself is both attacked and reinforced.

Polyglot was yet another tactic of linguistic noise at the Cabaret Voltaire. In speculating on the genesis of Hugo Ball's famous set of six sound poems, Rudolf Kuenzli offers the following explanation: "Ball's experiments with sound poems might even be taken as an attempt to overcome the language barrier in the Cabaret Voltaire, since the audience consisted of Russians, French, Poles, Italians, Germans, etc., who were all living in Zurich in order to escape the First World War."[10] Given the economic motivation for the Cabaret to stay open, Ball's sound poems were an attempt to break down the segregation of nights held for special language- and nation-based audiences. As Marcel Janco recounts, "We held Russian events where anyone could go up on the podium and sing popular Russian music, Romanian evenings with Romanian dancers and music, and so on."[11] Ball's move toward predominantly phonic content was therefore an attempt to generate a transcultural appeal within language, similar to the one already rehearsed within ideas of music as a universal communicator.

Kuenzli supports his claim by pointing out that the six sound poems were atypical of all of Ball's other writings and thus seemed to be pitched to the local concerns of the Cabaret Voltaire. Driven into the refuge of Swiss neutrality, Ball's *Verse ohne Worte* (poetry without words) was, additionally and perhaps more precisely, a verse without German language, with its militarist associations amid the other languages of the exile community. It could therefore serve Ball as the *vox humana* to express the disgust he had for his homeland. Neutrality meant meaninglessness. To this can be added Ball's vigorous support of the poetic codification of polyglot practice: the poem "L'amiral cherche une maison à louer" (The Admiral is looking for a house to rent). It was simultaneously recited in German, English, and French (as well as in nonsense words, vocables, singing, and whistling), moving in and out of relations of translation, by Richard Huelsenbeck, Marcel Janco, and Tristan Tzara at the Cabaret Voltaire on 29

March 1916.[12] Again, the polyglot has lost its specific qualities to become *the voice*, in this case, at risk in a world of noise. As Ball wrote:

All the styles of the last twenty years came together yesterday. Huelsenbeck, Tzara, and Janco took the floor with a *poéme simultan*. That is a contrapuntal recitative in which three or more voices speak, sing, whistle, etc., at the same time in such a way that the elegiac, humorous, or bizarre content of the piece is brought out by these combinations. In such a simultaneous poem, the willful quality of an organic work is given powerful expression, and so is its limitation by the accompaniment. Noises (an *rrrrr* drawn out for minutes, or crashes, or sirens, etc.) are superior to the human voice in energy.

The "simultaneous poem" has to do with the value of the voice. The human organ represents the soul, the individuality in its wanderings with its demonic companions. The noises represent the background—the inarticulate, the disastrous, the decisive. The poem tries to elucidate the fact that man is swallowed up in the mechanistic process. In a typically compressed way it shows the conflict of the *vox humana* with a world that threatens, ensnares, and destroys it, a world whose rhythm and noise are ineluctable.[13]

For Ball, the "mechanistic process" was part of a powerful belief in matter over the spirit that had produced the "modern necrophilia," and the machine was something that "gives a sham life to dead matter . . . death working systematically, counterfeiting life."[14] The mechanical process he loathes most is that associated with language and journalism: the printing press, the machine that in itself "tells more lies than any newspaper it prints." The repetition destroys human rhythms, just as the pacing of caged animals happens in repetitious patterns, and there is nothing more horrifying than "a walk through the noisy workroom of a modern printing shop. The animal sounds, the stinking liquids. All the senses focused on what is bestial, monstrous, and yet unreal."[15]

As Ball said in a statement given prior to reciting the sound poems themselves, "In these phonetic poems we totally renounce the language that journalism has abused and corrupted. We must return to the [Rimbaudian] alchemy of the word, we must even give up the word too, to keep for poetry its last and holiest refuge."[16] Ball's *holiest refuge* for poetry against a journalism and the noisy machines that printed it was grounded in Christianity. His *ohne Worte* was in actuality the sound of *das Wort*, a place where words are disassembled into the *voice* in order to leave the Word intact. It is true that the Cabaret Voltaire is not usually thought of as a crossroads between Bethlehem and Golgotha, but it was on such sacrosanct ground that Ball had already tested noise early in the month prior to reciting his six sound poems, with his staging of the bruitist *A Nativity Play*.[17] The onomatopoeia that had become submerged and subtle in his sound poems, "touching lightly on a hundred ideas at the same time without naming them,"[18] was much more imitative in the play, conventionally depicting the wind *(f f f f f fffff)* and animal sounds, Joseph and Mary muttering their prayers, and less conventionally depicting The Angel (sound of a propeller), The Star (*zoke, zoke, zzzzzzzzzzzooooooke*, etc.), among others. The audience did not let the noise get in the way of their reverence for Christmas in the summertime, even the nationalities in the audience whose devotion to Jesus Christ couldn't be taken for granted watched "with real astonishment." However, Ball was "ashamed of the noise of the performance, the mixture of styles and moods."[19]

In less than three weeks he was standing in a stiff bishop's costume performing his own brand of Edenic language of the sound poems. Moreover, while reciting them,

I noticed that my voice had no choice but to take on the ancient cadence of priestly lamentation, that style of liturgical singing that wails in all the Catholic churches of East and West. I do not know what gave me the idea of this music, but I began to chant my vowel sequences in a church style like a recitative, and tried not only to look serious but to force myself to be serious. For a moment it seemed as if there were a pale, bewildered face in my cubist mask, that half-frightened, half-curious face of a ten-year-old boy, trembling and hanging avidly on the priest's words in the requiems and high masses in his home parish. Then the lights went out, as I had ordered, and bathed in sweat, I was carried down off the stage like a magical bishop.[20]

It seems clear that the "half-frightened, half-curious face of a ten-year-old boy" Ball mentions in his description was himself, the actual boy whose kisses had worn down a spot on the wooden frame surrounding the picture of the Virgin Mary above his bed. Although his religious fervency may have gone dormant until his conversion back into Catholicism during the mid-1920s, Christianity remained Ball's touchstone throughout his Dada days. Within the sound poems themselves, along with the primitivist and onomatopoeic words, Richard Sheppard has detected the trace of some inadvertent sound poetry recited by Jesus Christ after hanging on the cross for nine hours. The nonwords "elomen elomen lefitalominai" in Ball's sound poem "Wolken" (Clouds) resembles Jesus' "ELI, ELI, LAMA SABACHTHANI?" (Matthew 27:46), which are the words "My God, my God, why hast thou forsaken me?"[21] Moreover, all the poems hearkened back to Corinthians: "For he that speaketh in an *unknown* tongue speaketh not unto men, but unto God: for no man understandeth *him;* how be it in the spirit he speaketh mysteries" (14:2). In this sense, the clatter of foreign tongues in the Cabaret Voltaire was countered with an even more foreign tongue.

Noise and Simultaneity

"One hears *shit* from every corner of the universe."
Blaise Cendrars[22]

Simultaneism in the avant-garde was closely associated with noise in two ways: as the product of an instantaneous awareness of numerous events occurring at any one time in space, whether that might be the space of a café or the entire earth, and the product of an additional collapse of time into that already collapsed space. Richard Huelsenbeck, in discussing its literary variants within Dadaism, thought that simultaneism attempted "to transform the problem of the ear into a problem of the face"[23]—in other words, the flow of time needed to understand individual speech versus the capability, when the face becomes a unified perceptual organ, to grasp a multitude of entities in an instant. Objects and events in time come to occupy the same spatial instant: "While I, for example, become successively aware that I boxed an old woman on the ear yesterday and washed my hands an hour ago, the screeching of a streetcar brake and the crash of a brick falling off the roof next door reach my ear simultaneously and my (outward or inward) eye rouses itself to seize, in the simultaneity of these events, a swift meaning of life."[24] Huelsenbeck goes on to explain how simultaneism was closely associated with the noise of bruitism. He cites music to seek a working definition of noise but not as a place where numerous tones can simultaneously exist in harmony and counterpoint: "Just as physics distinguishes between tones (which can be expressed in mathematical formulae) and noises, which are completely baffling to its symbolism and abstractionism, because they are a direct objectivization of dark vital force, here the distinction between a succession and 'simultaneity,' which defies formulation because it is a direct symbol of action. And so ultimately a simultaneous poem means nothing but 'Hurrah for life!'"[25] At another time he differentiates between bruitism and simultaneity, as the former melding the sound of a yawn with, again, screeching streetcar brakes, and the latter a melange of actions:

The Bruitist poem
represents a streetcar as it is, the essence of the streetcar with the yawning of Schulze the coupon clipper and the screeching of brakes

The Simultaneist poem
teaches a sense of the merry-go-round of all things; while Herr Schulze reads his paper, the Balkan crosses the bridge at Nish, a pig squeals in Butcher Nuttke's cellar.[26]

One simultaneous poem by Tristan Tzara (Zurich, April 1919) was fortuitously compounded by the audience's own *bruitism* and simultaneity; it was "performed by twenty people who did not always keep in time with each other. This was what the audience, and especially its younger members, had been waiting for. Shouts, whistles, chanting in unison, laughter . . . all of which mingled more or less antiharmoniously with the bellowing of the twenty on the platform."[27]

Huelsenbeck credited F. T. Marinetti and the Italian Futurists with the invention of literary simultaneity, but the Dada practice he referred to was limited to a coterminous utterance along the lines of *L'amiral cherche une maison à louer*, whereas Marinetti also entertained the function of wirelessness within simultaneism. Transmissional space shared the same atmosphere as acoustic simultaneity, however, whereas the cohabitation of a space by several speakers in a room could render the immediacy of speech nonsensical, the simultaneity of signals could potentially operate in a much more abstract way. For instance, Marinetti thought that all conventions of relationality, traditionally confined as they were to local and manageable structures and comparisons, would break down once they were pummeled with a global infinitude of possible relations all arriving at once with a newfound speed having "no connecting wires" and that the new disposition to this transmissional reality, the *wireless imagination*, required a radical response from among the arts.[28] Also, the polyglot of the cabaret took on other meanings when anywhere in the globe could be figuratively invoked.

Guillaume Apollinaire claimed to have originated the term *simultaneity* in 1912 in reference to the arts, against the similar claims made by Henri-Martin Barzun, who had argued for simultaneous poetry performances, some aided by a phonograph (*Voix, rhythmes et chants simultanés*, 1913). However, Apollinaire was concerned with painting and not literature and in particular the paintings of Robert Delaunay. Like Delaunay, Apollinaire's simultaneism was linked to the supremacy of sight: "Our eyes serve as the essential sensibility between *nature* and our *soul*. Our soul maintains its life in harmony. Harmony is engendered only by the *simultaneity* with which the measures and proportions of light reach the soul, the supreme sense of our eyes. This simultaneity alone is creation; everything else is merely enumeration, contemplation, study. This simultaneity is life itself."[29] Delaunay let it be known that his distaste was for things outside the service of color: "I am horrified by *music* and *noise*."[30] Nevertheless, no matter how simultaneism could be represented in vision, light, and color, it was best experienced through transmissional and acoustical means.

The simultaneity of noise mimics that of the signal in the first part of Cendrars's major novel *Dan Yack* (1927), where Antarctica becomes the Eiffel Tower[31] of the bourgeois world traveler. One pole gives way to another—Antarctica the nonnation gathering point of all nations, the place where citizenship is gravitationally pulled down into a frigid universalism. Instead of a wireless, Dan Yack comes equipped on the ship from Tasmania to Antarctica with means to invoke the rest of the world: six phonograph machines and a cache of recordings. Although "Music bores me stiff, I don't like anything except the nasal bleating of phonographs and the loud roar of gramophones,"[32] he is nevertheless able to imagine in such nasal bleating the desirable bodies of female singers: "Dan Yack swore that it was a buxom little blonde, wiggling her hips as she sang. 'I can just see her bare legs, Captain. There are little folds above her knees.'"[33] The Captain is apparently not amused, so Dan Yack offers to play him a recording of a sea lion getting its throat cut or the clubbing and skinning of 60,000 seals. Dan Yack steps out of the bath, puts on the phonograph and begins to shave:

In the silence one could hear the razor scraping through the hairs, then the click of the gramophone, then a deafening rumble and suddenly a frightful scream that filled the cabin. It was the sea-lion having its throat cut. Its cry rose to a crescendo. Then there was the far-off barking of a million seals, followed by a long moan. Next, the voice of a man shouting at the top of his lungs: "Kill it, John! Kill it!" A gunshot. Then no more. Then, once again, the baying, but retreating farther and farther into the distance. And finally, the hoarse sound of a ship's siren.

Or perhaps it was the beast's death-cry.

Dan Yack had stepped back into his tub. A smell of vetiver wafted through the cabin. The needle, at the end of its track, scratched and fretted.[34]

Once in Antarctica and after suffering its night, Dan Yack thinks he sees the spring sun in the play of long shadows (cinema?), but others are not convinced. To herald the sun Dan Yack sets up several phonographs and gramophones to play simultaneously. From these erupt the simulated sounds of nations all at once, as if they were flowing centripetally down along wireless longitudinal lines, the global simultaneity of silent transmissions is modeled through the ability for sounds to occupy the same space:

He wound up all his phonographs and all his gramophones and set them up on the big table in order of size. He put a record or a cylinder on each one. Then, moving as quickly as possible from one to the other, he set them all going. They were triggered off almost simultaneously. The turntables started to spin. There was a multiple whirring noise, then a nasal voice roared: '"The Marseillaise"! . . . played by the trumpeters of the Garde Républicaine!'

But before the phrase was finished, overlapping with it, two other machines struck up, a quarter of a turn later, like cannons firing a salute on a day of national celebration: *Bojé Tzara chrani*. Then the Garde Républicaine broke into the "The Marseillaise" with great fanfare of bugles and drums, while another machine burst forth with "God Save the King" played on the bagpipes!

There was a racket fit to wake the dead. The gramophones tried to drown each other out.

"The sun! The sun!" yelled Dan Yack.

He was beaming.

He started up the last phonograph and the languorous voice of Fragson joined in the tumult: *"Manon . . . voici le . . . sssolei!"* . . .

The gramophones started up again, louder than ever. The room echoed to the cries of the crowd, applause, thousands of voices, trumpets, the brouhaha of processions, a million shuffling feet.

At last the Tsar died on a final, dying all of *phew-phew;* then it was the King's turn to fall silent; "The Marseillaise" still rolled on, warlike and democratic; it stopped abruptly on a crash of the big bass drum.

rrrrrrerererereararararararararara . . . gasped the records in their death-throes.[35]

Fragson's anthem to love then served as the denouement to this cacophony of simultaneous nationalisms and the crowds and masses associated with them. The noise in this case was understandable—that is, because each song within this agglomerate had been repeated so often, each could be listened to and ignored. It was sufficient to know that each song existed and interacted among other songs at any one moment. The lack of a need to listen invited the eradication of the specifics of any one song, just as the idea of the nation eradicates the actual differences of the people living there. Those who sing certain anthems collapse themselves into the body of the head of state from where they sing a narcissistic praise song to their own disappearance.

It might seem like Dan Yack set the anthems resounding with one another to civilize the landscape—that it is a clinical case study for colonialism or, as Franz Fanon said of Radio Algeria, that "It is one of the means of escaping the inert, passive, and sterilizing pressure of the 'native' environment. It is, according to the settler's expression, 'the only way to still feel like a civilized man.'"[36] But Dan Yack was looking for just this type of ciphering of crowds to reproduce the pomp and circumstance appropriate for a procession of the sun. The cacophony of these combined crowds would lure the sun, which would provide the warmth that these absent crowds could not, and as these crowds die out they leave only the absence of love and the individual warmth it too might provide; in the nasal bleating of the phonographic death throes of the crowd he can imagine at least one body. If these sounds were supposed to signal the powers and pleasures of colonial civilization, their international dispersion, their pathetic simulation of crowds through decrepit technology, would have a poor chance against the transformations brought about by the sun.

In Dan Yack's multiple phonograph installation, noise was also under-scored by surface noise, skipping and repeating grooves, and the sound of the mechanism—its nasal bleating and the scratching and fretting needle at the end of its track. The exhaustion of materials, the fatigue of the spring, and the deterioration of the mechanism impinged on the age, health, endurance, and commitment of the human voice. What may begin as anthem may end as dirge. What captures vitality may choke it. Ord-Hume reported about the fate of many phonographic novelties when he cited the late-nineteenth-century cigarette dispenser that once asked the opener of the box, "Would you care for a cigarette?" but then wore down to "Aaahjjouaaakkmmenn?"[37] The funereal phonograph in Joyce's *Ulysses* was simply catching up with the moldering body beneath: "Kraahraark! Hellohellohello amawfullyglad kraaark awfully gladaseeragain hellohello amarawk kopthsth." Thus, on the other side of a dynamic, transgressive noise, the "trajectory of a word tossed like a screeching phonograph rec-ord,"[38] as Tzara said, we can hear the mournful lament at the decay of tech-nological enthusiasm.

The Future of War Noises

The most important single achievement in the early history of avant-garde noise was the Italian Futurist Luigi Russolo's *art of noises*. Included under this term were his manifesto of 1913, a book of 1916, the music he devel-oped through the design of his new noise-intoning instruments, the *into-narumori*, and a new form of notation. The art of noises seemingly came out of nowhere: there was no easily observable precedent for it within mu-sic, and it came from an unlikely person. Although Russolo belonged to a family of musicians, within Italian Futurism he belonged instead to the first group of painters. On his transition, he effectively displaced Balilla Pratella as the movement's in-house composer and became the public face for music and noise within Italian Futurism. Within the avant-garde as a whole Russolo's art of noises would become synonymous with noise itself, although often it would be wrongly attributed to the movement's impresa-rio F. T. Marinetti or to Italian Futurism in general. Besides the connec-tions with bruitism mentioned above, the composers who were provoked positively or negatively by Russolo's noise included Ravel, Debussy, Proko-fiev, Stravinsky, Antheil, Satie, Milhaud, Honegger, Varèse, and Cowell. The imitative sounds within Jean Cocteau's libretto, if not Satie's score, for

Diaghilev's production *Parade* derived from the art of noises. It had an impact on aspects of the Russian avant-garde, including the poetry of Mayakovsky and the films of Dziga Vertov, on Vorticism in England (including Ezra Pound), and on Moholy-Nagy and Mondrian. The latter addressed Russolo's ideas in two lengthy essays in an attempt to formulate his own *neoplastic* music. The influence of Russolo's noise eventually waned but was then revived in the wake of *musique concrète* in the 1950s and has become widely recognized as a precursor to a range of artistic activities as the second half of the century rolls to a close.

Russolo's art of noises appears to be an ineluctable expression of the machines and motors of modernity, yet if that were the case, an art of noises seemingly would have arisen much earlier elsewhere. Although Italy arrived late to the industrial revolution, its accelerated growth rivaled that of any spot on the continent: it was not so much modernism per se but modernism hitting the ground at full speed. The way this abruptness foreshortened the future amid Italy's agrarian past provided a local model for Italy's retrograde position among the European avant-gardes, especially from F. T. Marinetti's Parisian vantage point. Motivated by a combined nationalism and national embarrassment and buoyed by his family's wealth, Marinetti set off to shape his own avant-garde. The Italian Futurists could soon be heard berating Italy as the land where museums and ruins spread across the cultural landscape like a crop of tombstones and were leading them forward with Marinetti's revelation in *The Founding and Manifesto of Futurism* that a roaring car is more beautiful than the *Victory of Samothrace*. Russolo founded his art of noises on the same sentiment: "*We delight much more in combining in our thoughts the noises of trams, of automobile engines, of carriages and brawling crowds, than in hearing again the* Eroica *or the* Pastorale."[39] This, in itself, gave an urban and technological flavor to his modernism that distinguished it from the resident Italian Futurist composer Francesco Balilla Pratella, whose music allied itself to Futurism primarily on the program of a nationalism rooted in the peasantry. Pratella's *Manifesto of Futurist Music* (11 October 1910) did indeed state that Futurism ought to "express the musical soul of crowds, of the great industrial shipyards, the trains, the transatlantics, battle ships, cars and airplanes,"[40] but he was to say later that these were not his sentiments but those Marinetti interjected during the editing process.[41] Pratella had already composed and performed his Futurist music and penned three manifestos by the time Russolo took up his art of noise. As a gesture, Russolo's manifesto "The Art of Noises" appeared on 11 March 1913, exactly one year after Pratella's "Technical Manifesto of Futurist Music," and was published in the form of a deferential open letter:

Dear Balilla Pratella, Great Futurist Composer,
In Rome, at the very crowded Teatro Costanzi, while I was listening to the orchestral performance of your revolutionary MUSICA FUTURISTA with my friends Marinetti, Boccioni and Balla, I conceived a new art: The Art of Noises, the logical consequence of your marvelous innovations.[42]

The manifesto ends with equal respect: "to my dear Pratella, to your futuristic genius." The Pratella concert mentioned was in reality only a matter of days before the release of Russolo's manifesto, hardly enough time to develop ideas at the level of ambition and coherence displayed. The manifesto was apparently finished three months prior to Pratella's concert but postponed so as to not disrupt ongoing preparations and embarrass a fellow Futurist. Moreover, the opening and closing niceties are contradicted by the manifesto's central themes, which demean the conventional musical basis on which Pratella's music is founded.[43]

Pratella's music was dissonant for the time but hardly enough to inspire a radical break into noise. Yet music was not the only art using sound within Italian Futurism; there were also the onomatopoetic practices of Marinetti's *parole in libertà* (words-in-freedom, or free words). Russolo included in his manifesto a letter from Marinetti in which *parole in libertà* were used to report on the sounds of military combat at Adrianople, the ZANG-TUMB-TUUUMB of the cannons, the taratatata of the machine guns, and other sounds interspersed with musical instructions and allusions. Here is just an excerpt of the "marvelous *free words* the orchestra of a great battle"[44] that Russolo included in the manifesto:

Far far back of the orchestra pools muddying huffing goaded oxen wagons *pluff-plaff* horse action *flic flac zing zing shaaack* laughing whinnies the *tiiinkling jiiingling* tramping 3 Bulgarian battalions marching *croooc-craaac* [slowly] Shumi Maritza or Karvavena *ZANG-TUMB-TUUUMB toc-toc-toc-toc* [fast] *crooooc-craaac* [slowly] cries of officers slamming about like brass plates pan here *paak* there *BUUUM ching chaak* [very fast] *cha-cha-cha-cha-chaak* down there up there all around high up look out your head beautiful![45]

The passage ends with the image of "the orchestra of the noises of war swelling under a held note of silence in the high sky round golden balloon that observes the firing."[46] The graphic element of a surveillance balloon as a musical note, foreshortens the noises of war below into an orchestra, just as Marinetti's plane rides above battlefields had foreshortened military action into the orthographic form of *parole in libertà*.[47]

By citing Marinetti's *parole in libertà* text within his own text, Russolo achieved several things. He deferred to the authority of Marinetti as the founder and leader of Italian Futurism, an authority supported by Marinetti's ability to bankroll the movement's activities; for Russolo, Marinetti was "my dear and great friend . . . who is still vibrating from the great acoustic emotion of his experience assisting in the siege of Adrianople."[48] Within the context of the text itself, the violent fact of war acted as a rhetorical device, persuading the reader-listener of the inevitability of noise through its disciplinary role in the negotiation of lives and nations. War noises also staked a claim within the avant-garde land grab of the future because they were *the newest noises* and required new artistic means for their expression.[49] Finally, war noises were valued by Russolo because he valued war. Thus, the emphasis conferred on the fighting sounds of Marinetti's combat *parole* situates militarism at the founding of Futurist noise. The incursion of militarism into the musical project of Russolo's art of noises can thus be understood as an auditive negotiation between music and war.[50]

War was a longtime preoccupation for Marinetti. The bombast of his pre-Futurist writings, where his words were projected out over the endless ocean was but a rehearsal for a voice that could trumpet the scope if not the decibel level of massive scenes of destruction. He officially let loose the battle cry with his first manifesto in 1909: "We will glorify war—the world's only hygiene—militarism, patriotism, the destructive gesture of freedom-bringers, beautiful ideas worth dying for, and scorn for women."[51] Marinetti's report "from the trenches of Adrianopolis" was included in Russolo's manifesto under the guise of a personal correspondence, but Marinetti had actually been performing the piece publicly prior to the publication of the manifesto, and he had linked military sounds and *parole in libertà* already the year before.[52] As Marinetti recounted, "I finished that short synthesizing noise-making poem while witnessing the machine-gunning of three thousand horses ordered by the Turkish general who was the governor before the fortress fell."[53] He transmitted these sounds as he traveled from the front with its "long worms we swallowed from the necks of the bottles filled with water from puddles"[54] to aristocratic drawing rooms and bohemian haunts of Sofia, St. Petersburg, Berlin, London, Paris, Rome, Milan, and elsewhere. Velimir Khlebnikov marked Marinetti's visit to Russia with a letter addressed to "You untalented loudmouth. . . . I am convinced that we will meet one day to the sound of cannons, in a duel between the Italo-German coalition and the Slavs, on the Dalmation coast. I suggest Dubrovnik as the place for our seconds to meet."[55] Aleksei Kruchenykh, the Russian Futurist exponent of *zaum*, was likewise unimpressed for other reasons, "The Italian 'amateurish' Futurists, with their endless ra ta ta ra ta ta, are like Maeterlinck's heroines who think that 'door' repeated a hundred times opens up to revelation."[56] A visit to Berlin in 1913 left Rudolf Leonhard with the recollection that Marinetti "loved and worshipped war, because it made a noise and because he had no desire to know what else it did. With his noise for noise's sake he genuinely but unintentionally caricatured art for art's sake."[57]

Just weeks before World War I, C. R. W. Nevinson witnessed Marinetti perform in London: "Marinetti recited a poem about the siege of Adrianople with various kinds of onomatopoeic noises and crashes in free verse, while all the time the band downstairs played 'You made me love you. I didn't want to do it.'"[58] The poet Harold Monro admired Marinetti's inventiveness but thought as poetry his declamations were nothing more than "an advanced form of verbal photography."[59] Henry Nevinson, father of C. R. W. Nevinson and like Marinetti a war correspondent, explained that he himself had "heard many recitations and have tried to describe many battles. But listen to Marinetti's recitation of one of his battle scenes . . . the noise, the confusion, the surprise of death, the terror and courage, the shouting, curses, blood and agony—all were recalled by that amazing succession of words, performed or enacted by the poet with such passion and abandonment that no one could escape the spell of listening."[60] Wyndham Lewis, alluding to Erich Maria Remarque's *All Quiet on the Western Front*, remembered it this way:

It was a matter of astonishment what Marinetti could do with his unaided voice. He certainly made an extraordinary amount of noise. A day of attack upon the Western Front, with all the "heavies" hammering together, right back to the horizon, was nothing to it. My equanimity when first subjected to the sounds of mass-bombardment in Flanders was possibly due to my marinettian preparation—it seemed "all quiet" to me, in fact, by comparison.[61]

Marinetti in his manifesto "Dynamic and Synoptic Declamation" detailed a performance at the Doré Gallery (28 April 1914) in London:

Dynamically and synoptically I declaimed several passages from my *ZANG TUMB TUUMB* (the *Siege of Adrianople*). On the table in front of me I had a telephone, some boards, and matching hammers that permitted me to imitate the Turkish general's orders and the sounds of artillery and machine-gun fire.

Blackboards had been set up in three parts of the hall, to which in succession I either ran or walked, to sketch rapidly an analogy with chalk. My listeners, as they turned to follow me in all my evolutions, participated, their entire bodies inflamed with emotion, in the violent effects of the battle described by my words-in-freedom.

There were two big drums in a distant room, from which the painter Nevinson, my colleague, produced the boom of cannon, when I told him to do so over the telephone.

The swelling interest of the English audience became frantic enthusiasm when I achieved the greatest dynamism by alternating the Bulgarian song "Sciumi Maritza" with the dazzle of my images and the clamor of the onomatopoeic artillery.[62]

Marinetti argued for a poetics open to the forces exerted by the new technologies of transportation, communication, and information, all of which were thrown, among other purposes, into the conduct of military combat.[63] In the Italo-Turkish War he had witnessed the first use of airplanes in modern warfare, and it was the whirling propeller of an airplane that had "taught" him the destruction of syntax.[64] Another new technology of modern warfare was the observation balloon equipped with wireless telegraphy, both the vantage point of the balloon and the collapsing of distance in telegraphy having the some capacity for foreshortening and abstraction. Marinetti represented these balloons in the "round golden balloon that observes the firing" (in the *parole in libertà* quoted in Russolo's manifesto) and the orthographic poem "Captive Turkish Balloon," where one of the ephemeral lines of TSF (wireless telegraphy), which would normally report troupe movements, transmits to "Tsarigraad."[65] For Marinetti, the poet too was supposed to receive and transmit vibrationally, to become a wireless observer of the grand panorama of the battlefield, to "telegraphically transmit the analogical foundation of life with the same economical speed that a telegraph imposes on the swift accounts of reporters and war correspondents."[66]

But Marinetti, Russolo, and other Italian Futurists sought much more than poetics and rhetorical ploys within warfare, and World War I gave them all they had bargained for. Perhaps least among their worries was how the war interrupted the series of Russolo's concerts, which no doubt would have secured him wider fame. According to one report a total of about 30,000 spectators were in attendance over the course of twelve performances at the London Coliseum, and the tour was just beginning:

From London we should have gone on to Liverpool, to Dublin, Glasgow, Edinburgh and Vienna, and then started another long tour that included Moscow, Berlin and Paris. The war caused it all to be postponed. Meanwhile in Italy, the long period of neutrality started. And there began our long struggle for intervention, which lasted until that glorious May when war was declared. Then, abandoning everything to enlist voluntarily, I left for the front, together with my futurist friends, Marinetti, Boccioni, Piatti, Sant'Elia, and Sironi. And I was lucky enough to fight in the midst of the marvelous and grand tragic symphony of modern war.[67]

Italy's reluctance to intervene caused great frustration among the Futurists. In protest, Russolo, Marinetti, Boccioni, and others staged an interventionist demonstration at the Teatro dal Verme during a performance of Puccini. The next evening they burned an Austrian flag and, after fighting with audience members, were arrested and detained for five days. Six months later, Russolo was successfully inducted, served briefly in a cyclists battalion, later became an Alpinist, and, in November 1915, engaged in combat for the possession of several ridges. Umberto Boccioni could hardly wait for the threatening sounds of battle: "Zuiii Zuiii Tan Tan.

Bullets all around. Volunteers calm on the ground shoot Pan Pan. Crack shot Sergeant Massai on his feet shoots, first shrapnel explodes. We arrive hearing a shout we throw ourselves to the ground: shrapnel explodes twenty steps away and I shout: At last."[68] The war had permeated Marinetti's thinking so completely that he even argued for full-scale militarism within his "Manifesto of the Futurist Dance" (8 July 1917), outlining the "first three Futurist dances from the three mechanisms of war: shrapnel, the machine gun, and the airplane."[69] In part 1 of the *Dance of the Shrapnel* he wanted to "give the fusion of the mountain with the parabola of the shrapnel. The fusion of the carnal human song with the mechanical noise of shrapnel. To give the ideal synthesis of the war: a mountain soldier who carelessly sings beneath an uninterrupted vault of shrapnel. *Movement 1:* With the feet mark the *boom-boom* of the projectile coming from the cannon's mouth," etc.[70] The dances were to be accompanied by the *organized noises* and *special effects* of Russolo's intonarumori.

Russolo devoted an entire chapter of his book *The Art of Noises* to "The Noises of War." In it he implies that the battlefield serves as a model for modern listening and an art of noises since in combat the ear is much more privileged than it is in daily life: it can judge with "greater certainty than the eye!"[71] "From noise, the different calibers of grenades and shrapnels can be known even before they explode. Noise enables us to discern a marching patrol in deepest darkness, even to judging the number of men that compose it. From the intensity of rifle fire, the number of defenders of a given position can be determined. There is no movement or activity that is not revealed by noise."[72] The most remarkable thing about this chapter is that it concentrates almost entirely on ordnance and ignores the sounds of dying humans or animals; the closest Russolo gets to the sounds of the species endangered by war is the *katzenmusik* of shrapnel.[73] It is interesting, in this respect, to contrast Russolo's acoustic account of the battlefield with Erich Maria Remarque's *All Quiet on the Western Front*, or in the original German *Im Westen nichts Neues* (1929). On the one hand, Remarque better describes the *aesthetics*, literally the heightening of the senses (compare with anesthesia), of combat:

The moment that the first shells whistle over and the air is rent with the explosions there is suddenly in our veins, in our hands, in our eyes a tense waiting, a watching, a heightening alertness, a strange sharpening of the senses. The body with one bound is in full readiness.

It often seems to me as though it were the vibrating, shuddering air that with a noiseless leap springs upon us; or as though the front itself emitted an electric current which awakened unknown nerve centers.[74]

The experience of combat engenders a new relationship a person has with the earth, animals, other humans, as well as what Walter Benjamin called the unwitting *wooing of the cosmos* involved in modern warfare.[75] This sense of spirituality, spectacle, and attunement would be well suited to an argument for a new art form if Remarque did not also describe the absolute horror accompanying the seduction.

Like Russolo, Remarque details the prioritization given the ear in combat, whether it is for listening for troupe carriers behind the enemy lines; for the bells, gongs, and clappers to warn of that other counteraction of sight—gas; or for differentiating the sounds of artillery shells.[76] However, whereas Russolo will describe the sounds of shells using musical terms, Remarque will concentrate on matters of life and death: "[The young recruits] get killed simply because they hardly can tell shrapnel from high-explosive, they are mown down because they are listening anxiously to the roar of the big coal-boxes falling in the rear, and miss the light, piping whistle of the low spreading daisy-cutters."[77] Remarque also details the sounds of injured, dying, and dead soldiers. One wounded soldier can be heard for three days but he cannot be found; he must be lying face-down "for it is only when a man has his mouth close to the ground that it is impossible to gauge the direction of the cry. . . . He grows gradually hoarser. The voice is so strangely pitched that it seems to be everywhere."[78] The first night he calls for help, the second his cries are mixed with delirious conversation with his family back home, the third he simply weeps, and then he is silent until one last death rattle. But it does not stop there, for the dead refuse to remain silent: "Many have their bellies swollen up like balloons. They hiss, belch, and make movements. the gases in them make noises."[79]

The sounds of an enemy soldier dying, indeed, accompanies the most important turning point in *All Quiet on the Western Front*. The protagonist seeking refuge in a shell hole repeatedly stabs a soldier who stumbles in. It is the first time he has injured or killed anyone in hand-to-hand combat, without the consolation of distance, and as if to impress the immediacy of the act further, he shares the shell hole with the wounded man, who pathetically gurgles for hours on end as he dies: "It sounds to me as though he bellows, every gasping breath is like a cry, a thunder—but it is only my heart pounding."[80] The soldier is too weak to cry out, so he will not have to be stabbed in the throat. The protagonist wants to close his ears to the gurgling, but that would also render him deaf to the signals of the continuing battle; instead, he must listen as every gasp lays his heart bare. The most unbearable sound is the silence after the soldier dies. He fills the silence frantically with his own speech: "You were only an idea to me before, an abstraction that lived in my mind and called forth its appropriate response. It was that abstraction I stabbed."[81] He eventually calms down and promises the dead man, "Today you, tomorrow me. But if I come out of it, comrade, I will fight against this, that has struck us both down."[82]

Russolo wrote "The Noises of War" during a break in his service in 1916 before returning to the field, and, although sounds produced by the human voice were absent, in the *Art of Noises* manifesto of 1913 he did include as one of the *"6 families of noises* of the futurist orchestra that we will soon realize mechanically" a number of sounds that could easily have been encountered on the battlefield: "shouts, screams, shrieks, wails, hoots, howls, death rattles and sobs."[83] Within this family of noises, *howling* formed a class of intonarumori: the *ululatori*, "the most musical of the noise instruments. The howling that they produce is almost human; and while they recall the siren to some extent, they are also a little like the sounds of the string bass, the cello, and the violin."[84] Whether it was immersing oneself in the sonic surrounds of battle and fixing on the acoustical descriptions of shrapnel or of immersing oneself in the sounds of the world and extracting a music, Russolo appears to be involved at every point in the same process of abstraction that Remarque's protagonist decried, "that abstraction I stabbed."

The sounds of actual pained voices became more of a personal reality for Russolo after returning to the front where, serving as an alpinist, he suffered a serious head injury from an exploding grenade (17 December 1917). Prefigured in Marinetti's *Dance of the Shrapnel*, he also became a sad realization of a poetic prophecy made by Marinetti in "Let's Murder the Moonshine" (1909): "And we ourselves will give the example, abandoning ourselves to the raging Tailoress of battles who, when she has sewn us into handsome scarlet uniforms, gorgeous in the sun, will anoint our hair with flame and brush it smooth with projectiles."[85] Russolo required eighteen months of hospital care and harbored a partial paralysis lasting years longer. In 1921, during a concert in Paris that was disrupted by the Dadaists, Marinetti appealed to the audience on behalf of Russolo because of his war wounds:

The Italian *bruitistes*, led by Marinetti, were giving a performance of works written for their new instruments. These works were pale, insipid and melodious in spite of Russolo's noise-music, and the Dadaists who attended did not fail to express their feelings—and very loudly. Marinetti asked indulgence for Russolo, who had been wounded in the war and had undergone a serious operation on his skull. This moved the Dadaists to demonstrate violently how little impressed they were by a reference to the war.[86]

Marinetti had also been seriously wounded in the war, and Futurist architect Sant'Elia, Russolo's close friend Umberto Boccioni, and millions of others were killed. Long afterward, the war continued to resonate among the bodies that were left. George Antheil wrote of the 1920s, "Negro music made us remember at least that we still had bodies which had not been exploded by shrapnel."[87]

The violence encouraged and the carnage suppressed within Russolo's engagement with war noises was present at the founding of the art of noises with the inclusion of Marinetti's onomatopoeic reportage. Modernism in general played a role, certainly, but it played a more specific role through the noises produced in a clash of modern warfare, of an industrial technology given over to the quick kill instead of its usual protracted grind among the cogs. Although Russolo would eventually become antifascist, during the second decade of this century he was never antiwar. Warfare as an intensification of modernism never promised a peace through accelerated cycles of technological development, as Walter Benjamin wrote: "Now and then one hears of something 'reassuring' such as the invention of a sensitive listening device that registers the whir of propellers at great distances. And a few months later a soundless airplane is invented."[88] Russolo's battlefield never invented its way into silence. Instead, his invention relied on the theater of war, where the newest speeding metals cannot help but make an impression on their listeners in accordance with the two highest attri-

butes Marinetti prescribed for manifesto writing itself: violence and precision. The ear *will* become more attentive because "in modern warfare,
mechanical and metallic, the element of sight is almost zero. The sense,
the significance, and the expressiveness of noises, however, are infinite."[89]
In this way Russolo's well-known words—"Let us cross a large modern
capital with our ears more attentive than eyes"—sounds like marching orders, even though within discussions of twentieth-century music and the
arts his gait is most often confused with the saunter of a *flâneur* or the
focused mycological prowl of John Cage.[90] In the same respect, and as we
shall see in the celebrations of other emphatic sounds of modernism, turning a deaf ear to the violences will not silence them.

Part II

Drawing the Line:

Music, Noise, and Phonography

I frequently hear music in the heart of noise.

George Gershwin

Sea, wind, leaves, thunder, waters, cows lowing, the cattle market, cocks, hens don't crow, snakes hissss. There's music everywhere. Ruttledge's door: ee creaking. No, that's noise.

James Joyce, Ulysses

Music is like sound to my ears.

Paul DeMarinis[1]

Within the history of Western art music, noises were not intrinsically extramusical; they were simply the sounds music could not use. The determination of extramusicality rested not in a hard and fast materiality but in the power of musical practice and discourse to negotiate which sonorous materials will be incorporated from a world of sounds, including the sounds of its own making, and how. In the latter half of the nineteenth century, this task was aided by acoustics, itself still associated with that realm of scientific inquiry known as music. At the same time acoustics was separating itself out from music using new techniques of *visible sound* derived from graphic techniques and automatic recording instruments. Although increasingly alienated from one another, acoustics and Western art music were both in the business of determining what was music and what was noise. Sometimes they agreed, and sometimes they did not, but even in disagreement they were usually complementary. Two *lines* played an important role in this determination—the graphic line, whether visible or figurative, inscribed by hand, mind, machine, and nature, and the conceptual dividing line between noise and music, between sound and musical sound.

The line between sound and musical sound stood at the center of the existence of avant-garde music, supplying a heraldic moment of transgression and its artistic raw material, a border that had to be crossed to bring back unexploited resources, restock the coffers of musical materiality, and rejuvenate Western art music. To make extramusical material musical, the sounds of the world were processed in numerous ways. First, the sounds of the world were to be themselves categorized, explicitly or implicitly, into referential sounds and areferential *noises*, such that a noise could be incorporated into the areferential operations of music. Thus, there was an operative exchange between the distinctions of sound and musical sound from the perspective of music and sound and noises within the sphere of extramusicality, whereby the *sound* of the former was recuperated through the *noises* of the latter, with a remainder of sound usually dismissed as *imitative*. Second, these privileged *noises* of the sphere of extramusicality would align themselves with already existing musical attributes and elements, such as dissonance, timbre, and percussion. Third, these noisy correspondences within music were emphasized as themselves bearing traces of the world of true extramusicality; this was the basis of what I call the practice of *resident noises*. Fourth, sounds were technologically selected or manipulated to render them suitable as musical material, as in phonographic practices such as *musique concrète*, and finally, sounds were processed through the operations of aurality, a feature of John Cage's dictum to hear *sounds in themselves*.

The underlying presumption of all these was that the nature of music was sonic, thereby the importation of worldly sounds into music meant diminishing or eradicating sounds that were too significant. Most important, this process displaced significance to music itself, such that the most common way to make noise significant was to make it music, but by doing so the significance of sounds was rendered insignificant.

Resolve against the mimetic ran up against the changed conditions of aurality in the latter half of the nineteenth century represented most significantly by phonography, the mimesis machine that incorporated all classes of sounds. By *phonography*, within this context, I mean the phonograph as the technological device for recording and reproducing sound (including phonautographic and visible sound practices that predated and paralleled the inventions of Charles Cros and Thomas Alva Edison, the later developments of optical sound film, and so on) and also phonography as an emblem for a dramatic shift in ideas regarding sound, aurality, and reality from that time. Phonography was associated with a number of crucial developments: it foregrounded the parameters of *a sound* and *all sound*, presented the possibility of incorporating all sound into cultural forms, shifted cultural practices away from a privileging of utterance toward a greater inclusion of audition, placed the voice of presence into the contaminated realm of writing, and linked textuality and literacy with sound through inscriptive practices. The promise of phonography, before and after the actuality of the phonograph, added another player to older discourses and practices based on musical technologies, and when it pointed more toward the production and not the reproduction of music, phonography necessarily invoked the world of *all sound*. The pressure of worldly sound brought to bear on musical practice was exacerbated in the 1920s with the marked development of auditive technologies and institutions—particularly improvements in microphony and the phonograph and the development of sound film—as practiced within music, radio, and cinema. It was within this complex that dramatically new approaches to sound began to materialize.

To make my way through the entanglements of Western art music, noise, and phonography, I concentrate on the inscriptive practices involved through the concentrated figure of the line. The line can draw the boundary between musical sound and noise by being the threshold at which too much of the world is detected. In this way the line is a sonic buffer, a silencing device. The line can also inhere the world of all sound, the most familiar instance being the intensification of the world packed into the jagged phonographic line, replaying what it has heard to make the world thicker with sound. Or the line can do both, remaining within music or demarcating music from the world while being suffused with its own plenitude. The inscriptive processes examined here cover a number of artistic practices up to the mid-twentieth century.

CONCERNING THE LINE

The line is a point where the meeting of *audio* ("I hear") and *video* ("I see") has been particularly conspicuous. The alphabet is the most obvious example, but I would like to avoid those places where lines are articulate only because they belong to a local series or set of similar configurations. Although it is ultimately futile to avoid alphabets altogether, for the simple reason that lines tend to drift among different inscriptive systems and practices, I am most interested in a simple line, as separate as possible to functioning within a system. This does not preclude this same simple line from subsequently being used within some larger type of arrangement, but by then there would be at least a double system of articulation. Likewise, this does not preclude a simple line itself being complex; in fact, this is the present topic.

Lines have received short shrift among people who think about them in a modernist way or, more precisely, a narrowly modernist way, especially when a line is understood to be but a *trace* in the sense of a remnant, even a remnant that exerts power as a predisposition. This is effectively the minimalist notion of a line, a line in an elemental sense, resting at the end of reduction. This minimalist notion should not be criticized too much since in large part it is the predominant case; yet it is not the only one. Many lines are productive and reproductive; they can be intensifications and not just rarefications, and, most important, they can be both at once. In other words, the line exists as a reservoir and not a residue, and as a reservoir *and* a residue. Consequently, the trace may be a much more lively place than commonly perceived. In modernism, however, this plenitude does not come without a price. The trade-off is that the line *contains* noise, in both senses of the word *contain*. It stores noise in its intensification while suppressing noise in the purity and simplicity of the line, and a similar process takes place when noise is controlled discursively by a line of demarcation, whether posing as a considered theoretical position or appearing as plain common sense. The line in this sense could be unraveled within its proper domain of *video*, giving another perspective on perspective and another representation of representation, extending to the limits of turbulence and chaos. However, we are restricting ourselves here to a few places where *audio* and *video* meet, conspicuously, within modernism.

Yet the life of the line is hardly limited to modernism since, historically, lines of sound have been called on to be so much more than what they initially appear to be. The best early example is the single string of the Pythagorean monochord, which vibrated in accord with the cosmos ever since the Pythagorean narrator at the end of Plato's *Republic* joined music to the motion of the spheres.[1] Pythagorean ideas of the universe, or universality, and music mediated through mathematics, if at times only simple proportionality or the unconscious musical math of Leibniz, have had a remarkable longevity through the ages, and central among these ideas was that the cosmos assumed harmonious proportions, tonalities, and ultimately, as we shall see, periodic frequencies. It did not matter that in the lore of Pythagoras his own music was never without words and sounded strange to the tastes of the day or that his insight into the mathematical basis of music was mythically sparked by the percussive sounds of a blacksmith's hammers. Linked through the ages by the traditional *Quadrivium* of *mathematica* (arithmetic, music, geometry, and astronomy) and reinvigorated in distinct periods of neo-Pythagoreanism, by the nineteenth century Pythagoreanism in music was associated with instrumental music, a high regard for consonance, and little regard for percussion, despite the lore of the blacksmith's hammer. The legacy of neo-Pythagoreanism within modernism, however, has been fairly peculiar, as it pertains to both notions of the breadth of *all sound* and the capability of a line to represent many attributes of the world, including a range of sounds.[2]

In terms of the universality of *all sound* during the late nineteenth and early twentieth centuries, the strains of neo-Pythagoreanism were detectable in two main places: synesthetic systems and Western art music. Although the acoustic space elaborated by neo-Pythagoreanism was ultimately a conceptual one (the loudness of the music of the spheres could not be heard on earth), the auditive practices (music and speech, and not just any music and speech but the phonics of poetical speech and the tonalities of music) through which it was elaborated could indeed be heard. In other words, neo-Pythagoreanism was required to invoke the universe and its universality through limited auditive means, through privileged forms of utterance. Thus, all sound was not only reduced to an anthropocentric determination; it was further reduced by being limited to what humans uttered (spoke, performed) within elite cultural practices and by excluding what humans heard apart from these utterances—what they heard of the rest of the world.

There was another magnitude of reduction, a further proscription of certain sounds, a noise abatement, in how Pythagoreanism was underscored by the single string of the monochord with its traffic in music, at one time the powerful nemesis of noise. The musical reinvigoration of Pythagoreanism within the ranks of Romantic music is well known, whereas its legacy within synesthetic systems, which traded in speech as well as music, is less obvious.[3] Even when they were wrenched from their mimetic relationship with the cosmos, synesthetic systems were constituted through relationships that deflected one perceptual and affective register to another, creating a complementary space of proportionate relations. Human participation within the auditive aspects of this space was channeled through speech (almost always the acoustic periodicity of vowels) and musical performance (with the periodicity of tones). Yet in the course of listening to humans alone, synesthesia gave status to neither consonants nor aperiodic musical sounds, let alone sounds of the world not uttered or performed within poetry or music.[4] How might universes based on the inharmonious aperiodicity of consonants and musical noises behave? What would follow from cultural practices not keyed to the centrifugal trajectories of human utterance? These were the types of questions against which Western art music and synesthetic systems unwittingly protected themselves, fortifications within which the universal could still be invoked by the distant, background sound of the monochord mapping the heavens. The figure of the monochord kept the cosmos at hand and noise at bay. Thus its single string was simultaneously rendered a fecund and discriminating line, an intensification and a reduction, an inclusion of everything and a boundary against much.

The physics and cosmology of sound were transformed dramatically when, beginning in the late eighteenth century and pervading the nineteenth century, two new inscriptive practices loosened the reliance of acoustics on music: the application of graphical techniques to visible sound and automatic recording instruments as represented by the phonautograph and phonography. There had of course been numerous means in the past to visualize sound, but the ability to make the invisible visible and to hold the time of sound still entered into a new phase. The concentric rings on the surface of water that had since antiquity provided a visual analog in time for advancing spheres of sound within the air[5] gave way in 1785 to the inscriptive stasis and intricacy of Chladni's sound figures of sand on the surface of plates and subsequently to other instrumental means for tracking and trapping time. These in turn gave way to the wavering line of automatic recording technologies such as the phonauthograph and phonograph, which brought down sound from its astronomical heights to etch audible events physically onto surfaces and onto the surface of the earth.

The universality of the line of the monochord shifted to a universality found here on earth. Édouard-Léon Scott's phonautograph, which inscribed sound-wave impressions on lamp black but unlike the later phonograph could not replay these inscriptions, was primarily put to experimental uses more concerned with analytical than analogical matters[6] and, as such, restrained the line to a terrestrial sphere. Scott himself had grander plans for his device. It was not enough to imagine the immense expanse of *all sound;* he wanted to give the earth a stylus with which to write its vocabulary for a universal language, for phonautographic inscriptions were to be the stenographic, if not hieroglyphic, means to "force nature to constitute herself a general written language of all sounds."[7] Noise abatement also persisted from earlier traditions. Whether a stone was thrown into the water by Vitruvius in the last century B.C. or Helmholtz in the nineteenth century, it was in effect a noisy act of percussion graphically muted by the surface tension of the water and rendered in regular wave patterns. The earliest automatic recording instruments (and this included those not applied to sound) and other early visual sound technologies valued mellifluousness and repetition through time more than sounds of short duration or the momentary noise of percussion. Sounds sustained through bowing, vocalization, and the rotary motion of instrumental cranks and registered on rotating recording surfaces were more easily observable to the eye. However, by these very actions musical tones and vowels were privileged. The discourses surrounding phonography proper inherited the ideas developed among the pre-Edisonian sound transcribers and then coupled them with a practice and potential of actual audibility, and it was through this audibility, as opposed to the visual privileging of earlier mechanisms, that finally gave credence to figures of *all sound*. The phonograph was not merely a speaking machine or a writing machine; it was also a listening machine.

When the modernist arts engaged these inscriptive techniques, the fecund and discriminating capabilities of the single string of the monochord were carried over to invest the single line of inscription with unlimited signs of life, as well to reduce noise and demarcate boundaries among the arts. The line, in other words, should not immediately be understood as enacting reduction on a richer phenomenal reality since, from the perspective of the line itself, there was so much it could contain that might far exceed normal expectations of a reducible reality. Whether parodic or deeply serious, the perceived ability to inhere complex and proliferous phenomena overrode the reduction of phenomenality, even while existing simultaneously with such reduction.

The intensification of inscription was nowhere as pronounced as in instances involving a simple line, as opposed the accumulation of simple lines arrayed in an alphabetic system that could be grouped, read, and written or an array of lines topographically extended into a space. Alfred Jarry was particularly interested in such a line to assist him with the Rabelaisian density of his *Exploits and Opinions of Doctor Faustroll Pataphysician* (posthumously published in 1911). Toward the end of the story, the itinerant Faustroll drowns after his sieve boat fails, the water "swirled hissing around their feet, with a noise opposite to the deglutition of an emptying bathtub."[8] In the next chapter, entitled "Concerning the Line," his soggy corpse becomes but a simple "letter from God" open to a profound reading by the Marine Bishop who "remembered that, following the proposition of the learned Professor Cayley, a single curve drawn in chalk on a blackboard two and a half meters long can detail all the atmospheres of a season, all the cases of an epidemic, all the haggling of the hosiers of every town, the phrases and pitches of all the sounds of all the instruments and of all the voices of a hundred singers and two hundred musicians, together with the phases, according to the position of each listener or participant, which the ear is unable to seize."[9]

If so much could be unraveled from one line a single curve, no matter how lengthy, what could one expect then from "the wallpaper of Faustroll's body . . . unrolled by the saliva and teeth of the water," like a musical score? Nothing less than "all art and all science were written in the curves of the limbs of ultrasexagenarian ephebe, and their progression to an infinite degree was prophesied therein."[10] Indeed, this procession of the heavy investment into single lines elaborated into the graphic designs of corporeal wallpaper ultimately reveals nothing less than the fourth dimension, where Faustroll, "finding his soul to be abstract and naked, donned the realm of the unknown dimension."[11] Thus, the fecundity of the line sets into motion a supercession of any phenomenality, of which it is meant to be a mere reduction, to proceed to another dimension altogether.

Jarry's passage was generated in part through a parody of Sir William Thomson's (Lord Kelvin) *Popular Lectures and Addresses,* specifically an 1883 address entitled "The Six Gateways of Knowledge." The gateways of knowledge are the senses, the sixth one being the result of breaking the sense of touch into the sense of heat and the sense of force. The gateways do not fully discriminate among perceptual functions. For instance, sound does not just enter the gateway of hearing; it can also be perceived through the sense of force, and to this end he gives the example of how "the greatest master of sound" (he is speaking of Beethoven) "used to stand with a stick pressed against the piano and touching his teeth."[12] In fact, Thomson makes the argument that "all the senses are related to force" and, in particular, that "the sense of sound . . . is merely a sense of very rapid changes of air-pressure (which is force) on the drum of the ear."[13]

In a graphic rendering of sound, time is the independent variable while air pressure is the function. Indeed, only the slowness in the variation of, say, barometric pressure in the atmosphere prevents it from being heard. Ostensibly, within the progress of Thomson's text this would be a demonstration where all other complications are eliminated such that a range of complications in air pressure could alone be observed.[14] Instead, it becomes a demonstration of his adulation of "the potency of mathematics"[15] to represent complex phenomena with the simplicity of a line. In the process, the air pressure complications that might give rise to a representation of noise are never entertained. Noise is here deferred or forever postponed, lost to a fascination with mathematics. This was no oversight, since he repeats his requisite formulation for so many treatises on music and acoustics—that musical sounds are periodic, that noises are aperiodic, and although they meet at certain junctures for cultural reasons, that they are fundamentally distinct by dint of physics.[16] As he says in another context, following Lord Palmerston, "Dirt is matter in its wrong place."[17]

Enter into Thomson's text (and from there to Jarry's text) Professor Cayley, the mathematician who had demonstrated in a lecture the ability of a simple curve to represent the price of cotton over time or mortality over the course of a plague (drawing on the legacy of William Playfair and his *Commercial and Political Atlas* of 1785—the same year, by the way, that Chladni announced his sound figures). For Thomson this was applicable to musical sound, where a "single curve, drawn in the manner of the curve of prices of cotton, describes all that the ear can possibly hear," whether it might be the "single note of the most delicate sound of a flute" or "the crash of an orchestra."[18] The latter most excited him for here was an nearly unimaginable complexity expressed within the simplicity of a line. It was so complex, with so much of the sound no doubt being "less distinctly periodic," that he had to enlist another means of noise reduction—"the superposition of the different effects," which was nothing less than "really a marvel of marvels."[19] In other words, noise was in effect crowded out by complexity, the complexity in the case of the orchestra being the score written by the composer, the subtleties of interpretation given by each instrumentalist in an orchestra of 100 instruments, along with 200 voices of a chorus singing along with the orchestra (for Jarry it was 200 musicians and 100 singers).[20] We could add to that the acoustic chaos of noise in the *crash* of an orchestra. Of course, it becomes tautological that the subsumed complexity of music will produce a simple line and not a fractured line of noise—not music. Consequently, the marvelous analytical power of mathematics, the simplicity of graphical representation, and acoustical discourse within the framework of science at that time enforced cultural practice; noise was eliminated, and music bolstered within the given confines of musical sound.

Resident Noises

Hermann Helmholtz, like Lord Kelvin, had many adherents among the arts, especially composers who had read his monumental study *On the Sensations of Tone* or any of the books by others popularizing his findings. Two elements in the book were particularly influential: the delineation between noise and music and the use of specialized instruments and devices, especially sirens. Avant-garde composers reacted against the former with *resident noises*, while the same composers were interested in a more positive manner in the musical possibilities for the siren's generation of glissandi. Whether they agreed or disagreed really did not matter in the end, since the discursive and sonic use of noise, sirens, glissandi, and sliding tones came to function similarly in their relationship to the sounds of the world and worldliness in general. Within the inscriptive manifestations of noise represented visually in the microscopic figure of the wave form, all that was required to invoke the world was a slight irregularity, whereas the glissando, fully evident to the ear, was the revenge of the regular wave form writ large.

As could be expected, Helmholtz felt compelled to rid his study of noise from the outset: "Noises and musical tones may certainly intermingle in very various degrees, and pass insensibly into one another, but their extremes are widely separated."[21] He directed his readers away from the noise and noisy figures of "the splashing of water . . . the splashing or seething of a waterfall or of the waves of the sea" and directed their imagination instead to a stone dropped into calm water.[22] Russolo, however, took exception to the cultural claims of acoustics: "Acoustical science, which is indubitably the least advanced of the physical sciences, is particularly applied to the study of pure sounds, and until now has completely neglected the study of noises. This is perhaps because it was thought that sounds must be sharply divided from noises—an absurd division . . . which has no reason to exist at all."[23] Russolo singled out Helmholtz in rejecting the neat division between sound and noise. He stated the issue in this way:

Sound is [usually] defined as the result of a succession of regular and periodic vibrations. *Noise*, instead, is caused by motions that are irregular, as much in time as in intensity. "A musical sensation," says Helmholtz, "appears to the ear as a perfectly stable, uniform and invariable sound." But the quality of continuity that sound has with respect to noise, which seems instead fragmentary and irregular, is not an element sufficient to make a sharp distinction between sound and noise.[24]

Since all that is needed, according to Russolo, to establish *continuity* in the ear is something vibrating at sixteen times per second, then an aperiodic wave form at sixteen times per second will constitute a noise that makes a sound. In this determination, he necessarily relied on inscriptive practices of representing sounds lasting only one-sixteenth of a second, since it would be impossible to distinguish with the naked ear whether such a sound was repeated. In terms of the quality of the vibrations themselves, Russolo pointed out that what were commonly understood as musical sounds were themselves characterized by the acoustical irregularities that produce an instrument's timbral signature and were thus in effect instances of noise in the midst of music. He valorized "the great variety in the timbres of noises in comparison to the more limited ones of sounds."[25] Noises were preferable, in other words, because musical sounds were merely limited, not pure: "Thus, the *real* and *fundamental* difference between sound and noise can be reduced to this alone: *Noise is generally much richer in harmonics than sound.*"[26] In keeping with the graphic attributes of water, he demonstrated these properties by asking his readers to imagine waves emanating on the surface of water from a rowboat as it is launched, if the boat is shaken a little.[27] Russolo's rowboat was thus pitched between Helmholtz's total noise of splashing water and the music of a stone dropped into calm water; it was directed toward the world but never left music.

Russolo's argument, as we have seen in the previous chapter, was not just formulated in formal, acoustic terms but replaced notions of purity with a richness of noise meant to correspond to the richness of life, especially modern life, including the richness of destruction and vitality of killing. Russolo argued that music had become anachronistic, its self-referentiality had afforded no link with the world while life all around it had energetically advanced into the modern world. His stated goal was, on the one hand, to open music up to the plenitude of all sounds—the subtle and delicate noises of nature and rural settings, the brutal noises of the modern factory, city, and war—while, on the other hand, avoiding *imitation*. For Russolo, noise constituted an apparent confusion that simultaneously disrupted both musical sound and imitative sound and was recuperated into music attracted by the existing suppression of timbres and restriction of other musical sounds. In other words, this unstable material could be absorbed because of the limitations of music and any apparent confusion was resolved easily through a familiar process of domestication: "the ear must hear these noises mastered, servile, completely controlled, conquered and constrained to become elements of art."[28] Once so controlled, noise had the advantage of coming from life and recalling it and thus could exceed music while remaining within it.[29] He did not in the end argue for a fundamentally different notion of auditive materiality, which would have guaranteed a degree of autonomy for his art of noises, or transform a relationship to nature to be more amenable to a new artistic aurality but was instead satisfied with his efforts at what he called a "great renewal of music."[30]

Thus, Russolo's noise presented timbre as a *resident noise* that invoked the world without incorporating it. Musical sound and noise thus could not be separated in Helmholtzian style because noise was deeply imbedded in musical materiality, while the hermetics of music from worldly sound that Helmholtz's figures implied was maintained by discovering within music a world of noise. Russolo was not alone in thinking along these lines; perhaps the most succinct statement about the resident noises within Western art music can be found in Henry Cowell's article "The Joys of Noise" (1929). By 1929 there was not simply a well-established familiarity with noise within music and the other arts. There was heightened attention directed toward aurality in general, due in part to radio and sound film and also to the introduction of music from other parts of the world. Moreover, the constitutive features of noise were themselves well enough known that it was a fairly easy exercise for Cowell to retrieve arguments about the extramusical origins of noise and apply them internally to Western art music. It was not necessary to go "outside" the confines of this particular type of music, he said, but it was possible to locate and release repressed forms of noise already existing "inside" music: "I shall attempt to show that the noise-makers are developing a little-considered, but natural, element of music, rather than dealing with extra-musical material."[31] He had already shown it in his own technique of playing *tone clusters* on the piano.

Many things already belonging to music were considered to be noisy, including dissonance, entire classes of musical instruments (such as percussion), other types of music, and music from other cultures, and these categories could, of course, be combined. Cowell was moved to comment on the so-called *noise-sounds* of percussion instruments in the music of *primitives* and how "noise-making instruments are used with telling effect in our greatest symphonies, and were it not for the punctuation of cymbal and bass drum, the climaxes in our operas would be like jelly-fish."[32] He also appealed to the acoustic dimensions of voices and musical instruments by distinguishing, along the lines made popular by Helmholtz, between *tone* and *noise*, the former consisting of periodic vibrations, the latter consisting of nonperiodic vibrations. Because singers use language, they not only use the tone-like periodic vibrations of vowels; they also use consonants with their noisy aperiodic vibrations (Russolo made a similar argument in the "Noises of Language" chapter of *The Art of Noises*). Cowell also asserted that there is no such thing as a pure tone emanating from a musical instrument because any sound produced necessarily contains aperiodic vibrations. Pure periodicity can be produced only in an acoustics laboratory, but "even there it is doubtful whether, by the time the tone has reached our ear, it has not been corrupted by resonances picked up on the way."[33] In other words, noise effectively exists at all times and certainly at all times within music.

But how can one begin to think about something at once so pervasive and so despised? Cowell concludes by suggesting that practitioners of music could think of noise in terms of food (cultured) and sex (repressed): "Since the 'disease' of noise permeates all music, the only hopeful course is to consider that this noise-germ, like the bacteria of cheese, is a good microbe, which may provide previously hidden delights to the listener, instead of producing musical oblivion. . . . Although existing in all music, the noise-element has been to music as sex to humanity, essential to its existence, but impolite to mention, something cloaked by ignorance and silence. Hence the use of noise in music has been largely unconscious and undiscussed."[34] Cowell's own interest in noise developed after he listened to Varèse's "Hyperprism" for the first time. The noise in this case was generated by the existence of percussion instruments, seventeen of them with only four melodic instruments, and thereby he had found that he had fallen prey to the musical pleasures consisting proportionately of "seventeen twenty-firsts noise, yet noise is not a musical element!"[35] Cowell, like Varèse himself, had largely retreated from the rhetoric of worldliness used to great effect by Russolo to remain unambiguously within music and its dedicated noises. Russolo had relied on the suppression of timbre within Western art music to make the first formal avant-garde argument for noise as worldliness, whereas Cowell argued the same but enjoyed the added rhetorical advantage of *noise* itself having already established itself as the marker of the avant-garde. Whereas resident noises may have once been limited to wolf tones or the spare wayward sound, entire classes of extramusical sounds were now identified in the midst of music and ready to serve as a material resource fulfilling the emancipatory rhetoric of avant-garde music. Music could thus become an auditive world unto itself, replete with transgressions and appropriations across its own internal demarcations of musical and extramusical sounds. It was necessary not to go outside music for the rejuvenation that noise could bring but only to release the repressed within music itself.

The Gloss of the Gliss

The impulse animating ideas of resident noise was also responsible for the prominence of glissandi within modernism. Like Professor Carey's graphic line within which so much of the world was intensified, the glissando was the simplest of lines, one that commanded a presence by always falling short of becoming a melodic line. Like melody, however, it was firmly ensconced within music. The glissando was not uncommon prior to the twentieth century, but within modernism it took on an entirely new emphasis, becoming at once the site and the product of intense negotiations between sound and musical sound. It was similar to resident noises in the way that it signaled worldliness while remaining within music, but it did so in a more oblique manner. The glissando could allude to foghorns and sirens, which themselves strung together disparate noises and rounded out the angularity of the urban environment, while also alluding to the expanse, continuity, and mellifluousness of nature; indeed, it was nature that provided the rhetorical basis. Unlike the line of noise, which was negotiated at the microscopic level, the glissando was as large as life and could envelope listeners in its smooth contours. It was a line of plenitude within music, a life line that could wave toward the infinity of nature and freedom.

Technologically, glissandi became associated with the rotary motion of the siren and Russolo's intonarumori and would eventually be found in the spiraling groove of the phonograph disc and spooling reels of film. Modernist glissandi were first heralded by the siren, particularly the clinical instruments adopted by Helmholtz for his acoustical research but also those sirens that welcomed the new days of industrialism, urbanism, and militarism. In 1922 the Russian Sergei Yutkevich of FEKS (Factory of the Eccentric Actor) announced, "The electric siren of Contemporaneity bursts with a mighty roar into the perfumed boudoirs of artistic aestheticism!"[36] Sirens cried out in public in an already abstracted sound, scanning the auditive range in order not to leave anyone out and, in the process, created a unique push-pull signature yelling *come here* or *stay away* that people failed to take notice at their own peril. It seemed to be the perfect modernist anthem.[37]

Within the techniques and technologies of music, the modernist glissando alluded to worldliness by being set in contrast to the segmentation of both temperament and instrumental design. The silenced sounds between notes, between microtones, were seen as markers of a lack of freedom, of restricted movement within a comprehensive and infinitely fine universe, and the gradient of all possible pitches was considered to be typical of the wealth of lived experience outside music. Glissandi were attractive to composers also because they were very modern. They could formally outdo dissonance, touching on an infinite gradation of the pitches they traversed, while at the same time evoking a grand lyricism, a gestural sweep stringing together the more disparate and wayward elements of a composition. Noise was an atomistic element that signaled an abundance apart from itself, whereas the glissando contained infinity itself while attracting elements in its vicinity. Noise invoked the world, whereas the world dwelt within the glissando. A modernist glissando was not so much a trace of the world as a tracing with it.

Extending into the second half of the century with such notable compositions as James Tenney's *For Ann Rising!* and Alvin Lucier's sine-wave pieces, the roots for modernist glissandi can be traced back to the future-looking *New Atlantis*, where Francis Bacon describes the Sound Houses, which included the capacity to generate "Harmonies *which you have not, of*

Quarter-Sounds, *and lesser* Slides of Sounds. *Diverse* Instruments *of* Musick *likewise to you unknowne.*"[38] Closer to the twentieth century, the Italian composer Ferruccio Busoni in his "Insufficiency of the Means for Musical Expression" (1893) urged for a fuller utilization of existing musical capabilities and for the development of "new instruments of the future" that would complete the potential breadth of orchestral sounds and techniques.[39] In his famously influential essay *Sketch for a New Esthetic of Music* (1911), he contrasted the limitations of temperament and segmentation of keyboards themselves against the limitlessness of nature: "Keyboard instruments . . . have so thoroughly schooled our ears that we are no longer capable of hearing anything else—incapable of hearing except through this impure medium. Yet Nature created an *infinite gradation—infinite!* who still knows it nowadays?"[40]

For Busoni's student Edgard Varèse the glissando was part of a tactic, along with the strewn and skewed pitches of percussion, to saturate and blanket temperament and, thus, to draw a line describing the infinite gradation of nature.[41] With this use of percussion and glissandi combined, they underscored a flanking maneuver over and against the nature of the piano keyboard (itself a percussion instrument given over to temperament) and the constitution of the symphony orchestra. In Varèse's tactic, each compensated for the weakness of the other. The infinity of specific points in between notes along the line of a glissando, which were only touched on lightly during (theoretically) an infinitely small amount of time by the ascent or descent of the passing tone, both was freed from the reduction of the line and also infused the line like a strange attractor, by the surrounding complexity of individual percussive sounds from a variety of instruments, each strike an abbreviated package of noisy timbre. Correspondingly, what was lost in the restricted pitch mobility of percussion was gained in the diapasonic movement of microtonality along the line of the glissando. Indeed, for all the attention subsequently paid to the role of percussion within the development of his musical strategies, Varèse himself maintained a special emphasis on the role of glissandi:

I began to resent the arbitrary limitations of the tempered system, especially after reading at about the same time, Helmholtz's description of his experiments with sirens in his *Physiology of Music.* Wanting to experiment myself, I went to the *Marché aux Puces,* where for next to nothing you could find just about anything, and picked up two small ones. With these I made my first experiments in what I later called spatial music. The beautiful parabolas and hyperbolas of sound the sirens gave me and the haunting quality of the tones made me aware for the first time of the wealth of music outside the narrow limits imposed by keyboard instruments."[42]

Varèse held extramusical associations for his glissandi, even though this would seemingly contradict his criticism of Russolo's art of noises. On the one hand, he characterized himself in his early years as "sort of a diabolical Parsifal on a quest, not for the Holy Grail, but for the bomb that would explode the musical world and allow all sounds to come rushing into it through the resulting breach, sounds which at that time—and sometimes still today—were called noises."[43] Yet in Francis Picabia's *391* (1917), he railed against "certain composers [who] have nothing in view in their works but a succession of titillating aggregations of sound—material for the most part of terrifying intractability—and [who] have no intellectual concern with anything but external sensorial effect,"[44] although the precise demarcation between his *organized sound* and a "succession of titillating aggregations of sound" might not be so easy to make. And like so many others, he mistakenly equates the art of noises with reproduction ("The futurists imitate, an artist transmutes"), whereas "There's nothing imitative or descriptive or futurist about me; I have nothing like the *Iron Foundry* or Mossoloff, or *Pacific 231*. Mr. Honegger's locomotive doesn't travel very fast, does it?"[45] Besides, as Louise Varèse reports, he found cars and urban noise tedious, so why honor the tedious through imitation?[46]

Nevertheless, around the time Louise Norton and Varèse were contemplating marriage, he moved into her apartment on Fourteenth Street in Manhattan, "far enough west so that as he worked, all the river noises entered his room and he discovered the music in the foghorns. . . . He listened to the 'parabolas and hyperbolas' of the fire-engine sirens with the haunting music, which he had, thanks to Helmholtz, discovered so long ago. Under the sirens' spell, he transposed their tracings to a number of glissandi within the score he was working on, to which he was to give the title *Amériques: Americas, New Worlds*."[47] There might be the mythical call of the sirens at play here, for there he was safe in the embrace of love while entrancing songs of peril emanated from over the water and in the city, but Varèse remembered it this way: "When I wrote *Amériques* [composed

1918–1921], I was still under the spell of my first impressions of New York—not only New York seen, but more especially heard. For the first time with my physical ears I heard a sound that had kept recurring in my dreams as a boy—a high whistling C sharp. It came to me as I worked in my Westside apartment where I could hear all the river sounds—the lonely foghorns, the shrill peremptory whistles—the whole wonderful river symphony which moved me more than anything ever had before."[48] Varèse was required to maintain his criticism of imitation in the music of others since joining his glissandi too tightly with specific sounds in the world would have removed them from their mapping of the infinite gradation of nature. He was able to do this because glissandi were firmly embedded in music as a form and consisted of nothing else than entirely acceptable musical sound; it was not a matter of importing sounds, he could argue in a frame not dissimilar to the rhetoric of resident noises, just adding new emphasis to already existing musical sounds. Perhaps more important, and this is an instance of modernist aurality later find exemplified in John Cage, he could be assured that he was not imitating the sounds of the river and the city in his music because he already heard these sounds as music.

Russolo, like Varèse indebted to both Busoni and Helmholtz, was likewise fascinated by glissandi. Busoni's call for the infinite of nature was elaborated by Russolo through the idea of enharmonics, associated most immediately with Balilla Pratella, his predecessor as Italian Futurism's premier composer, yet he took some liberties with the idea. In his art of noises enharmonicism was no longer a means to account for smaller intervals on alternative scales; it became the ability to land on any pitch whatsoever and to invoke a gradient in itself. In this project Russolo appealed to both nature and machines: "All the sounds and noises that are produced in nature, if they are susceptible to variation of pitch (that is, if they are sounds and noises of a certain duration) change pitch *by enharmonic gradations and never by leaps in pitch.* For example, the howling of the wind produces complete scales in rising and falling. These scales are neither diatonic nor chromatic, they are *enharmonic.* Likewise, if we move from natural noises into the infinitely richer world of machine noises, we find here also that noises produced by rotary motion are constantly enharmonic in the rising and falling of their pitch."[49] Russolo with his partner Ugo Piatti (and with Helmholtz in the back of his mind) designed this "enharmonic" capability into the mechanism of the intonarumori through the incorporation of a rotary crank, using the same motion as a siren. Thus, the source of noise was to be found in the heart of musical sound, and the expedient way to find this world of internal noise was to glide.

Cowell conducted experiments with sirens as early as 1914 while he was at the University of California, and by the time he had completed his book *New Musical Resources* in 1919, he had already developed a position on the use of glissandi and sliding pitches. Writing within the context of an argument for a sophisticated use of overtones, Cowell asserted that very fine gradations of pitch could be perceived and thus should be used within the stock of compositional material: "Professor Dayton Miller, well-known acoustician and author of *The Science of Musical Sound*, speaks of having heard the forty-fourth overtone with his unaided ear . . . [and] Professor Leon Theremin in a demonstration of his electrical instruments, showed that the interval of one-hundredth part of a whole step can be plainly discerned by an audience."[50] Because such determinations were but stops along the way of a glissando, it was natural that he consider them an appropriate compositional device. His argument was remarkably similar to Russolo; although the use of glissandi within *our* music, as Cowell said, was infrequent and "a very frequent use has been considered in bad taste," he stated that their abundance in the natural world should be taken as a sign to incorporate them into music, albeit in an abstracted manner in order to avoid imitation:[51]

Natural sounds, such as the wind playing through trees or grasses, or whistling in the chimney, or the sound of the sea, or thunder, all make use of sliding tones. It is not impossible that such tones may be made the foundation of an art of composition by some composer who would reverse the programmatic concept. . . . Instead of trying to imitate the sounds of nature by using musical scales, which are based on steady pitches hardly to be found in nature, such a composer would build perhaps abstract music out of sounds of the same category as nature sound—that is, sliding pitches—not with the idea of trying to imitate nature, but as a new tonal foundation.[52]

And following his own procedure of discovering the repressed element within a given situation, he found sliding tones in the heart of temperament, by opening up the piano and producing glissandi directly on strings, such as *Piece for Piano with Strings* (1923) and *The Banshee* (1923).

If Cowell was looking for a composer who would build an abstract music, then the Australian composer Percy Grainger, known mostly for the gentility of a work such as *Country Gardens*, might seem an unlikely candidate, yet there was no one quite as glissandi-mad as Grainger. He made them a central feature of his lifelong investigation into Free Music, his Busonian term for a radically new form of music and the means for its realization, a project that belonged squarely within the avant-garde music tradition of this century. Beginning in 1903, Grainger was yet another student of Busoni and like his teacher probably better known for his piano recitals than his own composition. It would be sensible to assume that some of Busoni's grand plans for music rubbed off on Grainger, if it weren't for the fact that Grainger was already entertaining ideas of nonharmony, gliding tones, total independence of voices, and what he called "beatless music" as early as 1899, when he was seventeen years old. Nevertheless, despite Grainger's avowed dislike for Busoni's own compositions, the scope of his teacher's ambitions could not help but legitimate and nurture his own. Grainger kept working on his Free Music throughout his career and devoted concentrated attention to it during the last fifteen years of his life.

Grainger thought that music was unique among the arts by its woeful dependence on the type of segmentation inherent in temperament, as he wrote in 1942: "Current music is like trying to do a picture of a landscape, a portrait of a person, in small squares—like a mosaic—or in preordained shapes: straight lines or steps."[53] Indeed, in his statement "Free Music," he attributes a set of visual cues to the genesis of Free Music: "My impression is that this world of tonal freedom was suggested to me by wave-movements in the sea that I first observed as a young child at Brighton, Victoria, and Albert Park, Melbourne."[54] He faithfully kept clear from all the programmatic waves or streams soaking Western art music because, within the odd tensions of modernist music, too much of an attachment to worldly sound would likewise be a constraint on freedom. Instead, "For me, of course, my free music seems entirely inspired (heard in the inner ear) & that is why I feel so much duty towards it. It seems to me the only type of music that tallies our modern scientific conception of life (our longing to know life AS IT IS, not merely in a symbolistic interpretation), and clearly the kind of music to which all musical progress of many centuries has been working up."[55]

The "modern scientific conception of life" was, of course, very conducive to making music with machines. In his statement "Free Music,"
extending Busoni's yearning for a composer's piano with an orchestra
inside, Grainger wanted the composer to have a direct route to performance without having to go through the performer: "A composer wants to
speak to his public direct. Machines (if properly constructed and properly
written for) are capable of niceties of emotional expression impossible to
a human performer. That is why I write my Free Music for theremins—the
most perfect tonal instruments I know."[56] The *theremin* was an instrument
capable of producing glissandi up and down all day long. In fact, this was
the source of its biggest problem, and although it seems to be designed for
the gestures of a conductor, it did not escape Grainger for long that this
was just another form of performance in disguise. He opted out of the
theremin in favor of an instrument that could play more directly from the
inscriptions of a composer and not from the human movements arising
from these marks. He was also more interested in a machine that came out
of music, not vice versa.

Grainger's desire for a composing machine led him into his fruitful
collaboration, beginning in 1946 and lasting the rest of his life, with Burnett Cross, whom he met while living in White Plains, New York. Unfortunately, there has yet to be an adequate account of the progression of their
collaborative experiments in sound and instrument design, and this is not
the occasion for such an undertaking.[57] There were a great variety of experiments and a number of false starts and dead ends for manual, mechanical,
electric, and photoelectric play, everything from the small "Butterfly Piano" to an inscribed movie sound track (drawn sound). All attempts were
characterized by a remarkable resourcefulness, as Grainger's biographer
Jon Bird described it: "At times Ella and Percy would don their finest
clothes to avoid police suspicion and spend part of an evening rummaging
amongst the piles of rubbish by the back doors of department and furniture
stores. Eventually the [Free Music] machines employed such improbable
articles as pencil sharpeners, milk bottles, bamboo, roller-skate wheels, the
bowels of a harmonium, linoleum, ping-pong balls, children's toy records,
egg whisks, cotton reels, bits of sewing machines, carpet rolls, a vacuum
cleaner, a hair drier and, of course, miles of strong brown paper and
string."[58] Whereas other composers sought the high-technology route,
Grainger and Cross reached for things close at hand.[59]

With all these composers, the glissando was a line that circumscribed the world by recording its diapason while filtering out sounds not already belonging to music. As a tactic, it resembled that other avant-garde tactic of incorporating hitherto extramusical sounds—noise—into music by eliminating or reducing the associative aspects of sound, but because the glissando was already within music, it was more akin to the safer enterprise of the elaboration of resident noise. Just as the curvilinear Doppler united the physical world of sound with that of light, the glissando undulating through space and warping in time was a delineation of all that was outside. In this way, it was not merely a line of sanitized noise; it was, for these composers, a sweeping generalization made from within music.

Beethoven at Fifty Times per Second

Edison and Beethoven had more in common than their deafness; they had similar means to compensate. Just as the *greatest master of sound*, Lord Kelvin reminds us, could be found with a stick in his mouth, so too Edison would bite down on the horn of his phonograph. He was not frustrated with the workings of his new device; his odd behavior was instead a means to use an alternative gateway for hearing, conducting sound through bone. The difference between the locked jaw ensemble of Beethoven's skull fused to stick and piano and that of Edison's skull fused to his phonograph was that the phonograph opened up other possible perceptual gateways for the simple reason that it too could listen, speak, write, and compose.

Developed within a technological environment informed by the telephone, telegraph, and phonautograph, Edison's phonograph was born among imperatives to fuse speech and writing. Prior to inventing the phonograph, he sought to develop a device that could take the phonautographic signatures of vocal sounds and automatically transcribe them into the appropriate letter. This was, in effect, a phonograph where the playback was printing instead of sound. His hope that inscription might find its own voice was given a boost when he read an article entitled "Graphic Phonetics," a report on the research (commissioned by the French Linguistic Society) by Professor Étienne Marey et al. on the mechanical recording of graphic representations of vocal vibrations and speech organ movements.[60] Even on hearing the first sounds of his phonograph, he imagined its inscriptions as dots and dashes similar to Morse code—that is, he concentrated on the mediation of the lived temporality of the voice and the inscription of mechanical code. He was, in other words, tied to the scriptual domain of Leon-Scott's phonautograph instead of turning his attention directly to the characteristics and qualities of sound. It should be kept in mind that the technical promise of legible speech belonged to other promises and realizations of universal alphabets, universal languages, colonial normalization of speech, and aurality, as well as the assault against deaf language and culture.

Edison was not alone in harboring such hopes. Less than a year after the invention of the phonograph there was enough speculation about a phonographic alphabet that Alfred Mayer felt compelled to issue a warning. It was futile, he said, "to hope to be able to *read* the impressions and traces of phonographs, for these traces will vary, not alone with the quality of the voices, but also with the differently related times of starting of the harmonics of these voices, and with the different relative intensities of these harmonics."[61] A word was already too different from its sound to be unambiguously transcribed, let alone reinscribed and heard, but there was another problem more relevant to our present topic: the simple inscription could be infused with more than what might be immediately apparent. How could one tell how much was recorded in an inscription when all sounds were condensed into the fluctuations of a single stylus, the type of "superposition of different effects" that Lord Kelvin had mentioned? How could multiple, superimposed sounds be untangled from their simultaneous occurrence at the time of recording but also through mixing done with the device itself? Mixing, after all, was attempted during the earliest days of the phonograph. In one public demonstration several recordings were superimposed over the other in a primitive mix with a result that "the phonograph was equal to any attempts to take unfair advantage of it, and it repeated its songs, and whistles, and speeches, with the cornet music heard so clearly over all."[62]

Despite four decades of such explanations by Alfred Mayer and others, their warnings did not reach or deplete the enthusiasm of László Moholy-Nagy, who during the early 1920s argued for extending the phonograph from simply a machine for reproducing sound to one for producing sound:

An extension of [the phonograph] for productive purposes could be achieved as follows: the grooves are incised by human agency into the wax plate, without any external mechanical means, which then produce sound effects which would signify—without new instruments and without an orchestra—a fundamental innovation in sound production (of new, hitherto unknown sounds and tonal relations) both in composition and in musical performance. . . . The primary condition for such work is laboratory experiments: precise examination of the kinds of grooves (as regards length, width, depth etc.) brought about by the different sounds; examination of the man-made grooves; and finally mechanical-technical experiments for perfecting the groove-manuscript score. (Or perhaps the mechanical reduction of large groove-script records.)[63]

He went on to develop these ideas in a 1923 article called "New Form in Music: Potentialities of the Phonograph" and in an article a decade later ("New Film Experiments") he was able to point to drawn sound on film as confirmation of his earlier ideas. He even imagined that "the creation of the ideal synthetic tenor is within reach."[64] He also went on to make his own film, now lost, entitled *The Sound of ABC*, where letters, lines, and profiles were drawn onto the optical sound track, prompting him to ask one person, "I wonder how your nose will sound?"[65]

It was perhaps reasonable to expect so much from the line of sound film inscription, since the first attempts at the invention of sound cinema were animated by a similar desire. We have, of course, Edison's famous statement: "In the year 1887, the idea occurred to me that it was possible to devise an instrument which should do for the eye what the phonograph does for the ear, and that by a combination of the two all motion and sound could be recorded and reproduced simultaneously."[66] Given the complementary rotations of the zoetrope and phonograph cylinder, was not it only a matter of bringing them together? Of all the possible solutions for what was called the kineto-phonograph, common sense dictated that the photographic be subsumed within the phonographic, doing for the eye what had been done for the ear: "The initial experiments took the form of microscopic pinpoint photographs, placed on a cylindrical shell, corresponding in size to the ordinary phonograph cylinder. These two cylinders were then placed side by side on a shaft, and the sound record was taken as near as possible synchronously with the photographic image, impressed on the sensitive surface of the shell."[67] Even after enlarging the photographs to the grand size of one-eighth of an inch, the materials failed, the general design was abandoned, and entirely different approaches were pursued. The important facet of this enterprise, though, was that the world of visual images was to be installed at the site and scale of phonographic inscription.

The possibility for the phonographic playback of any inscription literally caught the corner of Rainer Maria Rilke's eye when he saw the coronal suture, the jagged lines atop the skull inhabiting every good poet's den. Skulls, of course, had been mapped with the scalp still on, but phrenological reading was a poor cousin for a writing that could cut to the bone. What would happen if this line were decoded, now that the machine for sonorizing lines had been invented? This was the basic question Rilke asked in his essay "Primal Sound" (1919): "What would happen? A sound would necessarily result, a series of sounds, music. . . . Feelings—which? Incredulity, timidity, fear, awe—which of all the feelings here possible prevents me from suggesting a name for the primal sound which would then make its appearance in the world?"[68] He could not say what sound might be produced, but he was not too shy to imagine a truly ubiquitous recording, one in which the entire visible world would become soundful through the phonographic tracing of a needle: "What variety of lines then, occurring anywhere, could one not put under the needle and try out? Is there any contour that one could not, in a sense, complete in this way and then experience it, as it makes itself felt, thus transformed, in another field of sense?"[69] Rilke had noticed a similar confluence of the senses in Arabic poetry, while to an unnamed woman he attributed the observation that such confluence was nothing more than "the presence of mind and grace of love." He was thereby compelled to diagram the technical motives in the perceptual spatiality or nonspatiality of lovers and poets.[70] Because the phonograph might decode the inscriptions of the entire visible world and unlock so many of its mysteries, it promised to become the technology of choice for investigating the conflict and correspondence between love and poetry. In this way it surpassed other technologies of perceptual extension, such as the telescope and microscope, since their experiences remained remote—can you smell Mars, walk through its canals, or feel the contours of plankton?—whereas one could become sumptuously immersed in the sonorized secrets of all lines.

Despite such enthusiasm, there was something else intensifying the complexity of the line, making it more capable of writing the world and at the same time frustrating its transparency and legibility. Its simplicity

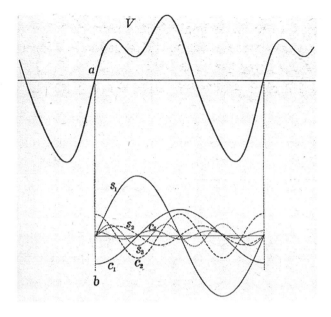

| Figure 3.1 |
Curve of a violin tone and its sine and cosine components.
From Dayton Clarence Miller, *The Science of Musical Sounds* (1916).

could mask the fact that it was the product of an underlying harmonic complexity. This was the case within mathematical modeling and graphic representation, including representation by mechanical instrumentation, quite apart from its relevance to phonographic inscription, which by its nature assume another scale of complexity altogether. It was Baron J. B. J. Fourier who in 1822 showed that any periodic wave form can be analyzed through its sinusoidal components; this meant that there were deeper-running, constituent harmonics within sound waves that were not rendered within their graphic inscription[71] (see figure 3.1). The intensification of the line of the wave was, however, tempered by the way the component parts were required to obey the mandates of periodicity; in essence, the constituent waves were required to start and end at the same place. It was another matter to analyze waves when their constituent parts were out of phase, let alone analyze them when they were of greater irregularity still. In this way Fourier's analysis was unhelpful in the analysis of noise and, by the range and power of its actual analytical capabilities, was predisposed to noise abatement and musical convention.

A case in point was an unusual demonstration by the American acoustician Dayton Clarence Miller in his influential book *The Science of Musical Sounds*, first published in 1916 and widely available to midcentury.[72] Miller challenged the acousticians who came before him when he rejected the equation of musical tone with periodicity and of noise with aperiodicity and unwittingly agreed with the resident noise composers of the time when he pointed out that many instances of musical sound were aperiodic and many periodic sounds were perceived as noise. For Miller noise was better defined as "a sound of too short duration or too complex in structure to be analyzed or understood by the ear."[73] Complexity was gauged by a person's perceptual capabilities or predisposition or by cultural norms—such as the complicated construction of Wagner's "Tannhäuser Overture," which could be heard as noise by some and as music by others.[74] That an individual's confusion can produce noise meant there was nothing intrinsically noisy about the physical attributes of a sound. With that qualification made he quickly contradicts himself and retreats. Noise will be dealt with only after "we understand the simpler and more interesting musical tones. *Tones* are sound having such continuity and definiteness that their characteristics may be appreciated by the ear, thus rendering them useful for musical purposes."[75] Thus, Miller managed noise rhetorically and excluded it through the perceived necessity of scientific study that naturally evolved from the simple to the complex, instead of incorporating a notion of the complex at the simplest level. But the techniques, technologies, and aesthetics of Western art music music would not be the only device for demonstrating *appreciation*, codifying simplicity and eliminating noise; he would also use new instrumentation and woman to bring noise into line.

To demonstrate the workings of harmonic analysis and synthesis, Miller drew a line profile from a photograph of a woman and then ran this line through two of his machines. The first converted the line into an equation of thirty terms—"but the coefficients of the terms above the eighteenth were negligibly small"—and the second used the equation to synthesize a replica of the line profile of the woman[76] (see figure 3.2). At this juncture aesthetics and desire are plied back into this machine inscription: "If mentality, beauty, and other characteristics can be considered as represented in a profile portrait, then it may be said that they are also ex-

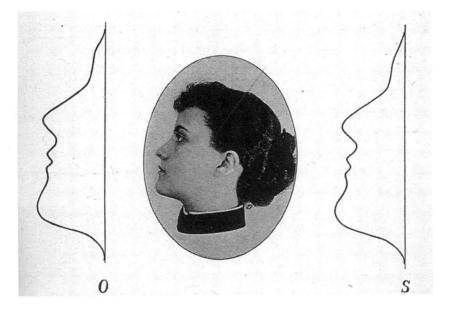

| Figure 3.2 |
Reproduction of a portrait profile by harmonic analysis and synthesis.
From Dayton Clarence Miller, *The Science of Musical Sounds* (1916).

pressed in the equation of the profile."[77] The simple beauty of the female expressed in the line thus becomes also the simple beauty of mathematics, graphic representation, and instrumentation, let alone mediation and reproduction, involved in the production of the equation and profile. Thus, we move beyond Lord Kelvin's fascination with a beauty of mathematics to a fascination with a mathematics of beauty.

If there was any question about the presence of beauty, then it was a simple matter to render the line sonorous and musical. The simple curves compounded within this profile could be expressed as simple tones, and the resulting sound wave could be repeated periodically to produce a sound. For Miller, this demonstrated that the "beauty of form may be likened to beauty of tone color—that is, to the beauty of certain harmonious blending of sounds"[78] (see figure 3.3). In this respect, he belonged to a patriarchal tradition that equated women with music and pitted female beauty against female noises. Auguste Villiers de l'Isle Adam in his novel *L'Eve Future* (Tomorrow's Eve) may have employed phonography as the

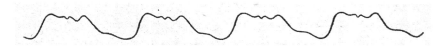

| Figure 3.3 |
Wave form obtained by repeating a portrait profile.
From Dayton Clarence Miller, *The Science of Musical Sounds* (1916).

basis for a gynoid that would retain feminine beauty while eliminating the noise he found in women's speech and refusal to reproduce. Miller synthesized a woman whose capacity to be calculated and technologically reproduced, whose beauty and harmony would eliminate noise.

Although this technique never went very far in practical application, its appeal was obvious. It could slip in and out of semiotic registers while keeping one foot in the indexical; some sound would always be reproduced in accord with the representation. Directly inscribing sound promised a notational form circumventing the vagaries and economies of musical instrumental interpretation (*qua* Busoni), promised a new-found technical control, promised technical control at subperceptual levels where control could go unobserved, and promised a fusion of the arts—a connection between the visual arts and music, if not the more extensive connections possible once voices and sounds could be synthesized. As we see in chapter 5, this technique was entertained on numerous occasions, especially in the 1920s and 1930s, when there was a concerted investigation into the artistic possibilities of phonography (sound film and the phonograph proper) in music, radio, and cinema, as well as the development of new electrical musical instruments.

Miller's demonstration did find its way to a 1937 article by John Cage entitled "The Future of Music: Credo."[79] More than a decade before Cage's dictum of *letting sounds be themselves* came into being, he was interested instead in *capturing and controlling sounds*. He was also interested in the control possible through new means of synthesizing music: "It is now possible for composers to make music directly, without the assistance of intermediary performers. Any design repeated often enough on a sound track is audible. Two hundred and eighty circles [*sic*] per second on a sound track will produce one sound, whereas a portrait of Beethoven repeated fifty times per second on a sound track will have not only a different pitch but a different sound quality."[80] Cage apparently thought that this technique was viable because twelve years later he was still celebrating "adventurous workers in the field of synthetic music," for whom "twenty-four or n frames per second is the 'canvas' upon which this music is written."[81] Nevertheless, his choice of a profile of Beethoven, the masthead of the symphonic repertoire, was obviously parodic. A line drawing makes a poor death mask, especially for Beethoven, since it fails to show where the bones and ears were removed during autopsy to determine the cause of his deafness. For Cage, the singular genius humbly assumes a position within avant-garde musical materiality as one pitch and tone-color among an infinity of others. Cage maintained Beethoven as his chief antagonist for many years to come, especially as he championed Erik Satie and campaigned against self-expression within art.[82] Cage's Beethoven writ small at fifty times per second was, in this way, not a demarcation from noise but a declaration from a music founded on noise to demarcate itself from musical convention.

"I, the Accelerated Line"

Attempts at the intensification of the inscription betray a certain violence when they are seen as a compensatory maneuver for the reduction of phenomenality, and this would be apart from the normative restraint involved in describing certain artistic bounds. This is nowhere more evident than where the object of inscription and process of investing inscription returns from other bodies to one's own. Cage's *50-Beethovens per second* is just one instance of inscribed bodies within a modernism rife with bodies stretching without pain to accommodate the suturing of montage or wireless disembodiment and telematic displacement. But Henri Michaux's description of a dramatic overdose of mescaline, in his book *Miserable Miracle* (1956), is most vivid in describing what it would be to enter the corporeal warp of inscription and in the process gives a glimpse into the violence involved in a reduction of phenomenality. At one point, lines and furrows raced through his body then oscillated into outlines of faces "stretched and contorted like the heads of aviators subjected to too much pressure that kneads their cheeks and foreheads like rubber."[83] But then he "WENT DOWN" to a place where he became what he beheld: "at this incessant, inhuman speed, I was beset, pierced by the electric mole boring its way through the essence of the most personal part of myself. . . . Caught, not by anything human, but in a frenzied mechanical agitator, a kneader-crusher-crumbler, treated like metal in a steel mill, like water in a turbine, like wind in a blower, like a root in an automatic fibre-shredder.[84] Mentally sound people live their lives as spheres, but he experienced the absolute helplessness of being "nothing but a line. . . . I, the accelerated line." Michaux experienced his transplantation into the place where inscription meets signal, where the line becomes electrical, as the ultimate horror. From here it becomes apparent that it is easier to reconnoiter a reduction of phenomenality when that reduction takes place outside the phenomenon of oneself. He does not describe the sound of this line, so one can only imagine what harmonies the collapse of body and being might produce.

THE SOUND OF MUSIC

Demarcated Sounds

There has been a line drawn between sound and musical sound, describing disciplinary demarcation and maintaining musical integrity at an historical juncture in which there were the means to do otherwise. In the absence of any practical challenge from the other arts, music was considered the *sine qua non* of the arts of sound, and what appeared to be a challenge mounted by avant-garde music was instead primarily a recuperation of sound into musical preoccupations. What little pressure was put on musical practices to change was largely discursive and had little positive effect in actual sonic practice. During the heyday of the avant-garde, some of the most provocative artistic instances of sound came from literature and other writings and were distant from the development of the arts or aurality of the time. In the latter half of the 1920s, with the increased technological sophistication of film sound, radio, amplification, microphony, and phonography, as well as a changed aurality shaped by mass-mediated culture, the questioning of musical integrity started to become more pronounced, as we see in the next chapter. Soon, however, economic collapse, consolidation and expansion of authoritarian regimes, exile and repression against artists and intellectuals, and military activities would remove what conditions had existed for major artistic revision and elaboration. Nevertheless, although the sporadic activities during the late 1920s and early 1930s failed to assume the broader continuities of an artistic practice, they did indicate a qualitatively different artistic approach toward significant sound.

The tradition of what is called avant-garde, modernist, and experimental music during this century is usually understood as the radical edge of the larger practice of Western art music, a small minority of composers

and other practitioners important for the evolution or assertion of different philosophies, poetics, politics, techniques, technologies, styles, and so
forth within the larger realm of composition—a way to keep pace with the
present. It can also be understood as an adaptive maneuver by which arts
in the West confronted larger transformations in the social conditions of
aurality and kept the full extent of their social, political, and poetic provocation at bay by recuperating significant sound into musical materiality.
While the first understanding is regularly rehearsed and the second seldom
so, they are in many instances functionally interdependent.

Despite the concentration of the bulk of Western art music activity
on the music of past centuries, played on vintage classes of instruments
couched within equally vintage rites, the actions of venturesome contemporary avant-garde composers grappling with changing conditions of aurality have given rise to an impression that Western art music as a whole has
the capacity to respond to the world in which people presently live. Whether
they responded admirably in musical terms is not the question here. It is
merely whether, through the discursive dint of associating musical sound
with sound in general, or through other aspects on an historical scale quite
apart from the personal integrity or the value of the music of this or that
composer, they responded as well they could to the changing conditions of
sound and aurality. Likewise, the process of musicalization does more than
act to rejuvenate Western art music practice, expanding the material and
technical base while maintaining the autonomy of musical practice. More
significantly, it casts musical premises far afield of their natural habitat,
where music is further situated and supported through its incorporation
into other practices and discourses of culture and aurality. Thus, from the
timbral tactics of Russolo's art of noises, through the homegrown legitima-
tion of resident noise, through John Cage's musicalization of aurality itself,
Western art music has developed a number of means through its avant-
garde to maintain its integrity and expand its resources in the changing
auditive environments of this century.

One thing that remained tenaciously extramusical, however, was what
was usually called *imitation*. However it may have been invoked past or
present—noise, sound, reproduction, representation, meaning, semiot-
ics—the primarily sonic has been recuperated into music with relative ease
while significant sound has met with great resistance. Only the briefest and
most infrequent instances of worldly sound were allowed into Western art

musical practice, while its broader applications of imitation, such as program music, were commonly considered to be lower life forms. Contraptual sounds produced by noninstrumental objects were banished to the circus, variety theater, novelty music, vaudeville, theatrical sound effects, and folk traditions, and even quotation from musics outside one's own tradition could be an exercise in extramusicality.

It was more difficult to keep "imitative" sounds at bay after the advent of viable phonographic techniques. Unlike the verisimilitude that painting and drawing were relieved of by photography, music was not relieved of any tradition or aspiration toward phonographic realism. Phonography did, nevertheless, promise an alternative to musical notation as a means to store sonic time and, in the process, deliver all sound into artistic materiality, and musical discourse responded by trivializing the complexity of significant sounds and their settings. Indeed, after a certain historical point, it was not so much the potential for musical practices of imitation that were debased as it was the concept of imitation within musical discourse. Only by distancing itself from attempts at a comprehension of the conditions of aurality within a particular time and place, including the operations of music itself within those conditions, could music protect itself from sound.

How could this be the case within the radical transformations that occurred during the vigorous days of modernism and the avant-garde? How could Western art music be so successful in protecting its own domain when, at the very same time, so many other arts inverted their representational modes? If painting could jettison the recognizable for the nonobjective, how could Western art music not follow suit and jettison the nonobjective for the recognizable? What was the source of this sensorial asymmetry in modernism? One line of reasoning has to do with the conservatism of Western art music itself, against which a relatively modest departure would appear to be transgressive. Dissonance comes immediately to mind, but for our purposes a better case in point would be the reaction that avant-garde music incurred through its use of percussion, a reaction based on the failure to reproduce a certain set of instruments, conventions, and sounds. That percussion fell within the bounds of a musical materiality meant that it only had (decreasing) strength as a sign for extramusical sounds. In this way, modernist conflicts over representation could be reproduced internally, without appealing to an external sense of representation. This was played out in terms of noise, resident noise, and figures of worldliness such as the glissando and eventually in the sphere of sound recording.

Another line of reasoning pertains to institutional and societal factors. The early avant-garde had relatively little to do with music; in fact, prior to midcentury the term *avant-garde music* was nearly oxymoronic. Relatively few composers frequented the bohemian haunts of artists and writers, breeding grounds for radicalism of all types, because their attendance could be better spent elsewhere. Unlike writers or painters, who needed relatively affordable technologies (pen and paper, brush, paints, canvas, and the like) to complete their art, composers were closely linked to string quartets or symphony orchestras to hear common forms of their practice realized. The artistic and literary avant-garde looked like a cottage industry when compared to the big factory of musical modernism. To gain access to their technologies, composers were required to circulate in the upper reaches of society, participate within the formal rites of high musical culture, and speak through the discourses attending these scenes. Edgard Varèse, one of the few composers to intersect with the ranks of bohemia, described in 1924 the stifling effects operating within a generational and class logic: "There is little hope for the bourgeoisie. The education of this class is almost entirely a matter of memory, and at twenty-five they cease to learn, and they live the remainder of their lives within the limitations of conceptions at least a generation behind the times."[1] The Surrealist Philippe Soupault put it more succinctly: "The area of music, a colonial possession inhabited by snobs."[2] John Cage understood it less as a class phenomenon and more a difference arising between individual and institutional modes of support: "The people who control taste and who give funds to buy things in the field of art are individuals. I think institutions in the case of art follow the lead of those individuals and individual collectors. Whereas in music, institutions get in the way in the very beginning and they close the doors to what they would consider to be rabid experimentation."[3]

According to Félix Guattari, the institutions and practices of music worked against music itself: "One has here to contrast the abstract machines of music (perhaps the most non-signifying and de-territorializing of all!) with the whole musical caste system—its conservatories, its educational traditions, its rules for correct composition, its stress on the impresario and so on. It becomes clear that the collectivity of musical production is so organized as to hamper and delay the force of deterritorialization inherent in music as such."[4] If music has the deterritorializing capacities that Guattari attributes to it, then its inability to challenge basic premises regarding its artistic materiality can be traced in part to these conventions, economic, and institutional conditions. As we see below, however, Guattari would have disagreed since moves toward signification would deterritorialize the deterritorializing capacities he found inherent in music as such.

Another reason that music was not compelled to radicalize its representational means relative to the other arts was the privileged position that music itself held among the arts. Music was valued as a model for modernist ambitions toward self-containment, self-reflexivity, and unmediated communication. Its abstracted character was thought to have already achieved what the other arts were attempting. Apollinaire, in championing analytic cubism, was most interested in the relationality music had elaborated through polyphony, rhythm, counterpoint, harmony, melody, and so on. Simultaneity, the cohabitation of space underpinning cubism, was child's play for all types of music. What the aural equivalent to synthetic cubism would have been—with its incorporation of actual objects or, as with Picasso's chair caning printed on oil cloth, representations of actual objects—is another question entirely. Gabrielle Buffet-Picabia, a musician in a world of visual artists, was in a good position to make a statement typical of the time:

I had been initiated into the organization of sounds into music, into the strict discipline of harmony and counterpoint, which make up its complex and artificial structure. The problems of musical composition became for me a constant source of amazement and reflection. Consequently, I was well prepared to hear Picabia speak of revolutionary transformations in pictorial vision, and to accept the hypothesis of a painting endowed with a life of its own, exploiting the visual field solely for the sake of an arbitrary and poetic organization of forms and colors, free from the contingent need to represent or transpose the forms of nature as we are accustomed to see them.[5]

Music ceases being mere legitimization and becomes even more central to the work of many painters. Among the innumerable cases we could examine, let the obvious cases of Wassily Kandinsky and Piet Mondrian suffice. Although music was for Kandinsky a powerful model for nonrepresentation, this produced a second-order imperative to avoid *the representation of music*. He confronted this problem in two phases marked by a change in his attitude toward Wagner's use of leitmotivs. At first an avid admirer of Wagner, he considered leitmotivs to operate as something more than a simple mode of identification, a motivated sound involved in naming. Instead, he associated identification with essence and considered its expression to be auratic, a radiance occupying the space of sound: "Wagner began to use the medium of his art—sound. The heroes of his operas are expressed not only by material form, but also by sound—the *leitmotif*. This sound is, as it were, the spiritual aroma surrounding and expressing the hero: each Wagnerian hero 'sounds' in his own way."[6]

However, as Kandinsky developed his notion of *inner sound*, a deeper and more pervasive vibrational being of which radiance would be an externalization belonging to the mundane world of appearance, his attitude toward Wagner changed. Kandinsky now thought that Wagner was preoccupied with externals; he had rendered music subservient to text and imitation, made it into a type of mechanical reproduction of the already apparent: "The hissing of red-hot iron in water, the sound of the smith's hammer, etc., were represented musically."[7] Wagner's recourse to leitmotivs represented a degeneration into unabashed identification: "This obstinate recurrence of a [particular] musical phrase at the appearance of a hero finally loses its power and gives rise to an effect upon the ear like that which an old, well-known label on a bottle produces upon the eye. One's feelings finally revolt against this kind of consistent, programmatic use of one and the same form."[8]

His change of heart toward Wagner pivoted on an association with the already degraded form of program music—that is, exercises in extramusicality using musical instruments unsuited to the task. This inadequacy of musical technology and thought consequently restated the perception of an ingrained difference between sound and musical sound. As he wrote in *On the Spiritual in Art:*

How lamentable are attempts to use musical means to represent external form is shown by program music in the narrower sense. Such experiments have been made right up to the present time. Imitations of frogs croaking, of farmyards, of knives being sharpened, are worthy of the variety stage and maybe very amusing as a form of entertainment. In serious music, however, such excesses remain valuable examples of the failure of attempts to "imitate nature." Nature has its own language, which affects us with its inexorable power. This language cannot be imitated. If one tries to represent a farmyard musically in order to recapture the mood of nature and to put the listener in this mood, then it becomes clear that this is an impossible and unnecessary task. This sort of mood can be created by every art form; not by the external imitation of nature, but by the artistic recreation of this mood in its inner value.[9]

Here was an example of the well-rehearsed differentiation of *serious* music from other, lower forms of Western art music practice—specifically, program music and musical imitation—in the face of a nature too powerful to be imitated. This model provided Kandinsky with the rationale for his own amimetic art: "Music, which externally is completely emancipated from nature, does not need to borrow external forms from anywhere in order to create its language. Painting today is still almost entirely dependent upon natural forms, upon forms borrowed from nature. And its task today is to examine its forces and its materials, to become acquainted with them, as music has long since done, and to attempt to use these materials and forces in a purely painterly way for the purpose of creation."[10] Since nature's language was too powerful to imitate and music was self-sufficient and emancipated from nature, music became infused with the autonomy and power of nature. Thus, when Kandinsky wrote, "I do not want to paint music,"[11] he meant that he did not want to make his own painting programmatic of any music; he wanted his painting to have the same relationship Western art music already had to the program music within its own ranks. This would not make painting a purely personal social phenomenon, for the autonomy from nature would be only an apparent nature, and there would be resonance among all realms of existence at the deeper vibrational level of inner sound. Communication among humans—for instance, between Kandinsky, his painting, and viewers of his painting—would take place vibrationally, unmediated by signs. Similar to the general tactic of avant-garde musical noise with its exchange along a correspondence between the areferential sounds outside music and the noisy elements already existing within musical sound, Kandinsky circumvented imitation by setting up conduits of cosmic vibrations behind apparent reality.

Piet Mondrian—one of the high practitioners of modernist purgation, the painter of *Broadway Boogie-Woogie*—would go to wherever the music he loved was being played, even if it meant sitting through a string of circus acts just to hear a jazz interlude. Indeed, prompted by Luigi Russolo's noise music, in two long essays written in 1921 and 1922—"The Manifestation of Neo-Plasticism in Music and the Italian Futurists' *Bruiteurs*" and "Neo-Plasticism: Its Realization in Music and in Future Theater"—he went so far as to propose a new type of music with its own venue. Mondrian described his new music across a range of features, and when it came to the question of materiality, he not only exercised the usual proscription against imitation; he thought that Western art music itself was too close to nature: "Sounds in nature are the result of *simultaneous and continuous fusion.* The old music partially destroyed this fusion and continuity by decomposing noise into tones and ordering them in a definite harmony. But this did not transcend the natural. *This definiteness is not sufficient for the new spirit.* 'Scale' and 'composition' show regression to natural sound, fusion and repetition. *To achieve a more universal plastic, the new music must dare to create a new order of sounds and nonsounds (determined noise)."* [12]

Mondrian generally favored the *bruiteurs* (intonarumori, the noise-intoning instruments Russolo devised to play his art of noises) since he saw them as a step away from the old music and toward his new Neo-Plastic music, a mechanical music that would achieve a *"perfect determination of sound"* by eliminating human touch. [13] However, despite their actual nonimitative restriction to the resident noise of timbre, they likewise treaded too close to nature: "Naturalism, in the sense of the imitation of natural sounds (including machines), causes degeneration in music. Reality was introduced into music with the intention of making it more universal; but by following reality too closely, music on the contrary became more individual. *Natural reality did not achieve its true expression because it was not transformed into abstract plastic.* This is clearly shown by the *bruiteurs* whose noises remain reproductions of natural sounds." [14] In the new type of hall for playing Neo-Plastic music, people could come and go freely without missing anything because the compositions would be repeated just like in movie theaters. Long intermissions would provide time to view projected images of Neo-Plastic paintings, the electrical playback equipment would be hidden, and the space would meet the "new acoustical requirements of 'sound-noise.'" [15] Neo-Plastic music would be mechanical and electric because "human touch always involves the individual to some degree and prevents the *perfect determination of sound*,"[16] and man, once he has "attained complete maturity" will "free . . . himself of his animality and achieve pure exteriorization of his deepest 'self.' Only then will animality be destroyed in art. *After this there will be no need either for the old plastic means or for the vocal organs of man.* Man will prefer sounds and noises produced by inanimate nonanimalized materials. He will find the noise of a machine more sympathetic (in its 'timbre') than the song of birds or men."[17]

About twenty-five years of Neo-Plastic maturation later, after moving to London, Mondrian wrote to his brother to detail his own revanchist animal instincts. These took the form of a fascination for Disney cartoon characters with special attention given to Snow White and the seven dwarfs. Moreover, he chose to fill his own room with the strains of a different type of music. Referring to his new neighbors, Mondrian's letter suggests the possibility of an infantilism operating in his valorization of music: "In the evening when the dwarfs return from work, I hear their music in the distance, a very cheering sound. . . . I have my gramophone here too with 12 of the latest records that I managed to save out of the many that I possessed. So I also have a record with the music of the dwarfs on it, and quite often play it. Sneezy and the others like that too."[18] Underscoring this specific instance of a high modernist traffic in music, in a neighborhood quite distant from Lautréamont's cruel ecosystem, the rejection of animality, nature, and signification was definitely a move to a less complicated time, or, rather, it was a time for a move toward less complication.

Drawing the Line in Theory

Demarcative procedures were likewise practiced throughout philosophies, theories, and commentary on music or anywhere music was used as a rhetorical entity. Although different composers or musics served as signposts for different thinkers, who themselves may have been composers, there was surprisingly little variation among different schools of thought in recourse to the line. If an historical census could be taken mapping the meandering of this line negotiating the difference between sound and musical sound, it would show the line was more adamantly inscribed the greater the proximity to phonography, noise, and other signs of the world. For a conservative philosopher like Roger Scruton extramusical sounds posed a specific threat to music: "When music attempts the direct 'representation' of sounds it has a tendency to become transparent, as it were, to its subject. Representation gives way to reproduction, and the musical medium drops out of consideration altogether as superfluous."[19] It may come as a surprise to discover that *superfluousness* for Scruton begins with musical quotation, with its emblematic composer being Charles Ives, whose "evocation of sounds of Central Park [demonstrates] a constant tendency on the part of the musical medium to collapse into the sound represented. . . . All that we are left with is a succession of brass-bands, jazz groups, cries and murmurs, which stand out in the music as isolated particulars bearing no musical relation one to another, just like the sounds in Central Park."[20]

If quotation could prove so vexatious, what then of the pressures brought on music by phonography? One measure can be found in the lamentations of Pierre Schaeffer, founder in 1948 of *musique concrète*. Using phonographic recording equipment to make his early compositions (only later moving to tape recorders), he rejected his very first composition *Étude aux chemins de fer* (1948) soon after completion because the train station sounds remained too recognizable. He thereafter employed a variety of manipulation techniques that would more assuredly diminish or entirely eradicate any associative properties a sound might have. Once such severance had taken place, music was inevitable: "From the moment you accumulate sounds and noises, deprived of their dramatic connotations, you cannot help but make music."[21] Yet over the course of time even in this formulation was not immune to rejection: "You have two sources for sounds: noises, which always tell you something—a door cracking, a dog barking, the thunder, the storm; and then you have instruments. An instrument tells you, la-la-la-la [sings a scale]. Music has to find a passage between noises and instruments. It has to escape. It has to find a compromise and an evasion at the same time; something that would not be dramatic because that has no interest to us, but something that would be more interesting than sounds like Do-Re-Mi-Fa."[22] The intrinsic despair of "compromise and evasion" finally developed into Schaeffer's remarkable dismissal of his entire career: "Musique Concrète in its work of assembling sound, produces sound-works, sound-structures, but not music."[23] He returned to the notion that no music was possible outside of conventional musical sounds: "It took me forty years to conclude that nothing is possible outside DoReMi. . . . In other words, I wasted my life."[24] In 1988 I had occasion to describe Schaeffer's lament to John Cage over the dinner table. He quickly responded, "He should have kept going up the scale!"[25]

To rationalize his new-found conservatism Schaeffer sought recourse in the structural anthropology of Claude Lévi-Strauss: "I'll bring in Lévi-Strauss, who has said again and again that it's only things that change; the structures, the structures of humanity, stay the same—and the uses we make of these things."[26] For Schaeffer to invoke Lévi-Strauss to account for the failure of *musique concrète* was an act of insult on injury bordering on masochism, since Lévi-Strauss had already criticized *musique concrète* in his best-known book, *The Raw and the Cooked*. Given the architectonics of his thought and the central role music played, it was inevitable that Lévi-Strauss would draw the line at what was and what was not music, and he found it in *musique concrète*, which, it seems, had abdicated the significance of sound but failed to find significance in music:

It is precisely in the hierarchical structure of the scale that the first level of articulation of music is to be found. It follows that there is a striking parallel between the ambitions of that variety of music which has been paradoxically dubbed concrete and those of what is more properly called abstract painting. By rejecting musical sounds and restricting itself exclusively to noises, *musique concrète* puts itself into a situation that is comparable, from the formal point of view, to that of painting of whatever kind: it is in immediate communion with the given phenomena of nature. And like abstract painting, its first concern is to disrupt the system of actual or potential meanings of which these phenomena are the elements. Before using the noises it has collected, *musique concrète* takes care to make them unrecognizable, so that the listener cannot yield to the natural tendency to relate them to sense images: the breaking of china, a train whistle, a fit of coughing, or the snapping off of a tree branch. It thus wipes out a first level of articulation, whose usefulness would in any case be very limited, since man is poor at perceiving and distinguishing noises, perhaps because of the overriding importance for him of a privileged category of noises: those of articulate speech.

The existence of *musique concrète* therefore involves a curious paradox. If such music used noises while retaining their representative value, it would have at its disposal a first articulation which would allow it to set up a system of signs through the bringing into operation of a second articulation. But this system would allow almost nothing to be said. To be convinced of this, one has only to imagine what kind of stories could be told by means of noises, with reasonable assurance that such stories would be both intelligible and moving. Hence the solution that has been adopted—the alteration of noises to turn them into pseudo-sounds; but it is then impossible to define simple relations among the latter, such as would form an already significant system on another level and would be capable of providing the basis for a second articulation. *Musique concrète* may be intoxicated with the illusion that it is saying something; in fact, it is floundering in non-significance.[27]

As Stanley Diamond has written, "Lévi-Strauss' central metaphor is music, which he considers the most basic of all art forms precisely because it is wordless, hardly cognitive, a pristine syntax of sounds, of harmonic and rhythmic contradictions and progressions—structuralism incarnate."[28] Lévi-Strauss's musical tastes for sonatas, symphonies, cantatas, fugues, and musicians like Stravinsky and especially Wagner ("If Wagner is accepted as the undeniable originator of the structural analysis of myths"[29]) lead him to elitist and ethnocentric positions, endemic to many practices of anthropology. He fixes on the Western forms emanating from the lone mind of the composer,[30] circumvents collectivist musics both within and outside Western culture, and adopts the "hierarchical structure of the scale" begged by *mathemusic* as a means toward his own thought.[31]

Karlheinz Stockhausen, in an electronic music laboratory competing with Schaeffer's studio, also had *musique concrète* in mind when he valorized electronic sounds over "all instrumental or other auditive associations; such associations divert the listener's comprehension from the self-evidence of the sound-world presented to him because he thinks of bells, organs, birds or faucets."[32] So too Pierre Boulez: "Sound which has too evident an affinity with the noises of everyday life . . . any sound of this kind, with its anecdotal connotations, becomes completely isolated from its context; it could be integrated. . . . Any allusive element breaks up the dialectic of form and morphology and its unyielding incompatibility makes the relating of partial to global structures a problematical task."[33] And as Dmitri Shostakovich stated, or stated with the aid of a censor, "'Concrete music' is extremely primitive. By the way, a collection of the sound-imitating and noise effects of this form of 'art' can be used for certain episodes of radio-telefilm with an appropriate subject, or in certain instances for sound effects on the stage: for example, shipwreck, fire, railway accident, earthquake, etc. . . . We cannot be too emphatic in stressing the fact that all these anti-humanistic trends are entirely alien to socialistic realism, as well as to the requirements of Soviet people in general and creative artists in particular."[34]

Along with *musique concrète* the other dominant sound or musical sound signpost in the postwar years was John Cage. He earned this role for his championing of noise, use of recorded and transmitted sound, his idea that all sounds can be music, his championing of sound and listening *per se*, and so on. His attitude about *musique concrète* itself was somewhat conflicted. After years of musing and theorizing about the use of recorded sound for musical purposes, he became moved to action—but only after meeting Pierre Schaeffer in Paris, the person who had beaten him out of this particular artistic gate. Cage's first audiotape work, *Williams Mix* (1952), part of the Music for Magnetic Tape project, consisted of minutely and obliquely cut pieces of magnetic audiotape, chosen and spliced together through chance operations from a stock of 500 to 600 recorded sounds in six categories—city sounds, country sounds, electronic sounds, manually produced sounds (including the literature of music), wind-produced sounds (including songs), and small sounds requiring amplification to be heard with the others. It required an incredible effort on the part of several people to construct and still only lasted about four and one-half minutes (at fifteen inches per second), when played back on eight tracks deployed spatially with speakers encircling the audience. Although both *Williams Mix* and works of *musique concrète* are premised on the musicalization of sound, the former made sure that not only imitation but also any subjective factors attendant on composition would be banished.

People familiar with *Williams Mix* will know that whatever associative properties the recorded sounds might have once possessed are almost entirely obliterated, except for what sounds like crickets (high-pitched sounds identify themselves quickly). Familiarity with *Williams Mix* usually derives from its inclusion on the Twenty-Five-Year Retrospective album. In the album's notes Cage writes, "Since the pioneer work of Pierre Schaeffer at the Radio Diffusion of Paris in 1948, the making of tape music has become international. (The different approaches of the various world centers— Paris, Cologne, Milan, New York are excellently set forth in an article by Roger Maren in *The Reporter*, issue of Oct. 6, 1955, pages 38–42.)" Looking at the Maren article that Cage so enthusiastically recommended, we find an interesting tripartite categorization. One category pertains to work where tape is used but nothing radical is attempted, as with Luening and Ussachevsky. More interesting is the categorical wedge Maren drives between Schaeffer's *musique concrète* and Cage's work. Because "the strong referential significance attached to certain noises" have not been sufficiently eradicated, Schaeffer's *musique concrète* is, according to Maren, therefore, "closer to cubist poetry than to music. . . . This does not necessarily nullify the value of the work. It simply places the work outside the domain of pure music." In the third category Maren distinguishes Cage's work, as well as the tape work of Messiaen, Boulez, and Varèse, as *pure music* because recorded sounds are "manipulated to the point where they lose all referential significance. The composer's interest is in the sound itself and the patterns into which it can be formed." Thus, the quality of general organization of recorded sounds—the formidable compositional means of Cage, Messiaen, Boulez, and Varèse versus the relatively simplistic arrangements of Schaeffer and company—signaled the extent to which referentiality persisted, despite the attempts to eradicate it. By referring people to the Maren article, in other words, on the occasion of a major retrospective release of his work, Cage conforms to a view that *musique concrète* is not really musical. In many other instances, of course, Cage not only understands *musique concrète* as musical but too conventionally musical, indicting Schaeffer later on for, among other things, simulating solfeggio by imposing a twelve-tiered taxonomy on the expanse of sound.

A demarcative use of Cage's own music comes from an unlikely source, that of Gilles Deleuze and Félix Guattari. One would suspect they might share Cage's musical radicalism, yet they thought Cage went too far, and, more surprisingly, the offending works were not among his most raucous but were instead the fairly benign prepared piano pieces. They begin with a paean: "Varèse's procedure, at the dawn of this age, is exemplary: a musical machine of consistency, a sound machine (not a machine for reproducing sounds), which molecularizes and atomizes, ionizes sound matter, and harnesses a cosmic energy. If this machine must have an assemblage, it is the synthesizer."[35] Deleuze and Guattari's synthesizer will not be entirely recognizable to electronic music buffs, since it would be philosophical: "like a thought synthesizer functioning to make thought travel, make it mobile, make it a force of the Cosmos (in the same way as one makes sound travel)."[36] That sound could not travel too far across the never-ending vacuum of the cosmos would not prevent it from traveling back in time to dust off a few stellar pages from Schopenhauer. Letting actual sound travel freely where it might across the terrestrial spaces where it travels best would be "opening music to all events," which might rupture the type of "machine of consistency" by coming too close to that most feared phenomenon of all space travel—the black hole of Cage's prepared piano pieces:

Sometimes one overdoes it, puts too much in, works with a jumble of lines and sounds; then instead of producing a cosmic machine capable of "rendering sonorous," one lapses back to a machine of reproduction that ends up reproducing nothing but a scribble effacing all lines, a scramble effacing all sounds. The claim that one is opening music to all events, all irruptions, but one ends up reproducing a scrambling that prevents any event from happening. All one has left is a resonance chamber well on the way to forming a black hole. A material that is too rich remains too *territorialized:* on noise sources, on the nature of the objects . . . (this even applies to Cage's prepared piano).[37]

This will surely be difficult to understand among people who think *only* Cage's prepared piano music could be called music. What terrestrial and territorial hazards drove Deleuze and Guattari away from Cage's music? Their portrayal of Varèse's music as a synthesizer would be appropriate to his percussion-laden music but not, say, *Poème Électronique* (1958), which used new technologies to both produce and reproduce sound. The prepared piano was an act of melding a percussion ensemble with the piano (itself an instrument already equipped with percussive functions) following Varèse's own formidable forays into percussion. The specific occasion for its development was a dance by Syvilla Fort at the Cornish Institute in Seattle. Fort, an African-American choreographer and dancer, wanted music with an African feel to it, but the stage was too small for a percussion ensemble, thus its miniaturization under the lid of a piano. In this way, Deleuze and Guattari's complaint does not synthesize thought but reproduces the tradition of Europeans hearing non-European music, especially percussion music in a modernist response to *primitivism* as noise. Why was it, then, that their interpretation of musical events so easily sailed skyward to the unpopulated vacuum of the cosmos and not south?[38]

Many of these problems could be credited to a general lack of understanding about sound; there is, after all, little discourse on sound. Moreover, if we leave it to the type of candor expressed by Jean Baudrillard in acknowledging his lack of understanding about sound, then the situation may not improve very soon. When asked about the theoretical implications of sound he said, "I have some difficulty replying to this question because sound, the sphere of sound, the acoustic sphere, audio, is really more alien to me than the visual. It is true there is a *feeling* [spoken in English] about the visual, or rather for the image and the concept itself, whereas sound is less familiar to me. I have less perception, less analytic perception, of this aspect." Yet he could not refrain from saying in the very next sentence: "That is not to say that I would not make a distinction between noise and sound."[39]

Synesthesia as Noise Abatement

The historical incidence of synesthesia among the arts has produced its own forms of noise abatement. Found in the works of Baudelaire, Rimbaud, René Ghil, and others in France, the Russian avant-garde, Der Blaue Reiter group, the Italian Futurists, "visual music" abstract films beginning in the 1910s and continuing through to Oskar Fischinger's impact on Walt Disney's film *Fantasia*, colored-light organs, optophones, and elsewhere, synesthesia's relatively short life span within the heyday of modernism should not mask the fact that the ideas underpinning it were time honored. From Pythagorean and Platonic ideas and their recurrence through the centuries of relating pitches and scales to planets (producing most familiarly the music of the spheres), modernist synesthetic systems derived a cosmic coordination of essences along mathematical and musical lines, at once spiritualistic and rationalistic, one in which elemental, minimal, and pure foundations could generate an all-encompassing space. From the tradition of Cratylus in which the relationship between language and the world was coordinated eponymously and onomatopoetically came phonemes and letters, mostly vowels, that resonated with musical sounds, with other phenomena, and, in turn, with the universe. From St. Augustine's *simultudo*, manifested through such notions as Emanuel Swedenborg's correspondences and representations and Charles Fourier's analogies, and from Herder's Book of Nature, came the idea that sounds, among other worldly phenomena, acted as ciphers of the universe. From Newton came the idea that sound and light were simply traveling at different speeds and thus spectral and harmonic systems could be aligned as expressions of the same vibrational universe.[40] These sources fed into modern occult doctrines such as theosophy, new sciences such as psychology, and cultural ideas that promoted the merging of various artistic disciplines, which in turn fed back into specific synesthetic systems. Supporting these claims were persuasive anecdotal and clinical demonstrations of individual synesthetic experience, whether inherent in a person's psychological makeup or associated with exceptional states brought on by drugs or psychoses.

Conforming to the anthropocentric projection of utterance over audition, actual sound in synesthetic systems occurred as speech and musical sound, which then might correspond to each other; to colors; to intellectual, emotional, affective, or characterological attributes; or to other phenomenal or cosmological traits. The musical practices associated with the pitches within synesthetic systems were themselves well rehearsed in suppressing noise—beginning most immediately with percussion, timbre, amplitude, and other aspects attending the production of music itself. When it came to the sounds of language, vowels were overwhelmingly preferred for their ability to mimic the sustainable pitches of musical tones, while the fricatives and other noises of consonants were poorly represented in the universe. Also, because the vowels were Indo-European, only certain cultures could claim privileged relationship to the cosmos. A sound could never exist autonomously but once invoked would immediately be deflected to its corresponding stations among other traits of the system. A sound was always elsewhere, and this elsewhere would ultimately become the cosmos as repeated deflection from one register to another generated a totalizing space. Such deflection was commensurate with the ephemerality, temporality, movement, and spatial character of sound in general, and it was practical that it should become figural, conceptual, spiritual, and silent only in service of such a grand cause. At the same time, a sound was also always in one place, fixed into place in an interdependence of elemental and cosmological. If not dampened by the fixed set of correspondences, then movement within a register of sound or between the cardinal points of pitches or phonemes might be implied, but so was a proportionate reconfiguration of the system. Moreover, because a single sound was already a cipher for so much, noise would not merely disrupt a perceptual or aesthetic reception but would raise havoc with the cosmos.

The sensory formalism of modernist synesthetic systems was also capable of reducing and eradicating the worldly and otherworldly characteristics of its own ancestors: gone are the mythological attributes in the Myth of Er section in Plato's *Republic*. Closer to home was Charles Baudelaire's famous poem "Correspondences." The poem was so often referred to in conjunction with subsequent instances of synesthesia within the arts that the word *correspondence* itself served as a synonym, yet the poem's stanzas provide two very different views, only the second one being privileged within the synesthetic legacy:

Like long-held echoes, blending somewhere else
into one deep and shadowy unison
as limitless as darkness and as day,
the sounds, the scents, the colors correspond.[41]

It is from this association that *correspondences* came to be closely associated with the purely sensory aspects of synesthesia, where sounds, scents, and colors were qualities quite apart from the meaning of things in the world, which happens to be the topic of the second stanza:

The pillars of Nature's temple are alive
and sometimes yield perplexing messages;
forests of symbols between us and the shrine
remark our passage with accustomed eyes.

For Baudelaire, the realm of sensory correspondences was not the first line of experience but a distant place where the perplexity of nature coalesced amorphously in *one deep* and *shadowy unison*. It certainly was not distributed within a structured and sensible whole expressible in a table of relations. Synesthetic systems are, in this respect, a circumnavigation of the forest of symbols and a revenge of rationality. Indeed, if we go deeper into the shadowy sources of Baudelaire's idea of correspondence itself, to the eighteenth-century Swedish theologian Emanuel Swedenborg, then we find even greater variability, multiplicity, and meaningfulness. The register of the sound of speech, for instance, is not limited to pure sensation but arrayed across a range of chatty spirit personalities speaking out loud, murmuring and belching out words. In Swedenborg's "The Universal Human" from the *Arcana Coelestia* (1747–1753), hearing is explicitly associated with the hearing of spirit voices, with the respective character of these spirits corresponding to the position they occupy to the ear: "These are the ones who relate to its particular organic parts—to the outer ear, the membrane called the eardrum, the more inward membranes called the fenestrae, the hammer, stirrup, anvil, cylinders, cochlea, and who relate to still more inward parts, even including those nearer the spirit but clothed with substance and those that are even within the spirit, and finally those most closely united to the element of inner sight."[42]

In a remarkable text, Swedenborg details a number of spirits, their location, the nature of their voices, their character, and how their character was derived from their previous embodied lives. Spirit voices from people upset because in their lives they had prayed for something and received no response reside on the outer ear or earlobes. Toward the back of the earlobe a spirit who had not reflected on what other people said but allowed their words to enter his own ears unimpeded. Swedenborg could tell the spirit's own words were inconsequential by the way he belched them out. In general, "people like this, who give little heed to the meaning of things, belong to the cartilaginous and bony part of the outer ear."[43] Former gossips muttered just inside the ear, although in the "other life" this muttering was louder than regular speech. Former logicians and metaphysicians spoke loudly from inside his body to get out and report that their lives were wretched—because "they had buried their thinking in these matters with no end in view but gaining a reputation for learning and attaining prestige and wealth as a result" and because they had not absorbed any useful learning ("Their speech was slow and barely audible").[44] There were a number of others as well. We could set up a table of Swedenborg's spirit voices and their various correspondences, and it would become quickly obvious that no synesthetic system within the legacy of correspondences undertook such quirky and precise elaboration. Scampering about the sides of his head their vocal character is varied and not phonemically reduced to vowels. They inhabit symbolic positions on the human body, not a space regulated by mathematical proportions, and the complexity of their personification far exceed the capacity of the elements of synesthesia.

The phonemes of most synesthetic voices belong to vowels instead of consonants, again conforming to the distinction between musical tones and noise.[45] Certainly the best-known example is to be found with Arthur

Rimbaud's poem "Voyelles," especially when combined with his boast: "I invented the color of vowels!—*A* black, *E* white, *I* red, *O* blue, *U* green."[46] Ignoring the range of readings given over the decades to this poem, it is of little surprise to find anecdotal evidence relating to musical sound. Pierre Petitfils has made the case that "Voyelles" had as its background a youthful idea for a universal language that would, as Rimbaud wrote, "be of the soul and for the soul, embracing everything, scents, sounds, colors, thought catching thought and pulling," but was motivated more immediately by the barman Ernest Cabaner (described as "Jesus Christ after three years of absinthe" by Verlaine), who, in teaching Rimbaud how to play the piano, used a beginners system where keys were color coded and attached to the vowel-laden solfège.[47]

Synesthetic systems accrued legitimacy, of course, through the simple existence of synesthetes and synesthetic experience, even though ultimately there was little confirmation to be had. Kandinsky in *On the Spiritual in Art* cited a synesthete who associated colors and taste. Although this did not keep Kandinsky from being fascinated with certain features of synesthesia, it made him skeptical of a general system whereby "one might assume that bright yellow produces a sour effect by analogy with lemons,"[48] for the obvious reason that there are very few blue foods. We can only conjecture what the actual experience of Kandinsky's synesthete might have been, just as we can only wonder how one young French woman in the late eighteenth century could have stomached colors, considering she "was insensitive in her whole body with the exception of her epigastrium, to which all her senses seemed to have been transferred. She could hear, see, and smell only through her epigastrium."[49] Other people experienced synesthesia on ingesting certain substances, as did Anaïs Nin with LSD:

I ceased looking at the garden because on the plain door now appeared the most delicate Persian designs, flowers, mandalas, patterns in perfect symmetry. As I designed them they produced their matching music. When I drew a long orange line, it emitted its own orange tone. . . . The murals which appeared were perfect, they were Oriental, fragile, and complete, but then they became actual Oriental cities, with pagodas, temples, rich Chinese gold and red altars, and Balinese music. The music vibrated through my body as if I were one of the instruments and I felt myself become a full percussion orchestra, becoming green, blue, orange. The waves of the sounds ran through my hair like a caress. The music ran down my back and came out of my fingertips.[50]

Alcohol and music mixed in an apotheosis of bourgeois delectation with the lengthy literary construction of Des Esseintes's *mouth organ* in J. K. Huysmans *A Rebours* (1884).[51] As Roland Barthes has said in another context, "Taste implies a philosophy of trifles."[52] Baudelaire was more interested in the vocational uses proposed in Hoffmann's *Kreisleriana*: "The conscientious musician should avail himself of champagne to compose a comic opera. In it he will find the light and frothy gaiety called for by the genre. Religious music requires Rhine wine or Jaraçon. In these there is the same intoxicating sorrow that underlies profound thoughts. On the other hand, Burgundy is indispensable to heroic music."[53]

One of the best-known cases of sustained synesthetic behavior was chronicled by the Russian psychologist A. R. Luria in his book *The Mind of a Mnemonist*. The man, referred to as S., sported a memory so vast and precise it interfered with his daily life. Operating through synesthetic means, he not only saw colors when he heard sounds and voices, but he also saw images and lines, blurs, puffs, and splashes, and these images served as the foundation of his mnemonic powers. S. told Vygotsky, "What a crumbly yellow voice you have."[54] I know of no instance where an artist appealed to S.'s case to legitimate a particular synesthetic system, yet S. did describe what it was like listening to Sergei Eisenstein speak: "It was as though a flame with fibers protruding from it was advancing right toward me. I got so interested in his voice, I couldn't follow what he was saying."[55] The acuteness of these images was the source of his problem; for example, a person's voice over the telephone in the morning would generate a different image than the same person's voice in the afternoon, just because of the slight changes within the voice over the course of the day.

Even when he was subjected to the sonic neutrality of a clinical setting, his images diverged from even the most generalized synesthetic schemes of dark color/low tone and light color/high tone as cultural constructs. For instance, sustaining 30 cycles per second at 100 decibels generated the mental image of "a strip 12–15 cm. in width the color of old, tarnished silver. Gradually this strip narrowed and seemed to recede; then it was converted into an object that glistened like steel. Then the tone gradually took on a color one associates with twilight, the sound continuing to dazzle because of the silvery gleam it shed."[56] It would be difficult to agree with Kandinsky when he said that "our hearing of colors is so precise that it would perhaps be impossible to find anyone who would try to represent his impression of bright yellow by means of the bottom register of the piano, or describe dark matter as being like a soprano voice."[57] Indeed, what this demonstrates is that most synesthetic systems within the arts rarely reflect the possible complexity of the experience of actual synesthetes.

The exception, of course, comes in those cases where synesthetes are themselves artists. The composer Olivier Messiaen experienced a sustained and complex correspondences of musical sound and color: "One note-value will be linked to a red sonority flecked with blue—another will be linked to a milky white sonorous complex embellished with orange and hemmed with gold—another will use green, orange and violet in parallel bands—another will be pale gray with green and violet reflections—another will be frankly violet or frankly red."[58] The American composer Mitchell Clark had a short phase of synesthetic capabilities in which he could identify semitones according to the colors they generated, once astonishing the composer Kenneth Gaburo by picking out a difficult pitch in one of his compositions, aided by a puce. Yet Clark during his spell of synesthesia would have seen tones differently from Messiaen, and both would differ from S. or any other synesthete. This need not detract from the potential of synesthetic perception and devices as productive means within the arts, but their arbitrariness cannot be extended to the social sphere, let alone to form the rationalistic spiritual laws of the cosmos. Synesthesia more properly belongs to another class of consideration where private experience is mistaken as public, such as the schism involved in the voice one hears while speaking versus the voice others hear, or the celestial music and cosmic vibrations heard by a person at the time of death as opposed to the gurgling death rattle heard by everyone else.

UBIQUITOUS RECORDING

The Rotary Revolution

In the mid-1920s a media revolution began that continued into the 1930s. A time not unlike our own, much excitement surrounded the artistic possibilities of new communications technologies. Whereas our present media upheaval is driven by the computer, earlier this century it was driven by audiophonic technologies: radio was new on the scene; film and animated cartoons were moving to sound; dramatic improvements were occurring in phonography, microphony, and other audiophonic technology; and the prospect of television was in the air. Likewise, the convergence involved in the digital mix of today had its forerunner in a mix of audiophonic equivalencies: sound began to complete the picture as phonography combined with film and promised to fuse the radio and cinema into television; recorded sound stretched over film sound, film music, music composition and performance, and the new realm of radio and threatened to establish its own autonomous artistic domain. Within this overall media environment, the rotary revolution shifted gears from the cranking motion of the siren and intonarumori to the steady spooling of the optical sound track and the gently tugging torque of the phonograph record's spiraling grooves.

Against the obstacles of musical thinking, the case for auditive imitation became increasingly compelling, and with it came a new sense of artistic possibility, a marked increase in theoretical and practical activity in the artistic use of significant sound and important experiments in asynchronous film sound. Unfortunately, radio art, audio art, and film sound experimentation based on recording technologies was cut short and postponed for decades. That radio or audio art was not firmly established early on has no doubt contributed to the fact that the true potential of a radically asynchronous sound film has, to this day, not been adequately explored. The discontinuity of these artistic traditions stands as an historical lesson that, even though the technological and conceptual requirements exist and have generated sporadic material realization, these requirements are still insufficient for maturation into an artistic practice. For instance, as discussed below, although much has been made of the development of *musique concrète* by Pierre Schaeffer beginning in 1948, it was for lack of proper institutional settings, not for want of ideas or technologies, that it failed to occur some twenty years earlier. If compelling ideas could drive the production of artwork, then we would now be watching and listening to a much more interesting and sophisticated cinema thanks to Vertov, Eisenstein, and others from the ranks of Russian Revolutionary cinema.

The shift in the rotary revolution was experienced individually by the composer George Antheil, who happened to busy himself with both sirens and phonographs. Cranking the siren did not always wrench glides and gradations from the world; turning the crank could also place the performer among revolutionary circles. Antheil saved his siren for the climactic end of the American premiere of *Ballet Mécanique* in New York (1927), but it ended in climactic embarrassment. When the conductor Eugene Goossens gave the cue, the siren player cranked and then cranked feverishly, but absolutely no sound was produced:

The moment for the siren was by now long past, and Goossens was turning to the last page of the score. Disgustedly the effects man stopped turning the crank, as the last bars of the *Ballet* crashed out. And then in the silence that followed there came the unmistakable sounds of a fire siren gathering speed. Louder and louder it came as the last notes of the *Ballet* died away, and as Goossens turned to bow to the audience and Antheil rose from the piano, it reached its full force. We had all of us completely forgotten the simple fact that a fire siren does not start making any sound until it has been energetically cranked for almost a full minute. And also we had forgotten that it does not stop shrieking simply because you stop cranking. We remembered both of these things now as the wail from the infernal red thing on the stage kept dinning in our ears, drowning out the applause of the audience, covering the sound of the people picking up their coats and hats and leaving the auditorium.[1]

The siren in *Ballet Mécanique*, especially in the context of the other instruments, was an unabashed sign of modernism, which the formalism of a glissando could have masked only with great difficulty. Sirens signaled modernism in various ways—to call workers to mechanistic labor and, after the revolution in Russia, to call emphatically to the future. During the early 1920s in Russia, the proletarian zeal of the Smithy Poets could be heard in their love of "the power of steam and of the force of dynamite, the song of sirens and the motion of wheels and shafts."[2] It was the same with the steam-whistle sirens in the versions of the *Symphony of Sirens* directed and described by Arseni Avraamov. These symphonies were on the grand scale of other spectacles in the early years of the revolution, at times employing the sirens of many factories, ships' horns and bells, the noises of trucks and seaplanes, fireworks, gunshots, machine gun volleys, and artillery charges. There was also a specially made "steam-whistle machine" that would toot *The Internationale* and "On the half verse, a joint brass orchestra sounds and the automobile chorus with the *Marseillaise*."[3] The symphonies were not merely praise songs to industrial life; they also echoed the collectivist cries and military actions of the new nation: "Then the revolution came. Once, at night—an unforgettable night—Red Petersburg sounded with a many-thousand mighty chorus of horns, whistles and sirens. And in response, thousands of trucks rushed to the outposts throughout the city bristling with bayonets. The Red Guard rushed to encounter Kornilov's vanguards. In this formidable moment, the shrieking chaos had to be tied together with one single will in order to substitute the cries of alarm for the victorious hymn of *The Internationale*. The Great October Revolution!"[4]

Antheil flatly denied any connection between his *Ballet Mécanique* and things industrial, let alone politically proletarian: "It had nothing whatsoever to do with the actual description of factories, machinery—and if this has been misunderstood by others, Honegger, Mossolov included, it is not my fault. . . . It is true that at the time I did consider machines very beautiful, and I had even advised aesthetes to have a good look at them; still, I repeat again and again, even frantically, I had no idea (as did Honegger and Mossolov, for example) of *copying* a machine directly down into music, so to speak."[5] He nevertheless found himself implicated, in the eyes of Wyndham Lewis, in a utopic vision of musicalized factories on the basis of a remarks made by his friend Ezra Pound: "It is possible to imagine music being taken out of the chamber, and entering social and industrial life so completely and so splendidly that the whole clamor of a great factory will be rhythmically regulated, and the workers work, not to a deafening din, but to a superb symphony. The factory manager would be a musical conductor on an immense scale, and each artisan would be an instrumentalist. You think perhaps that George Antheil and I are foolish visionaries."[6]

Antheil may have had no desire to copy a machine directly into music, but he was interested in the music made with the copying machine known as the phonograph. It had the advantage of being modern and, at the same time, more versatile in its connotations than other machines. Antheil had plans to use phonographs in *Cyclops*, his unrealized opera based on the episode in James Joyce's *Ulysses* and animated by a huge mechanical ecstasy: "I saw thousands of electric lamps strung in the heavens and illuminated from one switchboard to create God; vast cinemas projected a new dimension in the skies; music machines large enough to vibrate whole cities."[7] Unfortunately, its main impact at the time was a three-page extract of a piece called "Mr. Bloom and the Cyclops" in a 1925 issue of *This Quarter*. The score lists the following instrumentation: voice (from electric amplifier), chorus (from electric amplifier), sixteen mechanical pianos operated from a master roll and controlled from a switchboard, eight xylophones controlled from a switchboard, amplified gramophones containing all of the ordinary orchestral instruments registered on gramophone record and amplified and controlled from a switchboard, four bass drums, four electric buzzers, four pieces of steel, an electric motor (wood attachment), and an electric motor (steel attachment). Antheil, confident in the fidelity of gramophones, explained in a letter to Pound how the "phoneygraphs" will create a revelation of artifice:

The opera progresses. Orchestras and hugely augmented phoneygraphs both play simultaneously THE SAME THING . . . the orchestra stops, and one discovers the xxxxxxxxxx phoneygraph HAS BEEN PLAYING SOME-THING ELSE. All of the combinations to make your belly give up. Colossal orchestra for a change . . . mostly mechanical. Like Ulysses . . . encyclopedic. Entirely different from Bal. MeK. Must come down in June to show you. After the Bal& Meca.[8]

In the second decade of the century composers began in earnest their experiments with mechanical musics (reproducing pianos and organs, automata, clockwork musics, and the like), and phonographs, and by the late 1920s such experiments were not uncommon. Phonographs were used as secondary aids to music, such as Nikolai Kulbin's suggestion that "the improvisation of free tones may for the time being be taken down on Gramophone records" as a means of notation, or Cowell's use of the phonograph to demonstrate complex rhythmical patterns.[9] A more active approach could be found in Kurt Weill's "Tango-Angèle" (1927), in which a gramophone recording acted as a soloist: "I proposed achieving the [climactic] effect through a completely new sound form, and for me this was the gramophone, which enters for the first time as a soloist while the orchestra is silent, and whose melody is countered by the singers."[10] Artistic experiments proper sought to manipulate musical sound through the mechanism of the phonograph in recording or playback or to directly manipulate the recording itself. Darius Milhaud reportedly conducted experiments as early as 1922, and there were many more by the time Varèse partook of his phonographic studies in 1936. One writer described the gramophone experiments presented in Berlin by Paul Hindemith and Ernest Toch in 1930: "This made-for-phonograph-record-music was accomplished by superimposing various phonograph recordings and live musical performances, by employing variations in speed, pitch height and acoustic timbre which are not possible in real performance. The result was an original music which can only be recreated by means of the gramophone apparatus."[11] László Moholy-Nagy writing in 1933 described the experiments in terms of the voice:

The composers Hindemith and Toch have achieved some startling results by the application of the mechanical process of the phonograph. Thus, with the help of mechanical procedures, Hindemith transposed a vocal composition four octaves lower for one part, and four octaves higher for another. By increasing the speed with which he recorded a fugue made up of vocal parts only, Toch was able to produce an as yet unrecognized aspect of the human voice. Toch did the same with a choir composed of many voices, when he recorded a text that is simple but hard to pronounce ("Popokatepetl liegt nicht in Afrika, sondern in Mexico") at increasingly greater speeds; at high speed the recording gave back a perhaps never before suspected aspect of the human voice, one never even heard before, impossible to produce in any other way. This is the principle of sound-time expansion.[12]

Most composers were interested in the manipulation of musical sounds for musical purposes; some sought to import extramusical sound for musical purposes. One such person was Russian-American composer Nicolai Lopatnikoff (1903–1976). In 1931, while Lopatnikoff was still living in Germany, Henry Cowell praised him as the composer "writing for mechanical instruments in the most penetrating fashion." Cowell believed Lopatnikoff was alone among composers because he wrote music for recording instruments that could only be performed mechanically, being "impossibly fast, [or with] combinations impractical for the hands of players, no matter how many should take part in a performance."[13] Cowell also noted Lopatnikoff's "plans to make phonograph records of various factory and street noises, synchronizing and amplifying them as a percussion background for music written for keyboard recordings."[14] (It is significant that percussion, once again, was to act as the musical intermediary with noise.)

Turntable phonographics were concurrent with similar experiments using sound recorded on film. With both sound could be sped up and slowed down, reversed and amplified, but the advantages of film included the way sound could be edited and generated through "drawn sound" techniques (not to mention the advantages of inhabiting the realm of moving pictures).[15] These techniques proved to be well suited to integrating music in an innovative manner into different cinematic contexts. Maurice Jaubert used sound track reversal, splicing, and variable-speed-turntable methods in a number of his film scores, most notably for Vigo's *Zéro de conduite* (1933), and, as Richard Schmidt James put it, "He might well have taken part in the development of *musique concrète*, itself, if the war that temporarily stifled his art had not also taken his life in June of 1940."[16] Arthur Hoérée, at times in collaboration with Arthur Honegger, used reversible sound and collage techniques for his film scores, as well as drawn-sound techniques in which shapes photographed, drawn, and painted on the sound track were used to generate an early form of electronically synthesized sound and music. Drawn sound enabled him to visualize the long-standing periodic-aperiodic distinction between *musical sound* and *noise*, as discussed previously, and to entertain the ambiguity involved: "The sound written like this, you see [indicates a sine curve with his hand], by a sinusoidal curve is a musical sound but noise is less symmetrical. When it is written like this [indicates a somewhat irregular sine curve], it is somewhat musical and somewhat non-musical, it is a mixture."[17]

This class of phonographic experiments, where music and cinema met, point out a certain irony about the intonarumori, the instruments that Luigi Russolo devised to play his art of noises. For all the claims of Futurism, they are constructed as a composite of some very old instrumental technologies; the most modern element lurking within their design was the crank, which summoned up the rotary motion of Helmholtz's clinical sirens. He might have exploited the phonograph had he actually been interested in bringing sounds of the world into musical or artistic practice. As it was, phonography was to haunt him in one form or another for years and finally spell the end of his career. After assiduously avoiding imitation in the early development of his *art of noises*, during the 1920s he designed a new class of instruments premised, in part, on a capacity for imitation. The three different types of *rumorarmonio*, based on the intonarumori, had the capacity to imitate wind, water, animals, and the like, and thus, Russolo thought, they could be marketed for use in silent film accompaniment. One was installed in the late 1920s in the Studio 28 in Paris, where it was damaged during the ransacking of the theater by right-wing groups following the showing of Luis Buñuel's *L'Age d'or* (3 December 1930). Russolo's hopes for commercial success would be dashed, since they were based on trying to design a version of the sound-effects organs already used to accompany silent films,[18] at a time when sound film technology itself would soon eliminate the need for either. In short, the ascent of sound film signaled the descent of Russolo's musical career. The filmmaker Eugene Deslaw was curiously positioned on either side of Russolo's demise. In 1930 he announced that his film *Towards the Robots* would be accompanied by Russolo's "rumharmonium."[19] The very next year he made a sound film and submitted a composer to an exercise using its material: "I had ten sounds extracted from my film projected to a friend who is a composer. He only recognized and identified three. He thought the others were the result of unknown and new musical instruments. And there were no limits to his enthusiasm after the projection. 'What marvelous perspectives for the art of tomorrow.' I can still hear his phrase in my ears."[20] Deslaw left this composer unnamed. It would be a surprise if it had been Russolo; if it was, then he clearly chose not to translate his enthusiasm into instrumental design and musical practice.

Carol-Bérard (1881–1942) was a French composer and theorist who composed a noisy pre-Russolo *Symphonie des forces mécaniques* (Symphony of Mechanical Forces) (1908) using motors, electric bells, whistles, and sirens as well as *L'Aéroplane sur la ville* (n.d.) composed with phonograph recordings of noises. In 1929 he wrote an article criticizing Russolo for not following up on his initial breakthrough: "The noisemakers were dedicated in purpose to the music of the future, but their realization fell far short of the goal. For all the hammers, the exploders, the thunderers, the whistlers, the rustlers, the gurglers, the crashers, the shrillers, and the sniffers of the 'futurist' orchestra obey the same laws of execution as the common violins, violoncellos, flutes, oboes, and other instruments in the traditional orchestra. No matter how new the acoustic effects they create, they are always in need of performers."[21] Still, he believed that "noise . . . holds the secret of the future" for music and that the secret could be unlocked "if we take a definite noise, capture and associate it with other noises according to a definite design; an act of composition is [thus] performed and a work of art authentically created":[22]

Why, and I have been asking this for fifteen years, are phonograph records not taken of noises such as those of a city at work, at play, even asleep? Of forests, whose utterance varies according to their trees—a grove of pines in the Mediterranean mistral has a murmur unlike the rustle of poplars in a breeze from the Loire—? Of the tumult of the crowds, a factory in action, a moving train, a railway terminal, engines, showers, cries, rumblings? . . . If noises were registered, they could be grouped, associated and carefully combined as are the timbres of various instruments in the routine orchestra, although with a different technique. . . . We could then create symphonies of noise that would be grateful to the ear. There are plenty of symphonies today which are anything but agreeable, while at large and unregistered are a myriad of delightful sounds—the voices of the waves and trees, the moving cry of a sailing vessel's rigging, an airplane gliding down, the nocturnal choruses of frogs around a pool.[23]

He was willing to admit phonographic sounds directly into music without either intimating them through timbral effect, as had Russolo, or manipulating them beyond recognition, as *musique concrète* would do twenty years later. He nevertheless avoided venturing too far from conventional musical signification: "Once registered, naturally no significance other than that of sound can attach to individual noises. They will cease to be the creaking of a bus axle, the rumbling of a cauldron, the roaring of a cataract. They will have become merely noise factors, as saxophones, clarinets, violas or oboes are factors of musical sound."[24] These sounds may not need performers to be played, such was his criticism of Russolo's intonarumori, but he did not want them to depart materially from the identity of sounds trafficked by conventional musical instruments.

There were others who imagined artistic uses of phonographic and sightless cinematic recording that would incorporate extramusical sounds to such an extent that the result might not be music. In the early 1920s Moholy-Nagy, as he began to propose experimentation with sound film, effectively called for an autonomous phonographic art because he stated that sound should initially stand on its own before being integrated with visual images.[25] In Russia, Dziga Vertov, as we see below, attempted a phonographic art as early as 1916, an impetus that lead him into film itself and into his innovations with film sound; Serge Eisenstein argued for an asynchronous sonic counterpart to his sophisticated notions of visual montage; and Grigori Alexandrov attempted to "play with sound" in his ill-fated film *Romance Sentimentale*. In France, Raymond Lyon suggested in 1930 that one need not be restricted by the aural primacy of music and the voice; instead, by using recorded sound on film stock, with which one could "impose and direct the deformations of phonographic reproductions," a person could "splice phonographic scenes, from whence the phonograph gains access to all the techniques of representing associations of ideas, symbols, and memories employed in the cinema."[26] In Germany during the Weimar republic, Hans Flesch, the director of the *Berlin Radio Hour*, promoted the artistic possibilities of using sound film in the context of *Hörspiel* production. He was responsible for commissioning Walter Ruttmann's 1928 audio montage *Wochenende* (Weekend), which Hans Richter called "among the outstanding experiments in sound ever made. There was no picture, just sound (which was broadcast). It was the story of a weekend, from the moment the train leaves the city until the whispering lovers are separated by the approaching, home-struggling crowd. It was a symphony of sound, speech-fragments and silence of women into a poem."[27]

The combination of the context of radio, the next technology of film sound, and Ruttmann's background as a painter and activity as a filmmaker served well to break through genre demarcations of the literary and theatrical expectations of radio, as well as the limitations of musical signification attendant on a purely acoustical work. And F. T. Marinetti used recordings to present indexical sounds such as baby cries, motors, water lapping, fire crackling, the sound of a boxing match, birds, and airplane engines in his radio *sintesi* and poetry recitations, as well as theorizing, in collaboration with Pino Masnata, the artistic use of radio in the manifesto *La Radia* (1933).

However, the sum of this phonographic activity amounted to so little that, during the same period individuals were pointedly asking why more was not happening or had already happened. If we following the clock back from 1929 when Carol-Bérard declared "and I have been asking this for fifteen years," we arrive at 1914, the year after Russolo's *Art of Noises* manifesto during which he began his European tour. In Cowell's discussion of Lopatnikoff in 1931 he said that "The field of composition for phonograph records and player rolls is wide and offers many prospects, but the workers have been few and too little has been done to try to summarize the results."[28] When Rudolf Arnheim was writing his book *Radio* in the mid-1930s, he believed he was engaging in an anachronistic activity. Radio, he thought, was about to go in the historical dustbin because a mass culture of television, with its visual images *radiophonically* transmitted with the sound, seemed to be just around the corner. He nevertheless championed sound film strips and sound archives for use in radio and then wondered why people were not taking advantage of them:

In many cases, it is practicable and commendable to make up the sound-content of a radio scene from a mixture of several individual records, instead of doing everything at once in the studio at the time of the broadcast. Firstly, this makes it possible to use records of the original sounds, above all for sound effects. This has already been done to some extent, but this expedient is not nearly so much exploited as it might be, and in any case it is done with impracticable gramophone records instead of sound-strips. The use of the former on broadcasts of radio plays largely depends on choosing certain little bits of the records, and, in spite of the finest adjustment, it is a matter of chance, even for the most skillful and experienced people, whether they will manage to put the needle in the right groove at the right moment in the broadcast. A film-strip, on the other hand, can be cut at will, so that it fits quite exactly into the play.

Nevertheless gramophone records already enable us to utilize the whole range of naturalistic sounds for radio drama, and for a real radio dramatist there can be nothing more exciting than the study of the archives of those records. Besides records of famous political events and speeches and interpretations by world-famous singers, instrumentalists and conductors, there is a wealth of naturalistic records:

> And now the smiling librarian, a new record in her hand, goes up to the gramophone: the little room is filled with the deep breathing of a man, as loud as if a giant were snoring! . . . Then the narrow walls seem to fade away, a landscape appears, enlivened by the prattling and splashing of rushing streams. Then cars go racing through the tiny room, rumbling omnibuses and little rattling tin lizzies; a storm crackles and thunders by; noises of the stock-exchange emerge and turn into children's voices; we hear the wheezy organ on the merry-go-round and the subdued roar of the fair. . . . Again space dwindles to the size of the room, and suddenly invisible hands begin brushing clothes, crumpling paper, blowing noses, and then, in bewildering contrast, the walls extend into a factory with machines stamping and engines humming, harbor-noises surge up and mills creak, and so it goes on almost indefinitely: laughter of girls and growls of rage, battle-cries, drumrolls and trains puffing. . . . The young lady smiles again, conscious of the astonishment in store for the listener: an entire zoo with its thousands of voices appears! Monkeys scream and chatter, the walrus snorts, the polar-bear yawns, deer bell, dogs of all sizes and breeds bark, the tiger growls, the lion "speaks his mind," a pig grunts, bees hum—and birds trill and whistle and sing, from the canary and the nightingale to the kestrel. (From a newspaper article by Curt Corrinth)

. . . A large number of these records can be played at once, and they can be combined with what is being produced for the first time in the studio. Thus, for instance, it will be quite superfluous to imitate the bark of Frederick the Great's greyhounds by the more or less realistic yelping of a few worthy wireless officials—a genuine greyhound-bark can be obtained.[29]

He thought that the opportunity presented was "not nearly so much exploited as it might be" because this exploitation was the means toward the goal of a distinct radio art: "wireless claims the whole attention of the theorist of art because for the first time in the history of mankind it makes practical experiments with an entirely unexplored form of expression in pure sound, namely, blind hearing."[30] Although this *experimentation*, in Arnheim's usage, primarily meant the development of innovative techniques within an industrial practice and not experimentation within an avant-garde sense, the two were by no means mutually exclusive, and the former could have laid the institutional basis for the latter.

The rift between the artistic possibilities presented by phonography and the lack of activity that took advantage of these possibilities was a commonly expressed theme prior to midcentury. It cannot be explained by a shortage of ideas or the lack of proper technology, and although the period was marked by economic depression, authoritarian regimes, war, and censorship and exile of artists, all of which had a profoundly disruptive effect, even these events in themselves (as we shall see) cannot provide the total answer. Instead, it appears that the primary reason for inaction was to be found within the role of institutions and the machinations of class in matters of access to technologies, institutions, and the arts in general. For instance, although German artists and producers found a setting for their work on radio, it was short-lived because sponsors could not rationalize continued deployment of funds based on the small size of the listening audience. What commitment might have been made after a certain point would have been quickly scuttled by the pressures of the Great Depression and then by the Nazi *coordination* of cultural life, as it was called, although Ruttmann did manage to fit into this coordination as a filmmaker.[31]

Carlos Chavez in his book *Toward a New Music: Music and Electricity* (1937) was well aware of institutional constraints facing composers and other artists interested in the new auditive media of electric phonography, sound photography (optical sound film), and electronic instruments yet invented. He dispelled the conceit that the new technology was too complicated to work with by pointing out that the piano itself was once a complicated new technology that composers were able to sufficiently master. Chavez thought that the consequence of the alienation of artists from the institutions housing new technologies left a gap populated by technical personnel: "The composers of the present need large fields of experimentation in which to develop new instrumental aptitudes. It is very natural that, for the moment, no hints of new productions are at hand, since the artists are far from the instruments, while the only ones who know them are the engineers. Piano music would never have existed if the instrument had not come into the hands of artists. Only providing composers and artists with the means of knowing and familiarizing themselves with the new media will pave the way toward the birth of new art forms."[32]

Also rushing into this breach, according to Chavez, was an institutional layer of pseudo-composers who engineered music as much as engineers engineered technology: "Composers go on writing only classical symphonies, symphonic poems, string quartets, operas, masses, sonatas for piano and violin, etc., and the arrangers of the producing firms control the production of the films. The former live comfortlessly, with sparse elements of life and action, agonizing to achieve a Paris or New York performance of their works, directed or interpreted by some celebrated artist. The arrangers live in ease."[33] These arrangers are guilty of the musical crime of *pasticcio,* the type of un*organized* sound that Varèse characterized within Futurism as nothing but *a succession of titillating aggregations of sound.* Chavez thought that "No musical creations taking advantage of the wealth of the film's sound resources have yet appeared. Up to the present day there have as a rule only been what might be called musical salads, concocted of the most vulgar and sentimental tunes and realistic sound-imitations, giving the ensemble a naturalistic character of the poorest sort."[34] The world would open up once composers and artists carved out an institutional niche legitimated through a scientific model, a "world of new and unlimited artistic possibilities, huge and almost virgin . . . revealed to us when we consider the musicalization of a film with all the resources of a laboratory."[35]

In 1937, the same year Chavez's book was published, Cage gave a lecture in Seattle on "The Future of Music: Credo" in which he restated similar technical and institutional imperatives laid out in the book. He began, "Wherever we are, what we hear is mostly noise," and in what would be an anathema a little over a decade later he said, "We want to capture and control these sounds, to use them, not as sound effects, but as musical instruments." In his capacity as a composer he then points to the treasures that lie within the *laboratory:* "Every film studio has a library of 'sound effects' recorded on film. With a film phonograph it is not possible to control the amplitude and frequency of any one of these sounds and to give to it rhythms within or beyond the reach of anyone's imagination. Given four film phonographs we can compose and perform a quartet for explosive motor, wind, heart beat, and landslide."[36] What these new means could produce would no doubt abuse the sensibilities of conventional Western art music: "If this word, *music*, is sacred and reserved for eighteenth- and nineteenth-century instruments," he says, then it can be replaced with the Varèsean term *organization of sound*. If the music of the past is to be repeated, then let it be the "portrait of Beethoven repeated 50 times per second on a sound track."[37] The new means would carry forth the developing musical tradition associated with noise and phonography, but before anything could come to fruition, composers needed to get their hands on the equipment. Thus, Cage ended his essay, *pace* Chavez, by calling for the establishment of "centers of experimental music. . . . In these centers, the new materials, oscillators, generators, means for amplifying small sounds, film phonographs, etc. available for use. Composers at work using twentieth-century means for making music. Performances of results. Organization of sound for musical and extramusical purposes (theater, dance, film)."[38] He remained committed enough to this idea to take concrete action a few years later. In a letter to George Antheil written in 1940, Cage sought his assistance in finding support for a center of experimental music, so-called, to be set up at Mills College in Oakland or the School of Design in Chicago:

I am doing every thing I can to establish a "center of experimental music." The purpose of this center will be to do research, composition and performance in the field of sounds and rhythms not used in the symphony orchestra; the ultimate purpose will be the use of electrical instruments which will make available the entire desirable field of sound. Recently my father, who is an inventor, designed an instrument which should give rich possibilities in the variation of the overtone structure of a tone. This instrument will be constructed soon. I also have recordings of two of the percussion concerts. I think you would enjoy hearing them.[39]

He sent similar letters to a number of corporations, foundations, motion picture studios, universities, and individuals without result. When he finally did gain institutional access to a studio at Columbia Broadcasting

System, the result was not what he had hoped. In 1941 at his own initiative, he was commissioned to provide the sound score for the Columbia Workshop production of Kenneth Patchen's script *The City Wears a Slouch Hat,* a play about urban peripatetics that Patchen wrote while bedridden with the chronic back pain.[40] Cage had just moved to Chicago and "had made friends with the head of the sound effects department of CBS," who ended up misleading him about what was possible in the production of the play.[41] Someone explained to Cage that his "view of radio music was that it should follow from a consideration of the possible environmental sounds of the play itself; so that, if it was a play that took place in the country, it would be natural to have the sounds of birds and crickets and frogs and so forth. But, if it were a play that took place in the city, it would be natural to have the sounds of traffic. In other words, I wanted to elevate the sound effect to the level of musical instruments."[42]

With characteristic diligence, Cage produced a 250-page composition of sound effects based on his own peripatetic listening trips to the Chicago Loop. On presenting the score to the CBS Radio staff, he was told it was too expensive, ostensibly because of the use of compressed air,[43] and would not be realized as planned. He was forced to produce an entirely new percussion score, with a few simple recordings, within a week. After the show was aired, he appeared to be pleased with the result, although he may have been pleased only with the exposure the program brought. Yet neither was it what he had planned, nor did the project lead to his goal of working experimentally in a laboratory setting. It would probably be safe to say that his misfortune cannot be merely attributed to being misled, although this would certainly be the view from the composer's end. The episode needs to be set within the context of an absence of a tradition of working relations between artists and such institutions, which had they existed would have alerted the composer ahead of time to certain limitations or would have allowed the radio station staff itself to have anticipated such problems. In other words, as Chavez had pointed out in 1937, it was a failure produced by the general separation of artists from the technology, a stratum populated solely by the technical staff. Of course, it was ultimately the responsibility of the institution, with its power and resources, to take the initiative.

It is against this institutional backdrop that Pierre Schaeffer and *musique concrète* should be placed. Too often the historical break in 1948 represented by *musique concrète* is understood to be a technical, a technological, and an artistic one. The true achievement of *musique concrète* was that there was sufficient institutional support to elevate intermittent forays into the area to a sustained practice. The support did not suddenly begin in 1948 but was put into place as early as 1942 when Schaeffer, who was working at the Radiodiffusion Télévision Française (RTF) as a sound engineer, a member of the institutional stratum denigrated by Chavez, was able to initiate and direct a research program in musical acoustics. The date is especially important since, contrary to what one might know or suspect, the culturally stifling effects of World War II were not uniform. How else could Schaeffer have managed to lay the groundwork within an institution under control of the German occupation forces? He was able to carve out enough of a cocoon for himself to metamorphose from an engineer into a new type of composer. Indeed, the war continued to occupy Schaeffer after its end and was reenacted at the very inception of *musique concrète:* "We had driven back the German invasion but we hadn't driven back the invasion of Austrian music, 12-tone music. We had liberated ourselves politically, but music was still under an occupying foreign power, the music of the Vienna school. . . . I was working with turntables (then with tape-recorders); I was horrified by modern 12-tone music. I said to myself, 'Maybe I can find something different . . . maybe salvation, liberation, is possible.'"[44] Here was a twist on Chavez's scenario: the technical staff member becomes the composer. This would not make Schaeffer the equivalent to the easy-living musical *arrangers* that Chavez despised because Schaeffer took advantage of his institutional position to produce an important body of work that continues to be influential to the present day and because he directed the institution to engage a number of other composers, no matter how problematic some of those collaborations turned out to be.

Very soon after *musique concrète* had made its mark, there were accusations that neither Schaeffer nor Pierre Henry had properly acknowledged indebtedness to their predecessors. Maurice Lemaître in his introduction to the 1954 French edition of Russolo's *Art of Noises* said that Schaeffer in his book *Á la Recherche de la musique concrète* (1952) had not given adequate credit to Russolo and had even confused Russolo with Marinetti.[45] However, neither Schaeffer nor Henry was aware of Russolo when they first began their *musique concrète* compositions, their lack of recollection being part of a larger historical amnesia, and neither was willing to give unqualified acknowledgment on learning about the art of noises, since the genesis of *musique concrète* belonged to another tradition, that of recorded sound, which had in fact brought about the final demise of the art of noises. To account for the genesis of *musique concrète*, artistic precedent was virtually unnecessary since the technology involved was suggestive in its own right. Music was in the air—radiophonically—where it could easily make its own auditive connections with recorded sounds and, most important, one could sit in a movie theater with eyes closed and hear something similar to *musique concrète*. As Pierre Henry said, "the prefiguration of *musique concrète* was, indeed, relatively abstract, save, evidently, for the possibilities offered by the sound on film of cinema."[46]

Russian Revolutionary Film

At the same time that music composition experimented with the possibilities of optical sound film, a number of filmmakers proper began to develop complex approaches to sound and sound-image relationships. The most intense and radical combination of theory and practice within this realm took place within the Soviet Union, in particular, with Dziga Vertov and Sergei Eisenstein. There is a certain irony involved in Vertov's engagement with sound, since he came to be identified with the *kino-eye* among experimental film circles in the second half of the century. Yet not only was Vertov a very soundful filmmaker (just listen to *Enthusiasm* or *Three Songs of Lenin*), who kept sound in mind even in his silent films through tactics of implied sound, but he went into film in the first place because he was unable to do what we would now call audio montage. The kino-eye, in other words, was born of a keen but frustrated ear. His early aspirations can only be speculated on, but they seem to point to an actual art of noises and not one presented for rejuvenating music. Perhaps it was a deeper running documentary zeal and a background in both music and writing that led him to imagine such a possibility, yet it also seems that Russolo's art of noises itself played a role.

As a boy Vertov was a prolific writer, and at age sixteen he entered the Bialystok Conservatory of Music and studied violin, piano, and music theory for three years. In 1916, while attending the Psychoneurological Institute in Petrograd, Vertov was introduced to some of the major players of the Russian avant-garde, including Osip Brik, Alexander Rodchenko, and Vladimir Mayakovsky, who by that time were well aware of Italian Futurism and, for many of them, too aware.[47] A Russian Futurist almanac, *The*

Croaked Moon (Spring 1914), contained Mayakovsky's poem "Little Noises, Noises, Booms," generally understood as a derivation of Russolo's celebration of urban sounds in *The Art of Noises* manifesto, which had already been published in Russia.[48] Vertov was probably familiar with this poem since he was an avid admirer of Mayakovsky, committing many of his poems to memory, and had become personally acquainted with the poet.[49] For Vertov, the mix of writing, music, and noises within the adventurous milieu of the avant-garde "turned into an enthusiasm for editing shorthand records [stenographs] and gramophone recordings. Into a special interest in the possibility of documentary sound recording. Into experiments in recording, with words and letters, the noise of a waterfall, the sounds of a lumbermill, etc."[50] Toward the end of 1916, Vertov attempted to build a "Laboratory of Hearing" with a 1900 or 1910 model Pathéphone wax disc recorder:[51] "I had the original idea of the need to enlarge our ability to organize sound, to listen not only to singing or violins, the usual repertoire of gramophone disks, but to transcend the limits of ordinary music. I decided that the concept of sound included all of the audible world. As part of my experiments, I set out to record a sawmill."[52]

It has been assumed he became frustrated with the poor sound quality of the available technology. Indeed, he spoke of his transition to film in terms of the inadequacy of phonographic technology, remembering how "one day in the spring of 1918 . . . returning from a train station. There lingered in my ears the signs and rumble of the departing train . . . someone's swearing . . . a kiss . . . someone's exclamation . . . laughter, a whistle, voices, the ringing of the station bell, the puffing of the locomotive . . . whispers, cries, farewells. . . . And thoughts while walking: I must get a piece of equipment that won't describe, but will record, photograph these sounds. Otherwise it's impossible to organize, edit them. They rush past, like time. But the movie camera perhaps? Record the visible. . . . Organize not the audible, but the visible world. Perhaps that's the way out?"[53] Since determinations of sound quality usually prove to be creatures of the historical moment, not of some timeless measure of sonic realism, it is likely that other limitations of acoustic phonographs, primarily the difficulty of manipulating the inscribed sound materially, sent him packing into the kino-eye. Once there, however, he did not abandon his interest in sound but instead integrated sound into his writings on Radiopravda, Radio-Eye, and Radio-Ear. Indeed, in his 1925 essay "Kinopravda and Radiopravda"

(1925), with electrical phonography and breakthroughs occurring within the development of sound film in the United States and Germany, Vertov proposed documentaries of recorded audible events to take separate forms within radio, sound film, and television, all within a hopeful project of undercutting capitalism with the truth of reproduction:

If, with respect to vision, our kinok-observers have recorded visible life phenomena with cameras, we must now talk about recording audible facts. We're aware of one recording device: the gramophone. But there are others more perfect; they record every rustle, every whisper, the sound of a waterfall, a public speaker's address, etc. The broadcast of this record can, after its organization and editing, easily be transmitted by radio, as "Radiopravda." . . . Technology is moving swiftly ahead. A method for broadcasting images by radio has already been invented. In addition, a method for recording auditory phenomena on film tape has been discovered. In the near future man will be able to broadcast to the entire world the visual and auditory phenomena recorded by the radio-movie camera. We must prepare to turn these inventions of the capitalist world to its own destruction.[54]

He also invested the "Great Mute" of silent film with *implied sound.* Appearing in all his major films of the latter half of the 1920s were events denoting sound, objects, and sound technologies (a gramophone record, a radio, and other noisy objects are set in *Stride, Soviet* (1926) in a context of Lenin's call for electrification) along with formal motifs and movements suggestive of sound. Vertov himself listed some of the implied sounds within his 1928 newsreel *The Eleventh Year* in this way: "In the silent film *The Eleventh Year* we already see montage connected with sounds. Recall how the machines thump, how absolute silence is conveyed. At first there's the pounding of axes and hammers, the whining of saws, then it all ceases, followed by dead silence, and in that silence there beats the heart of the machine. [In another scene,] a 'sound' begins to grow, the pounding of hammers starts up, louder and louder, then the blows of a big hammer, and finally when a man appears and hammers on the cliff, a powerful 'sound echo' is conveyed. After the transition to radio-eye, all of this will resound impressively from the screen."[55]

Once sound film technology became available in other parts of the world, filmmakers in the Soviet Union, because of economic and policy factors beyond their control, were required to wait several years before they had their chance to use the new technology. This was especially frustrating, since their silent films were recognized as being at the forefront of international cinema. In lieu of actual production, they engaged in fervent debates about the pros and cons of sound film, especially how sound might interact with visual images. Perhaps because of Vertov's prior experience in sound, he tended to avoid the dogmas displayed by other prominent Soviet filmmakers and critics. He remained adamant about the documentary principle underlying the "unplayed film" and the political principle underlying all his actions. When it came to sound, the proletariat must use all means at its disposal, never the line of least resistance but "the line of maximum resistance . . . that of *complex interaction of sound with image*."[56] In an attack on the prescriptive use of asynchronous relationship between sound and visual image, laid out in the famous "Statement on Sound" (1928) signed by Sergei Eisenstein, Vsevolod Pudovkin, and Grigori Alexandrov, Vertov wrote: "Declarations on the necessity for nonsynchronization of the visible and audible, like declarations on the exclusive necessity for sound films or form talking films, don't amount to a hill of beans, as the saying goes. . . . Neither *synchronization* nor *asynchronization* of the visible with the audible is at all obligatory. . . . Sound and silent shots are both edited according to the same principles and can coincide, not coincide, or blend with one another in various, essential combinations. We should also completely reject the absurd confusion involved in dividing films according to the categories of talking, noise, or sound."[57]

Film historian Lucy Fischer has provided a valuable description of how Vertov produced his *complex interaction of sound with image* within the first section of his first sound film, *Enthusiasm: Symphony of the Donbas*. The fifteen categories included disembodied sound, sound superimposition, sound and visual time reversal, abrupt sound breaks, abrupt tonal contrasts, sound edited to create an effect of inappropriate physical connection to the image, synthetic sound collage, inappropriate sounds, mismatching of sound and visual distance, mismatching of sound and visual location, metaphorical use of sound, sound distortion, technological reflexivity, association of one sound with various images, and simple asynchronies of sound and image. In other places Vertov varied the speed of the sound, reversed it, and set up a symbology of sound production in general. He even engaged in sound synchronization.[58]

On another front, Vertov encountered resistance to the range of possibilities he wished to explore. In 1929, when he embarked on *Enthusiasm*,[59] the film critic Ippolit Sokolov wrote in "On the Possibilities of Sound Cinema" that the natural world of sound was not conducive to recording[60]—that is, a large part of the domain of documentary (the outdoors and the remote, the sounds of work, industry, celebration, public gatherings)—was not audiogenic: "Agitational and scientific films will be produced not in the lap of nature, not in the noise of the streets, but within the soundproof walls of the film studio, where no outside sound can penetrate. The sound movie camera will least of all film 'life caught unawares.' The unorganized and accidental sounds of our streets and buildings would become a genuine cacophony, a literally caterwauling concert."[61] Vertov understood Sokolov's "theory of caterwauling" to be "antinewsreel" and very much within the mold of formalist critics who preferred only actors and acting on the screen to his own idea of the *unplayed* film. He also rejected the exclusionary conceit derived from music that "everything which is not 'sharp' or 'flat,' in a word, everything which does not 'doremifasolize' was unconditionally labeled 'cacophony.'"[62] But Vertov felt that the true refutation of Sokolov's "theory of caterwauling" was *Enthusiasm*. For Vertov there was absolutely nothing do-re-mi in the "setting of din and clanging, admidst fire and iron, among factory workshops vibrating from the sound."[63] Moreover, he did not stay cloistered within "the soundproof walls of the film studio," as Sokolov recommended, but "penetrated into mines deep beneath the earth" and rode atop "the roofs of speeding trains" lugging twenty-seven hundred pounds of recording equipment developed specifically for the film, and *for the first time in history*, as he claimed, recorded in documentary fashion the basic sounds of an industrial region (the sound of mines, factories, trains, etc.).[64]

The necessity to get out of the studio provided Vertov with the basis to accuse Walter Ruttmann's use of studio-generated sounds in his crosscut film, *World Melody*, of being deceptive. He contrasted his own progress in getting outside the studio, all the way to the Donbasin region, where he was making his film *Enthusiasm*.[65] This was not technologically motivated, although he did bemoan the poor quality of film sound reproduction equipment throughout the late 1920s and 1930s and worked actively on a number of fronts to secure its improvement. It was instead politically important to Vertov that the workers were recorded speaking for themselves, surrounded by the sounds of their life. His tactics for remote recording can be summarized in this way:

1. opening the window at the Radio Centre and recording the outside
2. transmitting sound back to the studio using microphone wires
3. mobile sound unit used nearby
4. mobile unit used at greater distance to film a Party Congress
5. mobile unit used far away in many situations in the Donbas region
6. ultimately, the audio-visual sound transmission back to the studio will be accomplished via radio for both film and television[66]

Vertov may have rejected Sokolov's music-like exclusivity, but he didn't reject music, nor, with his experiences at the music conservatory, could he. He often referred to his role in filmmaking not as director but as *composer*.[67] He called *Enthusiasm* a "symphony of noises," and the film's second name, under which it was known in Russia, was *Symphony of the Donbas*. Among many of the aurally reflexive moments of the film, *symphony* signifies both the "harmonic" organization of the activities of the Five-Year Plan in the Don basin region and the parallel production of the film itself. For Vertov symphonies included noise and economic harmonies rattled with the sound of labor and machines; they were written amid an "enthusiasm of facts" and a literary process wherein sounds themselves were scripted before the film as a whole.[68] The result caught the ear of no less than Charlie Chaplin, who, in a note written from London (November 1931), said, "Never had I known that these mechanical sounds could be arranged to sound so beautiful. I regard it as one of the most exhilarating symphonies I have heard. Mr. Dziga Vertov is a musician."[69]

Although Vertov found Sergei Eisenstein's asynchronous approach to sound-image relationships unnecessarily restrictive, and although Eisenstein was never able to hear his early plans fully realized in actual sound, his ideas were nevertheless very compelling. To understand them we need to go back to the Russian avant-garde theater with its "eccentrism" and its opposition to the theatrical naturalism of the likes of Stanislavsky at the Moscow Art Theater. Eccentrism meant a fascination with popular culture in general and with American culture in particular, an appetite expressed across the entire European avant-garde for variety theater and music hall, clowning and the circus, ragtime and jazz, cowboys and Indians, cops and robbers and Chicago gangsters, the Salvation Army, slapstick pratfalls and sight gags, Charlie Chaplin—for all that was fast, funny, irreverent, and awash in artifice. It was discursively linked to sound film through the avant-garde theater's reaction to the *prospects* of a simplistic sound cinema. In 1913 Vladimir Mayakovsky said that theater, in the face of cinema, should give up its naturalistic copying of nature in the same way that painting had given up copying with the advent of photography. Otherwise, theater would be "merely the three-dimensional photography of real life."[70] Although sound film was still a number of years away on the world scene and even later for Russia, the very promise of the kinetophone lent even greater rhetorical presence to the reproduction of real life because "The only distinction between [theater] and cinema—silence—has been removed by Edison with his latest invention."[71] Naturalistic theater reproduced through a sound cinema would soon be nothing but a copy of a copy of nature—twice the reason to develop a new "anti-illusionist" theater.

Eisenstein's experience on the antinaturalistic theater stage was the platform from which he first issued his theories. In 1922 he cowrote an essay with FEKS (Factory of the Eccentric Actor) cohort Sergei Yutkevich that pitted "eccentrism" against cinematic illusionism and, retrospectively, against synchronized sound cinema circa 1905. Their essay quoted the French critic Claude Blanchard, who remarked, "People who visited the darkened halls in 1905–6 will of course remember the primitive imitation sounds that invariably accompanied the showing of a film (the crashing of waves, the roar of an engine, the sound of breaking crockery, etc. etc.)."[72] Blanchard himself thought little of such synchronization because the technical imperfections were too evident: "The illusion did not work!"[73] Eisenstein and Yutkevich questioned the desire for illusion in the first place. In addition, they were puzzled why in America, the wellspring of "eccentrism," filmmakers had not overcome "the temptations of illusion"[74] in their own films. America had not only given in to temptation, but it now housed the supreme *trompe l'oeil* artists, constructing the slums of Rio, Hindu temples, or the back alleys of San Francisco out of papier mâché in Hollywood studios. When the illusion of synchronized sound film finally did work in the late 1920s, Eisenstein would once again argue fervently against its technonaturalism and against the illusionism of the type trafficked by the United States, through his commitment to the "Statement on Sound" (August 1928).

Signed collectively by Eisenstein, Pudovkin, and Alexandrov, the "Statement" was in response to a threatening set of circumstances. The year before, the film *The Jazz Singer* signaled the commercial viability of sound film in America, and on the international scene England, Germany, and France were close behind. In Russia, however, it was clear that sound film would not be available for any time in the foreseeable future. It would be impossible, therefore, for Eisenstein and other Russian filmmakers to compete artistically at the international level at which they had become accustomed. Thus, they could not help but be removed from their leadership role in international film art, a leadership they had just been able to achieve through their development of montage. Hollywood would not develop sound film in terms of montage, but Eisenstein and others were sure they would use sound to emulate theater. Worse yet, sound meant the addition of speech, and that meant specific languages. The international traffic in film, which had not only bolstered Russian film's role in the cause of proletarian internationalism but had also made Eisenstein a celebrity, was aided immensely by the ease of splicing appropriate intertitles into the correct language, but the supple movement of lips set up nationalistic obstacles. With the advent of sound Stalin's doctrine of socialism in one country would enjoy its cinematic counterpart. Indeed, as Alexandrov reported, knowing that Eisenstein, Tisse, and he were headed to the United States to investigate sound, Stalin told them, "Study the sound film in detail. This is very important for us. When our heroes discover speech, the influential power of films will increase enormously."[75]

The "Statement" approached this problem by rehashing earlier Russian arguments, including the one put forth by Eisenstein and Yutkevich, about the importance of keeping cinema distinct from theater as an art form. It then went on to propose that sound montage be developed along the lines of visual montage and that the two should maintain an asynchronous relation to one another. Montage was a cinematic language of images and narrative developed in the absence of speech and sound. Eisenstein had earlier theorized that if film were to be its own art, it would need its own artistic raw material. That material was constructed on an elemental level by the shot and built up dialectically through a process of conflict. Sound threatened to smooth over the conflict by dictating a scene naturalistically at the slower pace set by the synchronization of speech emanating from bodies and sound from objects and actions. If a dialectics of antinaturalism were to be maintained, sound and visual images would themselves have to be set into asynchronous relationships of conflict. The "Statement" posed this relationship through the repeatedly emphasized metaphor of music: "*Only the contrapuntal use* of sound vis-à-vis the visual fragment of montage will open up new possibilities for the development and perfection of montage." The developmental process will be marked initially by "*a sharp discord*" and ultimately lead to "the creation of a new *orchestral counterpoint*" between sound and visual image.[76] This overarching play of musicality would diminish the role of speech enough to avoid the reduction of cinema to a "filmed play" and to mitigate against being locked into language-based markets.

It would be a number of years until Eisenstein had any serious engagement with actual sound film production, the first being the banned *Bezhin Meadow* (1935–1937) and then finally in *Alexander Nevsky* (1937–1938), but by then the giddy phase of experimentation had long passed into an increasingly pervasive climate of cultural conservatism, while his use of sound was sparing and overly reliant on music. Nevertheless, his earlier attempts bear close attention, beginning with *The General Line* (1929), re-named *Old and New*. He made plans to add sound after the fact, but financing for the project promised by a London firm was withdrawn. The sound script remains, however, and is very adventuresome, despite the fact that the story—about the efforts of a peasant woman Marfa to collectivize and technologize farming in her community—might seem an unlikely vehicle for major artistic experimentation.[77]

Eisenstein's lack of experience in sound sanctioned a wish list freed from practicality; many ideas would have been technically difficult or impossible to realize at the time. This was perhaps the only way to achieve an auditive montage commensurate in sophistication to visual montage as proposed in the "Statement." One way Eisenstein proposed to use sound was similar to the way conventional cinema would soon come to use music: to bridge the cut. Technically, there were perhaps more cuts in a normal Eisenstein film montage than in any other film at the time; if the quickness of the visual cutting had been paralleled with like speed in sound cutting, the result would have fallen on laggard ears. Historically, there had not yet been the cumulative decades of auditive mass media needed to produce a properly accelerated comprehension of code, the type operating in activities such as television channel surfing. Instead, Eisenstein could only rely on a pace typified by the trodding code of a Wagnerian leitmotiv. But the cutting in *Old and New* exists also as content, not just form. In an early scene where two brothers cut their hut down the middle and inefficiently partition their fields simply because they are separating from one another (a purported irrationality of peasant behavior), the sound in the script moves from a cross-cut saw, to a circular saw, to the "deformation of the saw sound (Zeitlup [slow-motion]) into sobbing"[78]—the sobbing signaling the poverty and suffering such irrationality imposes. This ability to stretch across the cut (of the hut and montage), to meld continuously from one "object" or entity to another, is a feature intrinsic to sound, and it has had little parallel within the cinema or videography until the recent computer-based capacity for morphing. Economically and politically, by bridging the cut sound enacts the subsumption and destruction of the peasantry under industrialism and the historical fatalism of the revolution.

At one point in the sound script for *Old and New* a fanfare is blurted out only to become shrill laughter; then saw sound is distorted into laughter, which itself melds into "animal laughter." There are at least two animal laughters here for Eisenstein: one is generated by the familiarity that the peasantry establish with their livestock before they are eaten, and the other is produced by cartoon animals that are born and bred to produce laughter, not meat. The cartoon sound connection is especially merited given Eisenstein's deep abiding interest in Disney and the unique characteristics of cartoon sound itself. Cartoons were, after all, creatures of both the high technology of their times and of American eccentrism. It was only through this rare pedigree that mock mice and rabbits and deer could ascend into the rarefied reaches of intellectual and artistic life. Oswald the Lucky Rabbit (September 1927) and Mickey Mouse (May 1928) had both announced their sound-image programs prior to the "Statement on Sound" (August 1928). After the resounding success of Mickey in *Steamboat Willie*, Disney tried to retrofit sound to Oswald the Lucky Rabbit episodes with little success, much like Eisenstein's plans to retrofit the silent *Old and New* with sound. A problem arose because "the finished products reveal their origins; because the animation was not done to a specific beat, and gags were not geared to particular sound effects or songs, there is no fusion between sound and picture."[79] In this way, Vertov's *Sound March*, the sound script to *Enthusiasm*, was more akin to *Steamboat Willie*.

In 1935, the British filmmaker John Grierson singled out the precedence of sound as the basis for Disney's success: "Out of the possibilities of sound synchronization a world of sound must be created, as refined in abstraction as the old silent art, if great figures like Chaplin are to come again. It is no accident that of all the comedy workers of the new regime the most attractive, by far, is the cartoonist Disney. The nature of his material forced upon him something like the right solution. Making his sound strip first and working his animated figures in distortion and counterpoint to the beat of the sound, he has begun to discover those ingenious combinations which will carry on the true tradition of film comedy."[80] That Grierson echoed the contrapuntal principle of the "Statement on Sound" was no accident; he was quite familiar with Russian film, and a year earlier he had written favorably on Pudovkin's use of sound.[81] The potent similarity between a "Statement" and cartoon sound was that both sought a continuous line of development out of the silent cinema, instead of either keying off ideas of verisimilitude or imagining a big break that many others thought would accompany the transition to sound. Whereas Eisenstein sought to find an auditive equivalent to his visually derived montage, Disney extended the elements of silent cinema into sound under the actuality (not metaphoricity) of music in such a way that the music and sound *performed* the visual elements of the film—its characters, objects, and actions. What may have once struggled awkwardly as an implied or otherwise compensatory sound made itself heard with a vengeance through every possible auditive technique. Voices, sounds, and music were spread out over the bodies of both characters and objects in a new form of homologous puppetry, whether a squeaking elbow joint, fly footsteps, flesh ripped off to play a rib-cage xylophone, or a piece of clothing mentioned in the title or verse of a familiar song. The exaggeratedly tight coordination of sound and image in the novel context of sound cinema meant that the visual experience of animated cartoons was itself animated by sound.

This coordination, in itself, was a carryover from how the muted voices of silent film manifested themselves in the performed gestures of the actors' bodies. Mary Ann Doane has pointed out that these familiar gestural exaggerations—akin to those of commedia dell'arte, which were developed to assist the voice to telegraph meaning beyond the normal range of projection—were produced in silent film as a compensatory voice:

"The absent voice reemerges in gestures and the contortions of the face—
it is spread over the body of the actor."[82] The logical cartoon extension of
the voice-performing body in silent films was extended bodies. In fact, the
elasticity of bodies immediately preceded and accompanied the coming of
sound to Disney's animated cartoons. Stretching gave Disney his early success with Oswald the Lucky Rabbit just prior to *Steamboat Willie*. Oswald's
selling point, as Leonard Maltin has written, "was a rubbery kind of movement that tied into fresh and amusing gags. In *Oh, What a Knight*, Oswald
wrings himself out to dry, and later, when kissing a fair maiden's hand, he
pulls an endless length of arm from her sleeve in order to have more to
kiss! In *Trolley Troubles* even Oswald's electric car is flexible, widening and
flattening to accommodate the unpredictable changes in the tracks beneath it."[83]

Sound stretching across the cut drew from the same elastic force that
worked on bodies. In terms of cinematic montage, sound did not resemble
a suture, which as a figure is too inscriptive; it resembled a gum or a glue,
an adhesion that could stretch. When Eisenstein gave into his fascination
and finally wrote about Disney Company cartoons, the main concern was
this type of elasticity. He found precedent in Lewis Carroll, the German
caricaturist Walter Trier, and etchings by Toyohiro, Bokusen, and Hoku-
sai, and he could have found it in Mayakovsky's long telecommunications
neck in his unfinished poem "The Fifth International" or in Salvador Dalí's
drooping, filleted forms.[84] He called it *plasmaticness* and considered Mickey
Mouse in possession of "this plasmation *par excellence*."[85] He briefly entertained the idea that its secrets are held in a prenatal, even cellular memory,
a standard from which to gauge the morphing of growth and shrinkage.
To explain the "prelogical attractiveness" of Disney cartoons in the United
States, he said that the plasmatic "all-possible diversity of form" finds its
ground as a counter to a "social order with such a mercilessly standardized
and mechanically measured existence."[86] He then went on at length to generalize such transformations to fire,[87] a fire "assuming *all* possible guises"[88]
in an aural-like flux where borders dissolve and things are born and die
in a moment, and through fire back to music: "herein also lies the secret
of the fascination of music, for its image too is *not stable*." In fact, he put
it bluntly: "'Music'—the element of Disney." While Eisenstein reveled
in the action in Disney's foreground, however, he thought that "Disney is
amazingly blind when it comes to *landscape*—to *the musicality of landscape*

and at the same time, to *the musicality of color and tone.*"[89] *Bambi*, for instance, lacked the lyricism of Chinese landscape and painting "in its treatment of fluffy beings—monkeys or fledglings."[90]

The cartoon connection with *Old and New* is actually more immediate. As a preface to the sound script Eisenstein lists *kinds* and *degrees* of sound, among other categories. The three kinds of sound are (1) musical, (2) natural surroundings, and (3) animated cartoon. The three degrees of sound are (1) slow motion, (2) animated cartoon (an exaggeration of number three above), and (3) special types of distortion of a purely acoustic sort (to be found). Eisenstein, faced with the problem of associating certain sounds to the changes wrought by rapid visual cutting, used the quick, often disjunctive sound and visual image relationships of the early sound cartoons as a means to accelerate sounds into at least some proximity of association. You can hear him convincing himself: "Must find ecstatic gradations of timbres, corresponding to the ecstatic gradations of the shots."[91] The problem he did not anticipate and never had to face (the sound version of the film was never realized) was that a cartoon shot was much longer in duration than a flurry of Eisensteinian shots. To coordinate the exaggerated synchronization of "animated cartoon sound," what would later be called in filmmaking jargon "Mickey Mousing" nevertheless found its place within *Old and New*, among animated animals no less, although unlike Disney characters, they had genitals. When the collective's baby bull Fomka grows to full size, in a series of shots constructed in an animated way much like the awakening stone lion sequence in *Battleship Potemkin*, he then inseminates his "bride" in one of cinema history's rare cross-species point-of-view camera shots:

Wedding—"lyricism"—Negro chorus. Parody on
Fomka's motif with Hawaiian guitar
Growth of Fomka—crescendo of Fomka's leitmotiv.
Choppy. With each jump in Fomka's growth the sound
gets stronger. Without transition. This same figure is
repeated in Fomka's running. There they fuse
The "Attack"—terrifying increase
Cow spreads her legs—complete pause. Then sound of
gunfire and an apogee of mooing.[92]

Eisenstein's second brush with actual sound occurred when Grigori Alexandrov, his close associate and cosignatory of the "Statement on Sound," and he undertook to make a film called *Romance Sentimentale* commissioned by Léonard Rosenthal, a wealthy merchant known as the Pearl King, to set the song stylings of his Russian lover Mara Giry into cinema. The Russian connection was there, but so was there a connection with the high bourgeoisie, yet they felt that it was worth the bother to acquire practical experience with sound film and to get paid. His last film had been about the collectivization of agriculture, but Eisenstein reluctantly joined in this rich man's bauble to assist Alexandrov with the script and the design of some shots, especially within the opening sequence. He even spent time at the Tobis Klangfilm Studio working on ideas for the sound, but then he left Alexandrov and Tisse to finish the film. Once completed, the producer of the film refused to release Alexandrov's fee unless Eisenstein's name was attached to it, for sake of both prestige and monetary return. Eisenstein, who was in the United States, conceded to become reunited with Alexandrov as quickly as possible.[93] The film was greeted widely as a debacle— especially embarrassing was the moment the singer seated at her piano reaches sufficient fervor that both she and her piano are whisked up into the clouds, accompanied by what appears to be stars scratched directly on the film stock and drawn sound that ends up sounding like a toy sliding bird whistle. Once catapulted into the clouds her piano becomes white, coordinating nicely with the swans who happen to be swimming past at that very moment. Eisenstein distanced himself from the film and attempted to rationalize the whole affair by pointing out that because scientists are allowed their white mice for experimentation, artists should be allowed their white pianos.[94]

It is no doubt the case that, of the two, Alexandrov was the one most interested in practical sound experimentation and the one most responsible for the realization of *Romance Sentimentale*. Nevertheless, during the same year of *Romance Sentimentale* Eisenstein was quite willing to associate himself with its sound experiment. In an address given in Hollywood on 17 September 1930 he said, "As we have proclaimed (and as Alexandrov tried to show in humble essay form in that piece of irony, *Romance Sentimentale*, so grievously misunderstood in its intentions)—with the coming of sound, montage does not die but develops, amplifying and multiplying its possibilities and its method."[95] Most interesting is a letter written five days earlier to Léon Moussinac: "You know very well there's not a lot of me in it (to say the least)—except for the principles and possibilities of sound utilization that are popularized in it. . . . In any case, we got what we wanted from the movie: we made some *very valuable* montage experiments and . . . we had enough money to stay in Paris until the transatlantic journey."[96] Most of the film is taken up with Mara Giry's song, which, except for very brief segments, contained nothing remarkable in terms of either montage or sound. Therefore, when he points to "the principles and possibilities of sound utilization" put forth in the film, he must be speaking instead about the sound and montage concentrated in the opening sequence of nature shots. The visual images that accompany these sounds are of quick and repetitive successions of large waves crashing against the rocks, turbulent clouds, tall trees falling or appearing to fall because of the upsweep of the camera motion, and trees flanking a roadside passing quickly by. This opening sequence is where the experiments are concentrated. The techniques—manipulating the optically recorded sound film, reversing it, drawing on it, and cutting it—were discussed by Alexandrov with the American film critic Harry Potamkin as means of "playing with sound":

Alexandrov, Eisenstein's co-director whom I have just seen off westward, has told me he has mounted sound in his brief experiment. *A Sentimental Romance*, which he made in Paris and sold to Paramount-Publix. He has done in this film a number of things I have thought basic in "playing with sound," such as: running the sound-track backwards, inscribing or designing the sound (sound is after all only inscription). He cut the sound inscription. By such method one may retard or accelerate sound movement. Let us say a note is banged on the piano, impressed on the negative. Immediate cutting—and there are a variety of ways—will change the character of the sound and give it an absoluteness. That is to say, it will not be associated with the instrument from which it will have emanated. One may record a jazz-band and then play around with the sounds as impressed, and get thereby any number of possible arrangements. The same can be achieved with speech: it may be clipped, stretched, broken into stutters, made to lisp, joined with all sorts of sound combinations either in discriminate mélange or in alternating, repeating motifs.

Alexandrov, so he told me, has played with the designs of sound by inscribing it directly on the negative and allowing light to make the final registration. Direct inscription of visual motifs on the negative has been attempted. And direct inscription of sound is more feasible, since in the visual movie human images are wanted, whereas in sound expressive utterances, which can be fabricated, are ultimately desirable. By studying the inscriptions closely one may come to an exact knowledge of these inscriptions and read them as easily as one reads musical notes for sound. The inscription for speech and that of sound differ only in the composition of the intervals and a close student will come to recognize the peculiarities of the different impressions. Actually sound will be created without being uttered![97]

Potamkin was himself very excited by these technical possibilities, particularly the ability to manipulate sound through its inscription, either by cutting a sound's representation at different points or by drawing directly onto the film and generating a new sound, what would today be familiar as digital editing and an attempt at synthesis. He was obviously aware of these possibilities prior to his conversation with Alexandrov because in an article published nearly a year and a half before he had confidently remarked, "graphic sound—the key to the sonorous film."[98] In fact, by the late-1920s the idea of "drawn sound" was well in place among artists and technologists and was being concretely investigated, mostly through the technique of photographing shapes on the sound track. One of the main investigators in Russia was Arseni Avraamov, who had earlier been involved in the *Symphony of the Sirens*. He contributed a drawn sound track of optically generated music (from photographed triangles) to Abram Room's *The Plan for Great Works*, a documentary on the Five-Year Plan credited with being the first Russian sound film (released in March 1930), and to other films and cartoons.[99] Alexandrov and Eisenstein would no doubt have been aware of such efforts.

If Eisenstein could not see the principles in the "Statement on Sound" realized in *Romance Sentimentale* or *Old and New*, then he could at least witness them within Kabuki theater and other aspects of Japanese culture. Eisenstein's celebration of Japanese culture within the context of film theory is well known, as is his idea that the combinatory attributes of Japanese script added up to montage.[100] In terms of sound cinema he was perhaps even more committed: "Just as painting owes an irredeemable debt to the

Japanese for Impressionism and contemporary left sculpture is indebted to the child of Negro sculpture, so sound cinema will be no less indebted to those same *Japanese!*"[101] In particular, he noted an *unexpected juncture* between Kabuki theater and sound cinema operating through a *monistic ensemble* where "sound, movement, space and voice *do not accompany* (or even parallel) one another but are treated as *equivalent elements.*"[102] This monism spread, for instance, to the different parts of the body creating a decomposition of elements with a remarkable resemblance to the isolation and independent action found in animated cartoons: "Act with just the right arm. Acting with one leg. Acting merely with the neck and head. The whole process of the death agony was decomposed into solo performances by each 'party' separately: the legs, the arms, the head."[103] For Eisenstein, this directly relates to his efforts within sound cinema: "In our *Statement* on sound cinema we wrote about the contrapuntal method of combining visual and sound images. To master this method you have to develop within yourself a new *sense: the ability to reduce visual and sound perceptions to a 'common denominator.'*"[104]

Once elements have reached their monistic status through the decomposition of larger complexes, the very process of decomposition has lent them a nonnaturalistic autonomy from which they can combine with other elements outside the conventions of synchronization. For instance, although the action of a pivoting elbow will not normally make noise, if it is isolated with a similarly isolated sound, it will produce a nonnaturalistic effect of the sound animating the action or the action giving rise to the sound. Eisenstein interpreted this phenomenon within a mechanics of synesthesia: "Watching Kabuki, you involuntarily recall the novel by an American writer whose auditory and optical nerves were transposed so that he perceived light vibrations as sounds and air tremors as colors; that is, he began to *hear light* and *see sounds.* The same thing happens in the Kabuki! We actually 'hear movement' and 'see sound.'"[105] Thus, sound and visual image could be exactly concurrent, but they would still not constitute synchronized sound. He gives a concrete example of a concurrent but contrapuntal sound of "a *hand movement* of Itsikawa Ensio as he slits his throat in the act of hara-kiri with the *sobbing sound* off-stage that *graphically* corresponds to the movement of the knife."[106] Thus, in this auspicious cut, the sobbing looks as though it is animating the knife, or vice versa, while at the same time each have an autonomy, thereby establishing in the immediate relationship between these decomposed elements an ability to reconfigure into a new complex of affect and meaning. What Eisenstein doesn't mention is how the rhythmic sobbing, because of its asynchronous relationship to the action, might have preceded or continued after the hand and knife movement, carrying meanings to interact with and be transformed by other actions. In any case, he could not be more enthusiastic about what he had witnessed in this scene, for it had achieved in actuality the possibilities for sound cinema he could only imagine: "There it is: 'The notes I can't reach with my voice I'll point to with my hands.' But here the voice does reach and the hands do point! . . . And we stand numbed by such perfection . . . of montage."[107] What, through circumstance, he could not achieve himself, he was willing to acknowledge elsewhere.

The Impossible Inaudible

Visuality overwhelms aurality in the cultural balance of the senses. The light that sparks the presence of objects and environments seems to be instantaneously everywhere and thus assumes a state of being that has proved to be particularly attractive to Western culture, whereas the actions that produce sounds appear scattered in space and time, tied to events that merely take place within a larger state of being. John Cage set out to tilt the balance in favor of the ear, and many people have heard the world differently because of his efforts. Yet they may not have heard all he had hoped to hear, for he wanted to hear all. His attempt began with adopting the avant-garde strategy of noise, prefigured in phonography and latent within percussion and other forms of resident noise, whereby all sounds were fair game for musical materiality, given certain conditions for their incorporation. He then followed with another tactic, associated most notably with his composition *4'33"*, which entailed rejecting the importance of whether a musical sound was present or absent within a composition and, in the process, extending the field of artistic materiality to all the nonintentional sounds surrounding the performance—that is, by shifting the production of music from the site of utterance to that of audition. This musicalization was then extended to all sounds, inside and outside the performance space, since the ability and willingness to listen were the only requirements, and these abilities in turn were extended, with the aid of amplification and other technological devices, to small sounds and hitherto inaudible sounds. The latter move was associated with his famous visit to the anechoic chamber, where he heard the ever-present sounds of his body, the low sound of his blood circulating, and the high-pitched sound of his nervous system in operation. This was a very important moment since it was here that *all sound* was joined to *always sound*. He went further still to rhetorically use the promise of technology to extend *all sound* and *always sound* outside the operations of his body to hear the vibrations of matter. Thus, sound was no longer tied to events but existed as a continuous state as it resonated from each and every atom. This certainly tipped the balance of the senses the other way since where one might expect night to remove light and give vision a rest, aurality would still exist. Everything always made a sound, and everything could be heard; *all sound* and *always sound* paralleled *panaurality*.

This sketch of Cage leading from noise to panaurality will be unfamiliar to most acquainted with his work, but this is simply the product of examining Cage on the terrain that he himself described—that of sound and aurality—whereas hitherto representations of Cage have relied exclusively on the regime of sound known as music. Consequently, some of the simplest questions regarding his work have not been asked—for example, the question of silence, which has been readily given over to repetitions of Cagean lore (generated by Cage and others), to metaphorical extension, and to simple speculation. Chapter 6 attempts to answer the question: how was Cagean silence generated? The chapter is based on an examination of Cage's first proposal for a silent composition entitled *Silent Prayer* (1948) and not the normal jumping off point, *4′33″*, composed four years later. Unpacking his proposal reveals a different Cage than the one to whom we have grown accustomed. Some may take this as a critique of Cage, whereas I would argue that he merely begins to look like someone of his time.

Cagean silence, we find, was dependent from the very beginning on silencing; this alone would run counter to the emancipatory rhetoric with which he was associated, the one he had internalized from the avant-garde wing of modernist music. Silencing would, in fact, run concurrently with his progressive opening up to all sound, and at the most fundamental level, it would entail a silencing of the social and ecological within an ever-expanding domain of music. The emancipatory drive coupled with the musical silencing of the social would eventually lead to his hopes for a new aurality out of the practical world of sound and into the realm of myth, out of the quotidian experience of hearing and into a world of the impossible inaudible. He began by liberating small sounds and then, on the wings of technological promise, smaller and smaller sounds until all matter became sonorous and musical. Once in the realm of myth, histories of music are of limited value. We must resort instead to a long-standing tradition of impossible sounds, voices, and aurality within Western culture. The last section of chapter 6 discusses how the generation of Cagean panaurality based in small sounds and technology moved into the realm of impossibility, and then chapter 7 places his impossible inaudible in a schematic of mythological inheritance, from antiquity to the present day.

In negotiating his new world of sound, Cage replaced the opposition of sound and silence with a gradient of all sound extending from small sounds to loud sounds. However, Cage's modernist enthusiasm for *discovery* and *emancipation* within this *totality* could not be played out evenly over this expanse of sound, as if over the reach of a keyboard. He believed he could approach them equitably—in effect, democratically hearing sounds in freedom by listening to each in themselves. Instead, he unwittingly encountered an imbalance, an asymmetry between small sounds and loud sounds, with the latter fitting awkwardly into his overall thought. In chapter 8 Cage's disposition toward small and loud sounds is contrasted to practices of a younger generation of artists during the late 1950s and early 1960s, and his awkwardness becomes their opportunity.

JOHN CAGE: SILENCE AND SILENCING

That a disagreeable noise should be as grateful to the ear as the sweet
tones of a lyre is a thing I never shall attain to.

*Meister Eckhart, cited by Ananda K. Coomaraswamy in The Transforma-
tion of Nature in Art*[1]

John Cage's ideas on sound, easily the most influential among the postwar
arts, were developed with a great deal of dedication, imagination, and good
will, within a complex of technical, discursive, institutional, cultural, and
political settings, forever changing over the course of a long and productive career. They matured within the sphere of music, and, until he began
to branch out into other artistic forms, most of the ideas he adopted from
elsewhere were brought into the fold of music. He was known for stepping
outside the usual confines of Western art music to usher noise and worldly
sounds into music and for proposing a mode of being within the world
based on listening, through hearing the sounds of the world as music. The
importance of his artistic role within the second half of the century is undeniable, if only evidenced in how he courses through the length of this
book; however, the brighter the light, the longer the shadow. When questioned from the vantage point of sound instead of music, Cage's ideas become less an occasion for uncritical celebration, and his work as a whole
becomes open to an entirely different set of representations. What becomes apparent in general is that while venturing to the sounds outside
music, his ideas did not adequately make the trip. The world he wanted for
music was a select one, where most of the social and ecological noise was
muted along with other more proximal noises.

Moreover, his ideas did not make the trip at a time when the social conditions of aurality and the nature of *sounds themselves*, in Cage's term, were continuing to undergo major transformations not immediately amenable to music as practiced. By midcentury, two decades after the first large onslaught of auditive mass media in the late 1920s, radio, phonography, and sound film had consolidated in the United States and expanded their overlapping positions. These media introduced on a social scale a newly pervasive, detailed, and atomistic encoding of sounds, gathering up all the visual, literary, environmental, gestural, and affective elements they brushed up against. Sounds proliferated by incorporating a greater diversity of cultural codes and worldly sources and generated still greater variety through internal means; the sheer number of sounds increased as they became freighted with multiple, shifting allusions and meanings. *Sounds themselves* took on multiple personalities, and the nature of sound became less natural. Through the redundancies trafficked by means of mass culture, many sounds became naturalized and were capable of being perceived with greater speed. Under the guise of a new aurality, an opening up to the sounds of the world, Cage built a musical bulwark against auditive culture, one founded on a musical identification with nature itself. During the 1960s when his interests shifted from musical to social issues, there was no corresponding shift to reconceptualize the sociality of sounds. At this point he opted to enter a tradition of mythic spaces by circulating the sociality of sounds through an impossible and implausible acoustics.

In this chapter, I examine Cagean sounds at the amplified threshold of their disappearance—silence, small and barely audible sounds—and how the social, political, poetic, and ecological aspects correspondingly disappear. I do not venture far into Cage's stated politics, or explore how he dealt with the theatrical, organizational, or institutional practices of Western art music, or discuss Cage's compositional prowess. I concentrate primarily on how his concept of sound failed to admit a requisite sociality by which a politics and poetics of sound could be elaborated within artistic practice or daily life. The immediate objection arises that he was just a composer, just making music, nothing else. Let us not confuse him with Elliott Carter. The core of Cage's musical practice and philosophy was concentrated on sounds of the world and the interaction of art and life. There is a musical specificity to be had within Cage, but it would be insufficient to understand his work. Indeed, my approach here takes Cage at his word when he says *let sounds be themselves.* I merely refuse to accept how Cage reduces sounds to conform to his idea of selfhood. When he hears individual affect or social situation as an exercise in reduction, it is just as easy to hear their complexity. When he hears music everywhere, other phenomena go unheard. When he celebrates noise, he also promulgates noise abatement. When he speaks of silence, he also speaks of silencing.

Silence has served as Cage's emblem. As a key to his developing work, silence (an absence of sound) was placed nicely between the odd materiality of sound and the organizational concerns of Western art music composition and theory. Organizationally, silence offset musical sound within duration and thereby established the basis by which rhythm and structure could accept all sounds indiscriminately, raising them over and above the specific attributes of musical sound—harmony, pitch, and timbre—that he considered to be outside duration. Silence shared duration with musical sound and would not contradict the extramusical sounds that Cage had already incorporated in his music. In this respect, silence took over where percussion, or rather the auspices of percussion, left off. Indeed, the rhetorical model for the ascendancy of silence in Cage's thought in the late 1940s can be found within his ideas of percussion and noise in the mid-1930s and thus in the *all sound* rhetoric of phonography and the avant-garde musical strategy inaugurated by Russolo. At midcentury, once within the context of indeterminacy, silence then turned into its opposite: sound. At first, it was nonintentional sound—for instance, the sounds occurring within the concert space when musical sound was not being intentionally made. Just as with the older form of silence, these sounds of silence were heard (intentionally) as music. Eventually codified in the publication of *4′33″*, an ultimate *silent piece* could occur anywhere and anytime, all sounds could be music, and no one need to make music for music to exist. As one indication of how much this new Cagean silence departed from common usage, loud sounds too could be silence:

Silence is all of the sound we don't intend. There is no such thing as absolute silence. Therefore silence may very well include loud sounds and more and more in the twentieth century does. The sound of jet planes, of sirens, et cetera.[2]

The next step was to interpolate sound (and thereby music) back onto a seemingly intransigent silence of objects. If silence was actually sound, then all matter too must be audible, given the proper technology to detect the soundful activities at the level of subatomic vibrations. Matter is dissolved as technology denies inaudibility and forbids silence.

Before tracking the development of such a powerful nothingness, it is crucial to understand how for Cage sound and silence come back to music. With regard to the line separating sound and musical sound, as discussed previously, Cage played a unique role in that he took the avant-garde strategy to its logical conclusion. Russolo initiated the strategy whereby extramusical sounds and worldliness were incorporated rhetorically or in fact into music to reinvigorate it. Cage exhausted this strategy by extending the process of incorporation to a point to every audible, potentially audible, and mythically audible sounds, where consequently there existed no more sounds to incorporate into music, and he formalized the performance of music to where it could be dependent on listening alone. He not only *filled music up*; he left no sonorous (or potentially sonorous) place outside music and left no more means to materially regenerate music.[3] He *opened music up* into an emancipatory endgame.

At the same time, Cage *made music more musical*. He criticized what everyone took as music in the same manner that the inclusion of noise in music itself had been criticized—that is, sound (musical sound) was not meant to carry extraneous meanings. His best-known campaign, of course, was against self-expression, which he equated most commonly within the German Romantic tradition and the classicism of Beethoven: "Are sounds just sounds or are they Beethoven?"[4] He eventually extended this concept to include a number of elements present both inside and outside Western art music. He credits Varèse for having "fathered forth noise" but then berates him for subjecting sounds to his imagination: "Rather than dealing with sounds as sounds, he deals with them as Varèse."[5] When it came to "jazz," Cage saw problems with ego-driven improvisation, along with measured time ("It is useful if I have to catch a train, but I don't think that catching a train is one of the most interesting aspects of my living"), orature and collectivism ("The form of jazz suggests too frequently that people are talking. . . . If I am going to listen to a speech then I would like to hear some words"), among other attributes.[6] And after a certain point communication, ideas and intention were also to be expunged so all that was left was a *sound in itself.* This tendency in Cage was a measure of the degree to which he was lodged within Western art music and how willing he was to carry further its processes of exclusion and reduction with respect to sound in general.[7] It was as though he could legitimately extend the bounds of musical materiality only by proving an unflinching fidelity to musical areferentiality on its own turf.

Cage's battles within music informed the most fundamental features of his thought, including how he heard and conceptualized worldly sounds, how he understood the operations of signification, and how he formulated the role of the artist, in particular, his campaign against ego investment and his concomitant interest in Asian religious thought and Christian mysticism. These considerations make their first coordinated impact on his thinking during the critical years 1948 through 1952, when he first entertained the idea of a silent composition, *Silent Prayer* (1948), to his most notorious composition, *4′33″* (1952).[8] The link between these two silences, moreover, demonstrated how he developed techniques and rationale, while engaging the sounds and silences of the world, to musically silence the social.

Much to Confess about Nothing

In *4′33″*, commonly known as the *silent piece*, the performer sits at the piano and marks off the time in three movements, all the while making no sound.[9] An unsuspecting audience (if one still exists) might attempt to reconcile the silence with its expectations before discovering, perhaps, what the piece might be. The initial absence of music might be taken as an expressive or theatrical device preceding a sound. When that sound is not forthcoming, it might become evident that listening can still go on if one's attention (and this is Cage's desire) is shifted to the surrounding sounds, including the sound of the growing agitation of certain audience members. Ostensibly, even an audience comprised entirely of reverential listeners would have plenty to hear, but in every performance I've attended the silence has been broken by the audience and become ironically noisy.

It should be noted that each performance was held in a concert setting where any muttering or clearing one's throat, let alone heckling, was a breach of decorum. Thus, there was already in place in these settings, as in other settings for Western art music, a culturally specific mandate to be silent, a mandate regulating the behavior that precedes, accompanies, and exceeds musical performance. As with prayer, which has not always been silent, concert-goers were at one time more boisterous; this association was not lost on Luigi Russolo, who remarked on "the cretinous religious emotion of the Buddha-like listeners, drunk with repeating for the thousandth time their more or less acquired and snobbish ecstasy."[10] *4'33"*, by tacitly instructing the performer to remain quiet in *all* respects, muted the site of centralized and privileged utterance, disrupted the unspoken audience code to remain unspoken, transposed the performance onto the audience members both in their utterances and in the acts of shifting perception toward other sounds, and legitimated bad behavior that in any number of other settings (including many musical ones) would have been perfectly acceptable. *4'33"* achieved this involution through the act of silencing the performer. That is, Cagean silence followed and was dependent on a silencing. Indeed, it can also be understood that he extended the decorum of silencing by extending the silence imposed on the audience to the performer, asking the audience to continue to be obedient listeners and not to engage in the utterances that would distract them from shifting their perception toward other sounds. Extending the musical silencing, then, set into motion the process by which the realm of musical sounds would itself be extended.

Silence can be derived from the idleness of an instrument or from the object status of the accouterments of music; thus, any sheet music or instrument becomes music *in potentia*, or the corpse of a music that has lived its life. In her 10 May 1951 diary entry Judith Malina wrote about a concert in which there was a performance of "*Imaginary Landscape No. 4 . . .* scored for 12 radios and 24 players. Silence is an important component." After the concert the instruments are moved out to the sidewalk, and a friend drives up in a hearse to take them away: "John and Remy [Charlip] pile the silent music into the vehicle, which drives off trailing a funeral gloom."[11] A similar objecthood overtakes certain performers in an orchestra when they are instructed by the score to remain silent; they join a tableaux as still and mute as their instruments and sheet music. The only difference between them and the performer of *4'33"* is that the latter is performing solo.

4'33" was not a gesture for Cage but something he sincerely took to heart and one of the key moments within the development of his mature philosophy and practice. From this point on he would typically make comments such as, "If you want to know the truth of the matter, the music I prefer, even to my own or anybody else's, is what we are hearing if we are just quiet. And now we come back to my silent piece. I really prefer that to anything else, but I don't think of it as 'my piece.'"[12] What could have moved him to legitimize and compose (or vice versa) such a radical piece? Numerous reasons have been offered by Cage and others, which should come as no surprise considering how it provides a clean slate, silence, absence, a nothingness rife with potentiality, a blank screen on which so much about so little can be projected. The earliest precedent occurred, as Cage recollected (we shall propose an earlier, deeper constituent), in 1940 while Cage was living in San Francisco:

I had applied to be in the music section of the WPA, but they refused to admit me because they said that I was not a musician. I said, "Well, what am I? I work with sounds and percussion instruments and so forth." And they said, "You could be a recreation leader." So I was employed in the recreation department, and that may have been the birth of the silent piece, because my first assignment in the recreation department was to go to a hospital in San Francisco and entertain the children of the visitors. But I was not allowed to make any sound while I was doing it, for fear that it would disturb the patients. So I thought up games involving movement around the rooms and counting, etc., dealing with some kind of rhythm in space.[13]

With its rules regarding silence, the hospital resembles the setting for a music concert. Recreation introduces performance into this space because recreation, unlike a concert, turns everyone into performers. Thus, in keeping kids quiet Cage is keeping both the audience and performers quiet, ostensibly while a grander therapy ensues all around, and by doing so thus extends the hospital's requisite silence.

Cage's recollection, which came during a conversation with Peter Gena, is interesting because it was raised so rarely (perhaps once?) in reference to the genesis of *4' 33"*. Instead, for Cage the most obvious motivation for the piece arose from his interest in Eastern thought. When he first thought of the idea in 1948, he was "just then in the flush of my early contact with oriental philosophy. It was out of that that my interest in silence naturally developed: I mean it's almost transparent."[14] By *oriental* Cage mainly meant South Asian and East Asian, although early Christian mystical texts and practices were often included and inferred. By 1952 Cage was familiar with several individuals and many texts that could have served as sources bridging orientalism and silence. Since the number of possible sources increased in retrospect over the years as Cage commented on *4′ 33″*, commentators have had difficulty in convincingly pointing out what may have played a key role and how. Thus, more precise determinations of what Cage called *oriental philosophy* are hard to come by, and, as will be argued, the restriction to "oriental" itself is not very accurate. The more accurate term at the philosophical locus of his generation of silence would be, if anything, *perennial.*

Cage also said that *4′ 33″* was provoked by his encounter with the white paintings of Robert Rauschenberg. Cage had probably seen them in New York at the Betty Parsons Gallery. Irwin Kremen, to whom Cage dedicated a version of *4′ 33″*, remembers seeing the white and black paintings of Rauschenberg (December 1951) in Cage's New York apartment—in other words, prior to Cage's incorporating of the white paintings, along with Rauschenberg himself, into his 1952 Black Mountain event:[15] "Actually what pushed me into it was not guts but the example of Robert Rauschenberg. His white paintings. . . . When I saw those, I said, 'Oh yes, I must; otherwise I'm lagging, otherwise music is lagging.'[16] He noticed how, on a canvas of nearly nothing, notably absent of the expressive outpourings characteristic of the time, another plenitude replaced the effusiveness in the complex and changing play of light and shadow and the presence of dust. Correspondingly, environmental sounds rushed in to fill the absence of musical sound in *4′ 33″*. Rauschenberg's paintings may have provoked Cage's *silent piece* or given him the courage to go ahead with it, but in this case their influence cannot be confused with an earlier development of the piece, since Cage had already had the idea in mind since at least 1948.

If we look back to 1948, to the first glint of the whiteness of what was to become *4′ 33″*, we find a number of factors that, in their totality, require a general reappraisal of Cage. The key factor is a document entitled "A Composer's Confessions," the text of a lecture delivered at the National Inter-Collegiate Arts Conference held at Vassar College (28 February 1948). When asked in a 1982 interview about the type of silence involved in *4′ 33″*, Cage replied, "I'd thought of it already in 1948 and gave a lecture which is not published, and which won't be, called 'A Composer's Confessions.'"[17] The curious thing about this statement is not that he had already been thinking about doing a silent piece four years prior to the 1952 date of composition of *4′33″*, but why in 1982—nearly thirty-five years later in the context of a discussion about the thirty-year-old piece *4′33″*—would Cage assert that the lecture *won't be published*? This interjection may have been just an offhand comment underscored by largely inconsequential considerations about the administration of his writings. On the other hand, the text of the lecture is very long and informative and, in retrospect, indispensable for understanding Cage's career and the genesis of his notion of silence. In it he proposed a new composition called *Silent Prayer* that would consist of three to four and a half minutes of sustained silence (the maximum time being just three seconds short of *4′33″*) to be played over the Muzak network. Most texts from the period were published in *Silence and A Year from Monday*, several of them much less important and none that would duplicate the material covered in "A Composer's Confessions." Was this a departure from his usual openness? Was he concerned about this text being touched by the light of day? Why would Cage wait to have it published until around his eightieth birthday?[18] One could speculate that Cage chose not to publish the text because it would have unnecessarily complicated the specter of silence as it had developed over the course of the 1950s—that is, the folkloric Cage first presented in *Silence* (1961) would have run counter to the Cage involved in the silencings at the birth of silence.

What are these complications? To begin with, in the supposed *transparency* of Cage's oriental thought there are several relevant texts, individuals, and activities leading up to 1948, many of which will never be known.[19] David Patterson has summarized many of these and observed Cage's overall predilection for South Asian references, a shift to East Asian ones, with a "rhetorical lurch" occurring between "Forerunners of Modern Music" (1949) and "Lecture on Nothing" (1950).[20] In this respect, the South Asian sources would be of greatest relevance for Cage's Vassar lecture, and, thus, the original genesis of Cage's silence would be Indian and not related to East Asian, or more specifically Zen, sources as has often been noted in discussions about *4′33″*. Among the most notable South Asian sources were his friendship with Gita Sarabhai, who assisted Cage in learning about Indian music and aesthetics; Joseph Campbell; texts by Ananda K. Coomaraswamy, including *The Transformation of Nature in Art* (1934) and, to a lesser extent, *The Dance of Shiva* (1948); and *The Gospel of Sri Ramakrishna*.[21] Yet as we shall see, there are at least two more texts that play an important role within "A Composer's Confessions": Carl Jung's *The Integration of the Personality* (1940) and Aldous Huxley's *The Perennial Philosophy* (1946).[22]

What becomes apparent when these texts are examined is that all, with the exception of *The Gospel of Sri Ramakrishna*, are transparently concerned with cross-cultural perspectives.[23] Coomaraswamy and Huxley both subscribe to Leibniz's *philosophia perennis*, evidencing the same global reach as Jung's *collective unconscious*. Therefore, although Cage's texts through 1949 cite South Asian and Christian mystics, his operant sources were much broader.[24] For instance, Cage's motto—"Art is the imitation of Nature in her manner of operation"—was not from Coomaraswamy, as Cage repeatedly states, but from St. Thomas Aquinas, from whom Coomaraswamy had borrowed the idea: *Ars imitatur naturam in sua operatione*.[25] In all of these perennially philosophical sources—tranquillity, quiescence, austerity, blankness, nothingness, emptiness, and any number of other ideas related to silence, including silence itself—were quite common. Jung summed it up when he wrote, "We are always surprised by the fact that something comes out of what we call 'nothing.'"[26] It should come as no surprise, then, that there are so many nothings and that they should be, all of them, so fecund.

The reason for Cage's reading in spirituality has been attributed to changes in his personal life during the 1940s, yet it was also significant that he, as an American, was attracted to timeless, global ideas during and after the World War II.[27] The war and its aftermath presented the United States with a cultural problem: how to estrange the character of its enemies while securing sympathies from certain domestic populations? For instance, one of Cage's compositions, *A Book of Music* (1944), was used by the Office of War Information, renamed *Indonesian Supplement No. 1*, and broadcast to the South Pacific "with the hope of convincing the natives that America loves the Orient."[28] This schism became intensified immediately following the war, since the domestic American populace was required to reconcile the decimation of the civilian populations of Hiroshima and Nagasaki with appeals to global commonality. The universalism and world betterment fervor that swept the United States after the war—after the world had become its oyster, especially as it served as the ideological frontline in the cold war—provided the cultural environment for popular projects of self-improvement; that most were detached, touristic, imperialistic, and appropriative did not rule out the possibility for more plausible engagements with cultures outside the Eurocentric sphere.

In this respect, the war repeated a problem posed by Jung in *The Integration of the Personality*. The "white man," as the translation went, was unable to contemplate the metaphysical conundrums by Lao Tze in the *Tao Tê Ching*, let alone answer them, because "he is forced to reject [it] as if it were a foreign body, for his blood refuses to assimilate anything sprung from foreign soil."[29] There are indications that Cage read Jung's text closely, yet he chose to frame the sentiment through reference to Coomaraswamy, who "convinced me of our naiveté with regard to the Orient. At the time—it was at the end of the war, or just afterwards—people still said that the East and the West were absolutely foreign, separate entities. And that a Westerner did not have the right to profess an Eastern philosophy. It was thanks to Coomaraswamy that I began to suspect that this was not true, and that Eastern thought was no less admissible for a Western than is European thought."[30] Jung had suggested, in the tradition of perennial philosophy, that Westerners assume a disposition toward the wisdom of *the East* which, although they could not hope to repeat it, would at least lead them to traditions closer to home:

One must be able to *let things happen*. I have learned from the East what it means by the phrase "Wu wei": namely, not-doing, letting be, which is quite different from doing nothing. Some Occidentals, also, have known what this not-doing means; for instance, Meister Eckhart, who speaks of "sich lassen," to let oneself be.[31]

For Jung, the *way* of the Tao was to be developed in the West through the development of the personality, and the key to this development was the integration of the different parts of the psyche, primarily conscious mind ("the ego and the various mental contents") and the unconscious.[32] A non-integrated psyche was not merely an obstacle to spiritual development; it impacted on all psychological matters and a range of physiological conditions:

Medical psychology has been profoundly impressed with the number and importance of the unconscious processes that give rise to functional symptoms and even organic disturbances. These facts have undermined the view that the ego expresses the psychic totality. It has become obvious that the "whole" must include, besides consciousness, the field of unconscious events, and must constitute a sum total embracing both. The ego, once the monarch of this totality, is dethroned. It remains merely the center of consciousness.[33]

Many American artists during the 1940s, under the influence of Surrealism, Freud and Jung were interested in dethroning the monarchy of the ego to tap the unconscious. Such a mission provided ample opportunity for individuals to engage in self-expression while imagining an ineluctable communication at a level above or below society and culture (oneiric, instinctual, archetypal) and for a socialization of figures of the unconscious in ideas of a *primitivism* based in the body. Jung in *The Integration of the Personality* believed in a connection between the Eastern and Western psychic states that subtended the ego: "The psyche called the superior or the universal mind in Hindu philosophy corresponds to what the West calls the unconscious."[34] Yet he was unwilling to subscribe to the body disciplines by which adepts reach the state of contact with universal mind: "This is all very well, but scarcely to be recommended anywhere north of the Tropic of Cancer."[35] Cage was not interested in self-expression, whether it was in music or in painting; he was also becoming less sure about communication, and his appropriation of other cultures for musical purposes was centered more on the operations of the mind than the body. Like Jung, Cage was interested in choosing among the ideas of the adepts without taking up any body practices. Over the course of a thousand pages Sri Ramakrishna was forever slipping off into *samadhi*, but Cage's interest remained solely with his wisdom and not in the practices that lent to its development. Overall, Cage was less interested in getting the ego out of the way to enable the unconscious to come out into the world than in removing the ego so more of the world could get *in* unobstructed. He wanted to be open to "divine influences" but not to the extent of fusing them with a world within.

"A Composer's Confessions" consists primarily of a long autobiographical sketch, the bulk of which pertains to a time before his most recent activities. At the very moment in the text in which Cage moves into the present and recent past he invokes Sarabhai, Coomaraswamy, and Jung: "After eighteen months of studying oriental and medieval Christian philosophy and mysticism I began to read Jung on the integration of the personality."[36] He reiterates Jung's concerns regarding psychological and physiological health and applies them to the topic of people's occupations in contemporary society as a basis from which to focus on the vocation of composition.[37] Composers, like everyone else, are prone to neuroses; however, "If one makes music, as the Orient would say, *disinterestedly*, that is, without concern for money or fame but simply for the love of making it, it is an integrating activity and one will find moments in his life that are complete and fulfilled."[38]

The term *disinterestedness* thereby becomes a tangible link between Cage's orientalism and his initial formulation of silence. I have not been able to locate where Cage might have derived the specific word—although it has cropped up in several texts, it has not occurred with the emphasis that might explain adoption into his vernacular—but there is no shortage of sources when it comes to the concept. Sentiments similar to "letting things happen" and "not-being" can be found in Coomaraswamy's discussions of self-naughting, dementation, anonymity, and impersonality,[39] and more specifically, both Cage and Coomaraswamy mention a similar disposition as it pertains to musicians. Coomaraswamy quotes the great poet Rabindranath Tagore in describing Indian musicians: "Our master singers never take the least trouble to make their voice and manner attractive. . . . Those of the audience whose senses have to be satisfied as well are held to be beneath the notice of any self-respecting artist [while] those of the audience who are appreciative are content to perfect the song in their own mind by the force of their own feeling."[40] Cage emphasizes disinterestedness in performers and does so with a source from the Orient ("if one makes music, as the Orient would say, *disinterestedly*"). Within "A Composer's Confessions" Cage explained that he found a concert of music by Ives and Webern pleasurable because "when the music was composed the composers were at one with themselves. The performers became disinterested to the point that they became unself-conscious, and a few listeners in those brief moments of listening forgot themselves, enraptured, and so gained themselves."[41] Making and listening to music disinterestedly is the means to integrate the personality "and that is why we love the art."[42]

Disinterestedness is also associated with Aldous Huxley's explanation of self-mortification and nonattachment in *The Perennial Philosophy*, including his own observation that "spiritual authority can be exercised only by those who are perfectly disinterested and whose motives are therefore above suspicion."[43] He also cites St. François de Sales's "holy indifference" and Chuang Tzu's story of Confucius lending advice to a disciple regarding "the fasting of the heart," which links indifference with a model for Cagean listening: "Cultivate unity. . . . You do your hearing, not with your ears, but with your mind; not with your mind, but with your very soul. But let the hearing stop with the ears. Let the working of the mind stop with itself. Then the soul will be a negative existence, passively responsive to externals. . . . Living in a state of complete indifference—you will be near success."[44] Fortified through its opposition to self-expression, *disinterestedness* remained an operative term through "Lecture on Something" (1951–1952) and was abandoned only as chance and indeterminacy transformed it from an attitude and disposition into a reproducible and consistent technique.[45] Later, disinterestedness took the most familiar form of a supercession of taste, which itself superseded style and genre, extramusicality and silence. Recounting its roots, Cage said in a 1984 interview:

I wanted to be quiet in a nonquiet situation. So I discovered first through reading the gospel of Sri Ramakrishna, and through the study of the philosophy of Zen Buddhism—and also an important book for me was *The Perennial Philosophy* by Aldous Huxley, which is an anthology of remarks of people in different periods of history and from different cultures—that they are all saying the same thing, namely, a quiet mind is a mind that is free of its likes and dislikes. You can become narrow-minded, literally, by only liking certain things, and disliking others. But you can become open-minded, literally, by giving up your likes and dislikes and becoming interested in things.[46]

Canned Silence

Disinterestedness, despite signaling the presence of a cultural other, when used within the context of "A Composer's Confessions" becomes implicated within an array of not-so-foreign values. It also becomes a means to commend the music of certain composers and celebrate the love of art, against the Western art music repertoire with its inflated importance, its claims to genius, posterity and masterpieces. And it becomes a means to counter academization and commercialization of the arts, self-expression, and art appreciation. In short, *disinterestedness* is the best response to all matters animated by "sheer materialistic nonsense."[47] The first call for silence in Cage's lecture comes when his disinterestedness shifts from the sheer materialistic nonsense of Western art music and the arts in general to commercial music proper and the mass media in general. He invoked silencing through the power of someone who had already in effect silenced music, James Petrillo, president of the American Federation of Musicians (AFM): "Since Petrillo's recent ban on recordings took effect on the New Year, I allowed myself to indulge in the fantasy of how normalizing the effect might have been had he had the power, and exerted it, to ban not only recordings, but radio, television, the newspapers, and Hollywood."[48]

When the vitaphone, the system that synchronized the phonograph with cinema, was introduced by Warner Brothers Studios in the late 1920s, many musicians whose job it was to accompany the silent film were no longer necessary; sound film made them even less necessary. Since in the 1920s such musicians constituted 30 percent of the AFM membership, the union was from that point on acutely conscious of the effects of recording technologies and over the next two decades countered by demanding proper remuneration from those who profited handsomely from the disembodied repetition of their members' performances. Petrillo and the AFM responded in 1942 with a strike to enforce their decree that record companies pay royalties to their musicians on every pressing. The strike lasted for over two years during the middle of the war and cost AFM members millions of dollars in lost wages. Since Petrillo's base of operation was in Chicago, his presence must have been felt by Cage, who was living in Chicago in 1942 and working with professional musicians during the Columbia Workshop (CBS) radio production of *The City Wears a Slouch Hat*, his collaboration with Kenneth Patchen. Indeed, Petrillo's reputation would have been unavoidable, for he was notorious for aggressively pursuing grievance not only through legal union tactics but also through gangsterist means at home in Chicago. In this respect, was Cage being tongue in cheek when he pondered whether Petrillo "had the power, and exerted it?"

In his lecture (28 February 1948) Cage was referring to Petrillo's second assault on record company practices, when a decree was issued (midnight on 31 December 1947) that extended the labor action to dance halls and radio shows dependent on recorded music. In Cage's fantasy, he wanted to extend Petrillo's silencing further still, to all of radio and other forms of mass media, whether they were audible or not. However, with the experience of the first decree in mind, the record companies put contingency plans in place, and, consequently, only working musicians were silenced.[49] Cage did go on to state what he hoped for from his fantasy: "We might then realize that phonographs and radios are not musical instruments, that what the critics write is not a musical matter but rather a literary matter, that it makes little difference if one of us likes one piece and another; it is rather the age-old process of making and using music and our becoming more integrated as personalities through this making and using that is of real value."[50] Of course, for nearly a decade Cage had used phonographs and radios as musical instruments—phonograph records, turntables, a radio station in 1939 in *Imaginary Landscape No. 1,* and a radio again in 1942 in *Credo in Us*—and was liable to use absolutely anything to make music. He was, in this instance, speaking rhetorically from inside Western art music as a practitioner and purveyor of "live" goods and even more immediately as a listener. Seemingly, by arguing for *liveness,* Cage was siding with the AFM against the record companies, but by 1948 the issue was not between live and recorded; it was a labor issue that seemed to Cage to be a distraction from the real social project of music. Phonographs and radios, the targets of the AFM decrees, are not important. In the terms of the text itself he was still attending the performance of Ives and Webern as a listener, where disinterestedness in *making and using music* had already led to "and that is why we love the art," but then he directed his attention to the performances reproduced on phonographs and radios, which followed a very different program.[51] Instead of acknowledging the obvious differences between the two spheres of music or contemplating the political realities of working musicians outside Western art music who act in an *interested* manner regarding their occupations, he returns again to the question of the integration of the personality and attempts to socialize it by implicating all musical activity in self-improvement. From where he sat in the text listening to music, all of music became "music," and the politics of music dissipated among the dispositions of individual personalities.

There is certainly the possibility that Cage's fantasy may have been an offhanded remark, a quick way to snub commercialism in favor of the integrity of the individual. However, there is more than just the kernel of truth in this particular jest, since the fantasy of a grand silencing of society had long been within his personal repertoire:

One of the greatest blessings that the United States could receive in the near future would be to have her industries halted, her business discontinued, her people speechless, a great pause in her world of affairs created, and finally to have everything stopped that runs, until everyone should hear the last wheel go around and the last echo fade away. . . . then, in that moment of complete intermission, of undisturbed calm, would be the hour most conducive to the birth of a Pan-American Conscience. Then we should be capable of answering the question, "What ought we to do?" For we should be hushed and silent, and we should have the opportunity to learn that other people think.[52]

This was the text of Cage's speech "Other People Think" for the Southern California Oratorical Contest in 1927, where he represented Los Angeles High School and won first prize. The rhetorical device of imagining a large social silencing was placed in a context very similar to that in "A Composer's Confessions."

Both instances of silencing create conditions for asking questions, which in turn lead to large transformations in consciousness. The social silencing in "Other People Think" provides the opportunity to ask the question "what ought we to do?" and to learn *that*, not *what*, other people think ("It is the produce of the mind of man, and in that it is truly great"),[53] and this in turn promises a Pan-American Conscience. Within "A Composer's Confessions" a smaller quiet provokes the key question about making and using music with which the remaining text is concerned. Cage had moved into a "new apartment on the East River in Lower Manhattan which turns its back to the city and looks to the water and the sky. The quietness of this retreat brought me finally to face the question: to what end does one write music?"[54] And then this question soon leads to a larger social silencing if Petrillo "had the power, and exerted it, to ban not only recordings, but radio, television, the newspapers, and Hollywood,"[55] in recognition of the unimportance of reproduced commercial music, music critics, and musical tastes versus the real value of making and using music, integrating the personality, and cultivating disinterestedness and the wisdom of the Orient.

In "Other People Think" Cage implied only that the social transformation would come about through individual transformation of consciousness, whereas in "A Composer's Confessions" social transformation would come about only through personal acts by legions of solitary individuals: "That island that we have grown to think no longer exists to which we might have retreated to escape from the impact of the world, lies, as it ever did, within each one of our hearts."[56] Both instances share what Yvonne Rainer has called Cage's "goofy naiveté" when it comes to politics,[57] the earlier speech in thinking that United States imperialism within Latin America would be moved by conscience (an opinion that might be expected from a high school student) and the Vassar lecture in conflating an issue of the political economy of music with self-improvement.

The second call for silence in "A Composer's Confessions" narrowed down the scope of the fantasy from silencing all the mass media to silencing just one aspect: Muzak. He planned "to compose a piece of uninterrupted silence and sell it to Muzak Co. It will be 3 or 4–1/2 minutes long—those being the standard lengths of 'canned' music—and its title will be *Silent Prayer*. It will open with a single idea which I will attempt to make as seductive as the color and shape and fragrance of a flower. The ending will approach imperceptibility."[58] In the late 1940s Muzak was piped over telephone lines into restaurants, workplaces, and other institutions and was thus primarily a transmissional service like radio. The company was just beginning to make a transition to recorded systems situated in-house. Although it would be difficult to say whether the Muzak Co. would have been amenable to Cage's idea, failure to realize the project would not have been due to a lack of courage on Cage's part to approach the company. The unbridled confidence for which he was known had been boosted by the nationwide reception, in both senses of the word, of *The City Wears a Slouch Hat*, and his *Book of Music* was broadcast throughout the South Pacific on military radio. He had always been very enterprising, unafraid to approach anyone who might be able to advance his projects, including a number of companies when he sought support for his Center of Experimental Music. There should be no reason to believe that his proposal was a ruse.

There are several possible art connections. It is obvious that *4′33″* is just three seconds over the upper limit for canned music, and, although much happened in the four years between the two pieces, if it was indeed chance that finally arrived at this duration, then it was at least a moment of objective chance, unwittingly, in the Surrealist sense. The fact that it was *canned* recalls the *ready-mades* of Marcel Duchamp, with whose work Cage was quite familiar. Although Duchamp transposed a mass-produced object into an art venue whereas Cage wanted to place an art object of canned silence alongside the other cans on the narrow-casted Muzak shelf, *Silent Prayer* could be thought of as a musical version of *Air de Paris*, Duchamp's bottled air. Then there was Ferruccio Busoni's well-known *Sketch of a New Esthetic of Music* (available in English translation from around 1911), in which he stated that consummate players and improvisers "most nearly approach the essential nature of the art" during their employment of holds and rests. If properly isolated, the product of such playing could very well describe one of the bases for Cagean silence: "The tense silence between two movements—*in itself music*, in this environment—leaves wider scope for divination than the more determinate, but therefore less elastic, sound."[59] I am not saying that Cage was thinking of Duchamp or Busoni at the time, and he certainly was not aware of F. T. Marinetti's radio *sintesi* written in the early 1930s and entitled *I Silenzi Parlano fra di Loro* (Silences speak among themselves), the most notable precedent of an artwork in which silence took on its own presence.[60]

The most plausible connection with the past becomes apparent when we ask what could have attracted Cage to Muzak in particular, among all the other forms of mass media? What more so than Erik Satie's *furniture music?* Cage had a long-standing interest in Satie (he arranged the first movement of the *Socrate* for a Merce Cunningham dance, *Idyllic Song*, in 1945), and by the time of his Vassar lecture he was deeply engaged with Satie's work. He was no doubt preparing for the Satie Festival lectures and concerts to be held at Black Mountain College that summer. At Black Mountain, concerts took place in the dining hall, or pieces would be played by Cage on the piano in his cabin while people roamed about outside, the latter suggesting the ambiance of furniture music.[61] Anyone involved in even modest research would have known about the two primary biographical texts on Satie—if Rollo Myers's *Erik Satie* (1948) was too late, then Pierre-Daniel Templier's *Erik Satie* (1932) was not—as well as the prominence of the "Erik Satie and His *Musique d'Ameublement*" section in Constant Lambert's *Music Ho!* (1934).[62]

Although usually solely attributed to Satie, *musique d'ameublement* (furniture music or furnishing music) was a collaboration with Darius Milhaud. It first took place in 1920 at an art gallery to act as an interlude for a play by Max Jacob. The introduction, read by Pierre Bertin, was included in Myers's book: "We present for the first time, under the supervision of MM. Erik Satie and Darius Milhaud and directed by M. Delgrange, 'furnishing music' to be played during the entr'actes. We beg you to take no notice of it and to behave during the entr'actes as if the music did not exist.

This music . . . claims to make its contribution to life in the same way as a private conversation, a picture, or the chair on which you may or may not be seated."[63] To put music in the intermission required an unobtrusive music—otherwise it would be another performance and not an intermission at all—and this not-to-be-listened-to music evokes immediate comparison with Muzak. The association with Muzak would have been particularly noticeable in Templier's book where he cites a note from Satie assigning certain of his compositions their respective *musique d'ameublement* settings: "*The Banquet*—'Musique d'ameublement'—For an assembly-hall . . . *Phèdre*—'Musique d'ameublement'—For a lobby . . . *Phédon*—'Musique d'ameublement'—For a shop window."[64] This type of shift in settings from art to nonart and vice versa has been a regular feature of art through the twentieth century, having perhaps its most notable demonstration with the institutional tactics of Duchamp's ready-mades, while eliciting a certain circularity in the relationship of Cage's *Silent Prayer* and Satie's *musique d'ameublement*. Satie's performance was a displacement of one of his café haunts (people talking, ignoring the music) into an artistic space, whereas *Silent Prayer* returns to the cafés and other nonart settings to replace Muzak with silence—that is, an unobtrusive music with something even more unobtrusive. Cage was not, like the protagonist in Heinrich Böll's story "Murke's Collected Silences," inside the institution trying to patch together some reprieve but was instead trying to seek a bit of reprieve, an *entr'acte*, from a daily life where Muzak had become obtrusively and insultingly pervasive. And there may have been a special consideration for choosing to silence Muzak among other forms of auditive mass media: if one was to be involved in silencing, there was little danger of being accused of censorship, for in its unobtrusiveness Muzak had already assumed a certain self-censorship, and a hiatus of four and a half minutes would do nothing to disturb the pervasiveness. Silencing would only impose a brief intermission.

In his book Myers also discussed Satie's composition *Cinema* (1924) as another instance of *musique d'ameublement*. Indeed, it was likewise intended to take place within an intermission, yet this time it did not stand alone but accompanied René Clair's film *Entr'acte*, which was to function as the intermission to Francis Picabia's ballet *Relâche* (the name *Relâche*, posted when a performance is canceled, is itself suggestive of the revoked performances of *Silent Prayer* and *4'33"*). *Cinema* was comprised of segments of music, incidental both in itself and to the images in the film, cut in regularly measured lengths with no regard for conventional continuity (the simple structure is perhaps the clearest statement of Satie, the measurer of sounds). Cinema in general affords its own unobtrusiveness and silence with regard to sound in at least two ways. First of all, since film music must as a rule never overwhelm the images, action, or speech, it is relegated to a music heard but not to be listened to. Silence enters the picture with segments of *Hörspielstreifen*, the delicate atmosphere of recorded silence whose purpose is to imperceptibly confirm the presence of a reproduction under way and not frighten the audience into thinking there has been a technical malfunction (which would require a break in the silence of the audience itself). The silence of cinema audiences is—like that of concertgoers, people praying, and kids being entertained in hospitals—culturally specific, and a true silence, without the presence of the *Hörspielstreifen*, would have the same effect as *4′33″*.

Apart from *musique d'ameublement*, another influence on *Silent Prayer* could have been derived from Cage's understanding of how structure in Satie's music worked to equalize the status of silence with that of sound. In his lecture "Defense of Satie" at Black Mountain College, Cage gave a great deal of importance to structure, specifically as practiced by Satie and Webern and heralded by music from, following his *perennial* motif, Asia and the middle ages.[65] Both Satie and Webern worked in a *short form* conducive to canned music, but Cage had more fundamental concerns. He figured that structure was determined by duration, which sound and silence shared, and in turn determined being from nonbeing: "Music is a continuity of sound. In order that it may be distinguishable from nonbeing, it must have structure."[66] Pitch, loudness, and timbre, although they could be heard in musical sound, were not intrinsic to the being or nonbeing of music because they did not require duration, whereas "silence cannot be heard in terms of pitch or harmony: it is heard in terms of time length.[67] This line of reasoning was one of Cage's platforms against harmony (thus Beethoven) and could be found in his earlier arguments for percussion and noise. Indeed, Satie's structure was "extramusical in its implications . . . into Satie's continuity come folk tunes, musical clichés, and absurdities of all kinds."[68] Cage now called Satie's structure into service to privilege yet another element historically downplayed within Western art music: silence. Music was composed most fundamentally of sound and silence, and silence became a way of hearing time within the *being* of musical structure. Nevertheless, he was still thinking of sound and silence as being conventionally distinct from one another, a presence and an absence of sound. By the time of *4' 33"*, silence became only the absence of an intentional sound, whereas musical sound had become ever-present and omnipresent, filled with intentional or unintentional sound. Thus, *Silent Prayer* was not underscored by the same sense of silence as *4' 33"*; it was not a way to begin hearing and musicalizing the surrounding sound. If anything was meant to be heard, it was conventional silence—in this case, the absence of the sound of Muzak, along the measured lengths of canned music.

But why the *prayer* in *Silent Prayer?* I believe the reason can be found in Aldous Huxley's *The Perennial Philosophy*—specifically, at the juncture of chapters 15 and 16, entitled "Silence" and "Prayer," respectively. Huxley's book consists of his commentary on perennial philosophy, with substantial quotes from mystics, saints, monks, philosophers, and psychologists. Among the people quoted—many passages are nothing but a sequence of quotes—one can find all the individuals and approaches favored by Cage; moreover, one could find them within a relatively secular context. The problem with Coomaraswamy, Eckhart, and others, after all, was the difficulty of appropriating spiritual ideas without committing oneself overtly to deism. Huxley's chapter on silence is one of the shortest in the book, perhaps because three-quarters of the chapter is devoted to appeals to stop talking. The remaining section consists of one paragraph consisting of Huxley's own appeal for silence over the mass media. It is only one paragraph, but it cannot be taken lightly. Throughout the book Huxley maintains an evenhandedness about timeless, global matters. Here he steps out of character and forthrightly condemns the present-day media:

The twentieth century is, among other things, the Age of Noise. Physical noise, mental noise and noise of desire—we hold history's record for all of them. And no wonder; for all the resources of our almost miraculous technology have been thrown into the current assault against silence. That most popular and influential of all recent inventions, the radio, is nothing but a conduit through which prefabricated din can flow into our homes. And this din goes far deeper, of course, than the ear-drums. It penetrates the mind, filling it with a babel of distractions—news items, mutually irrelevant bits of information, blasts of corybantic or sentimental music, continually repeated doses of drama that bring no catharsis, but merely create a craving for daily or even hourly emotional enemas. And where, as in most countries, the broadcasting stations support themselves by selling time to advertisers, the noise is carried from the ears, through the realms of phantasy, knowledge and feeling to the ego's central core of wish and desire. Spoken or printed, broadcast over the ether or on wood-pulp, all advertising copy has but one purpose—to prevent the will from achieving silence. Desirelessness is the condition of deliverance and illumination. The condition of an expanding and technologically progressive system of mass production is universal craving. Advertising is the organized effort to extend and intensify craving—to extend and intensify, that is to say, the workings of that force, which (as all the saints and teachers of all the higher religions have always taught) is the principal cause of suffering and wrong-doing and the greatest obstacle between the human soul and its divine Ground.[69]

If one needed spiritual impetus or moral justification to silence any aspect of the mass media—to remove the obstacles that would *prevent the will from achieving silence*, no less—here it was in an emphatic end to a chapter entitled Silence. On the facing page began the chapter called Prayer.

Silencing Techniques

4′33″ silenced music to hear the unintended, surrounding sounds, the noises, and ultimately the total environment. *Silent Prayer* silenced the sound of a music intended as environmental; Muzak was the surrounding sound meant to be as unobtrusive to the task at hand as audience sounds at a concert. Thus, during the twentieth-century Age of Noise, the most noted promulgator of musical noise was involved in the business of noise abatement. *Silent Prayer* was not alone in this respect because Cage, an inventor of techniques from an early age,[70] developed several other techniques for eliminating, diminishing, or displacing the source of the noise, transforming the noise into something else, or canceling the noise by playing back its image, so to speak, in the negative. He did not translate these techniques into technological devices of active noise control or act politically through popular protest and city ordinances to curb urban noises, but instead elaborated them through compositional, auditive, and physical means associated with music (the exception being his echoing of an anechoic chamber experience). Just as he incorporated noise as extramusical sound into music, so too did he accommodate urban noise through acts of composition and musical listening. Although he had railed against musical tastes, he also attempted through these techniques to transform what he personally found distasteful. These techniques have direct bearing on how *Silent Prayer* is understood, yet this composition cannot be understood without another composition proposed in "A Composer's Confessions" at the very same time, *Imaginary Landscape No. 4*, "a composition using as instruments nothing but twelve radios."[71] They need to be taken together, not only because he stated that the "two may seem absurd but I am serious about them"[72] but because they describe a paradigmatic range of noise-abatement techniques as applied to commercial music.[73]

An early mention of such techniques occurred during 1943 and arose within the context of personal betterment (as it would five years later in "A Composer's Confessions"), or perhaps personal adaptation, when he was quoted as saying, "People may leave my concerts thinking they have heard 'noise,' but will then hear unsuspected beauty in their everyday life. This music has a therapeutic value for city dwellers."[74] The noise in the city would not be physically diminished, but the city-dwelling concertgoers would accommodate themselves to it by appreciating it differently, removing the aggravation if not the noise, while both noise and aggravation would continue to exist for non-concert-going city dwellers. In further statements, such facility pertained to self-betterment—becoming more open to the world, trying to coexist peacefully with it—and to the negotiation of his own tastes. He was not averse to silencing things or at least to contemplate doing so. Two years after proposing to silence commercial music using *Silent Prayer*, and in the longer shadow of "Other People Think," he finished his "Lecture on Nothing" (1950) with a droll frenzy of destruction and silencing:

Would you like to join a society called Capitalists Inc. (Just so no one would think we were Communists.)? Anyone joining automatically becomes president. To join you must show you've destroyed at least one hundred records or, in the case of tape, one sound mirror [tape recorder]. To imagine you own any piece of music is to miss the whole point. This is no point or the point is nothing; and even a long-playing record is a thing. A lady from Texas said: I live in Texas. We have no music in Texas. The reason they've no music in Texas is because they have recordings. Remove the records from Texas and someone will learn to sing.[75]

Whereas *Silent Prayer* was a silencing of unobtrusive music such that true unobtrusiveness could exist and its time could be heard, removing recordings in Texas meant silencing the music that silences "live" music, silencing silence for music to be heard. Here again we have Cage the practitioner and purveyor of "live" goods, but instead of calling for Petrillo to extend his silencing beyond the AFM musicians, he fantasizes about destroying the recordings and the means for playback.

Just as silence against silence could produce music, noise against noise could produce silence. Cage was involved in noise abatement at a particular time within which the Age of Noise had reached crescendo proportions, as the noise of wartime shifted over to the immediate postwar period, which consisted of the combined noises of militarism and commercialism. In "Lecture on Nothing," Cage mentioned how the sheer magnitude of the war and of postwar American artifice, as it presumptuously equated itself with *life* and *time* (the magazines), had weighted him down and compelled him to offer something quieter: "Half-intellectually and half sentimentally, when the war came along, I decided to use only quiet sounds. There seemed to be no truth, no good, in anything big in society. But quiet sounds were like loneliness, or love or friendship. Permanent, I thought, values, independent at least from Life, Time and Coca-Cola."[76]

Two years closer to the war, in "A Composer's Confessions," he responded more directly with a two-pronged approach for noise abatement: becoming quiet and marshaling loudness against loudness:

Being involved in the complexities of a nation at war and a city in business-as-usual led me to know that there is a difference between large things and small things, between big organizations and two people alone in a room together. Two of my compositions presented at the Museum [of Modern Art, 7 February 1943] concert suggest this difference. One of them, the *Third Imaginary Landscape*, used complex rhythmic oppositions played on harsh sounding instruments combined with recordings of generator noises, sliding electrical sounds, insistent buzzers, thunderous crashes and roars, and a rhythmic structure whose numerical relationships suggested disintegration. The other, four pieces, called *Amores*, was very quiet, and, my friends thought, pleasing to listen to.[77]

Throughout the Vassar lecture Cage pitted personal integration against the forces of social disintegration. Big business, loud war, big orchestras, harmony ("a device to make music impressive, loud and big, in order to enlarge audiences and increase box-office returns")[78] and through music back again to *contemporary* Christian society, Western culture, acquisition of money and fame, and so on. He favored small and quiet things related to personal relationships in intimate situations, Asian thought, earlier Christian teachings, pleasure and religion, the island of the heart: "My feeling was that beauty yet remains in intimate situations; that it is quite hopeless to think and act impressively in public terms. This attitude is escapist, but I believe that it is wise rather than foolish to escape from a bad situation."[79] Just as he had sought to escape the Age of Noise during the war with the quietness of *Amores* and the raucousness of *Imaginary Landscape No. 3*, so too did he apply the two-pronged approach of noise abatement to commercial music and radio (early Muzak was transmissional) with *Silent Prayer* and *Imaginary Landscape No. 4*, silencing Muzak to side with the quiet and the integrated, and writing radio music to pit disintegration against disintegration, noise against noise.

Cage continued to employ such techniques throughout his life against the music that disgusted him, the music he otherwise no longer wished to hear, and the sounds of urban and domestic life. In "Composition as Process" (1958) he explained how *Imaginary Landscape No. 4* had enabled him to override his personal taste about the *sound* of radios, as had *Williams Mix* for Beethoven, *Imaginary Landscape 5* for jazz, and *Concert for Piano and Orchestra* for *bel canto*: "It remains for me to come to terms with the vibraphone."[80] Whatever bothered him about the vibraphone kept on bothering him until at least the late 1970s.[81] In a 1961 interview with Roger Reynolds, Cage still had not come to terms with Muzak: "If I liked Muzak, which I also don't like, the world would be more open to me. I intend to work on it. The simplest thing for me to do in order to come to terms with both those things would be to use them in my work, and this was, I believe, how so-called primitive people dealt with animals which frightened them."[82]

Reynolds revisited the question of persistent dislikes in an interview in 1977, but Cage did not single out Muzak.[83] This turn around might be explained by a plan Cage had to use Muzak in a composition. In 1962 his friend the sculptor Richard Lippold was commissioned to make a piece for the Pan Am building; however, he objected to his work sharing the same space with Muzak piped in by the building's proprietors. He asked Cage to provide the sound instead, so Cage proposed a sound work that used Muzak as source material to be manipulated. Perhaps because Cage's part of the Lippold commission was never realized, he became only partially accustomed to it, and by 1973 he had not completely come to terms with it. The Muzak company, he suggested in an interview, should consider including some of Satie's *musique d'ameublement* compositions because Muzak, "in a very weak way, attempts to distract us from what we are doing. . . . Whereas I think Satie's furniture music would like us to pay attention to whatever else it was that we were doing."[84] In essence, therefore, he was proposing another version of *Silent Prayer*, this time supplanting Muzak with *musique d'ameublement* instead of silence. However, this does not result in an easy equation of silence and *musique d'ameublement*, since after *4'33"* silence was nonintentional sound to-be-listened-to whereas *musique d'ameublement* was intentional and not-to-be-listened-to. By replacing Muzak with *musique d'ameublement* because it would better serve the ostensible function of Muzak, Cage was calling for a Muzak not-to-be-listened-to, he was attempting to *make Muzak more Muzakal*.

It may have been his way of dealing with a frightening animal, but the animal still had a bad temperament. All those cultural cues and tuneful hooks, no matter how mollified and defanged, still provided a *very weak distraction* whereas *musique d'ameublement* provided no *distraction*. A chapter in Huxley's *The Perennial Philosophy* concentrates on how to deal with distractions through "spiritual exercises": "Some of the most profitable spiritual exercises actually make use of distractions, in such a way that these impediments to self-abandonment, mental silence and passivity in relation to God are transformed into means of progress."[85] Such exercises were increasingly necessary because the Age of Noise was suffused with "a babel of distractions."[86] However, if Cage had helped Muzak realize itself through use of *musique d'ameublement*, then there would be no distraction. Thus, a *very weak distraction* remained, at least to 1984 during yet another interview.[87]

When it came to urban noise, at the time of "A Composer's Confessions" he could still write about how his quiet apartment on the East River moved him to ask about the reasons for writing music, but by the 1980s he faced the question of intrusive street noise: "I wouldn't dream of getting double glass because I love all the sounds. The traffic never stops, night and day. Every now and then a horn, siren, screeching brakes, extremely interesting and always unpredictable. At first I thought I couldn't sleep through it. Then I found a way of transposing the sounds into images so that they entered into my dreams without waking me up. A burglar alarm lasting several hours resembled a Brancusi."[88]

Musical noise no longer provided sufficient therapeutic value for city living; it became necessary to adapt to the new environment by combining the processes of musicalizing noise through listening and hypnagogic dreaming. What started out in the social realm of composition (city dwellers leaving a noise music concert to return more appreciatively to urban noise) retreated into techniques practiced by the individual alone. In addition to the inventiveness of this technique, he was still (in 1977) willing to engage in the old-fashioned technique of turning something off: "I think if I listened to [Conlon] Nancarrow for long, that I would have to finally say, please turn it off. The music that I don't have to turn off is precisely the music with us when we don't have any music . . . and that is the 'Mind' with the capital 'm.' That is what I meant by my silent piece in 1952, and it is *still* that piece which is my favorite music. That's why I have—if I do have—any difficulty with any other music (even if it's my own). It's because of that love that I have that difficulty."[89]

One of the central effects of Cage's battery of silencing techniques was a silencing of the social, a feature that was evident throughout but that was articulated in different ways and different degrees. There was a retreat from the social in the time between *Silent Prayer* and *4' 33"*, consisting of removing the silence from the public airwaves and placing it in the concert hall, silencing a piano instead of mass culture, arriving at four and a half minutes through organizational methods instead of industry standards, prying three movements into the time slot of canned music, acting directly against the Age of Noise, and developing an amenable position within it. In other words, *Silent Prayer* was immersed in the patently social, whether that was the labor activity of the AFM or the business of mollified music, whereas *4' 33"* was removed to the special space of Western art music where associations with the social are more oblique. Cage practiced social silencing rhetorically in "Other People Think" and "A Composer's Confessions," whereas he took explicit action through musical means, including musical listening, where a person's social situation became one of *being within music.* Cagean chance and indeterminacy, developed during this same period, were techniques not only to eliminate himself from his music[90] but to eliminate the social situations in which he found himself, particularly the one in which *Silent Prayer* and *Imaginary Landscape No. 4* were generated.

It should be stressed, however, that Cage's tack within the framework of *perennial philosophy* was not the only possible one, that spiritual techniques for dealing with the distraction of the social need not take recourse to *immediate* silencing of the social. If we go again to Huxley's *The Perennial Philosophy*, then we can imagine how a technique of listening could have been developed outside the socially deracinating influence of Western art music, one that could have led to silence without silencing. Among the spiritual exercises Huxley mentions that deal with distractions is one "much employed in India": "[It] consists in dispassionately examining the distractions as they arise and in tracing them back, through the memory of particular thoughts, feelings and actions, to their origins in temperament and character, constitution and acquired habit. This procedure reveals to the soul the true reasons for its separation from the divine Ground of its being."[91]

Applying this technique to aurality, if one begins with a notion that when humans hear and make sense of sound it is necessarily social, then, from the perspective of the individual, one's memory, thoughts, feelings, sensations, experiences, and actions will engender a knowledge of other things besides *the self* or a *sound in itself* and transform any understanding of being and acting within the world. Only then, as Huxley writes, "having made the resolution to do what it can, in the course of daily living, to rid itself of these impediments to Light, it quietly puts aside the thought of them and, empty, purged and silent, passively exposes itself to whatever it may be that lies beyond and within."[92] Cage merely skipped the first half of the exercise and went immediately to putting aside the thought of them.

Cage and the Impossible Inaudible

Cagean lore admits another key moment of silencing, his visit to an anechoic chamber, chronologically wedged between *Silent Prayer* and *4' 33":*

It was after I got to Boston that I went into the anechoic chamber at Harvard University. Anybody who knows me knows this story. I am constantly telling it. Anyway, in that silent room, I heard two sounds, one high and one low. Afterward I asked the engineer in charge why, if the room was so silent, I had heard two sounds. He said, "Describe them." I did. He said, "The high one was your nervous system in operation. The low one was your blood in circulation."[93]

The anechoic chamber was the technological emblem for Cage's class of silencing techniques. It was clinical and discursive, exhibiting attributes of both a *bona fide* anechoic chamber used in acoustical research and the anecdotal chamber diffused through Cagean lore. It absorbed sounds and isolated two of Cage's usually inaudible internal bodily sounds, but in the process there was a third internal sound isolated, the one saying, "Hmmm, wonder what the low-pitched sound is? What's that high-pitched sound?" Such quasi-sounds were, of course, antithetical to Cagean listening by being in competition with *sounds in themselves*, yet here he was able to listen and at the same time allow discursiveness to intrude in the experience because such sounds would be absorbed by clinical and scientific discourse, if not by the materials of the chamber itself, which historically had been allowed to intrude on musical listening. Cage once may have appropriated Dayton Clarence Miller's *The Science of Musical Sound*, but here he went to the site where acoustic texts themselves are produced to secure an experiential and scientific legitimization for his musical thought and to create his own anecdotal text, for the simple reason that he was in the process of extending music far past the assumptions exercised in any of the innumerable texts dealing with the acoustics of music. At the same time, acoustics was the music for the rest of the world. No longer constrained by musical parameters of sound production, Cage could still isolate an ostensibly asocial body through a clinical hearing cordoned off from worldly influences as a case in point for listening to the whole world musically.

As generator of a new silence, the anechoic chamber visit was a variant of *4′33″*, and while both took place in isolated spaces built for specialized audition, they muted different sounds and shifted attention in different directions—one to surrounding sounds, one to subtending sounds. *4′33″* muted the performer to shift attention to the sounds in the surrounding space and by implication to environmental sounds in general, while the anechoic chamber muted the sounds of the surrounding space, cordoning off all environmental sounds and dampening sounds inside its waffled walls to shift attention to Cage's internal bodily sounds and by implication to the impossibility of silence and the pervasiveness of music. The anechoic chamber certified for Cage the impossibility of silence by becoming a padded cell for the refractory sound of his own irrepressible vital signs; however, he resisted transposing the conventional figure of silence split between presence and absence of sound, which he was in the process of abandoning forever, into a presence and absence of life and death. The chamber itself was already as dead as possible to detect the most minute presence of sound. Sounds are absorbed by the wall design and materials (composed of sizes smaller than wave forms, their job is to fracture) and picked up by microphones and other sensing devices that are monitored by researchers who have abandoned the space. The anechoic chamber was a *dead* acoustic and depopulated space in which performativity shifted to the hitherto inaudible internal sounds of Cage, the living, fleshy inter-loper, as if his own body was constituted of material that also had absorbed sounds. Of course, his death would bring these vital signs to an end, along with the consciousness required to acknowledge them, but it would not bring silence. Obviously, sounds would still exist in the day-to-day world without him, people would exist who could hear them, but what he had discovered was that there would also be an entire region of sounds that people could not hear, and it was this revelation of a combined impossibil-ity of inaudibility and pervasive musicality that comforted him: "Until I die there will be sounds. And they will continue following my death. One need not fear about the future of music."[94] It is here that Cagean *all sound* melded forever into *always sound*.

The impossibility of silence and the pervasiveness of music were closely related to the development of indeterminacy, which also occurred in the time between *Silent Prayer* and *4'33"*. When a piece of music is pur-posefully purposelessly made, Cage asks, "What happens, for instance, to silence? That is, how does the mind's perception of it change?"[95] It no longer serves as a means of emphasis for taste or expressivity or as an ele-ment marking a predetermined or developing structure. When there are no goals, means become meaningless because nothing is meant to be hap-pening: whatever happens, happens. If there is no determination that the absence of musical sounds (silence, in the conventional sense) means the abeyance of a musical listening to any sounds, then what can be heard in the *silence*, as hitherto perceived, are the surrounding sounds: "Where none of these or other goals is present, silence becomes something else—not silence at all, but sounds, the ambient sounds. The nature of these is unpredictable and changing. These sounds (which are called silence only because they do not form part of a musical intention) may be depended on to exist. The world teems with them, and is, in fact, at no point free of them."[96] Consequently, silence itself disappears and transforms into its traditional opposite—sounds—and for Cage where there are sounds, especially a *world teeming in sounds*, there will be music. It should be made clear, in this respect, that the freeing of musical intention in Cage is specifically geared to the intention to make music. The idea that intention, let alone a formidable culturally laden discursive framework, is present within the act of hearing sounds as music does not receive equal attention.

Significantly, after the anechoic chamber experience, Cage would increasingly employ technology as a discursive means for musical listening and not just for practical musical production. Technology would enable the extension from the *always sound* of Cage's own vital signs to the (musical) vibrational resonances of all matter and to the conflation of a global atmosphere of transmitted signals with vibrational resonances and musics otherwise awaiting their reception. Through technology Cage could thus take the totalizing impetus of *all sound* to its logical conclusion. The anechoic chamber was joined in this project by another piece of tangible and fictive technology, the microphone, and both pieces of technology had the job of amplifying *small sounds:* one did it through subtraction, the other through addition. To *hear sounds in themselves* one must first hear them. Small sounds and amplification went hand in hand, although their overall role changed over time. Earlier in his career, the amplification of small sounds served the cause of noise as a practical means to increase the number of "more new sounds" in the constitution of a modernist material fount or to *free* them in Cage's rhetoric of sonic emancipation. With his commitment to the impossibility of silence the world was suddenly overrun with small sounds, and although it would seem there would have been less immediate need for amplification because a plenitude of sounds was ensured, amplification was still called on to perform rhetorically, far beyond its actual technological capabilities, to increase the number of possible sounds and to deny inaudibility. Small sounds also moved to inhabit the vicinity hitherto occupied by conventional silence. When silence became a type of sound, actual silence was merely a state of inaudibility, and everything known before as silence became nothing but small sounds contingent on amplification. Thus, the idea of small sounds became for Cage not only a negotiation between old and new silences but eventually a reason for his development of implausible and impossible amplification technologies, which, like other major developments in communications technology, presumed and produced different, perhaps only a revamped, world outlook.

Before considering Cage's amplified small sounds further, we need to ask about the practice of considering sounds according to *size*. In the realm of music, ideas about the sizes of sounds appeared at the turn of the century, when it became apparent that existing means of musical notation were inadequate to the tasks of denoting smaller and smaller intervals and of representing many of the salient characteristics of sounds in general. These ideas were accompanied by appeals to the vernacular experience of hearing and to acoustics, and their commonality occurring as acoustics continued, as it had since antiquity, to seek observational means for understanding sonic phenomena. While an individual might speak about the size of a sound, throughout the nineteenth century acoustics had busied itself with measuring and producing sounds through the development of visible sound (while at the same time mathematical modeling took acoustics further away from prosaic experiences of observation). Moreover, visualization meant that smaller and smaller increments and attributes of a sound became evident and, in turn, became the pride of acousticians who could publicly display them outside the laboratory. The avant-garde got quite a bit of mileage from affectionate parodies of the culture of science and technology, and no one got more than the French (Jarry, Roussel, Apollinaire, Duchamp). As we have seen, Jarry satirized the inscriptive impulse within ideas of visual sound; it was left to Erik Satie to take on the ideas of size implicit in acoustical measurement by claiming that he was in fact a phonometrographer, a measurer of sound, not a musician:

The first time I used a phonoscope, I examined a B flat of medium size. I can assure you that I have never seen anything so revolting. I called in my man to show it to him.

On my phono-scales a common or garden F sharp registered 93 kilos. It came out of a fat tenor whom I also weighed.[97]

Meanwhile, developments of microphony and amplification in telephony, phonography, and radiophony concentrated on lowering the threshold to the transmission of smaller sounds. Western art music met these developments head on during the late 1920s in the technologically saturated space of the radio studio. Once the orchestra was transformed into a *radio orchestra*, the old amplitude hierarchies were warped, and small sounds could have their day: "a harp, for example, even when played pianissimo, [could] be audible through no matter what orchestration."[98] By the 1950s, the combined approaches to the sizes of musical sound had become so well established that an advertisement in the *Village Voice* for the 1958 New York premiere of Varèse's *Poème électronique* promised "big sounds, not fat sounds."[99]

Cage demonstrated an interest in small sounds and amplification early in his career. In "The Future of Music" (1937) he called for centers for experimental music equipped with "means for amplifying small sounds."[100] The magnetic audiotape piece *Williams Mix* (1952) was listed as one of the six categories of sonic raw material "small sounds requiring amplification to be heard with the others" (as was the task with radio orchestra amplification). The instruction appears to have worked, if we believe the report from Robert Dumm of *Newsweek*, who wrote in 1954 that he heard in *Williams Mix* a little sound "like a fly walking on paper, magnified."[101] *Cartridge Music* (1960) also used "microphones and cartridges . . . connected to amplifiers that go to loudspeakers, the majority of the sounds produced being small and requiring amplification in order to be heard."[102] Then, starting in 1962 with *0' 00"* Cage began using amplification to render audible a range of small and inaudible sounds belonging to states and actions of the body, to other types of action, and to the signals of transmissions and radiation. Most important, he amplified amplification, extending audibility (thus musicality) to increasingly smaller sounds and to all sounds all the time. *0' 00"* itself was an electronic extension of music into everyday life and all fields of action. As Cage wrote, *0' 00"* is "nothing but the continuation of one's daily work, whatever it is, providing it's not selfish, but is the fulfillment of an obligation to other people, done with contact microphones, without any notion of concert or theater or the public, but simply continuing one's daily work, now coming out through loudspeakers."[103] Cage claimed that "the piece tries to say . . . that everything we do is music, or can become music through the use of microphones. . . . By means of electronics, it has been made apparent that everything is musical."[104]

From this point on Cage was thorough in how he introduced technology, audition, and music absolutely everywhere. The air was saturated with activity and could give up its sounds when signals were thought to be sounds and radios and other receivers were thought to be amplifiers:

The air, you see, is filled with sounds that are inaudible, but that become audible if we have receiving sets. . . .

There were [in *Variations VII* (1966)] ordinary radios, there were Geiger counters to collect cosmic things, there were radios to pick up what the police were saying, there were telephone lines open to different parts of the city. There were as many different ways of receiving vibrations and making them audible as we could grasp with the techniques at hand.[105]

The received all sound here was carried globally on the wave of a McLuhanesque prosthetic nervous system, even though Cage denied the synaptical signals of his own thought, let alone the political, military, and industrial barrage of what imperially and empirically pervades Lee de Forest's "Empires of the Air."[106] And according to Cage, the activities of the plant and insect worlds too awaited amplification:

That we have no ears to hear the music the spores shot off from basidia make obliges us to busy ourselves microphonically.[107]

I thought of sounds we cannot hear because they're too small, but through new techniques we can enlarge them, sounds like ants walking in the grass.[108]

The "music of the spores" imagines sounds having nothing to do with humans as music and puts Cage in a contradictory position with respect to his professed antianthropomorphism. At the minimum, it belongs to a nagging categorical imperialism in Cage's thought that should be taken into consideration in representations of his anarchism or ecology. Indeed, should there be some question about the nature of the influence of this aspect of Cage's thought on others, then it is helpful to refer to R. Murray Schafer's statement in his book *The Tuning of the World*. In this book, which has shaped *acoustic ecology* and underpinned much electroacoustic music, Schafer explicitly states his indebtedness to Cage and consequently goes on to say that "today all sounds belong to a continuous field of possibilities lying *within the comprehensive dominion of music.*"[109]

Cage completed the ubiquitous figure of musical sound when he extended amplification to the silence of objects and matter, which he would do wherever he happened to be at the time: "this table, for instance, around which we're sitting, is made experiential as sound, without striking it. It is, we know, in a state of vibration. It is therefore making a sound, but we don't yet know what that sound is."[110] Technology would not only let us know what the sound is but also render music "a revelation of sound even where we don't expect that it exists."[111] Thus, while he did not want to make his music into an object—this was his argument after a certain point against recording—he did want to make objects into music. In another circumstance, "If here, for musical pleasure, I could make audible to you what this book sounds like, and then what the table sounds like, and then what that wall sounds like, I think we would all be quite delighted."[112] Or again, returning full circle to the anechoic chamber, he says, "Look at this ashtray":

It's in a state of vibration. We're sure of that, and the physicist can prove it to us. But we can't hear those vibrations. When I went into the anechoic chamber, I could hear myself. Well, now, instead of listening to myself, I want to listen to this ashtray. But I won't strike it as I would a percussion instrument. I'm going to listen to its inner life thanks to a suitable technology. . . .

While in the case of the ashtray, we are dealing with an object. It would be extremely interesting to place it in a little anechoic chamber and listen to it through a suitable sound system. Object would become process; we would discover, thanks to a procedure borrowed from science, the meaning of nature through the music of objects.[113]

Cage's passion for striking tables and ashtrays (marking the philosophical status of the reality of this chair, that table) goes back to his meeting with the filmmaker Oskar Fischinger. In 1932 Fischinger began investigating the graphic synthesis of specific sounds on film. By the time he met Cage in around 1936, the correspondences between sign and sound had been enveloped by spiritism, and when he heard a sound, it was the *inner life* of an object speaking: "When I was introduced to him, he began to talk with me about the spirit which is inside each of the objects of this world. So, he told me, all we need to do to liberate that spirit is to brush past the object, and to draw forth its sound. That's the idea which lead me to percussion.

In all the many years which followed up to the war, I never stopped touching things, making them sound and resound, to discover what sounds they could produce. Wherever I went, I always listened to objects."[114]

Percussion was replaced by amplification as the means to listen to objects. Whereas percussion required striking objects or otherwise involving them in an action to hear their sound,[115] amplification (and the muting of the anechoic chamber) required no such action on the part of objects because the sound-producing action took place continuously at the atomic level. Therefore, all matter sounded all the time, and only the lack of proper technology prevented it from being music. Cage was not alone within modernist ranks, in which there was a long-standing notion that the soul, spirit, or essence of objects and matter was to be found within and communicated through vibrations. It is most familiar in terms of Kandinsky's *inner sound* but took on a more scientific cast when Richard Huelsenbeck said in passing, "Bruitism is a kind of return to nature. It is the music produced by circuits of atoms,"[116] or when the Italian futurists F. T. Marinetti and Pino Masnata wrote in their manifesto "La Radia" (1933): "The reception amplification and transfiguration of vibrations emitted by matter. Just as today we listen to the song of the forest and the sea so tomorrow shall we be seduced by the vibrations of a diamond or a flower."[117] Musically, it had been suggested by Varèse's *Ionization* and later in the work of Iannis Xenakis,[118] but it was Cage who situated it technically in a coherent theory of music.

Cage's dominion of *all sound* and *always sound* and of the corresponding capacity for *panaurality* is reminiscent of the totalizing reach of the Romantic utterance, resonating in voice or music throughout eternity and entirety, or of the nineteenth-century synesthetes who also used their utterances to insinuate themselves throughout the cosmos. It is true that Cage explicitly sought to subvert tactics based in human centeredness, yet all he did was shift the center from one of utterance to one of audition. He simply became quiet in order to attract everything toward a pair of musical ears. He achieved through centripetal means the same centrality of utterance achieved through centrifugal means. Indeed, Cage's musical renovation was built on a larger cultural association in which listening was thought to be intrinsically more passive, peaceful, respectful, democratic, and spiritual than speaking, as it intersected with Western art music, which, on the one hand, had produced itself through the sonicity of utterance and, on the other, promoted a proscription against speaking, signification, and mimesis. Cage's shift, in other words, entailed a production of music through the sonicity of audition while retaining all other features of Western art music. Again, although Cage introduced this feature systematically into music, perhaps the reason it resembles earlier forms of totalization carried out in a register of utterance is that there were also earlier forms based on audition. For instance, if we were to replace God's panaural ear with Cagean amplification, this passage from George Sand's *The Seven Strings of the Lyre* (1839) could be moved forward 125 years: "Hear the voice of the grain of sand which rolls on the mountain slope, the voice which the insect makes, unfolding its mottled wing, the voice of the flower which dries and bursts as it drops its seed, the voice of the moss as it flowers, the voice of the leaf which swells as it drinks the dewdrop and the Eternal hears all the voices of the Universal Lyre. He hears your voice, O daughter of men, as well as those of the constellations; for nothing is too small for him for whom nothing is too great, and nothing is despicable to him who created all!"[119]

The force of Cage's centripetal pull was likewise registered on the voice of technology. While describing the means to hear the inner life of the ashtray, he says that "at the same time, I'll be enhancing that technology since I'll be recognizing its full freedom to express itself, to develop its possibilities."[120] Seemingly, he ironically encouraged from technology what he discouraged among musicians—that is, expression—yet by "full freedom to express itself" he meant within the function of hearing a submolecular sound itself, where the technology becomes realized by becoming transparent. In fact, he masked the technology's "signature"—or rather the signatures of a specific piece of technology, the social exigencies built into any technology, and the meanings accumulated through use within different cultural settings—just as he omitted the mediational attributes of listening itself. Indeed, he was more attentive to the mediations of Jesus: "considering the lilies, which is a kind of silence; but now we know, through science, that the lilies are extremely busy. We could say that Jesus was not thinking microscopically, or electronically; but then we could agree with him, because the work of the lilies is not to do something other than themselves."[121]

Technologies are especially amenable to mediation when they happen to be communications technologies, the tools of the trade for Cage. By the

1950s, nearly three decades of full-scale auditive mass media (phonography, radio, and sound film) were followed by the dissemination of television. As the mass media introduced more and more sounds, individuals became generationally capable of apprehending sounds in their social complexity and at an accelerated pace. It was a period of media expansion that began to forcibly usher in the lightning-quick delivery of the din today. It was no coincidence that Cage's progressive expansion into *all sound* and *always sound* occurred at the same time, that his emblematic silence was founded on a silencing of communications technologies, that he diminished and eradicated the sociality of the sounds of the auditive mass media throughout the 1950s and 1960s (all their wayward empirical, semiotic, poetic, affective, cultural, and political noises), or that a shift toward listening occurred as listening became more of a consumerist imperative. In this way, Cage unwittingly aped the expansionist economies generating the media saturation in the postwar years and presented a figure of a din undifferentiated by power.

Cage completed the dominion of all and always sound during the 1960s at a time when he eventually became more interested in social and political issues. While his ideas of sound and sociality were becoming more global, sometimes literally so, he maintained a strict division between the two, "a being together of sounds and people (where sounds are sounds and people are people)."[122] He did not incorporate the social or the ecological, for that matter, into the immediate materiality of sounds but only simulated their compass and complexity through undifferentiated totalization. That his music of objects, matter, and air happened to be both everywhere and inaudible, its sounds heard only through a faith in technology, placed it squarely in a mythic heritage in the West established at the time of Pythagoras. Most important, Cage's own deafness amid all this inaudible sound—that is, his inability to hear the significance of sound—meant a depleted complexity of what could be heard in any *sound in itself*. Consequently, his elaboration of panaurality and sonic pervasiveness was compensatory: a space fulfilled by a dispersion of the density of the social and ecological. If he could not hear the world through a sound, then he would hear a world of sound.

NONDISSIPATIVE SOUNDS
AND THE IMPOSSIBLE INAUDIBLE

The human ear is an amazingly sensitive device since it "can detect movements of the eardrum about one hundred times smaller than the diameter of a hydrogen atom."[1] Despite this sensitivity, however, even the subatomic ear cannot hear certain sounds. As we have just seen, John Cage awaited the day when microphony would enable people to listen to molecular vibrations and when a world of mute matter could resonate and thus be musical. This desire was not born in the din of nineteenth- and twentieth-century technology; it belonged instead to mythological thought extending back to antiquity. With roots in rumors and frozen words, in the most fully realized form of this legend, all space becomes indelibly, inaudibly, or pervasively filled with voices and sounds awaiting to be heard by the right person (or personification) in the right place or by a person with privileged possession of the right device. In other words, the cacophony is not silent, just inaudible to all but a very few. Select individuals, personifications, and odd acoustics held sway until the right devices began to take over in the late nineteenth century. The development of phonography and other auditive technologies generated the desire for and promise of panaurality for all—the ability to comprehend the ubiquity of all sounds, including the most tenaciously inaudible, and to prevent them from dissipating. Many social concerns became absorbed into the ostensible neutrality of these listening technologies. Thus, it was on this base that Cage could build his musically indiscriminate panaurality, and it was at this point amid a greater legend of the impossible inaudible that Cagean musical thought entered the mythical.

Inaudibly Loud, Long-Lasting, Far-Reaching

Sounds are inaudible usually because they are small, they take place where we cannot hear, or we cannot hear them unaided. Or so it would seem. For the Pythagoreans there were some remarkably loud sounds that were in effect everywhere, but that, for some reason, could be heard by no one. Aristotle characterized their argument this way:

Some thinkers suppose that the motion of bodies of that [astronomical] size must produce a noise, since on our earth the motion of bodies far inferior in size and in speed of movement has that effect. Also, when the sun and the moon, they say, and all the stars, so great in number and in size, are moving with so rapid a motion, how should they not produce a sound immensely great? Starting from this argument, and from the observation that their speeds, as measured by their distances, are in the same ratio as musical concordances, they assert that the sound given forth by the circular movement of the stars is a harmony.[2]

One response a Pythagorean could use when facing the quandary of a sound at once so large and yet so inaudible was to say that the sound is embodied and sounding all the time within every person—in other words, a constant aurality resulting in a pervasive deafness. Aristotle was still not convinced: "It appears unaccountable that we should not hear this music. They explain this by saying that the sound is in our ears from the very moment of birth and is thus indistinguishable from its contrary silence, since sound and silence are discriminated by mutual contrast. . . . But, as we said before, melodious and poetical as the theory is, it cannot be a true account of the facts."[3] The Pythagoreans did not maintain that absolutely no one could hear the music of the spheres. Some said that only one person—Pythagoras himself—could and that through his lone ability he discovered the phenomenon in the first place.

Despite Aristotle's doubt or the Pythagoreans' credibility, the space of the music of the spheres is typical of a Western tradition of such mythic spaces. Many did not doubt its imaginary or allegorical status, whereas others were entirely literal. These spaces and quasi-spaces contained voices or sounds in perpetuity—sounds that continually sound, circulating within physical or social spheres, or that can be activated after having been recorded in matter or memory. Accompanying these sonic and phonic spaces of *all sound, all voices,* or *all* or *always sounding* is the capacity for panaurality to be invested within a single being or for other types of sensing ultimately to be manifested within sound. Between the sounds in perpetuity and panaurality is a process of negotiations called audibility and in turn at least one schism within audibility producing inaudibility. Certain beings (and like Pythagoras, they are usually exceptional) or things can hear, potentially hear, or hear with the aid of a technological device or the promise of such a device. Therefore, this is also the prehistory of amplification as we know it today: the amplification of sounds into audibility and the amplification of hearing into panaurality.

I would like to introduce a sampling of these spaces and quasi-spaces, each with their own correlation if not continuity of endurable voices and sounds (all sounded, all heard), knowing quite well that each instance needs to be better understood amid its respective historical situation. The intent here is to suggest the longevity of myth—that such ideas as *voices in perpetuity* are themselves in perpetuity. Besides the antiquity of the music of the spheres (which still haunts the twentieth century but not as loudly as it once did), the tradition goes back also to classical depiction of Rumour, a grotesque personification gendered female, who overlaps with Fame. Within the Latin and Greek *fame* is a saying, a report, or a rumor and thereby generally a public reputation, whereas *rumor* is a roaring, shouting, or yelling. In either instance, the female assumes a monstrous form for the power of her role in determining the character of reputation, in the simple diffusion of speech, and in the destructiveness of falsehood and exposure, as perceived by males accustomed to having power over both their own and others' speech. Rumor may lose its immediately pejorative connotations in some instances, but it always retains its capacity to assume grotesque proportions.

Rumor is a speech act with an odd symmetry, at once loud (amplified?) and inaudible, public and private. The word *rumor* relates, as I have mentioned, to a roaring, shouting, or yelling, whereas the activity itself happens behind the scenes out of earshot and out of control of those it most concerns. It may be entirely inaudible or an indecipherable murmuring. A rumor is generated from a vocalization that would otherwise dissipate within the air of the immediate moment and location, yet it takes on an uncanny public presence and permanence by spreading exponentially through a series of private conversations. Whether a truth some people would rather keep quiet, an outright lie, or something in-between, it then develops through numerous generations of inadequate or interested acts of hearing and retelling to a point at which nearly everyone everywhere has heard it and told it. In the *Aeneid* (IV:173 ff.), Virgil depicts Rumour as being unambiguously horrible for having told everyone of the lovers' liaison of Dido and Aeneas:

Rumour, the swiftest traveler of all the ills on earth,
Thriving on movement, gathering strength as it goes; at the start
A small and cowardly thing, it soon puffs itself up,
And walking upon the ground, buries its head in the cloud-base.
The legend is that, enraged with the gods, Mother Earth produced
This creature, her last child, as a sister to Enceladus
And Coeus—a swift-footed creature, a winged angel of ruin,
A terrible grotesque monster, each feather upon whose body—
Incredible though it sounds—has a sleepless eye beneath it,
And for every eye she has also a tongue, a voice and a pricked ear.
At night she flits midway between earth and sky, through the gloom
Screeching, and never closes her eyelids in sweet slumber:
By day she is perched like a look-out either upon a roof-top
Or some high turret; so she terrorizes whole cities,
Loud-speaker of truth, hoarder of mischievous falsehood, equally.[4]

Equipped with a feathered plethora of eyes, tongues, and ears, Rumour is perched close to the populace all seeing, all speaking, all hearing. In

Metamorphoses, Ovid favors her panaurality and places her far away from the populace:

At the world's centre lies a place between
The lands and seas and regions of the sky,
The limits of the threefold universe,
Whence all things everywhere, however far,
Are scanned and watched, and every voice and word
Reaches its listening ears. Here Rumour dwells.[5]

And her house is architecturally designed to tight acoustic specifications:

Her chosen home set on the highest peak,
Constructed with a thousand apertures
And countless entrances and never a door.
It's open night and day and built throughout
Of echoing bronze; it all reverberates,
Repeating voices, doubling what it hears.[6]

Besides rumor, the other source of repeating and doubling voices, of enduring speech cloaked in a phase of inaudibility, can be found within the tradition of *frozen words*, a notion recorded by Plutarch:

Quite in place here is Antiphanes' story, which somebody has recounted and applied to Plato's close acquaintances. Antiphanes said humorously that in a certain city words congealed with the cold the moment they were spoken, and later, as they thawed out, people heard in the summer what they had said to one another in the winter; it was the same way, he asserted, with what was said by Plato to men still in their youth; not until long afterwards, if ever, did most of them come to perceive the meaning, when they had become old men.[7]

In other words, someone who heard or read Plato in *his* youth may retain what was stated, but only the spreading warmth of wisdom in later years will melt those words into knowledge. For Plutarch, this comparison was key in explaining "How a Man May Become Aware of His Progress in Virtue."

The most famous version of this tale can be found in the "frozen sounds" episode of François Rabelais's *Gargantua and Pantagruel* (1532), which retains the humor and sheds the morality. Out at sea with little in sight, a strange assortment of sounds are heard. Pantagruel suggests to his shipmates that the sounds might be precipitants from an equilateral triangle formed by the contiguity of several worlds, the center of which holds nothing less than the truth, along with the "words, ideas, copies, and images of all things past, and to come."[8] After this and other explanations prove unsatisfactory, the skipper intervenes to put an end to speculation. Their location skirts the Frozen Sea, the site of a bloody battle during the winter between the Arimaspians and the Nephelibates. Such battle sounds would include the "words and cries of men and women, the hacking, slashing, and hewing of battle-axes, the shocking, knocking, and jolting of armours and harnesses, the neighing of horses, and all other martial din and noise." It was so cold that the sounds froze and fell to the ground and never reached the ears of the combatants; perhaps the whole battle was silent. Even though sounds in general might lack the humidity of the breath, it was as though they took the form of speech and speech became but a vaporizer of thought. Now that it was springtime, all these sounds long inaudible were being released and creating a racket, although not in their original temporal sequences of action.

Pantagruel found irrefutable evidence strewn over the ground of the island. These still-frozen sounds seemed "like your rough sugar plums, of many colours, like those used in heraldry." Friar John held what he thought was a big word in his hands. As it melted like snow, it gave off the sound of an uncut chestnut exploding in a fire; this was interpreted as the "report of a field piece." Handfuls of the multicolored plums, some not pleasant to the eye, were thrown onto the deck of the ship:

When they had been all melted together, we heard a strange noise, hin, hin, hin, hin his, tick, tock, tasck, brededin, brededack, frr, frr, frr, bou, bou, bou, bou, bou, bou, bou, track, track, trr, trr, trr, trrr, trrrrrr; on, on, on, on, on, on, ououououon, gog, magog, and I do not know what other barbarous words; which, the pilot said, were the noise made by the charging squadrons, the shock and neighing of horses.[9]

When the idea is put forth that some of the frozen sounds be preserved for later by packing them in oil and straw, Pantagruel objects, "'tis a folly to hoard up what we are never like to want, or have always at hand." Thus, by comparison, Rabelais himself was more attached to stored words than the Pantagruelists, for he alludes to many of them in the short span of this story, including Plutarch's remarks above on Antiphanes and Plato and Castiglione's story of the frozen words in *The Book of the Courtier* (1528), which took place more under the auspices of commerce. Indeed, it was in the printed book that one could find an affinity for recording and the perpetuity of voices. With printing still in its infancy and with orature remaining strong, the *black teeth*, as they were called at the time, of the blocky typographical characters through which voices spoke and were recorded gave words a more certain objecthood and permanence.[10] Consequently, the tale continued after Rabelais with Peter Heylyn's *Microcosmus* (1621), Ned Ward's *London Spy* (1698), and Addison's story in the literary journal *The Tatler*, no. 254 (1710).[11]

During the fourteenth century both Ovid and Virgil's versions of Rumour are evident within Geoffrey Chaucer's *The House of Fame*. Here Fame takes on the broad functions of both fame and rumor, has the grotesque appearance described by Virgil, dwells high above everything amid fantastic architecture, and processes and adjudicates speech as she does in Ovid. Also, as in Ovid, "every voice and word reaches its listening ears," as well as all sounds, yet not simply through Fame's uncanny perceptual powers or through the ascent of *pneuma* or *spiritus* to a higher judgment,[12] but through vibrations in the air. Since antiquity, one of the favored means for elaborating a vibrational acoustics was through correlating the action of ripples on the surface of water with sound through the air. One of the earliest recorded appeals to water for understanding was made by the Stoic philosopher Chrysippus (ca. 280–207 B.C.): "Hearing occurs when the air between that which sounds and that which hears is struck, thus undulating spherically and falling upon the ears, as the water in a reservoir undulates in circles from a stone thrown into it."[13] The architect Marcus Vitruvius Pollio(last century B.C.) used the same analogy to explain how voices are dispersed and *rise* among audiences sitting on the stepped rows of theaters: "While in the case of water the circles move horizontally on a plane surface, the voice not only proceeds horizontally, but also ascends vertically by regular stages."[14] With the designs inherited from the ancient archi-tects, who worked in conjunction with mathematicians and musicians, ev-ery member of the audience would be privy to voices of "greater clearness and sweetness."

Chaucer follows the ascending voices of Vitruvius, yet reverses the order of enunciation, such that the multitudes (as represented by the audience) who speak at once and the single voice (on stage) who hears everything with great clearness. Similarly, Chaucer uses the figure of ripples on the surface of the water but significantly appeals to the rings ad-vancing beneath the surface—in other words, to the unseen vibrations—to describe how utterances rise from their terrestrial locations to the House of Fame.[15] The descent of concentric rings is inverted when it comes to actual sounds in the air:

As I have proved of the water, that every circle causes a second, even so is it with air, my dear brother; each circle passes into another greater and greater, and bears up speech or voice or noise, word or sound, through constant in-crease, till it comes to the House of Fame.

Now I have told . . . how speech or sound by its very nature is inclined to draw upward; this I have well proved, as you can perceive; and that the abode to which each thing is inclined has in truth its particular location. Then it is right plain that the natural abode of every speech and sound, fair or foul, has its natural position in the firmament. . . . Then this is the conclusion: every speech of every wight, as I began first to tell you, moves up on high to pass to Fame's place, by its very nature.[16]

Speech leaves its speakers behind and travels to the House of Fame, where no beings of real corporeality reside. Instead, the speech collecting there "becomes like the same wight who spake those words on earth, and in the selfsame garb; and has so the very likeness of him who spake the words that you would trow it were the same body, man or woman, he or she."[17] Then the voices in different groups, categorically defined in their phantom bodies, come forth within a great hall to make appeals to Fame for a favorable judgment on the fate of their terrestrial repute. She was omnipotent, all seeing, all hearing, all saying: her feet touched the earth, her head reached the glow of the planets, she had as many eyes as a bird has feathers, and "she also had as many projecting ears and tongues as there be hairs on beasts."[18] Her decision could result in a blast blown by Aeolus from one of two clarions, Slander or Laud:

[Slander] went through every land as swift as ball from gun when fire is touched to the powder. And such a smoke came out of the end of his foul trumpet, black, blue, swarthy red, greenish, as comes all on high from the chimney, where men melt lead. And one thing more I saw well, that the farther it went the greater it waxed, as a river from its source; and it stank as the pit of hell. Alas, thus guiltless was their shame sounded on every tongue![19]

At another time the black clarion Slander was blown "as loud as winds bellow in hell, and eke in truth the sound was so full of mocks as ever apes were of grimaces. And that went around all the world, so that every wight began to shout at them and to laugh as a madman, such sorry visages men found in their hoods!"[20] Laud was a trumpet of gold that blew in the four directions as loud as thunder, and its breath "smelled as if men placed a potful of balm amid a basket full of roses."[21] Reputation could make a person's life a heaven or hell on earth and could, moreover, continue long after one's death to constitute an afterlife of eternal bliss or misery within the ether of terrestrial voices. Fame's determination was not divine but was more immediately felt. Thus, the original acoustical ascent of the rising voices did not correlate with the ascent of souls for judgment. But what was the inhalation that enabled the exhalation of Aeolus in a circulation of voices remaining tied to terrestrial life if not Mother Earth, the birthplace of Rumour as described by Virgil?

As the protagonist approached another castle, it emitted a continuous tumult, with sounds blasting forth through its walls, which were made of twigs and full of thousands of windows and holes. The blasts themselves set the twigs whirring and the entire construction squeaking and creaking and whirling around at great speed. And there was no quiet inside:

All the corners of the house are full of whisperings and pratings of war, of peace, marriages, rest, labor, journeyings, abidings, of death, life, love, hate, accord, enmity, of praise, learning, of gains, of health, sickness, of buildings, of fair winds, tempests, pestilence of man and beast; of divers changes of estate for men and nations; of trust, fear, jealousy, wit, profit, folly, of plenty, and of great famine, of ruin, of cheap times and dear; of good or ill government, of fire, of divers events.[22]

Whereas the procession approaching Fame in the great hall was orderly, this congregation was huge and roamed about in seemingly random fashion. This was the site not of reputation in general but of the unruly generation of rumor, for everyone was whispering into someone's ear or speaking aloud or listening to others:

But the most wondrous was this; when one had heard a thing, he came forth to another and straightaway told him the same thing that he had heard ere it was a moment older, but in the telling he made the tidings somewhat greater than ever they had been. And not so soon was he parted from him as the second met a third; and ere he was done, he told him everything; were the tidings true or false, he would tell them nevertheless, and evermore with greater increase than at first. Thus, every word went from mouth to mouth in all directions, evermore increasing, as fire is wont to kindle and spread from a spark thrown amiss, till a whole city is burned up.[23]

These words obeyed the acoustic principles of terrestrial sound and rose up and through the leaky building to the outside. If a semblance of truth still survived and tried to escape, it might meet a falsehood at a window too small to let them both pass; thus, they would become fused, and no one listening could ever separate the two. On escape all these voices would go to Fame for sorting; she allotted to "each its duration, some to wax and wane quickly," and then Aeolus blew them back to earth "twenty thousand in a company."[24] Fame was able to complete the task and so embodied the circulation of voices, by mimicking dialogue with the close proximity of her ears and tongues and sociality with their proliferation. With her perched all of communication, and, in this sense, her power was expressed through her judgment, which could be located with her alone. She was feared for the variation, proliferation, and diffusion of judgments that were difficult to contest.

Leonora Carrington's surrealist story "The House of Fear" (1937–1938) satirizes Chaucer on this count. The protagonist follows a procession of horses to the annual gathering at the Castle of the Mistress Fear. In keeping with the tradition of female grotesque, Fear is dressed in a gown made of live bats sewn at the wings, which would ostensibly allow her to fly blinded by night. From her position of omnipotence she instructs the throng of horses in the rules of this year's game:

You must all count backwards from a hundred and ten to five as quickly as possible while thinking of your own fate and weeping for those who have gone before you. You must simultaneously beat time to the tune of the "The Volga Boatmen" with your left foreleg, "The Marseillaise" with your right foreleg, and "Where Have you Gone, My Last Rose of Summer?" with your two back legs.[25]

Similar to the simultaneity phonographically realized in Blaise Cendrars's *Dan Yack*, Carrington invokes a pallid internationalism, a global noise. The polyrhythm of one horse would have been be difficult enough for most Western ears during the first half of the century and might have well been associated with the *noise* of polyrhythmic traditions within African music, but with a plurality of polyrhythms beat out by all the inhabitants of a huge room of horses, Fear would rule over noise guaranteed.

Charles Babbage in his *Ninth Bridgewater Treatise* (1837), an attempt to shore up religion against the onrush of science, kept his acoustics within the earth's atmosphere, dispersing atomized voices and sounds in such a way that they would not dissipate but could be recuperated in the future by those with the proper mathematical knowledge or by the One already equipped with a talent for the ultimate in calculation. The longevity of the voices and sounds was produced under the sign of conscience by using an improbable mnemonic device: recording memory within the air rather than in the circulation of speech or the peripatetic convolutions of the brain. Babbage's acoustics were developed under the sway of Newton's physics, Laplace's mathematics, and a universe of pervasive inscription. Babbage wrote:

The pulsations of the air, once set in motion by the human voice, cease not to exist with the sounds to which they gave rise. Strong and audible as they may be in the immediate neighborhood of the speaker, and at the immediate moment of utterance, their quickly attenuated force soon becomes inaudible to human ears. The motions they have impressed on the particles of one portion of our atmosphere, are communicated to constantly increasing numbers, but the total quantity of motion measured in the same direction receives no addition. Each atom loses as much as it gives, and regains again from other atoms a portion of those motions which they in turn give up. . . . The waves of air thus raised, perambulate the earth and ocean's surface, and in less than twenty hours every atom of its atmosphere takes up the altered movement due to that infinitesimal portion of the primitive motion which has been conveyed to it through countless channels, and which must continue to influence its path throughout its future existence.[26]

Although invisible and inaudible to the senses, these movements are demonstrable by reason. Thus, there might one day come a person so equipped with the mathematical knowledge of these motions that he or she will be able to predict the destiny of voices once uttered and to trace back the diffusion of others to their ultimate source:

Thus considered, what a strange chaos is this wide atmosphere we breathe! Every atom, impressed with good and with ill, retains at once the motions which philosophers and sages have imparted to it, mixed and combined in ten thousand ways with all that is worthless and base. The air itself is one vast library, on whose pages are for ever written all that man has ever said or woman whispered. There, in their mutable but unerring characters, mixed with the earliest, as well as with the latest sighs of mortality, stand for ever recorded, vows unredeemed, promises unfulfilled, perpetuating in the united movements of each particle, the testimony of man's changeful will.[27]

Technically, the complexity of these motions are not apparent as long as they remain in air, but they do become perceptible when inscribed on other media such as water. For Babbage it is on the waves where this vast record becomes one with conscience and the processes of terrestrial and ultimately heavenly retribution. He ends with an 1832 account of a slave ship that describes the horrific scenes of abducted Africans in the hold and of their drowning once cast overboard. It is addressed to the transcendent "infinite intelligence" who reads these motions with ease, although it could have just as easily been addressed to the parties involved in the insurance negotiations that went on at the time for nondelivery of goods. To make the difference patently cosmological instead of legal, retribution will be exacted at a jurisdiction where humans no longer exist:

When man and all his race shall have disappeared from the face of our planet, ask every particle of air still floating over the unpeopled earth, and it will record the cruel mandate of the tyrant. Interrogate every wave which breaks unimpeded on ten thousand desolate shores, and it will give evidence of the last gurgle of the waters which closed over the head of his dying victim: confront the murderer with every corporeal atom of his immolated slave, and in its still quivering movements he will read the prophet's denunciation of the prophet king. ("And Nathan said unto David—*Thou art the man*.")[28]

Charles Dickens cited Babbage's text to invoke the figure of the necessary diffusion of knowledge (not a knowledge of the diffusion), and, in turn, Babbage's ideas of lingering voices were impressed on the next generation. Dickens, as the newly elected president of the Birmingham and Midland Institute in 1869, enumerated the good works of its members:

The benefits of such an establishment must extend far beyond the limits of this midland county fires and smoke, and must comprehend, in some sort, the whole community. I do not strain the truth. It was suggested by Mr. Babbage, in his *Ninth Bridgewater Treatise*, that a mere spoken word—a mere syllable thrown into the air—may go on reverberating through illimitable space for ever and ever, seeing that there is no rim against which it can strike: no boundary at which it can possibly arrive. Similarly it may be said—not as an ingenious speculation, but as a steadfast and absolute fact—that human calculation cannot limit the influence of one atom of wholesome knowledge patiently acquired, modestly possessed, and faithfully used.[29]

The topic was self-improvement—the possibility for all with courage and perseverance to diligently raise their station, with "some savage African tribes" excluded from present company. It seems the acoustic atoms from the last pages of Babbage's treatise had yet to reach the midlands.

Machines of Nondissipation

An obscure American author named Florence McLandburgh devised a technology to hear hitherto inaudible voices and sounds in her story "The Automaton Ear" (1876), a tale in the style of Poe published the year before Edison invented his phonograph. The protagonist, a professor, runs across a paragraph describing how sound never fully dissipates and sets out to construct a device to aid the ear in hearing these wayward atoms. After a series of failed attempts he raises the trumpet of his invention to his ear:

Hark!—The hum of mighty hosts! It rose and fell, fainter and more faint; then the murmur of water was heard and lost again, as it swelled and gathered and burst in one grand volume of sound like a hallelujah from myriad lips. Out of the resounding echo, out of the dying cadence a single female voice arose. Clear, pure, rich, it soared above the tumult of the host that hushed itself, a living thing.[30]

The voice turned out to flow, as in the Babbage text, from the site of drowning—one place in particular:

and—hark! the Hebrew tongue: "The horse and his rider hath he thrown into the sea."

Then the noise of the multitude swelled again, and a crash of music broke forth from innumerable timbrels. I raised my head quickly—it was the song of Mirian after the passage of the Red Sea.[31]

The plot revolves around a deaf woman who, after regaining her hearing through the device, tries to run away with it and is murdered by the professor. When he once again uses the device, he hears her lingering voice. This moment of conscience disappears, along with the rest of the story, as he realizes that the whole episode has been the product of an elaborate bout of insanity.

That both conscience and technology were retracted puts McLandburgh's tale nicely on the cusp, since as the technological means for achieving nondissipative voices and sounds came to the fore, the teachings conducted by the persons and personifications who populated myth and teachings conducted on the natural forces of wind and water receded. New machines of sound simply made it more difficult to hear the virtues of Plutarch, the moral determinations of Chaucer's Fame, or the conscience in Babbage. Technology stood apart from humans like a new natural force, and questions of social conduct could be effortlessly abandoned to the task of explaining its wonders and workings, where power became first of all a determination of the capabilities of perception of those in possession of the new device. In particular phonography, although it did not abandon the lingering social voices of reputation or the internalized voices of conscience, encouraged the perception of the indiscriminate voices of the dead. At this point it became a device, or at least the foundation of a device, to hear the inaudible. After all, as a practical matter it could keep the voices of the dead alive or at least play them back, and as a discursive matter it could hear all sound and voices. It was no great leap, in other words, to link phonographic storage capacity to the massive inaudible ranks of the deceased, as well as of their fellow preternatural time travelers, the sounds and voices from the future. However, this death-denying feat failed to differentiate ethically among the masses filing through the House of Fame but instead deferred such considerations to a secondary role.

It becomes easier to secure McLandburgh's tale as a representative cusp of this larger transition given that her story appeared just one year before Edison filed his patent for the phonograph in 1877. Commonly referred to as the talking machine, the machine that talks, *die Sprechmaschine*, and the *phono*-graph (voice writing), it was a good machine for the rumor-like circulation of voices. It not only talked; it spoke all the languages of the world and could do so simultaneously. As one newspaper reporter in London wrote, "Mr. Edison's invention is considered first cousin to the prince of black art. My own impression after hearing it talk in English, French, German and Hungarian, all at once, was that I had gone mad."[32] Yet within the range of its own voice, it also listened. Cultural tropes of panaurality and *all sound, all voices*, began to proliferate the more it became a fixture within society. It was at this point that Edison sought to make it a fixture within all the society that ever had been—by inventing a machine to communicate with the dead. The communication itself was ostensibly indiscriminate; the specifications of the technology, however, betrayed its ethical dimensions.

The principle making his invention plausible enough to pursue was Edison's idea—an odd technical admixture of Theosophy and theories of organic memory—that different living beings are actually comprised of millions and millions of subperceptual, subatomic "life units" that are so small they cannot be seen with the most powerful microscope: "There is no limit to the smallness of things, just as there is no limit as to largeness. The electron theory gives us a reply which is wholly satisfactory. I have had the matter roughly calculated and have at hand the data of the calculation. I am sure that a highly organized entity, consisting of millions of electrons yet still remaining too small to be visible through any existing microscope, is possible."[33] Life units came from another developed sphere or spheres in outer space to colonize planet Earth, once it had sufficiently cooled down, and to get on with the evolutionary process. They group together in one swarm to make one type of living entity and in another swarm to make another. When that entity dies, the swarm disperses into life units that travel through the ether at very near the speed of light—for some reason Edison leaves unstated, mundane peripatetic or transport through the air would be too slow—and eventually regroup into another swarm.

When life units swarm, they do not do so amorphously. They just happen to be personified as little people who are grouped along class lines, act in accordance with bourgeois democracy, and perpetuate racialism, besides being little imperialists from outer space. A person's body is nothing but an aggregate of millions and billions of life units, and these life units are like little people in themselves: "There are many indications that we human beings act as a community or ensemble rather than as units. That is why I believe that each of us comprises millions upon millions of entities, and that our body and our mind represent the vote or the voice, whichever you wish to call it, of our entities."[34] However, just as the opinion of a person, given a position of power, can become a dictate, so too the voices and votes of the life units are differentiated by structuring the swarm into "ninety-five per cent workers and five per cent directors."[35] The "directing entities" or "master entities" were lodged in the area of the left frontal lobe, thought to be the cortical locus of speech by Paul Broca, where Edison gave them the function of personality and memory, the latter being within a logic of recording synonymous with the former.[36] From their perch they direct the entire corporation of life units and keep the records with the interaction with the world outside: "Everything we call memory goes on in a little strip not much more than a quarter of an inch long. That is where the little people live who keep our records for us."[37] Edison knows this because, as he says repeatedly, "eighty-two remarkable operations upon the brain have definitely proven that the meat of our personality lies in that part of the brain known as the fold of Broca."[38] That Edison should invest Broca's locus of speech with a recording strip laden with personality, memory, let alone the direction of the masses, betrays his phonographic agenda for speaking and recording in general and explains why "our body and our mind" would "represent the vote or the voice" of millions of life units.

Race, too, differentiates life units from one another—not so much within the internal structuring of a human but in how they might swarm from one generation to the next among the human population proper: "What we call 'inborn traits' are recollections of earlier experiences that the little peoples have brought along with them. Take an Indian baby, for instance. No matter how hard or how long you may try, you can never make a white man of that baby. The little peoples in the baby will not permit you to do so. They have their ideas, gained from preceding experiences, of what a human being should do. You may repress these little peoples to the point where you believe you have made an Indian into a white man, but, when you least expect it, they will jump out at you and startle you with a war whoop."[39] In fact, Edison holds a special place for race among the array of life-unit functioning and restricts movement for Native Americans in a way he would not do for plants ("Swarms do it all. The daisy has been the same for, say, 50,000 years. Then comes a variation. Perhaps the daisy becomes blue")[40] or for any other life units, which dissipate and regroup freely across different species and life forms. Edison's notion of racial memory—that race is indelibly recorded in reproduction—was itself a replay of Samuel Butler.

When either class or "minority" conflict arises in the body, harmony can be restored "If the minority is willing to be disciplined and to conform."[41] Those not willing to subject themselves to the higher ideals of the master units can then choose to leave or to go on strike and refuse to perform their work within the body. At this point, the person will become ill or die, and with death the bond of the swarm is dissolved, scattering life units out into the ether. But the life of proletarian life units does not include vacations: "The workers cannot loaf or stop, even though something may compel them from their habitat, that which has been the 'body' of a 'man.' They must go to something else to build, as, for instance, to corn, a tree, grass—whatever may be—always working under the direction of the higher type among them.[42] The directors, however, stick together and have enough time between jobs to have a little chat with the living, or so Edison was hoping.

It was now just a matter of building a device, at once extremely powerful and sensitive, that could detect the attempt of the lingering life units to have their last say, while they were still in a configuration identifiable as a discrete personality, before dispersal and reassignment. This "spirit catcher" would be a valve against which the "slightest conceivable effort is made to exert many times its initial power for indicative purposes. It is similar to a modern power house, where man, with his relatively puny one-eighth horse-power, turns a valve which starts a 50,000-horse-power steam turbine."[43] He did have some previous success in the realm of sensing and amplification technology. While investigating the improvement of the telephone, the carbon button speaker accidentally emitted what he called "molecular music," the result of the imperceptible stressed movements of the telephone handle. If sound existing among the tiny world of molecules could be heard, the carbon button could amplify small sounds to another unheard-of order of magnitude, or so his assistant Francis Jehl thought:

The passage of a delicate camel's hair brush was magnified to the roar of a mighty wind. The footfalls of a tiny gnat sound like the tramp of Rome's cohorts. The ticking of a watch could be heard over a hundred miles.[44]

A rapt public followed every move in Edison's attempt to break through to the Other Side, for he had come through for them so many times before. The front page headline of the *Times* magazine once read: "No Immortality of the Soul Says Thomas A. Edison. In Fact, He Doesn't Believe There Is a Soul—Human Being Only an Aggregate of Cells and the Brain Only a Wonderful Machine, Says Wizard of Electricity."[45] He assured them that his materialism was not an obstacle but a means to the spirit realm: "I have been working out the details for some time; indeed, a collaborator in this work died only the other day. In that he knew exactly what I am after in this work, I believe he ought to be the first to use it if he is able to do so."[46] The recently deceased William James was also thought to be the natural person, or spirit, to assist Edison with the demonstration of his device. If the device's effectiveness could be proven, then there of course would be a large and lucrative market, especially among the living who wished to contact those killed in World War I.[47] In this way, Edison's "spirit catcher" was greeted similarly to the phonograph; for instance, the lead editorial in *Scientific American* (22 December 1877) stated that Edison's invention heralded "the startling possibility of the voices of the dead being reheard through this device. . . . the voices of such singers as Parepa and

Titiens will not die with them, but will remain as long as the metal in which they may be embodied will last."[48] But what would happen if the aging Edison himself died before making his discovery—or worse yet, if he decided it was impossible? "If this apparatus fails to reveal anything of exceptional interest, I am afraid that I shall have lost all faith in the survival of personality as we know it in this experience."[49]

The instrumentality of phonographic listening became quite efficient once its complement was found within the desocializing tendencies and techniques of modernist music. Perhaps the earliest confluence came in 1911 when Ferruccio Busoni designed an April Fool's device through which phonography acted as an amplifier for an unusual class of sounds. Busoni's shill in this instant was one Kennelton Humphrey Happenziegh, the actual fictitious inventor of a "super-sensitive apparatus (intended for phonographic discs)":[50]

[It] resembles at first glance a drum disk with a super-sensitive epidermis, and possesses the quality of combining the utmost delicacy with the most complete power of resistance and is able to pick up noises which are inaudible or unintelligible to the human ear; moreover it has the power of dissecting complicated sounds into their constituent parts. If, for example, one plays a note on the violin, every accompanying noise is picked up separately; the sounds which arise from the hairs of the violin-bow; the resin, the pressure of the fingers which hold the bow, the most imperceptible vibration of a window pane are recorded on the disk. The contrivance is so extremely delicate that when a hand is passed through hair the crackling is *distinctly* audible; light steps in the next room are recorded by it, the slightest breath is impressed on it.[51]

Early one morning Happenziegh makes a recording and, on inspecting the inscriptions with a special microscope, finds some unexplained patterns. After separating out the usual patterns of early morning noise, he isolates what sounds like music—but like no music he ever heard before. After several months he makes his determination: "A scream fades away into tomorrow and the day after tomorrow and further, in corresponding strength—logically into yesterday and the day before yesterday also."[52] The same applies not just to the effective amplifications of screaming but to all sounds. Thus, the reason he never heard the music before is that the music is from the future (anywhere from twenty to three hundred years, probably around 150 years). Some of the more unusual attributes of this new music include "Sounds from trombones like Aeolean harps melt into a sound fog, and again other voices out of the void, without audible beginning, disappear into the atmosphere of sound. Sounds as if coming from tinkling water and burning fire assume melodic form, appear and disappear."[53] All the instruments sound as if they are being played *muted*, but this is most likely a side effect of the means of amplification. And the calculations for how far into the future are definitely out of register, since sound fog would soon settle in with Busoni's student Varèse and tinkling water began to flood into music in the 1950s.

Busoni was showing a modernist card when he imagined a phonograph-like device to listen to the future, whereas Babbage, McLandburgh, and Edison were interested in the dead or otherwise residual. Another noted attempt to listen to the dead is known under the term *Raudive voices* for Konstantin Raudive, who formalized a discovery in 1959 by the Swede Friedrich Jürgenson that one may hear afterlife banter using microphones, radios, and tape recorders. Just as McLandburgh found her professor in Edison, the device he was unable to invent was to be found in the unwitting tape recorder. Raudive describes one method, which is to place a tape-recorder microphone in an area where no voices are audible and to record. The investigator might lead things off with "Hello, hello, here is X.X.— I should be very happy to know that the unseen friends are here and are manifesting through the tape."[54] The auditors must be trained to listen and, at times, must know a number of different languages because apparently no Biblical universal language exists. The voices can be grouped according to three categories of audibility: group A are the most readily heard, even by the untrained ear, and can be subjected to repeated listening. Raudive "analyzed roughly 25,000 voices according to speech content, language and rhythm. By this method of repetition, the acoustic reality of the voices can be established beyond doubt, and hallucinations of the ear are excluded."[55] Group B voices are soft and fast and thus required trained specialists. Group C is the most difficult to hear and also the most interesting because of the wealth of *paranormal data* provided and perhaps because they rely on the promise of future technological developments: "Unfortunately, these can be heard only in fragments, even by

Nondissipative Sounds and the Impossible Inaudible

a trained ear, but with improved technical aids, it may eventually become possible to hear and demonstrate these voices, which lie beyond our range of hearing, without trouble."[56]

William Burroughs championed Raudive voices because they prove the case against "the whole psychiatric dogma that voices are the imaginings of a sick mind," but he then challenges Raudive's interpretation of where the voices might emanate. Raudive says they are not from the unconscious, but Burroughs challenges his assumption with one borrowed from L. Ron Hubbard's *Dianetics:* "Remember that your memory bank contains tapes of everything you have ever heard, including of course your own words. Press a certain button, and a news broadcast you heard ten years ago plays back."[57] Furthermore, a larger recording and playback expresses itself socially two ways through a worldwide redundancy, perhaps simply an imperial conquest of commercialism ("The rude clerk in Hong Kong bore a strong resemblance to the rude clerk in New York, and both used the same words to indicate they did not have what you asked for: 'I never heard of it'") and an historical accumulation ("Old war tapes. We all have millions of hours of it, even if we never fired a gun. War tapes, hate tapes, fear tapes, pain tapes, happy tapes, sad tapes, funny tapes, all stirring around in a cement mixer of voices").[58] Equipped with this idea of a ubiquitous recording, Burroughs characteristically improves on Raudive's theory (it would be his mission to propose impossible technologies to fulfill modernist and occult desires) by suggesting that a similar principle may be applied to listen into the future and not just to the representatives of the past:

Fifteen years ago in Norway, experiments indicated that voices could be projected directly into the brain of the subject by an electromagnetic field around the head. The experiments were in a formative stage at that time. So maybe we are all walking around under a magnetic dome of prerecorded word and image, and Raudive and the other experimenters are simply plugging into the prerecording.[59]

In other words, Babbage's atmosphere—atomistic and filled with conscience—now becomes electromagnetic and filled with destiny, no matter how prosaic it may be, and the eschatology of recording from Babbage through Edison becomes cosmologically pervasive and undifferentiated, adding prerecording to recording and transforming phonography into the functional principle for a time machine that would travel from one type of place to the same type of place. The question, of course, becomes by whom or what are the words and images prerecorded? Religious lifelines oscillate too much with good and bad deeds and would produce too many moral offshoots antithetical to Burroughs's general disposition. There is probably a magical inroad already explored by Burroughs and Brion Gysin while they were first in Paris together, but the magnetic dome itself alludes, in this case, to the congruent atmospheric envelopes saturated with Reichian orgone energy and the transmissions of mass-mediated culture. While the sexual tropes of Reich may produce a sense of reproduction, if not generational replication, the behavior-inducing powers of mass media, an entangling of realist modes with reality, as well as a dependence on technologies of reproduction—imbue life with predestination, perhaps only a return of the produced. Thus, there is everywhere a deafening sound, a blinding numinous light, which individuals can neither hear nor see in all its consonance, for it is silently constituted by signals saturating the substance of all space with the din of mass-mediated culture. As a dead Aristotle might have said: It appears unaccountable that we should not see or hear this din. They explain this by saying that the sound is in our ears and the image is in our eyes from the very moment of birth and is thus indistinguishable from its contrary silence . . . and darkness. But melodious and poetical as the theory is, it cannot be a true account of the facts. True, facts mean little, but they meant much to Burroughs.

An exception to the deferral of ethical attributes of technology can be found within a brief musing by Bertolt Brecht in 1927, in which he yearned for a device for the ubiquitous recording of monopolized airwaves:

I very much wish that this bourgeoisie would add another invention to their invention of radio—one that would make it possible to record for all time everything that can be communicated by radio. Later generations would then have the chance of seeing with amazement how a caste, by making it possible to say what they had to say to the whole world, simultaneously made it possible for the whole world to see that they had nothing to say.[60]

Of course, a recording device would not do. Instead, he really needed an *institution* of recording to detect such pervasive silence amid the redundant din of bourgeois broadcasting. However, the type of political impetus designed into Brecht's device was largely an exception among other technological desires within the twentieth century.

Finally, one technique local to the question of audibility is to found within the tradition of *deamplification*—muting or what would now be called *noise abatement*. Vladimir Mayakovsky stated after visiting the raucous environs of New York that one should not "extol noise but . . . put up sound absorbers we poets must talk in cars."[61] Tristan Tzara suggested that "everything which might make a sharp sound will be covered with a thin layer of rubber,"[62] and "time has made its nest damped down with much sound-absorbent insulation, with sponges long extinct yet relentlessly ponderous."[63] And Luigi Russolo included, in his 1916 book *The Art of Noises*, one of the tricks of trench warfare: "How many times have our wonderful soldiers had to take off their noisy hob-nail boots or wrap them with trench sacks so that the noise would not reveal their approach to enemy trench!"[64] When it came to silencing the noise of the city, numerous people such as Babbage and Schopenhauer protested how loud and disruptive sounds came in from the street to make the conduct of their intellectual activities, let alone their living, difficult. But it would be left to others, once the political attempts had failed, to think about the appropriate technologies to carry out the task. Karlheinz Stockhausen, mindful of sanitation, developed plans for his Sound Swallower. This device would be equipped with hidden microphones to pick up sounds on the streets and with a computer to analyze the sounds, create negative wave patterns, and return them to cancel out the original sounds—an idea first developed by Lord Rayleigh in the 1870s using organ pipes and electric tuning forks and now taken up under the rubric active noise control:

You're on the street talking to your friend, and all of a sudden he recognizes that you're just moving into a silent area and he tries to say something but you don't hear anything. Then people could go to the corner and do anything they liked. You'd also have a tiny switch with which to turn the sounds on and off. People could acoustically piss and shit in special acoustical toilets, but they wouldn't be bothering anyone else with their acoustical garbage.[65]

If that is not clean enough, then there is always Mangon in J. G. Ballard's short story "The Sound Sweep," who, equipped with a sonovac, removes sounds that settle on the floor and furniture: "He swept them methodically, moving the sonovac's nozzle in long strokes, drawing out the dead residues of sound that had accumulated during the day."[66] This device would seemingly work on all lingering voices and sounds, although care should be taken not to dispose of life units—or care should be taken to predispose them properly.

THE PARAMETERS OF ALL SOUND

During the 1960s a number of historical narratives and genealogies were constructed by artists to account for the flourishing new arts. In the panoramic pictures built by Fluxus impresario George Maciunas, John Cage was always exceedingly important, not because he was the origin of trends but because he consistently occupied the most crucial transitional role. The backbone of Maciunas's "Diagram of Historical Development of Fluxus and Other 4-Dimensional, Aural, Optic, Olfactory, Epithelial and Tactile Art Forms" was formed by the connection Cage made between the avant-garde of the early part of the century and artists of the postwar period. It was not meant to demonstrate the historical transmission of ideas—if that were the case, there would have been included any number of books, journals, exhibitions, salons, group discussions, personal relationships, and the like—but only the trail of ideas as exemplified by individual artists and different trends. Still, Cage would have held a similar position in such a representation. His classes at the New School for Social Research were particularly important in this respect, attracting the likes of George Brecht, Al Hansen, Dick Higgins, Allan Kaprow, and Jackson MacLow, who all played formative roles in the founding of Fluxus, Happenings, and related activities. For others, Cage was a personification of the Black Mountain aesthetic, and when he attended the exhibitions and performances of his younger contemporaries, something he continued to do throughout his life, they were frequently grateful for his presence and generosity.

Indeed, many artists freely expressed their indebtedness to Cage, and remarkably few, given the power of his influence, could be said to have been derivative.[1] Unlike the limiting discursive frame in which Pollock's drip painting became the *solution* to the *problem of painting*, the imposing figure of Cage abundantly bestowed license, directed as much toward artistic concerns as toward the conduct of daily life. Yet there was another side to this sense of artistic possibility. Cage had opened up so much that very little, in a modernist rhetoric of liberation, was left to be set free: "Every young artist tried to define himself/herself as going past Cage but this was very difficult because the Cagean revolution was very thorough," recalls composer James Tenney.[2] Filmmaker Stan Brakhage stated the problem in a different way: "Cage has laid down the greatest aesthetic net of this century. Only those who honestly encounter it (understand it also to the point of being able, while chafing at its bits, to call it 'marvelous') and manage to survive (i.e., go beyond it) will be the artists of our contemporary present."[3] Tenney also said that "Cage created a situation where we don't have to kill the father anymore,"[4] although what was Nam June Paik doing during his performance piece *Étude for Pianoforte* when he ran into the audience to cut off Cage's tie? The *great aesthetic net* of Cage proved to be both a safety device over which daredevil experimental feats could be attempted and also an obstacle preventing individuals from grounding themselves in something *beyond-Cage*. Nevertheless, the experimental drive Cage exemplified when applied to the latitude he granted ensured that many of those indebted to him would indeed succeed to be part of the *contemporary present* Brakhage mentioned.

The obvious difficulty in expanding on, let alone superseding, the modernist practice of musicalized sound so effectively colonized by Cage meant that Fluxus and other experimental artists were required to explore a number of strategic options. One popular recourse was simply to take

Cage at his word. When pushed to their logical conclusions, his ideas had the potential to open on concerns that sat only uncomfortably, if at all, within a Cagean aesthetic. In fact, Cage himself was just as capable of following his ideas into awkward areas as his younger cohorts, and at times he appeared to be following the directions they were taking. The problem, of course, was that Cage was limited by the gravitational pull of the formidable mass of his own aesthetic whereas younger artists were more free to investigate the attendant artistic possibilities.

This strategy was most evident when young artists in the late 1950s and early 1960s approached Cage's reworking of the modernist paradigm of *one sound* and *all sound*—specifically, the imperative *to hear a sound in itself*, the idea that all sounds can be music, and thinking about sounds according to their size. For instance, Cage structured works to defeat conventional musical relationality, but because the sounds were almost always in an agglomeration of other sounds, relations were easily contrived through listening. Fluxus artists, on the other hand, literally listened to sounds in themselves by radically isolating them, such as in George Brecht's *Drip Music*, which is discussed in chapter 10. Through their techniques of linking sound (often problematically) to an object, task, performance, or concept, Fluxus artists invited a range of corporeal, cultural, and political factors, many of which were generally anathematic to Cage. And, as we see below, Tony Conrad, LaMonte Young, and other artists took listening to sounds *in* themselves further by listening *inside* sounds.

Loud Sounds

The modernist drive to comprehend all sound was channeled by younger artists through paradigmatic ideas about the size of sounds—that is, small sounds and loud sounds—that tested Cagean totalization. On the small end of things, Fluxus artists explored borderline states of audibility, but to the extent these works relied on ideas of presence and absence of sound, this may not have been the best avenue toward superseding Cage. Once Cage supplanted ideas of noise with the operations of aurality, the arena of small sounds itself became privileged because of their proximity to questions of audibility and suppressions of inaudibility. Moreover, as a rhetorical carryover from his days of noise, small sounds were well suited to his emancipatory project, whereas loud sounds by their nature were quite capable of announcing and imposing themselves on circumstances and thus needed no assistance, let alone emancipation. He also associated loud sounds negatively with the use of harmony and in the big sound of the symphonic repertoire. Cage's emphasis on small sounds—on the barely audible, the improbably and impossibly audible—set up a material imbalance within his aesthetic. He wanted to open up to *all sound*, considering each sound in its own right, while in actuality his attention was much more fixed on one end of the scale. It was not a simple question of spreading his loyalties out more evenly, as some symmetrical exercise across the keyboard. Loud sounds would have required from Cage a different set of ideas that, quite simply, were outside his frame of reference. This did not mean that Cage would never incorporate loudness or other new ideas into his work, but by then he would have been following someone else's lead.

During his experimental composition class at the New School, Cage used the category of the *dimensions of sound* to discuss the parameters of sound, whether they existed in musical terms as multiple *pianissimi* and *fortissimi* or in the acoustic terms of "intensity 0–120 phones/inaudible-painful."[5] To Dick Higgins, one of his students at the time, Cage was not taking his own lesson to heart: "It was in the air in the late 1950s to consider the balances of sounds. The small sounds that John Cage tended to favor didn't seem complete to a lot of people. Many of us wanted sounds to have a real physicality that sometimes couldn't be perceived in the small sounds, as well as the larger ones."[6] The physicality of loud sounds that Higgins mentioned could be understood in a number of ways—as an ill-defined sonic force exerted *en masse*, as the conveyance of a materiality of sound that confounds the experience of sound as a nonphysical sign, as the establishment of a palpably saturated acoustic space, as the experience of the intensity of vibrations on the whole body as well as within it, as the unexpected corporeal experience of sound complementing the experience of hearing only with the ears and mind, as the physiological response to loud sounds as a potentially dangerous action, as a rhetorical basis for emphasis, and so on. Higgins's approach was realized in his *Loud Symphony*, where he set up a correspondences between a simple line of gesture and the harsh pealing of speaker feedback. Composed in 1958, *Loud Symphony* was perhaps the earliest amplified piece in a time in which loudness would soon become commonplace. It was also an early example of what by now must constitute a genre of feedback pieces, including Steve Reich's *Pendulum Music* (1968), and innumerable noise music works:

I was living on a very low budget and the only really loud sounds that interested me were the screeching sounds you could get by passing a microphone in front of a loudspeaker. Those kinds screaming feedbacks are what I used for my *Loud Symphony*, which was about one-half an hour long. I took the graphic notations I had composed up to that point, probably fifteen pieces or so, and I used those as movement scores for how to pass the microphones in front of the speaker. Holding the microphone in my right hand and the notation in my left I passed them back and forth according to the patterns that were indicated by my graphic notations.[7]

For Tony Conrad, artist, filmmaker, musician, and one-time member of the Theatre of Eternal Music, or Dream Syndicate, amplification was a practical means to hear very subtle aspects of sound. The Theatre of Eternal Music—which at one point in 1962 and 1963 included John Cale, Angus MacLise, LaMonte Young, and Marian Zazeela—was well known for its highly amplified concerts, where the air was thick with a complex, palpable mix of droning sound and delicate elaborations. People have described how painfully loud the music was, and this was before they opened the door to enter the concert hall! John Perreault described a "painfully loud" Young concert accordingly as "walking into a room full of brine and discovering that surprisingly enough it was still possible to breathe."[8]

Young used amplification earlier in his work for Anna Halprin's Dancer's Workshop, *2 Sounds* (1960), produced by scraping tin cans on glass and a drum stick on a gong: "When the tape ends after fifteen minutes, the ensuing silence comes as a shock: silence has somehow been charged."[9] The charging of silence takes on metaphysical overtones, but it was not charged merely because the loud sound rendered the absence of sound in stark contrast but also because it marshaled the physiological defenses of the body against injury and long-term hearing-loss: "Sometimes we produced sounds that lasted over an hour. If it was a loud sound, my ears would often not regain their normal hearing for several hours, and when my hearing slowly did come back, it was almost as much a new experience as when I had first begun to hear the sound."[10] The charged silence, moreover, was indicative of an obverse state of sound and aurality, one in which a person did not listen to a sound but listened inside a sound:

When the sounds are very long, as many of those we made at Ann Halprin's were, it can be easier to get inside of them. Sometimes when I was making a long sound, I began to notice that I was looking at the dancers and the room from the sound instead of hearing the sound from some position in the room. I began to feel the parts and motions of the sound more, and I began to see how each sound was its own world and that this world was only similar to our world in that we experienced it through our own bodies, that is, in our own terms. I could see that sounds and all other things in the world were just as important as human beings and that if we could to some degree give ourselves up to them, the sounds and other things that is, we enjoyed the possibility of learning something new. By giving ourselves up to them, I mean getting inside of them to some extent so that we can experience another world. This is not so easily explained but more easily experienced.[11]

The specific need for amplification within The Theatre of Eternal Music arose from the "long sound" of droning that served as the ground for the whole group. Each member had arrived at the sustained sounds through different sources. Young traces them back to growing up in a log cabin in Idaho, where he listened to the wind blowing steadily across chinks in the cabin as though it were a large flute, and by the constant sound of nearby electrical transformers, while Conrad locates another source in how Young's jazz saxophone playing, developed within the "cool jazz" of California in the 1950s, manifested itself in his Western art music compositions later in the decade: "Young . . . went cooler than any of the rest of them, and started incorporating cool, long spaced-out tones in his classical pieces."[12] As early as December 1961 Cage was able to notice that there was something distinctly un-Cagean going on that, nevertheless, brought to mind the microscope—that is, the visual counterpart in the field of amplification and small sounds:

La Monte Young is doing something quite different from what I am doing, and it strikes me as being very important. Through the few pieces of his I've heard, I've had, actually, utterly different experiences of listening than I've had with any other music. He is able either through the repetition of a single sound or through the continued performance of a single sound for a period like twenty minutes, to bring it about that after, say, five minutes I discover that what I have all along been thinking was the same thing is not the same thing after all, but full of variety. I find his work remarkable almost in the same sense that the change in experience of seeing is when you look through a microscope.[13]

Conrad's own interest harks back first to "slowly and carefully" negotiating the special tunings and timbres on his violin required in the playing the *Mystery Sonatas* of the seventeenth-century composer Heinrich Ignaz Franz Biber: "The slower and more exquisitely in tune I played the Biber sonatas, the more they sang out. My body merged with the body of the violin; our resonances melted together in rich dark colors, harsh bright headlights. Slower, slower."[14] The one source many had in common was that of classical Indian music. While different people found different things in the music, Conrad "focused upon the intersection of intonation, slow playing, and intervallic (rather than harmonic) listening"[15] and found support for his inadvertent droning on the Biber pieces.

The sustained tones performed within the Theatre of Eternal Music became an occasion for listening *inside* the sounds, in the sense of one's envelopment within the sound and in the sense of the attention paid to "microscopic" subtleties of the sounds that had hitherto gone unheard. Conrad describes his experience in this way:

I played two notes together at all times, so that I heard difference tones vividly in my left ear. The major second, as a consonant interval, has a very deep difference tone, three octaves below the sounded tones. Any change in the pitch of either of the two notes I played would be reflected in a movement of the pitch of the difference tone—but the difference tone would move eight times as fast as the actual pitches. I spent all of my playing time working on the inner subtleties of the combination tones, the harmonics, the fundamentals, and their beats—as microscopic changes in bow pressure, finger placement and pressure, etc., would cause shifts in the sound.[16]

Within the context of the group it became necessary to amplify Conrad's violin (and other instruments) to compete with Young's saxophone, just as it became necessary to amplify the sounds so the audience itself could dwell inside the sounds, feel the ubiquity, and discern the subtleties. Amplification became privileged because it meant that it was "no longer necessary to press upon groaning mechanical instrumentation to produce the terrific power and sonority necessary for dealing with partial complexity and without shattering the all-important sound—the throbbing reverberance that has fixed musical attention on consonance and formal design."[17]

There is some similarity here with Cage's amplification of small sounds. However, whereas Cage amplified small sounds to establish their presence, which may or may not have been loud, he was not interested in amplification as a means to divulge the contents or become immersed in its environment. On the other hand, Conrad, Young, and others turned up the volume to hear *inside* musical sounds and establish a common space of auditive being for both the musicians and the audience. Indeed, despite a philosophy founded on the shift of utterance to audition, from musical composition to musical listening, Cage's use of amplification to introduce small sounds into musical materiality conforms more readily to a musical logic of utterance than does Conrad's stress on very close *listening*. Perhaps this is why Conrad still had room to say that a "route out of the modernist crisis was to move away from composing to LISTENING"[18] while being in such close vicinity to Cage. Another reason was that Conrad used amplification in an area Cage had famously feared to tread. Cage had *no feel for harmony*, as he first told his teacher Arnold Schönberg and then so many others afterward, and he launched his contestation of Western art music by placing rhythm over harmony.[19] Indeed, Cage saw harmony as one of the means Germanic orchestral music used to impose their importance by making sounds *big*. Conrad and Young instead worked within a very specific *telos* of Western art music where hearing harmonies would become hearing liminal harmonic phenomena. Perhaps this fact was what moved Cage to say that "La Monte Young's music can be heard by Europeans as being European."[20]

Apart from the Theatre of Eternal Music, a number of artists and composers in the early 1960s combined sustained sound and repeated sounds with loudness and amplification to hear features of sound masked in a momentary or singular incidence of the sound. The phasing involved in a sound might reveal itself only when that sound is sustained for a long time, as might the way a sound interacts with the acoustic properties of a particular site, and the internal acoustical workings of sound and the situa-tions in which it occurs become even more complex when a battery of psychoacoustical realities is taken into account. Cage had championed Erik Satie's *Vexations* (1893), but what was repeated in this composition was a set of organized sounds, where any attempt to comprehend a single sound had to contend with how that sound related to others. In contrast, Young's *Composition 1960 #7* (1960) instructs the player to hold a B and F sharp are held "for a long time," and in his *X for Henry Flynt* (1960) a *loud sound* is re-peated steadily every one to two seconds, a great number of times; 566 has been a popular choice since the premier of the scored version by Toshi Ichiyanagi in May 1961.[21] By subjecting the sounds completely to time, both pieces attempt to pull sounds out of time, to hold them still within time, so that the acoustical intricacies might be perceived. What would soon become evident is that *a sound* is in fact *many sounds*, arising from both acoustical and psychoacoustical vicissitudes, creating their own vari-ations and modulations of time, and, given time, evolving their own organ-ization often richer than any given musical structures through which they might be directed. This then is another passage through a Cagean man-date. By setting up a situation more faithful to *hearing a sound in itself* than Cage himself, it becomes evident that there could be no such thing as *a sound*. Any sound, once it has time to be heard, is plural.[22]

Loudness and amplification also provoked questions about the bodies, surroundings, and the agency of listeners. In nineteenth-century Western art music loudness was generated by the lungs and limbs of performers grouped together in massive numbers. Oscar Wilde wrote in *The Picture of Dorian Gray* (1891) that Wagner's music was so loud that people could talk to one another the entire time without bothering anyone. When Cage sat in D. T. Suzuki's class, however, Suzuki's soft-spoken words were drowned out by airplane noise, although Suzuki would continue unperturbed.[23] In the 1960s, the powerful means of amplification enforced an inability to speak and left the individual body performing in tandem with a new agency of sound, or so it was in the New Bohemia described by John Gruen:

Sound, used to envelop the listener physically, becomes a manufactured envi-ronment. Having a quiet chat in even the remotest corner of the largest disco-theque is like attempting a conversation under water. Indeed, the entire notion

of amplification may be looked upon as a vehicle of assault on habitual response based on "who" you are, verbally. The self must now be defined in
physical action, but it is no longer the embrace of a dancing partner that defines the physical self. Since amplified sound touches all, equally, partners need
not embrace while dancing; sound becomes the *real* partner.[24]

The loudness that silenced speech could also be used to stifle the body.
With enough amplification any performance space could be turned into a
resonant chamber, much like a body of a very large instrument in which
humans are played. And just as there may be imperfections or loose parts
of an instrument, so too human bodies may prove to be too loose. During
a highly amplified La Monte Young concert at *Documenta 5*, it was not
people talking in the audience that disturbed him but people moving. He
stopped the performance to berate two people who had begun to move
with the music and explained later that he needed to set an example to
instruct people on the discipline needed for listening: "Otherwise, there'll
be people rolling around and doing all sorts of things. You see any movement in space moves the air and moves the frequency. And we're trying to
get the frequencies in tune and they're moving the air, so we can't hear."[25]
The space of Cage's *4′33″*—in which the performer remained silent while
the audience attended to environmental sounds, including the sounds of
their own making—had been returned to the type of proscriptions in place
at symphony concerts, with performers who were now louder than any big
sound composition in the repertoire.

Loudness brought awareness to bodies in a new way, but this did not
prevent them from being suppressed. Nor could protection from injury
be assumed, as the onset of deafness among a number of musicians who
reveled in loudness during the 1960s has demonstrated. Loudness is ultimately governed by injury, and in this way, the body refuses to indiscriminately allow *all sound*. This has crucial implications for Cage, since his
philosophy was dependent on the idea of all sound. A discourse on loudness, big sounds, and amplification can be culled from Cage's writings, but
it assumes a much lesser position than that supporting small sounds. While
attending a concert by the Spanish experimental group Zaj, Cage tried his
best to be impartial toward loud sounds, to let them be themselves even if
they were dangerous:

Some people object to loud sounds. They're afraid of hurting their ears. Once I had the opportunity to hear a very loud sound (the conclusion of a Zaj performance). I'd been in the audience the evening before. I knew when the sound was coming. I moved close to the loudspeaker from which it was to be heard and sat there for an hour, turning first one ear and then the other toward it. When it stopped, my ears were ringing. The ringing continued through the night, through the next day, and through the next night. Early the following day I made an appointment with an ear specialist. On my way to his office, the ringing seemed to have more or less subsided. The doctor made a thorough examination, said my ears were normal. The disturbance had been temporary. My attitude toward loud sounds has not changed. I shall listen to them whenever I get the chance, keeping perhaps a proper distance.[26]

For Cage loud sounds like small ones were first of all objects to be discovered, but there was a difference. Small sounds were to be detected through a supple direction of attention and more often using technological means, whereas loud sounds were to be *found* through a peripatetic trek that would place him in the vicinity of a loud sound. Small sounds were absolutely everywhere; loud sounds dwelled in certain locations and drew Cage himself in their direction, as if by gravitational pull of their mass. Loud sounds did not need Cage to detect or emancipate them because they were the rulers of their own presence and reigned over their own space.

There was a difference in how Cage discovered loud sounds experientially and how he discovered them rhetorically. When he actually confronted loud sounds, the limits of *all sound* were enforced by the physiological limits of the body, whereas thinking about them knew no such limits. More important, Cage discovered loud sounds through the auspices of small sounds, and because his mature notion of silence was tied to the fate of small sounds, loud sounds were a by-product and afterthought in the development of his thought. As we have seen, through the detection of small sounds in the anechoic chamber he certified that silence was not constituted by an absence but consisted of *all* and *always sound.* His longstanding concern for amplification was directed first of all toward hearing small sounds and not toward making loud sounds (in contrast to Conrad, who used loud sounds as a practical way to hear small sounds). Because small sounds were ever-present in vibrating matter, they were best suited to imagining a pervasive state for sound, while loud sounds were fixed to specific locations and too attached to actions and the quotidian to contribute rhetorically to his cosmology of sound.

There is an architectural and scientific aspect to this issue based on the remarkable fact that Cage defined the respective parameters of audibility on visits to two specialized rooms used in acoustical research. On the smallest end of the scale was his well-documented visit to the anechoic chamber, but the room on the loudest end of the scale is not as well known, with neither Cage nor commentators on Cage making much of the visit:

I have always sought out loud sounds, when I can find them, and I have asked people to make them louder . . . and most people run away from those situations. They put their fingers in their ears or protect themselves, something like that. I didn't find it necessary. The loudest one I think I heard was in a research center for architecture near London. They had a reverberation chamber, and I was able to hear very low sounds very, very loud. And I kept indicating I wanted it louder; finally, it was as though I was being massaged by the sound. It was quite a marvelous experience. Because the Japanese aesthetician, when I talked to him about hearing with the ears, you know, he said, "Remember that one can also hear with his feet."[27]

It is not surprising that he would set the parameters of audibility on visits to specialized listening spaces. Western art music still has its concert halls, which pride themselves on their acoustical design, and ever since *Imaginary Landscape No. 1* (1939) Cage had used the radio studio as a space of sound production. His early hopes for an experimental music studio demonstrate an affinity to the *bona fide* scientific spaces of the anechoic and reverberation chambers. The main difference is that Cage used the two scientific spaces to listen to and not to produce or refrain from producing sounds *(4'33")*. What he heard were sounds bereft of a natural habitat, in chambers that ensured isolation and deracination. These were, in other words, sounds fully conducive to musical materiality and occurring in spaces tuned to the tasks of the concert hall: the imposed silence of the anechoic chamber, the controlled sound of reverberation chamber.

However, even when granted their scientific and musical neutrality, the rooms were disproportionately weighted, and they opened up to very different places: the floor plan looked less like rooms balanced at either end of a long corridor than a black hole of small sounds pulling a dispersed mass of loud sounds into their infinite domain. The anechoic chamber housed the promise of panaurality, opening up far beyond the finitude of human perception and its prostheses, to the mythic realm of a pervasive and inaudible sound. Because of it he could write, "Many doors are now open (they open according to where we give our attention). Once through, looking back, no wall or doors are seen. Why was anyone for so long closed in? Sounds one hears are music."[28] Its hypersilence belied its role as an expansionist technology. While the anechoic chamber led absolutely everywhere, the reverberation chamber led nowhere. Its salient feature was its controlled preclusion of injury, and such control contradicted Cagean indeterminacy and acted to delimit the diapason of all sound.

All was appeased because the room turned out to be a massage parlor. The irony, of course, is that loudness, by exerting pressure on the whole body, might better quell the thinking that exerts pressure on the preferred areferentiality of musical listening, just as it had proven to drown out that type of sound so readily inhabited by meaning: speech. And would not loudness serve well as one of the emphatic sounds in modernism that begged the end of representation? Or would massages conjure a different thoughtfulness, one pertaining to the very body toward which Cage and Western art music generally have been indisposed? This would not only invite the vissicitudes of meat (as discussed in part 5), but it would also bring into play all three sounds of Cage's body inside the anechoic chamber—the low sound, the high sound, and the inner speech interrogating the two—and the contemplation in the resonance chamber of an entire body given over to aurality. How might have Cage's music evolved if he had listened with his whole body and not just listened to it? And how might his music evolved if small sounds too had their version of the finitude, bereft of technological promise, a finitude that frustrated the totalizing reach of all sound?

Conceptual Sounds

Fluxus also focused on small sounds. However, whereas Cage carried the promise of technology forward to the point where there was no such thing as silence, where inaudibility was impossible and all matter was sonorous, Fluxus played at the delicate threshold of audibility and then edged over into a liminality of conceptual dimensions whose impossibility was left to flourish in its own right. In other words, both Cage and Fluxus dealt in both real and imaginary sounds, in actual and impossible audibility, but Cage's denial of the imaginary and impossible committed him ultimately to time-honored myth of nondissipation and panaurality, while the embrace of the conceptual by Fluxus led to new art and poetics.

Audibility, for those who wonder, is usually the absolute minimum required for music to exist. Jean-Jacques Nattiez has written, for example, that "we can . . . allow (without too much soul-searching) that sound is a minimal condition of the musical fact."[29] It depends, of course, what one thinks is a sound, a fact, a soul and how one might search for each. What if an action presented within a musical setting produces both barely audible and inaudible sounds? La Monte Young's *Composition 1960 #2* (1960), "which consists of simply building a [small] fire in front of the audience,"[30] does precisely this. Would the fact of audible sound cease to exist when the action that produced it continued without interruption? Would what one thought and interpolated at this brink of audibility come into play with the music, or would music reside intracranially, going in and out of existence depending on the fluctuations of acoustics, physiology and cognition? Young's *Composition 1960 #5* (1960) pushes the question further, pursuing it over the edge of plausible audibility:

Turn a butterfly (or any number of butterflies) loose in the performance area.

When the composition is over, be sure to allow the butterfly to fly away outside.

The composition may be any length, but if an unlimited amount of time is available, the doors and windows may be opened before the butterfly is turned loose and the composition may be considered finished when the butterfly flies away.[31]

Young "felt certain the butterfly made sounds, not only with the motion of its wings but also with the functioning of its body and . . . unless one was going to dictate how loud or soft the sounds had to be before they could be allowed into the realms of music . . . the butterfly piece was music as much as the fire piece."[32] Young asked from the audience a moment of interspecies empathy and assumed that sounds exist for butterflies even though humans are unable to hear them unaided. It did not occur to Young to *busy himself microphonically*, as Cage suggested, let alone to confront the problems presented by the butterfly's fragility and mobility, although the plausibility of sound would suggest a recourse to technology was not out of the question.

But what if the first reflex were toward a poetical disposition (which might include a poetical disposition toward technology), where inaudibility was embraced, not denied, and remedied through the promise of technology? Take, for example, Yoko Ono's word score *TAPE PIECE III/Snow Piece* (1963):

Take a tape of the sound of the snow
falling.
This should be done in the evening.
Do not listen to the tape.
Cut it and use it as strings to tie
gifts with.
Make a gift wrapper, if you wish, using
the same process with a phonosheet.[33]

There is some indication that Ono might have derived her sound of snow during the night from Hakuin, the Zen master greatly appreciated amid the ranks of Fluxus, reading him in Japanese or as it was cited in D. T. Suzuki's *Living by Zen* (1949):

How I would have them hear,
In the woods of Shinoda,
At an old temple,
When the night is deepening,
The sound of the snow-fall![34]

Or she may have known of the radio piece written by Milan Knizak, the Czech Fluxus artist, consisting of the instructions "Snowstorm is broadcast," but she really needed no prompting to be astonished by the acoustical effects of snow falling. It is a sound of blanketing bereft of warmth, a massive field of intense activity that is oddly quiet, and because the accumulation of snow acts to absorb sounds and the minute crystalline structure of snow flakes breaks up sound waves at their own scale, it becomes progressively quieter as the snow mutes itself. Ono's score further muffles the snowfall by situating it at night, which, in most places, brings by itself a relaxation of the sound of human and other animal activity and in combination with snowfall, especially a new one, will subdue things further. The resulting calm is conducive to observation and self-observation—to humans listening to the sounds not of their own making and to the imagined sounds of their own thoughts. Indeed, the irony of snow falling is that it produces the conditions for listening closely but then absorbs the sounds that might be heard. But it will do nothing to the raucousness generated when one acknowledges that sounds will necessarily result from one object colliding with another (no two snowflakes are alike), just as Cage imagines that molecular vibrations will necessarily create a sound. Because the snowstorm fills the sky with impending action and covers the ground with its aftermath, there must be something happening in between. If the sky was the upper eyelid and the earth the lower, the deafening sound would explain the resultant silence:

Wink Talk
An intensity of a wink is:
two cars smashed head on.
A storm turned into a breeze.
A water drop from a loose faucet.[35]

Ono's *TAPE PIECE III/Snow Piece* involves much more than trying to listen, even though she has employed and displayed the technology of listening. She has actually employed a technology one imagines and a technology one ignores. Assume for a moment an impossible transparency of audiophonic technology: a saturation of mikes, a mix customized to each eventual listener's closely studied expectations, no noise in the signal, indeed no signal at all but a technology that stores and channels original vibrations without depletion or transformation due to interaction with surfaces, densities of medium, or other vibrations. A tape recording is made of falling snow using such technology and then ignored. Ono's score instructs the recordist not to listen to it because it is the best way to ensure its accuracy.

Finally, Ono's score overlays a person's relationship to the environment with a relationship to other people. A refusal to listen complements both the silence of the imagined sound of snow falling and the silences involved in the very act of gift giving. Whatever else can be said about gift giving, something is always left unsaid. Although speech may revolve around the act, the delicacy of the gesture, especially in Ono's score, acts to absorb the sound waves of speech. When the audiotape is used as ribbon, the environment of snow falling lies covertly inscribed along the length of the tape in patterns resembling the loops of the bow. The spatial volume of the environment is warped in time and space as it follows the loops of a bow and is condensed, immersing the object being given in the ambience of the gesture. Whatever may be the case, it seems at least that the concentrated figure of a massive field of an already progressively muted activity collapsed onto a silent surface, no matter how cold the original, reproduces the emotional warmth of the silences involved in gift giving. There is no denial that silence exists. On the contrary, there is an acknowledgment of a multitude of silences. The same holds true for many of Yoko Ono's word scores and those of Dick Higgins, George Brecht, Takehisa Kosugi, Mieko Shiomi, Alison Knowles, Bengt af Klintberg, Thomas Schmit, and other Fluxus artists. Hers was a silence that grew from poetics and philosophy, not from the techniques of music: "I think of my music more as a practice (*gyo*) than a music. The only sound that exists to me is the sound of the mind. My works are only to induce music of the mind in people."[36]

Water Flows and Flux

1952. After Jackson Pollock stopped dripping, John Cage started pouring. During the late 1940s, Pollock began to drip and pour paint over canvases laid flat on the ground—he explained why in his brief statement "My Painting" published in 1948—and stopped dripping and pouring in 1952. *Water Music* (1952), Cage's first work to move "towards theater from music,"[1] included among its forty-one events a duck whistle blown into a bowl of water and two receptacles for receiving and pouring water. Historically, *Water Music* fell within the avant-garde strategy in which extramusical sounds were used to reinvigorate Western art music: "I included sounds that were, just from a musical point of view, forbidden at that time. You could talk to any modern composer at the time and no matter how enlightened he was he would refuse to include banal musical sounds."[2] Cage had also "somewhere gotten the notion that the world is made up of water, earth, fire, etc. and I thought that water was a useful thing to concentrate on,"[3] so he "made a list of things involving water that would be theatrical . . . subjected it all to chance and composed it."[4]

Pollock's dripped and poured paintings and Cage's water sounds heralded a larger concurrence of fluidity, water, sound, and performance—the dissolution of media at midcentury in New York, which continued across the arts internationally for years to come. More immediately, it formally announced a period increasingly concerned with the ephemeral within practices where objects once reigned, a period of progressive dissolution of disciplinary constraints, and a flow of art into life and vice versa. This font welled up during the 1950s and spilled over to the next generation of artists, who, noisy, wet, and performative, came from many disciplinary and media backgrounds and worked at the interstices of many more. Many were interested in the ideas of Cage. Allan Kaprow and George Brecht—two visual artists whose names came to be closely identified with the new performance modes known as happenings and events, respectively—are not normally identified with sounds but were both responsible for innovative approaches to it. Prior to their links with Cage in the latter half of the 1950s, however, many of the same ideas of fluidity, noise, performance, disciplinary and media breakdown, and chance had already been introduced during the first half of the decade within the orbit of the ideas surrounding Pollock's work. In effect, what had washed over them were tendencies larger than both Pollock and Cage.

To notice an outpouring of this complex of water and fluidity, performance and sound, presumes a previous period that was dry, rigid, inactive, and silent. Such a period, of course, did not exist; programmatic water, metaphorical flows, performed objects, and all types of sounds had been everywhere in evidence. What did exist, however, was a scarcity of sounds made from actual water. This may seem like an insignificant distinction, yet only with the historical incidence of actual water did fluidity suddenly become implicated in the widespread dissolution of objects. In chapter 9 I present a mute desiccated modernism and then in chapter 10 show how a soundful, wet, late modernism developed among the concerns of the visual arts and music, specifically, Pollock and Cage, Kaprow and Brecht, and others in the orbit of midcentury New York. In the process of negotiating the relationship between and after Pollock and Cage, it will also be necessary to take time to challenge readings of the 1950s that elevate their antagonism to an historical plane or, rather, two distinct historical planes. In sum, this part simply proposes that after Pollock, in the wake of dripping the sound of actual water would come to signal a greater saturated and fluid state within the late-modernist arts and that the real event of 1952 should be characterized as the point at which water flowed from the liquidity of paint and spilled into the materials and techniques of the following decades. If we were to continue to divine water in the arts, it would necessarily invoke an ecological self-consciousness, including the nature of the body, where materials and techniques themselves become political.

A SHORT ART HISTORY OF WATER SOUND

Water Music

Water flowed in the arts prior to midcentury, of course, but it was restricted almost entirely to programmatic, depicted, or discursive water: water music, water scenes, water talk. A simple act, Cage's *Water Music* irrevocably introduced water sounds from actual water into Western art music, which, unlike many other musics around the world, was dry and slow to irrigate. There was water water everywhere in program music, but no one got wet. There were other water musics, but as Cage characterized his *Water Music* in a letter to Nicolas Slonimsky, "unlike Handel's, it really splashes."[1] The normal instruments of a symphony orchestra were ill suited to simulating water, and claims otherwise (such as Berlioz claiming a *tremolo* near the bridge of a violin resembled the sound of a powerful waterfall) were exaggerated for effect. The odd ancient or modern instrument utilizing water was never called into regular orchestral duty, while pooling within the opaque plumbing of the brass instruments formed a suppressed subterranean lake of orchestral saliva to be politely discharged like other bodily substances. During a 1965 interview Cage focused on this discrete sibilating vent in terms of performance and not on the sound: "Even a conventional piece played by a conventional symphony orchestra [is a theatrical activity]: the horn player, for example, from time to time empties the spit out of his horn. And this frequently engages my attention more than the melodies."[2] Vladimir Mayakovsky did hope in 1918 to "make the ocean waves pluck at strings stretched from Europe to America,"[3] but the revolution that was to herald this organological innovation never completely materialized, even though there has developed over more recent times a whole genre of (shorter) long-stringed instruments.[4]

Discursive water, at least since Romanticism, has flowed much more freely, albeit in the harmonic gushes that repulsed Cage. As Wagner wrote in *Art of the Future,* "We must not yet abandon our image of the sea for the nature of musical art. If rhythm and melody are the shores on which music touches and fertilizers the two continents of the arts that share its origin, then sound is its liquid, innate element; but the immeasurable extent of this liquid is the sea of harmony. The eye recognizes only the surface of this sea: only the depths of the ear understand its depths."[5] With Wagner's link with harmony, nearly all attributes of music at one time or another have been ascribed to figures and forms of water.[6]

There has been a long-standing association of water and sound in observational acoustics from antiquity through Chaucer to Helmholtz and beyond, with the sound of a stone hitting water producing a visual counterpart, which was then mapped back onto the invisible movements of sound waves. Russolo was, as we have already seen, the one to cast the first stone when he shook the boat atop the acousticians' water and formally launched noise into Western art music. He felt that water represented "in nature the most frequent, most varied, and richest source of noises,"[7] and as he did with other noises of the world, he incorporated them into music through the category of timbre and then specified them further using other musical attributes. Although he called one of his intonarumori a *gurgler,* his own disavowal of imitation failed to prevent one sympathetic listener from hearing in his music the rustling of "the sea in summer"[8] and another from hearing "a flood of water washing the town, children crying and girls laughing under the refreshing shower."[9] Likewise, there was no way to prevent one antagonistic critic in London from describing a concert as "the sounds heard in the rigging of a Channel-steamer during a bad crossing."[10] He managed to hold off imitation well into the 1920s when, in the developing force field of sound cinema, he promoted his instrument the *psofarmoni* (1924) replete with a "Second Register: imitates the water and the rain."[11] For that other musical figure of worldly sound, Henry Cowell, water was one of the sources of sounds generating the characteristic sliding tones of nature, and Percy Grainger began his obsession with glissandi as a young boy watching the waves in the waters of Victoria.

The use of actual water entered twentieth-century Western art music through percussion—specifically, percussion tuned by water, or *wet percus-*

sion. The first notable use of wet percussion was Erik Satie's use of the *boutelliphone* (a series of tuned bottles suspended from a rack, "a poor man's glockenspiel") in *Parade* (1918).[12] Satie may have followed Russolo in the avant-garde incorporation of noise, but he was nonetheless the wettest composer of the time, aided no doubt by sporting the driest sense of humor. In fact, the ground for wet percussion was first softened by his satirical writing "Water Music" (1914), in which he incorporated water sounds into the field of percussion and noise—the percussion associated with military music, the Italian Futurist noise associated with militarism, the programmatic percussion used in Wagner:

The mysterious frontiers which separate the domain of noise from that of music tend more and more to be obliterated. With a growing satisfaction, musicians annex for themselves these unknown territories so rich in sonorous surprises. The expansion given to the percussion by the most audacious of our modern orchestrators is, in this regard, quite characteristic. The percussive artillery expands from day to day in our instrumental armies. And witness how nature takes an interest in our musical games and can take part in our concerts. "The organs of the earth" of which the Taoist Louis Laloy speaks have gradually come to an agreement to permit that Stravinsky reserve a staff in their scores in the future. The elements take their A from our tuning fork. The hydrographic engineers tell us that all the waterfalls of the earth, whatever their social standing might be, yield a low F, clearly audible, upon which it so happens is built a perfect chord in C Major. What a marvelous resource! What a great contribution to open air festivals. What a beautiful natural pedal for the prelude—transposed—to *Das Rheingold* performed in Schaffausen, next to the *Rheinfall.* . . . The Water Company is elated: it is going to install carefully calibrated conduits in all the concert halls to offer musicians an entire chromatic scale of little cascades. How soon the first concert for two faucets obbligato and orchestra?[13]

Just the year before he had begun to edge into water on the backs of some its smallest inhabitants. *Embryons desséchés* (1913) (Dried-up embryos) (referring perhaps to the embryonic appearance of dried shrimp) was his composition known for its satirical take on the bravado of the final cadences of such works as Beethoven's Fifth Symphony. It also contains one of his most famous performance marks, "like a nightingale with a toothache." Its three parts are themselves named after little sea creatures—Holothuria, Edriophthalma, and Podolphthalma—and his notes inform us that Holothuria purr like cats and Edriophthalma have sad dispositions (in a similar vein, later in life while in Paris Kandinsky moved from the musical links of his earlier canvases to microscopic watery creatures). He invokes more voluminous commitments in his *Sports et Divertisements* (1914), where one can find "The Water Chute," "Fishing," and "Sea Bathing," all of which contain programmatic waters of one type or another. The American television comedian Ernie Kovacs summed it up perhaps when he set the life span of a drop of water to music by Satie.

Noise and percussion combined nowhere more noticeably than in Henry Cowell's *tone clusters*, a technique for playing clusters and expanses of keys on the piano with hands, fists, and forearms, and water was nearby. One story of how he formed the technique involved the waters of *The Tides of Manaunaun* (1912), which he composed at age fifteen for an outdoor pageant on Irish creation myths. The clusters were meant to depict the mystic waves of Manaunaun, the god of waters, as he brought order out of chaos. As one person described the tone clusters in action, they were "calm, ponderous, leisurely thundering waves and rumbling drumming accompaniment." Actual water entered his music when he used "8 Rice Bowls" tuned to no definite pitch using water for *Ostinato Pianissimo (For Percussion Band)* (1934). An avid student of world music, Cowell mentions in the score that the instrument had been derived from the Indian *jalatarang*, which literally means "water waves."[14] (He would later write that Cage's prepared piano reminded him of the jalatarang.[15]) As wet percussion, Cowell's instrument still negotiated realms of sound between music and noise in favor of music. His use of water-tuned bowls drew from three musical sources of noise—the noise of the other in world music, the resident noise of percussion, and the extramusical noise of water—yet in operation these noises acted against one another. In particular, percussion already acted at the time as an intermediary with the noisy world that water inhabited, while water ameliorated the noise of percussion by making it tonal. In other words, wet percussion was watered-down noise.

The same held true, with an important difference, for other water percussion occurring in the United States during the 1930s. In 1936 Cowell, in the *New Music Orchestra Series*, published several percussion works written over the previous three years by other composers that involved water or fluid-related instruments, including the water-tuned musical tumblers in Harold Davidson's *Auto Accident,* a bottle to be broken and a triangle stick on a ginger ale bottle in William Russel's *Three Dance Movements,* and rubber-covered sticks on pop bottles in Ray Green's *Three Inventories of Casey Jones.*[16] The bottles in these pieces (and in Harry Partch's instruments) and the water-tuned tumblers of *Auto Accident* were examples of wet percussion, even though some may have been in the spirit of the boutelliphone in a dry way.

However, in the intervening years between Satie's 1918 boutelliphone and its 1930s variants there was an important cultural shift in aurality associated with improved phonography, radio, sound film, and animated cartoons that brought about a different the approach to wet percussion evidenced in Davidson's *Auto Accident,* a work replete with sound effects. Beginning with Jovis Ivens's film *Regen* (Rain) from 1929, it started to rain and gush and gurgle on film, leaky faucets taunted cartoon creatures equipped with new types of hydrophones, reports from dramatic characters were transmitted from ships in distress, ocean waves were finally reunited with their programmatic progeny in music, which became ever more faithful in their mimicry, and so on. Communications media blended water sounds into a rich semiotic broth, mixing programmatic musical scores, timbral allusions, mechanically or physiologically generated theatrical imitations and other sound effects, recorded sounds and noises, discursive citations (such as a title or a verse from a song about water), as they became arrayed in common against narrative and imagistic elements. The arts and communications media found it easy to tap one another for sources of water.

Cage's first formal use of water came in his collaboration with Lou Harrison, *Double Music* (1941), in which Cage specified the use of a "water gong (small—12"–16" diameter—Chinese gong raised or lowered into tub of water during production of tone)." Harrison said that by the time they began working on the piece, the use of water was a well-accepted compositional device in percussion music and that it was Henry Cowell who had earlier encouraged Cage and himself to use non-Western and "junk instruments."[17] Cage instead traces his use of the water gong to 1937 at UCLA, where, acting as an accompanist, he sought a solution to the problem of providing musical cues to water ballet swimmers when their heads were underwater.[18] Water was again used for the tuning percussion, but the roles had been reversed: water was no longer contained in the instrument, but now the instrument was contained in the water. The tuning was not fixed but fluctuated when played, just as with other forms of wet percussion, but there was less control and predictability, more given over to the whims of the water from one stroke to the next. Water produced a variability within percussion that, as Cage understood in retrospect, was already characterized by variability. Thus, an inability to control pitch was added to the already noisy status of percussion. Most important, water produced the most marked instance of the variability that "prepared me for the renunciation of intention and the use of chance operations."[19] The material flows and turbulence of water and fluidity in general would, as we shall see, be called on during the 1950s to drain subjectivity from performers and other creators.

Cage's first mention of a use of water sounds in music occurred within "The Future of Music Credo" (1937, same year as the water ballet gong), where he included the sound of rain as one of the sounds that could be "captured and controlled" by means of film phonographs and other technological devices.[20] After the use of the water gong in *Double Music* (1940), he broke the link between water and percussion with *Water Music* (1952). It included among its events a duck whistle blown into a bowl of water, which recalled the tell-tale exhaust bubbles of his father's failed submarine design.[21] Cage composed the related work *Water Walk: For Solo Television Performer* (1959) for performance on an Italian television quiz show. The water-related instructions and properties are numerous and include a bathtub of water, an operating pressure cooker, a supply of ice cubes, a garden sprinkling can, a soda syphon, and many other objects.[22] Here the vaudeville and novelty music influences become obvious. During one performance of his *0′00″* (1962), he placed a contact microphone on his throat and drank a glass of water. One person remembered the swallow reverberating through the performance space "like the pounding of giant surf."[22] *Solo for Voice 83* from the *Song Books* (1970) repeats this same action, with the substitution of cognac for water. Contact microphones were also used to amplify the small sounds circulating inside the internal caverns of large conches in *Inlets* (1977). Cage produced other wet compositions, at times quite unplanned, as with the first performance of *4′33″* in Woodstock, New York, when it began to rain during the second movement.

Dripping

Musical water also appeared in literature and other artistic writing, a fine example being that of the huge white worm that dripped heavy water onto a zither found in Raymond Roussel's novel *Impressions of Africa* (1910). Having noticed the musical fascination demonstrated by the worm, which lived in a spring with water of unusual viscosity and weight, it occurred to the Hungarian musician Skariofszky that he could teach it how to play the zither. First he built a contraption consisting of a long trough made out of mica and clay propped up by branches above the zither. The worm, set in the trough, blocked an open groove running the length of the trough along the bottom:

Equipped with a gourd, it did not take him long to draw a few quarts of water from the spring and pour them into the transparent sluice. Subsequently, with the end of a twig, he lifted for a quarter of a second, a minute portion of the extended body. A drop of water escaped and struck a zither string which gave out a clear note.[23]

Skariofszky raised the worm's body in a succession of notes; the worm responded by twitching out the same phrase unassisted and then went on to display a remarkable memory by learning "various lively or melancholy Hungarian tunes" with great ease. It also learned to secrete two notes at once, and "In the end, multiplying the difficulties, Skariofszky tied a long twig to each of his ten fingers and taught the worm polyphonic acrobatics normally excluded from his own repertory."[25] This mnemonic worm was the ancestor of the mechanical musics of Hindemith and Nancarrow and of audiotape drip pieces such as Hugh Le Caine's *Dripsody: An Etude for Variable Speed Recorder* (1955) and Toru Takemitsu's *Water Music* (1960).[26] Drops of water were conducive to music because they could comfortably assume musical speeds and were amenable to total organization by the composer. It may come as a surprise, however, to what extent drops, to qualify as musical material, were required to avoid sonic impurities by shedding even the most minute fluctuations, the slightest palpitations on the skin of a drop of water. Take, for instance, Hugh Le Caine's description of the process for culling the material for his tape composition *Dripsody:*

A metal waste-basket was filled to a depth of two inches with water and water was allowed to drop from an eye-dropper held at a level of about ten feet from the basket. A microphone was placed in the basket, insulated from the water by a plastic cover. . . . From a one-half hour tape, the sound a single drop was chosen. Some of the sounds had wavering pitch which gave the drop a gurgling sound; others had pitch glides of over an octave. To simplify the problem of composition, the simplest and most formless sound was chosen, although the drops with complicated pitch changes were passed over with great regret.[27]

The music of less domesticated dripping could be found in the untamed wilds of the home wherever there was a leaky tap, its unpredictable pitches and rhythms effectively the equivalent of the book of nature read aloud. Aldous Huxley, by pondering this quotidian profundity in "Water Music" (1920), anticipated the importance of dripping water in Fluxus and, later, in chaos theory:

Drip drop, drip drap drep drop. So it goes on, this water melody for ever without an end. Inconclusive, inconsequent, formless, it is always on the point of deviating into sense and form. Every now and again you will hear a complete phrase of rounded melody. And then—drip drop, di-drep, di-drap—the old inconsequence sets in once more. But suppose there were some significance to it! It is that which troubles my drowsy mind as I listen at night. Perhaps for those who have ears to hear, this endless dribbling is as pregnant with thought and emotion, as significant as a piece of Bach. Drip-drop, di-drap, di-drep. So little would suffice to turn the incoherence into meaning. The music of the drops is a symbol and type for the whole universe; it is for ever, as it were, asymptotic to sense, infinitely close to significance but never touching it. Never, unless the human mind comes and pulls it forcibly over the dividing space.[28]

Kurt Schwitters's tap was less erratic, beating out a rationalistic universe in the plans for his Merz theater that called for "a water pipe [that] drips with uninhibited monotony."[29]

Dripping is a flow, marked by incipience and restraint. Can it be a surprise, therefore, that it becomes closely related to Marcel Duchamp's tight technical charting of libidinal plumbing and the general secretion of his hermeticism? With few exceptions, his complex relationship to water always tended toward the *closely dispensed;* only in the film *Entr'acte* does water pour all over his chess game. He liked America for her bridges and her plumbing, for these were things that kept him away from her flows, above the water, the flows channeled out of sight.[30] The libidinal plumbing of the "Bachelor Machine" of the *Large Glass* was supposed to lead, had it been finished, to a "Crash-Splash," and at one time the illuminating gas was to have congealed with spangles to take on a sedimented "condition resembling glycerine mixed with water" that would be "the only manifestation of the *individuality* (so reduced!) of the illuminating gas in its habitual games with conventional surroundings. What a drip!"[31]

Two of the found objects were water-related. Normal use for the *Bottle Rack* would have resulted in a veritable orchestra of dripping (it could also be understood as an expedient form of Tomas Schmit's *Zyklus*).[32] The thrice-desiccated *Fountain* (a fountain was brought indoors and set on its head; the water in both sets of plumbing—the fixture and the user [viewer]—was never connected) had the glory, among other things, to have christened the genitourological track within twentieth century art, a tradition which leads, as we shall see in the next chapter, to Pollock and beyond.[33] Duchamp made another contribution with his ejaculatory painting *Paysage fautif* (Wayward Landscape) included in a version of the *Boîte-en-valise* customized for Maria Martins) and also enlisted Rrose Sélavy to trade in *lazy hardware* in the form of an auditive faucet, a rigidly flacid phallus. "Among our articles of lazy hardware we recommend a faucet which stops dripping when nobody is listening to it."[34] *Lazy Hardware* was also the name he gave to the female mannequin with a faucet on her thigh constructed as part of a window display at the Gotham Book Mart in New York in 1945. One photo of Duchamp in front of the display shows him reflected in the window poised for phantom faucet fellation. There is a similarly erotic display among Salvador Dalí's watery pianos (following a pun on *piano à queue*/grand piano to *piano aqueux*) which render them gelatinous, as well as the snails that slowly slither over the female mannequin moistened by the constant drizzle inside his *Rainy Taxi* at the 1938 International Exposition of Surrealism in Paris.

Surrealism and Submerged Women

While Duchamp found the tap turned off on the mannequin in the window, the Surrealists and their forefather Raymond Roussel were remarkably consistent in portraying live women immersed in a concurrence of sound and water—in window displays, no less. First, there was Louis Aragon in *Le Paysan de Paris:*

Fancy my surprise when, attracted to the cane shop by a kind of mechanical drone which seemed to emanate from its display window, I saw the window suffused as if under water with a glaucous light, whose source remained hidden from view. It brought to mind the phosphorescence of fish, which I had had the chance to observe when a child on the jetty of Port-Bail in the Cotentin, but I was compelled to recognize that although canes may conceivably possess the luminous properties of sea creatures, no physical law seemed adequate to explain this preternatural light and especially the hollow noise filling the vault of the arcade. That noise I knew: it was the voice of seashells, which never fails to astound poets and film stars. The entire ocean here in the Passage de l'Opéra. The canes were gently swaying to and fro, like kelp. I hadn't yet recovered from this spell when I noticed a form swimming between the various strata of the display. She was slightly smaller than the average woman but in no way impressed one as dwarf-like.[35]

And then there was André Breton in "Soluble Fish," where ears become shells without having to divulge their cochlea:

We thus reached the city of Squirrel-by-the-Sea. There fishermen were unloading baskets full of earth-shells, with a great many ears among them, that stars circulating through the city were painfully cupping over their hearts to hear the sound of the earth. In this way they were able to reconstruct, to their pleasure, the noise of streetcars and great pipe organs, just as in our loneliness we seek out the sounds of levels under water, the purr of underwater elevators. We now belonged only to the despair of our song, to the sempiternal evidence of those words about the kiss. Very close to that spot we vanished, what's more, into a window display where the only thing the men and women showed was what is most generally visibly naked, that is to say, roughly, the face and the hands. One girl, however, was barefoot. We in turn put on the garments of the pure air.[36]

Finally, in Roussel's *Locus Solus,* a group on tour of the estate of the eccentric inventor Canterel come on a large diamond-shaped tank filled with a strangely radiant water:

In the center, a slender, graceful woman, in a flesh-colored costume, was standing upright on the bottom, completely submerged. Swaying her head gently from side to side, she struck many attitudes full of aesthetic charm. Her lips wore a gay smile and she seemed to be breathing freely in the liquid element which enveloped her on every side. Her superb head of blonde hair, hanging completely loose, had a tendency to swell above her, though without touching the surface. Each strand, surrounded by a kind of thin watery sheath, vibrated at her slightest movement as the layers of liquid rubbed against it; and the string thus formed gave forth a high or low note according to its length. This phenomenon explained the charming music we had heard on approaching the diamond. The skillful young woman produced it at will, expertly modulating its crescendos and diminuendos by varying the force and rapidity with which she oscillated her neck. The melodious rising and toppling of the scales, runs and arpeggios rippled over a compass of at least three octaves. Often, limiting herself to a slight and gentle rolling of her head, the performer remained confined within a very restricted register. Then, swaying her hips to impart an ample and continuous rotation to her bosom, she employed all the resources of her curious instrument, which then displayed its maximum range and volume. . . . The mysterious accompaniment ideally suited the young woman's sculptural poses, so that she seemed like some disturbing water-nymph. Because of the liquid medium in which the sounds were propagated, they had an extraordinarily plangent quality.[37]

What are we to make of all these women immersed in water? After taking LSD Anaïs Nin herself began to feel immersed in a fluid space as the doors, walls, and windows began liquefying: "It was as if I been plunged to the bottom of the sea, and everything had become undulating and wavering."[38] Through this experience she discovered *why women weep*: "IT IS THE QUICKEST WAY TO REJOIN THE OCEAN. You liquefy, become fluid, flow back into the ocean where the colors are more beautiful. . . . Everything is more wonderful underwater."[39] Similarly, when asked to explain her painting *Femme-pierre* (1938), Meret Oppenheim replied, "A stone woman is prevented from action but her legs are immersed in the stream. Which is to say it is a picture of contraries: sleeping stone and living waters. But she is not some ideal woman. . . . The stone is my inability to do any work, and the only really positive thing is the feet, which represent a connection with the unconscious."[40]

But that is the view from the inside; Roussel, Breton, and Aragon were on the outside looking in. Perhaps it was another instance of a male Surrealist gaze erotically relating the curves of a woman's body to waves or of transposing a kinaesthetic sense of undulation, the spirit of the undine, the gentle give and take of the flesh, floating immersed, buoyed against gravity, nonterrestrial, to the sight of water.[41] They would have been able to imagine the erotic nature of free-floating bodies through their own experiences at swimming and perhaps made an association with the amorous dances people are prone to do, accompanied by sets of sounds removed from the everyday that place them in another space. This was the intoxicated state of desire that formed part of the Surrealists' codification of the oneric, induced by a simple embrace or by the white noise heard in shells. Women become the cause and means of representation of an immersion within a psychological state, a dreamy state accompanied by the droning, modulating, oscillating sounds of gently swaying heads, hips, and canes, reminiscent of the magnetism Mesmer would invite through his use of Ben Franklin's armonica (glass harmonica). As Sibyl Marcuse tells us, "Before playing the Franklin harmonica, a performer thoroughly washed his or her hands. Then, after the rims of the glasses were moistened with a wet sponge, the glasses were set in rotation by the treadle, the rotation being toward the player. The tone quality of both musical glasses and harmonica was allegedly so enervating that Marianne Davies [the first concertizer with the instrument] had to abandon playing after four years, and it is said to have affected the nerves of many young ladies who were merely auditors."[42] Did Roussel, Aragon, and Breton know that Mesmer too was known for his abilities to sonically and psychically entrance his female clientele?[43]

Perhaps these men were gazing on and longing for their own former intrauterine immersion, their desire manifesting itself as nostalgia? That would be the view of woman as omniscient mother, harboring amniotic oceans. The vision of Georges Bataille, who would place the scene long before his mother's pregnancy, reserved a salient role for men in this evolutionary genesis. In "The Solar Anus" he described existence itself as an erotic product of the copula *to be*, in a world in which "air is the parody of water," exemplified in the movements of a coital sea:

Animal life comes entirely from the movement of the seas and, inside bodies, life continues to come from salt water.

The sea, then, has played the role of the female organ that liquifies under the excitation of the penis.

The sea continuously jerks off.

Solid elements, contained and brewed in water animated by erotic movement, shoot out in the form of flying fish.[44]

Intrauterine sound itself, of course, would relate to the vaunted maternal voice proffered in certain psychoanalytic scenarios. The sound would be a hydrologically filtered mother's voice promising the bliss of undifferentiation. However, the mother's voice in these internal matters are inexplicably privileged (fetal reading would allow recourse to textuality). There is clear evidence that external voices, music, and sounds are heard in the womb after a certain point of development and that the newborn can demonstrate a memory of these sounds. Moreover, all these voices and sounds would be heard on the constant backdrop of a full array of internal fluid sounds, although the constancy of the sound could not be equated with the sustained tones and drones, or mellifluousness associated with women and water. Then, of course, there are the intervening years of cultural code and the myriad voices of different women that would have to had developed and maintained unconscious contact with the primal fetal scene, whatever their social and historical setting might be.

However, when we move to the representation of women's voices in these three instances of immersion, what we find is that the voices are absent, supplanted by sounds as if in song or silent altogether, with sounds accompanying a dance of their presence, if not their actions. These women, in other words, have had their say in the matter dramatically reduced, both as mental and physical creatures, as occurs in many Surrealist texts and images. They are creatures after all, contained in a water in which creatures live, a water that man can live beside or on or gaze on, especially when the side of the sea is exposed as a fish tank posing as a window display. Man can imbibe this female brew into his psyche where it lives within him, but he cannot live within it; indeed, the actuality of women too is, like Ophelia, dead. The reduction of women's voice to sound is ostensibly redeemed by adoration, desire, and mesmerization. In his ambitious investigation of the concurrence of water and women in male texts, Klaus Theweleit looked back on a great number of instances not dissimilar from those above, except that his examples did not include a concurrence with sound. Even in these muted examples he notices too how water, fluidity, and flows were used to douse the spark of female agency. Theweleit finds "a specific (and historically relatively recent) form of the oppression of women—one that has been notably underrated. It is oppression through exaltation, through a lifting of boundaries, an 'irrealization' and reduction to principle—the principle of flowing, of distance, of vague, endless enticement. Here again, women have *no names*."[45]

The oceanic feeling that women instilled and the unconscious promised took on a distinctly global dimension on a scale that, as Sanford Kwinter reminds us, occurs on a predominantly water-covered planet misnamed as Earth.[46] But for the Surrealists, there was still, for their purposes, insufficient waters occupying the surface of the planet; more had to be found undisclosed. Oceans were suspect, in this regard, since blurry determinations of depth would have to be proffered. Instead, only the distinct separation of subterranean waters would suffice to construct the proper image of the unconscious. Thus, the oracular voice of the unconscious was no longer limited to the vented gases of the pneuma but was transformed to a spigot of oceans, in which to turn on was to invoke all. Aragon in his *Treatise on Style* (1928) traces the water of the unconscious from its discovery by Lautréamont to the effusive automatic speech of fellow Surrealist Robert Desnos during the *period of sleeps*. The typical reader of Lautréamont is understood by Aragon to be a worker who, digging into the earth, puts an ear to the bottom of his pit and hears

The ebb and flow of hidden waters, where everything merges. The listener rises. He will never forget this immense voice. . . . He will hail the abysmal mass, the foaming wide interior sea that flows beneath Paris as it flowed beneath Delphi. One and only meaning of the word Beyond, thou art in poetry, at that point where a Mediterranean of sounds awake. Completely. I remember a waterfall at the bottom of the grottoes. Someone I knew, a friend named Robert Desnos, was speaking. With the help of strange sleep he had discovered several secrets that had been lost to all. He was speaking. Well, what is called speaking. He spoke like no one speaks. The great common sea suddenly found itself in the room, which was any old room with its surprised utensils.[47]

The babbling of these subterranean waters was transmitted into the room through the buccal tap of a sleep-talking Desnos, as though he were but a puncture on the surface of the earth and of consciousness, tapping a universal consciousness. Desnos was such an avid *sleeper* that he eventually pressed the patience of his listeners too far, as evidenced by the episode when an intolerant Paul Eluard, to awaken Desnos, emptied a jug of water onto his chest, fighting water with water. It would be Artaud who would direct the unconscious, sound and an aqueous immersion into practical technique: "If dreams are the underside of life, if reality appears in dreams in a bewitching and magical form which the mind completely accepts, it is this nonillusory acceptance which I seek to force on the spectator. Thus, it is that in *The Cenci* the placing of the Loudspeakers maintains a public bath of sound, and a diffused storm *as* terrible [as the] volume [of an] authentic disturbance [a] natural storm."[48]

As one would suspect, water and fluidity insinuate themselves practically and discursively in a wide variety of ways within different artistic practices. It is the mimetic inclination of water to assume the shape of any vessel it occupies. Because of the different forms it already assumes, its powers of abstraction reach from the particularization of a drop to the atmospherics of humidity and immersion, from a brackish stagnancy to turbulence, from the pure linear figuration of waves to the chaotic mass of breaking waves. And in its relations to humans it can sustain life or destroy it. As we have already seen in chapter 1 with respect to the interpolation of water voices, it no wonder that Proteus, the old man of the sea, could assume so many disguises, and the same holds true for the use, interpolation, and interpretation of water sounds in general. Nevertheless, with our modest aim to demonstrate a technical distinction within the artistic uses of water and sound within the avant-garde and modernist traditions it remains that no matter how wet the soundful imaginations of writers were, the ink dried quickly on the page. Despite all the talk the use of actual water was kept to a trickle, and all the sounds doing discursive duty had yet to be heard.

IN THE WAKE OF DRIPPING:
NEW YORK AT MIDCENTURY

I am for an art that spits and drips.

Claes Oldenburg[1]

After Jackson Pollock stopped dripping, John Cage started pouring. The floodgates cracked open to a concurrence of sound, performance, and water and fluidity among the arts, a dissolution of disciplinary constraints and discrete bounds of the object, and an increased osmosis between art and life. The events of this concurrence did not flow in a chaotic manner, nor did they follow channels of influence usually attributed to Pollock and to Cage. Indeed, the plumbing of the postwar arts begins to look quite different. Rarely are Pollock and Cage considered in the same context, and when they are, they are often meant to represent two sides of a great divide of sensibility. It is true that Cage sincerely disliked Pollock. When asked by Lee Krasner to compose music for Hans Namuth's film on Pollock, Cage refused: "I couldn't abide Pollock's work because I couldn't stand the man." As Cage remembered, Pollock "was generally so drunk, and he was actually an unpleasant person for me to encounter. I remember seeing him on the same side of the street I was, and I would always cross over to the other side."[2] Whatever Cage's feelings may have been for Pollock and what he stood for, there were no sign of dislike, or even acknowledgment, in return. Pollock, after all, held center stage in the small artistic milieu of New York at midcentury where painting reigned, and his duel with Picasso for a place in history was no doubt more immediate to him than dealing with Cage on the street.

It is difficult to know what Pollock might have thought about a number of things since he was so reluctant to commit himself to print. Cage, on the other hand, was just beginning to produce the writings for which he would later become well known, and he trained his pen, in a very convoluted manner, on Pollock's famous short statement "My Painting" (1948). Cage no doubt felt compelled to distinguish himself from the artistic reign that Pollock typified, but he ran into some complications. Cage was enmeshed in the precepts of the same arts milieu of the late 1940s that produced Pollock, and to argue with him Cage was required to find the common ground on which a composer might argue with a painter and then to assert the priority for music in a milieu that so valued painting. Pollock's work, however, already drifted toward music. He said that his painting should be enjoyed "just as music is enjoyed"[3] (as had so many others within modernism). He explicitly incorporated performance, seemingly the province of music, into the object-oriented domain of painting, and many people associated Pollock's painting with jazz, as a pictorial and cultural complement and as improvisation. This did not deter Cage, who attempted to show that what was being championed in New York in the late 1940s was better achieved through music. In contrast to Cage's early resolve, during the 1950s many younger artists found the provocations of Pollock and Cage interchangeable. There were artists linked with Cage during the latter half of the 1950s who not only developed under the influence of Pollock but did so within areas commonly identified with Cage—noise, disciplinary and media breakdown, and chance—if not the performance and theatricality associated with his music.

This chapter discusses these two topics: the disciplinary drift in the terms Cage himself laid out in his response to Pollock—transience and stasis, performance and objecthood, the lived moment and recording—and the street-level reception of Pollock and Cage among younger artists, with a concentration on Allan Kaprow and George Brecht, at the heart of Happenings and Fluxus, respectively. It will also be shown that each time something was dislodged, it often sprung a leak or was swept along in another up-to-date current. At midcentury performance was imported into painting and dissolved the bounds of objecthood, whereas recording threatened to render musical performance into an object. In tandem, they attested to the artistic shift in object relations in the 1950s, where the object itself began to lose primacy, where boundedness and constraint in general became dissoluble. These in turn were concurrent with a proliferation of the sounds of actual water and a centrality of aqueous tropes, after the long period of modernist drought discussed in the last chapter. The incursion of water and fluidity, signaled by Pollock's dripping and Cage's pouring, and a sign in its own right of so much else, generated the elemental substrate that during the 1960s would assist the arts in confronting environmental and corporeal politics.

The Object of Performance

After Pollock stopped performing, Cage moved into theater. Cage's *Water Music* may have been his first move toward theater, but it was accompanied in 1952 by two works equally important to Cagean performance: the variably entitled "Black Mountain piece" or "Black Mountain event" (developed under the influence of Antonin Artaud's *The Theater and Its Double* and later known as the first happening) and *4'33"*.[4] The latter, no doubt Cage's most notable contribution to theater, achieved its theatrical ends the same way it achieved its musical ends: through withholding. In the realm of music where performance means so much, *4'33"* withheld performance. Just as musical sound was withheld so that all sound could be music, the composer and performer were withheld from the art work so that the art work could be everywhere. Also in 1952, Henry Cowell paraphrased Cage saying that "a brief series of sounds, or even a single combination of them, has come to seem complete in itself, and to constitute an audible 'event'."[5] The event was a way to draw expectations away from structural relations (let alone an organic whole) and direct attention toward sounds in themselves existing within their own time. It was also move toward conceiving of types of musical sound not amenable to conventional notation (Pierre Schaeffer was approaching the problem around the same time in terms of morphology). Composition for Cage would not thereby be the organization of constituent elements known as events but would instead be the provision of occasions where certain types of events could occur.

Cage moved to theater at a time theatricality had already moved far enough into painting that Pollock's dance above the canvas, along with painterly performances by others, could be captured by Harold Rosenberg in the idea of *action painting* in his famous article "The American Action Painters," also from 1952. Rosenberg likewise took recourse to the notion of the event, which for him was the temporal entity framing the action of painting, an entity that began to pull the painted object out of its own time and the objecthood out of painting: "At a certain moment the canvas began to appear to one American painter after another as an arena in which to act—rather than as a space in which to reproduce, redesign, analyze or 'express' an object, actual or imagined. What was to go on the canvas was not a picture but an event."[6] Rosenberg's events existed in a time gone by or, more precisely, in two times gone by: in the time of the execution of the painting, which transformed the object into a recording medium, and in a theatrical and mythic time of male heroic struggle, a struggle with the nature of things if not nature itself, when the painter "took to the white expanse of the canvas as Melville's Ishmael took to the sea."[7] The painted object was no longer the only object or goal of the act of painting but was instead a recording of a performance of physicality and materials and a theater of differing dispositions. They were in at least two places at once, driving the ambiguity between object and event (*painting* the noun and *painting* the verb) toward the latter. Consequently, although no less a thing, painting approached music as it became more in the doing.

The roots of this difference go back to 1948 and 1949. It begins when Pollock's statement "My Painting" was published in the first and only issue of *Possibilities* in 1948, an arts journal edited by Robert Motherwell, Harold Rosenberg, and Cage himself. Ironically for someone who was involved in pushing painting toward monumentality, not only was "My Painting" itself incredibly brief, but the scores of people who would try to find the threads of a philosophy straying from the notoriously tight-lipped artist hung on to two instances of a very short word: *in*. The two instances of the word were obviously important to Pollock, since both were italicized. The first *in* anchored a comparison of his method of painting on the floor to Native American sand painting: "On the floor I feel more at more at ease. I feel nearer, more part of the painting, since this way I can walk around it, work from the four sides and literally be *in* the painting. This is akin to the method of the Indian sand painters of the West."[8] This statement granted the act of painting and the painting itself a sense of spatiality, although at times it could also be read as a psychological space resulting both from an equalization of scale between the painting and the kinaesthetic body and also from the ritualistic associations with Native American cultural practice and performance in general. The second *in* was placed more directly in a psychologistic context (although it could still be read at the time as simply a matter of technique): "When I am *in* my painting, I'm not aware of what I'm doing."[9] Here, *painting* oscillated between noun and verb, with the interaction between the two being read as a relinquishing of ego similar to that of Surrealist automatism and jazz improvisation. Moreover, as the action of action painting moved attention backward in time to the process of painting itself, paint regained viscosity and flowed with the movements of the body. Prior to Pollock paint was meant to dry.

Cage responded to Pollock's statement in his article "Forerunners of Modern Music," which appeared in the March 1949 issue of the artists' journal *The Tiger's Eye*. Although Cage shifted the focus off an interpretation of the two *in*'s and alluded instead to "My Painting" through Pollock's mention of *sand painting*, his remarks were still grouped around the two concerns of technique and the psychologistics of art characteristic of other interpretations. Regarding technique, Cage placed sand painting into odd proximity with compositional techniques tied to recording technologies: "Just as art as sand painting (art for the now-moment rather than for posterity's museum civilization) becomes a held point of view," artists are beginning to use magnetic wire recording to make *synthetic music*, the important aspect of this technology being that "any music so made can quickly and easily be erased, rubbed off."[10] Not only was the use of wire recorders occurring at the same time that references to sand painting were being made within the art world, but the capacity to erase and record over the sound corresponded to the impermanence of sand painting. In this way, Cage dissociates sand painting from its appropriation by the painters of the "art for the now-moment" and claims it instead for composers who were using new technologies in music. In fact, at the time of writing "Forerunners of Modern Music" Cage gave a short talk at The Artists' Club (28

January 1949) in New York entitled "Indian Sand Painting or The Picture That Is Valid for One Day."[11]

Erasable sound recording technology shared the same transitory quality as sand painting but seemingly only from the position as a practitioner. While allowing the composer to manipulate sounds without locking the music indelibly into notation (the old means for recording music), once the composition was completed, it would nevertheless still be fixed and played back repeatedly for listeners (including the composer) and for posterity's sake. This problem narrows somewhat by acknowledging that recorded music when played back is still music and thus exists in time and will dissolve in the moment of its sounding. However, it should be remembered that the previous year Cage was effectively intent on erasing recorded music, with his composition *Silent Prayer* (1948), to hear silence among the offerings of Muzak. Cage seemed to want more than to sustain the *time* of lived experience, which would be reestablished with each playback. He was attached also to its original phenomenality, which would be debased by the exclusion of everything that accompanied the sound (say, the instruments, performers, audience, concert hall, pomp and circumstance, and so on). and dulled by its insertion during playback in a different time and setting. The answer, of course, was that these particular composers were not interested in using magnetic wire for replicating music but for making *synthetic music*. No problems of loss would occur because the process of production would have already eliminated what would have been lost. Thus, one could prefer the transitory quality of synthetic music over painting because time would still exist and so much less would be lost from it. Moreover, synthetic music would stand for music per se, as it encountered the devices of new technological surroundings to keep lived experience alive.

However, things become clearer when we look at the footnote reference to "sand painting (art for the now-moment . . .)":

This is the very nature of the dance, of the performance of music, or any other art requiring performance (for this reason, the term "sand painting" is used: there is a tendency in painting (permanent pigments), as in poetry (printing, binding), to be secure in the thingness of a work, and thus to overlook, and place nearly insurmountable obstacles in the path of, instantaneous ecstasy).[12]

Cage thus privileges the ephemerality of music in its time-bound sonic materiality, since this is produced both by performance and by synthetic music, whereas performance is eliminated by synthetic music (as conceived within modernism since Busoni). With performance signaling a being in time, the question then becomes whether Cage thought that Pollock's art form required performance or whether it was unduly secure in its thingness. The latter seems to be the case if we follow Cage's comments in a 1966 interview with Irving Sandler, where he described his speech, "Indian Sand Painting or The Picture That Is Valid for One Day":

Sandler: Did you allude to Pollock at all in [your speech]? He too once wrote about Indian sand painting; it was an influence on him.

Cage: I can see how it could have been; but his work had a permanence, so that he concerned really only with the fact of gesture, and perhaps of painting on a surface which was on the floor.

Sandler: And your primary point was. . . .

Cage: I was not thinking of gestures; I was thinking of impermanence and something that, no sooner had it been used, was so to speak discarded. I was fighting at that point the notion of art itself as something that we preserve. That was my intention in that speech.[13]

Cage reduced Pollock's performance to gesture, and transience was again identified with materials and techniques. If Pollock's painting was not performance due to its preservation, then no painting could typify the art for the *now moment.* Although it seems that all music would be preferable to any painting, Cage would later specify musical impermanence through his development of indeterminacy.

The now moment could also point to what it means to be modern, as contrasted to the fixed forms required by museums and other mechanisms of posterity. The latest developments in technology had long been at the center of modernist identity, and the United States had long been at the center of modernity. Cage alluded to the latest development in painting, that of Pollock, in his reference to sand painting, whereas sand painting itself in the sense used by Cage belonged neither to posterity (institutional or through modernist ideas of primitivism) nor to the lived culture of the

Navajo. Nevertheless, this did not eliminate a role for sand painting from late modernism. Pollock and other artists incorporated signs of Native American culture as a means to disrupt a continuity with European tradition and claim a uniquely contemporary status for American art. Cage did not reject European culture, just certain trends within it. In fact, he enlisted a European to separate himself from Europe when, in the "Forerunners of Modern Music," he quoted Paul Klee saying, "I want to be as though new-born, knowing nothing, absolutely nothing about Europe."[14] The interesting thing here is that this quotation formed Cage's footnote to "The use of technological means . . . ," the implication being that technology erases cultural memory in the land of technology, and, one would suspect, erasable technology does it better.

Finally, there were the psychological attributes of Cage's response to Pollock's statement. The composers of synthetic music were, in concert with technologists, "imagining brightly a common goal in the world and in the quietness within each human being."[15] This quiescence hearkens back to Cage's speech "A Composer's Confessions" (1948) in which he states that composers should be animated by *disinterestedness;* indeed, the prominence of Meister Eckhart in "Forerunners of Modern Music" was a clear pronouncement of his perennial philosophical concerns at the time. In this way, quietness would not relate directly to a concept of silence in music but would act as an alternative to a crass materialism fueled by permanence and accumulation and to the gestural displays of abstract expressionist painting. Music by its very nature and in any form would allow such quiescence and would be opposed to the tendency "to be secure in the thingness of a work, and thus to overlook, and place nearly insurmountable obstacles in the path of, instantaneous ecstasy."[16]

It might seem odd that Cage would resort to an exceptional psychological state of *instantaneous ecstasy* as a mark of accomplishment, since it was akin to Surrealist intoxication, expressionist rapture, or mythic transcendence traded in the New York arts scene, to which he was ostensibly opposed. Even though his version of ecstasy was, with its proximity to a quietness within each human being, decidedly less excitable than most, *instantaneous* as a revelation of the moment demonstrated that Cage still shared the imperatives of his peers. Nevertheless, in a similar way that he had invoked the European Paul Klee to remove Europe and Pollock's sand painting to remove Pollock, here he sets an epiphany against the remaining obstacles presented by permanence, fixed forms, objecthood, and all that would remove phenomena from time. Thus, Cage bases his skepticism about Pollock on one of the most common of aqueous aural tropes: musical time as flowing water. In fact, *String Quartet in Four Parts*, his composition written at the same time, contains the movement, literally, of "Quietly flowing along."

It would have been easy to disagree with Cage on several counts by pointing out that notions of performance fell disproportionately on painting and music and that the degree of performance Pollock's method afforded did much to destabilize his respective area of practice. Moreover, the destabilization of the object was not merely a critical assertion but could in fact be experienced by the viewer. One could also contrast the improvisation, arising from the association of Pollock's painting with jazz, with the static qualities of the notation Cage still employed at the time of writing "Forerunners of Modern Music" and conclude that the composer's score was equivalent to older forms of painting. It could also be said that *Williams Mix* (1952), Cage's meticulously spliced audiotape composition, took on object-like characteristics when it locked the chance operations used in its production into an endlessly repeatable, recorded form; in fact, Cage later leveled the same criticism at himself.[17] Relatedly, the disciplinary drift suggested by the phonographic hybrids occurring among music, radio, and sound film beginning in the 1920s, as discussed in chapter 5, might have demonstrated that recording, when considered in its semiotic role, should not have been equated with stasis. The main contradiction was, similarly, that Cage appeared to be unwilling to apply the principles of material and technical dissolution and to remove the obstacles to flowing between the disciplines—in this case, music and painting. He would later become identified with disciplinary drift but, then again, only in a personal cosmology in which music subsumed so much.

Apart from individual positions, however, the important matter here is that we are faced with a scenario in the late 1940s in which painting and music were close enough to one another that their terms could be commonly argued. This seems unremarkable in itself, yet it actually disturbs representations of the postwar arts in which Pollock and Cage are been placed in opposition to one another. Of course, they are rarely compared at all. In fact, during the 1980s in the formative discussions about the nature of postmodernism, Cage himself was rarely mentioned, and when he was, nobody really knew where to put him (a similar fate greeted Western art music as a whole). On the other hand, it often appeared that the entire theoretical project was built on the back of a caricatured modernism that, if it did not demonize Pollock, enabled a range of historical misrepresentations. More recently, Cage has finally begun to be considered within mainstream art history accounts, only to be constructed against Pollock and company. I am thinking specifically of an article by Caroline Jones—"Finishing School: John Cage and the Abstract Expressionist Ego."[18]

Jones identifies what she calls the *Abstract Expressionist ego*, a subjectivity imbued with a romance of masculinity and heterosexuality, and sets it against Cage, two of his younger compatriots—Jasper Johns and Robert Rauschenberg, and what she identifies as a homosexual subjectivity and aesthetic, if not Cage's own diminishment of the ego within art making.[19] While many things would support the existence of two camps, too many other things would confound such categorization, especially if the experience of the next generation of artists is taken into account. In fact, Jones supports her argument through an elaboration of Cagean aesthetics among younger artists: "In the perpetual contest to control the meaning(s) of modernism, Cage came to occupy a radically different perspective from his cohort [i.e., the Abstract Expressionists], serving to open a space for younger male artists whose names are legion (the list begins with Robert Rauschenberg and Jasper Johns but continues to include Allan Kaprow, Robert Smithson, Robert Morris, Walter De Maria, and countless others)."[20] Questions might arise about whether "the perpetual contest to control the meaning(s) of modernism" would itself evince un-Cage-like dispositions or, more likely, what relation this Cagean *space* of contestation would have to a space of Pollock or other Abstract Expressionists, and other spaces as well, among younger artists in the 1950s. I would suggest that because they both emanated from the same arts scene, what the next generation encountered was difficult to assign to specific individuals and, consequently, that it should be no surprise that Cage might hold some typical Abstract Expressionist dispositions and Pollock might in part appear Cagean.

We really need go no further than Dick Higgins's description, written in 1972, of the affinities existing between Abstract Expressionism and

Fluxus, the latter being deeply informed by a Cagean aesthetic, to get a sense that the reception among artists at the time did not admit such clear-cut distinctions:

One thing above all was foreign to Fluxus works: personal intrusion on the part of the artist. In fact there was a almost a cult among the Fluxus people— or, more properly, a fetish carried far beyond any rational or explainable level—which idealized the most direct relationship with "reality," specifically objective reality. The lives of objects, their histories and events were considered somehow more realistic than any conceivable personal intrusion on them.

Many would see this as a reaction against what is considered the personal, intuitive nature of Abstract Expressionism, which was, as a movement and as a whole, certainly a near-opposite of Fluxus. But I think this is because Abstract Expressionism is not far enough behind us to be seen clearly. Certainly Jackson Pollock's manifesto-statement in which he describes the only time he gets in "a mess" as being when he gets in the way of the life of his materials, certainly this attitude is actually very close to Fluxus. And most of the Abstract Expressionists of the late 1950s spoke more about "layering," "torque," and "linear configuration" than about their relationships to them. I would rather regard the impersonality of Fluxus work not as a reaction against this element of Abstract Expressionism, but as an extension of it (perhaps the only point in common between them) and as a translation of it into different terms and formats, more expressive of the attitude of the period than unique to Fluxus.[21]

We can expand on Higgins's observation by noting how the *spaces* of Cage and Pollock overlapped in other respects, no less, to the point of being fully interchangeable. A consideration of the cases of Allan Kaprow and George Brecht, both well placed with regard to major trends in the postwar arts, makes the 1950s look less like a pitched battle and more like an overlapping fade out and fade in, with Pollock waning and Cage waxing. We have already seen that in the late 1940s Cage could separate himself from Pollock only in an awkward manner. That Pollock would fade might itself have been forecasted around the same time, for there was Pollock from 1947 to 1952, having solved "the problem of painting" with his drip paintings but unable to pose another question, and there was Cage from 1948 to 1952, developing a rhetoric that would grant a sense of artistic possibility to several generations of artists to come. It is reasonable that it would take a decade to disentangle the pinnacle of achievement from the excitement in the incubator.

Allan Kaprow: Immersed Noisician

Beginning in the fall of 1956 John Cage conducted his composition and experimental composition classes at the New School for Social Research in New York City (summer 1958 through summer 1960). The catalog description for these classes read in part, "Experimental Music, a course in musical composition with technical, musicological, and philosophical aspects, open to those with or without previous training."[22] Among the participants in the class were several artists who were to play key roles within Happenings and Fluxus, including Allan Kaprow and George Brecht. Indeed, both Kaprow and Brecht created their first happenings and events, respectively, in the context of the class. It would be a sensible to conclude that the performative modes, sounds, and other aspects of happenings and Fluxus events could be attributed to Cage's influence. Although this would in large part be correct, both Kaprow and Brecht brought with them a range of attributes—including performance, sound and noise, aurality and immersion, chance, and dripping—which had their roots in Pollock and Abstract Expressionism, and each had his own interpretation of Pollock's *in*'s.

Kaprow's ideas on Pollock were first written down during 1956, the year Pollock died, published two years later in the widely read article "The Legacy of Jackson Pollock," and then elaborated later in his book *Environments, Assemblages and Happenings* and elsewhere. He interpreted the *in*'s primarily as a phenomenon of *immersion*, both spatial and psychological: "If Jackson Pollock spoke of being in his work while he painted, it was true in so far as he stood amongst the pools of paint he had just poured, while others were being formed as he moved about. With a little work a spectator before the finished painting could *feel into* the same state of immersion."[23] The pun of *fall into* to *feel into* was a homophonic means to submerge the spectator under the plane of sea level into a physiological and psychological sense of space, and, as we shall see, this spatiality was developed to an important degree in Kaprow's own work through sound. Although easily derived from "My Painting," the image of submergence was not simply rhetorical, especially after Kaprow had seen Hans Namuth's famous film of Pollock painting. The pertinent scene in the film was where Namuth set a piece of plate glass horizontally on two supports and placed the camera underneath, filming Pollock as he dripped and poured on the surface of the glass. The shot gave the distinct impression of painting in air or on the surface of water. While Jean-Jacques Lebel may have had this in mind when he claimed that Pollock was not *in* his painting, "he was on it, he was on the surface of it—like his painting was a lake and he was walking on it,"[24] other viewers of the film could easily imagine themselves inside the lake looking up.

As discussed in the last chapter, aqueous tropes in Surrealism included images of the unconscious as enveloping subterranean waters, the hydraulics of unconscious speech, the outpourings of automatism in general, and the immersion of women in sound and water. Pollock was informed by various ideas of the unconscious, although with the drip paintings it became, unlike automatism, physiologically distributed—"My concern is with the rhythms of nature, the way the ocean moves, I work inside out like nature"[25]—and his immersion was male (of the Shakespearean species), if we trace two titles in his first show of drip paintings (*Full Fathom Five and Sea Change*) to Ariel's Song in *The Tempest*: "Full fathom five thy father lies/ Of his bones are coral made/Those are pearls that were his eyes/Nothing of him that doth fade/But doth suffer a sea-change/Into something rich and strange."[26] Immersion can also mean drowning, especially when one is immersed in alcohol.[27] There were no doubt fluid implications for the material and psychological workings of his painting method to be found in the anecdote about his lunch with Franz Kline, recounted by Willem de Kooning, where pouring once again came into contact with the floor:

Half-way through the meal Pollock noticed that Franz's glass was empty. He said, "Franz, have some more wine." He filled the glass and became so involved in watching the wine pour out of the bottle that he emptied the whole bottle. It covered the food, the table, everything. He said, "Franz, have some more wine." Like a child he thought it was a terrific idea—all the wine going all over. Then he took the four corners of the table cloth—picked it up and set it on the floor. In front of all those people! . . . It was such an emotion—such life.[28]

According to Krasner, Pollock regularly immersed himself in sound: "He would get into grooves of listening to his jazz records—not just for days—day and night, day and night for three days running, until you thought you would climb the roof! Jazz? He thought it was the only other really creative thing happening in this country."[29] The multiple immersions produced by sound, alcohol, and psyche were brought into play when, toward his final days, he locked himself in his studio with a bottle of scotch and proceeded to play Jimmy Yancy and Fats Waller records at high volume. As Alfonso Ossorio remembered, Pollock was "obviously experimenting with his psyche full blast."[30]

For Kaprow, Pollock's painting produced a state of immersion for the spectator through the combined action of scale and a more local spatial effect associated with delirium, resulting in an extension of the painting out into the room toward the viewer. Thus, again, we have technical functions linked to psychologistic states, but unlike Cage, who denied Pollock any *instantaneous ecstasy*, Kaprow says that both painter and spectator experience a certain delirium. As if to emphasize the importance of scale in the genesis of environments and happenings, Kaprow juxtaposed his own photo in *Environments, Assemblages and Happenings* with a Namuth photograph of Pollock dwarfed by the painting *Little Man in a Big Sea*. The sea was perhaps the Atlantic, which for Pollock was an East Coast surrogate for vast landscapes of the West, the delirium perhaps that of Ishmael or perhaps a feeling more oceanic.[31] The large scale of the paintings attenuated peripheral vision enough to create a feeling of envelopment, providing a wraparound in which viewers could "with a little work" undergo a veritable hypnosis created by two phenomena: an oscillation of figure and ground and "an iterative principle of a few highly charged elements constantly undergoing variation."[32] In total they invited participation "in a delirium, a deadening of the reasoning faculties, a loss of 'self' in the Western sense of the term."[33] The viewer's delirium was matched by Pollock's "weaving body, with arms swinging in fierce delirium"[34] and was furthermore linked to "a kind of spatial extension . . . the entire painting comes out at us (we are participants rather than observers), right out into the room":[35]

By being inundated in his swirls of paint and by an enormous format which he could not assess in any one glance, he finally put the whole affair on the floor and stood in the middle of it. He created a quasi-environment in which reiterated pulsations of flung and dragged paint seemed to cause a trance-like, almost ritual loss of self, first in himself and, later, in the observer. This is not painting any more.[36]

The delirious states of artist and observer flanked the plane of painting; performance took over the object and imbued it with spatiality—not the flatness at the end of a modernist trajectory but a fusion of an *all-over* composition that rushed *out-from* the wall. All this activity within and through the painting created *extensions* (a key term in Kaprow's vocabulary) of these and other states, as well as the dissolution of the object, and these would form the habitus of his own work: "I wanted above all to be literally part of the work. I further desired something of my social world to be part of whatever I did."[37]

Kaprow's immersive tactics achieved extension and dissolution through performance and the enveloping spatiality of sound, with the performance deriving from the *action* of Pollock's painting and Rosenberg's essay: "My studies with Cage followed a direction I had begun to take a few years before when I was concerned with the implication that action painting—Pollock's in particular—led not to more painting, but to *more action*."[38] Kaprow's conception of sound is actually related to Pollock's action (stripped of any residual mythic struggle or oceanic character) and the fluidity of his paint. Having watched Namuth's film where Pollock is shot from below painting on a thick pane of glass, Kaprow observed how the space above the plane of the glass/canvas was infused with the loops and stretches of paint hanging foreshortened in midair before falling to be fixed on the surface. Quite remarkably, he likened these delicate quasi-objects delineated in air to the nature of sound and their inscriptive collapse onto the canvas as a form of recording. It was as if once the painting was placed upright against the wall, the recording would play back and the foreshortened inscriptions would once again assume their proper spatiality in the room.

Kaprow first simulated the out-from phenomenon of Pollock's paintings by incorporating relief elements in what he called "action collages," and then in 1956 (the year he began writing about Pollock) he began to incorporate "buzzers and bells that would go on at odd times, maybe because of the intervention of a visitor who crossed a beam of light, or pressed a button. They were part of assemblages and they started coming out off the wall."[39] The way that sound emanated off the wall, beyond relief, and into the room, filling it, suggested the possibilities of making environments: "I felt like I wanted to move as fast as possible out into the world in which those things occupied, rather than to pictorialize them, or make low-relief sculpture, which in effect it was. So, what with all the sounds in it, it was obvious to me that I could move very quickly and make the whole room the assemblage, and let people move in it and do various things. . . . This became the environment. That happened by 1957."[40] Jean-Jacques Lebel said something very similar: "All I did and all the happenings guys did was actually go from the surface of it, into it. In other words, we sank into it and the painting became—the thing that was a rectangular surface—became a room: a room with walls, a ceiling, and a floor."[41]

It was after this point, late in 1957, that Kaprow wanted to better integrate sound into his art work and to become, as he told his friend George Brecht, a *noisician*. The term was a deliberate one, he "was interested in the noise aspect of sound rather than the musical aspect of it."[42] At Brecht's suggestion he contacted Cage and soon thereafter enrolled in the class at the New School. He created his first happening in the context of the class, inspired among other things by the activities of fellow students, Cage's description of the theatrical piece at Black Mountain College, and get-togethers with artists held at his farmhouse and the sculptor George Segal's place. Self-described happenings were launched in 1959 when Kaprow published a script "Something to take place: a happening" and produced *18 Happenings in 6 Parts*. Both used sound in a varied and unique way for that time. The script, unhampered by technology or execution, included such things as boring sound, "low sound (pulsing at about seventeen cycles floor shaking)," sound produced through carrying out a task, "wild enduring noise," "brief sound of breathing . . . change to crackling almost pitchless rhythms," and "OLD MAN SCREAMS furiously turning wildly in all directions and is joined by impossible high-frequency sounds that come over loudspeakers from each corner of the room one after the other."[43]

Cage's class was crucial for the development of Kaprow's happenings but primarily in the way it directed an impetus already established in relationship to Pollock. The openness of Cage's aesthetic and pedagogy by that time assured that Kaprow, as one of "those with or without previous training" in music, could learn a composition that was not fixed to music. In practice, therefore, experimental composition was a composite of performance, sound (including Kaprow's noise), musical sound (including

Cage's noise), spaces and environments, concepts, and so on that could be composed independently of one another if so desired. Thereafter, Kaprow's happenings would become notable for their use of sound, and many would involve water. He was also the person who argued most radically for the dissolution of the bounds between art and life. Indeed, it was extension and immersion that led to inclusiveness, which was, in fact, the unsuspected legacy in the "The Legacy of Jackson Pollock":

[Pollock] left us at the point where we must become preoccupied with and even dazzled by the space and objects of our everyday life, either our bodies, clothes, rooms, or, if need be, the vastness of Forty-Second Street. Not satisfied with the suggestion through paint of our other senses, we shall utilize the specific substances of sight, sound, movements, people, odors, touch. Objects of every sort are materials for the new art: paint, chairs, food, electric and neon lights, smoke, water, old socks, a dog, movies, a thousand other things.

Everything was to be incorporated, including "entirely unheard-of happenings and events."[44] Since the forces that had dissolved the object could do the same to the conventional spaces of exhibition and performance, this would lead Kaprow's work to an increasingly quotidian, social, and ecological focus, including *Echo-logy* (1975), a work involving water, voice, and sound performed by a stream.[45] Although rarely if ever considered in these terms, Kaprow's desire for noisicianship, based on "the noise aspect of sound rather than the musical aspect of it," stands as one of the earliest and important moments in the burgeoning sound arts in the postwar period that were to lay the groundwork for a great deal of present-day practice.

George Brecht's *Drip Music*

While Kaprow's psychospatial notion of immersion was constituted through auditive elements and aqueous tropes, with George Brecht the connections between actual water and sound become explicit. Inextricably identified with Fluxus *events*, water and sound run throughout his work and are often found together, no more so than in one of the most characteristic events of Fluxus, *Drip Music*, the piece that made Brecht the world's second best-known art-dripper:

Drip Music (Drip Event)
For single or multiple performance.
A source of dripping water and an empty vessel are
arranged so that the water falls into the vessel.
Second version: Dripping.
G. Brecht
(1959–62)[46]

Brecht's indebtedness to Cage was admittedly much more pronounced than with Kaprow, and the New School class itself played a particularly important role: "I signed up for it and it really shook me up. That changed everything for me, almost without realizing it."[47] There are any number of connections between the Cage's and Brecht's ideas, but generally, Brecht transposed Cage's panaurality to performances and events (human and nonhuman): "I tried to develop the ideas that I'd had during Cage's course and that's where my 'events' came from. I wanted to make music that wouldn't be for the ears. Music isn't just what you hear or what you listen to, but everything that happens."[48] One would expect Brecht's emphasis on chance to be likewise derived from Cage, the person in the postwar arts most identified with it; however, even more directly than Kaprow's noise, it was linked to Pollock. Moreover, chance was from the very beginning associated with fluidity, which, with water and sound, would be regularly incorporated into Brecht's work and the work of other artists associated with Fluxus.

In 1957, Brecht wrote his long essay "Chance-Imagery" in which he outlined chance within science, mathematics, philosophy, and the arts and concluded with a set of instructions for generating chance. Most of the artistic references to chance relied on the account of the early avant-garde found in Robert Motherwell's 1951 anthology, *The Dada Painters and Poets*. He includes Surrealism and maintains special praise for Marcel Duchamp's pioneering work in a more mechanical approach to generating chance, even though he fails to mention Duchamp's chance music.[49] Most significantly, the contemporary practice of chance in art was given its own section, and the section was devoted entirely to Pollock: "Never before Pollock were chance processes used with such primacy, consistency, and integrity, as valuable sources of affective imagery."[50] In fact, Brecht identified Pollock so closely with chance that he called the drip paintings the "chance-paintings of roughly 1947–1951."[51]

Consistent with the general reception of Pollock among artists, Brecht concentrated on the *in*'s of "My Painting." However, Brecht emphasized technical and material concerns and was reluctant to allow a commensurate integrity to psychological functions. He maintained that Pollock's "lack of conscious control" while *in* his painting released materials and techniques into a liquidity suffused with chance, "the infinite number of variables involved in determining the flow of fluid paint . . . the paint viscosity, density, rate of flow at any instant."[52] This ran counter to Pollock's assertions that he was never out of control and there was no accident involved, to which Brecht responded that the final victory for chance was won by fluidity:

Aside from the lack of conscious control of paint application in these paintings, there are technical reasons for looking at this complex of interdependent forms as predominantly chance events. For one thing, the infinite number of variables involved in determining the flow of fluid paint from a source not in contact with the canvas cannot possibly be simultaneously taken into account with sufficient omniscience that the exact configuration of the paint when it hits the canvas can be predicted. . . . Even if we deny automatism, and claim omniscience for an unconscious modeled by a long learning period, it is obvious that in some of Pollock's paintings of the period (in *One*, 1950, for example) differently colored streams of paint have flowed into each other after application, resulting in a commingling completely out of the artist's hands.[53]

Contrary to Cage's *instantaneous ecstasy* and Kaprow's *delirium*, it was clear that Brecht was less interested in exceptional psychological states as they might occur in the painter or in viewing the painting than he was in the physical properties of paint itself—what it does in the air, breaking free of human agency as it enters the field of gravity, leading to its home in the chaos and turbulence of commingling pools. Thus, the "lack of conscious control" on Pollock's part would not be an end in itself but a means to get Pollock out of the picture and let the materials exist in their own right. Read back from this preeminence, the psychological loosening might be understood as a function of a more fundamental material disturbance.

He brought these principles to bear on his own paintings during the 1950s and, in particular, "with the sheet-paintings I was making in '56–7, where you crumple a bed-sheet and pour water on and then ink, depending on the quantity and distribution of the water, and the time you leave it till that crumpled mass is practically dry, you'll get hard edges. Whereas if you open it before it's dry you'll get more cloudy edges to the forms."[54] Cage was impressed with Brecht's chance paintings the first time they met. Soon after joining Cage's class later that year, Brecht realized that Cage and not Pollock had developed the most sophisticated approach to chance in the postwar period. In an afternote to the 1964 publication of "Chance Imagery," Brecht confessed that "In 1957 I had only recently met John Cage and had not yet seen clearly that the most important implications of chance lay in his work rather than in Pollock's."[55]

By 1959, *Drip Music* would be more complicated than any negotiation between Pollock and Cage could represent, with one drop having dissolved within itself a great array of influences and possibilities. To determine what these might have been for Brecht or could have been for others, I appeal to the three categories used by Brecht to understand his own work: Zen, science, and art.[56] Beginning with the last, we have already mentioned dripping in the arts, which, like almost all water, occurred in desiccated and discursive forms. In Brecht's own historical account in "Chance Imagery," Hans Arp could be found inadvertently valorizing the sonic singularity involved in *Drip Music* when he wrote, "One little sound might destroy the earth. One little sound might create a new universe."[57] By the late 1950s, dripping had been used by several composers as an element within tape music, most notably, Hugh Le Caine's *Dripsody: An Etude for Variable Speed Recorder* (1955). In 1959, Cage composed *Water Walk: For Solo Television Performer*, with its theatricality and contraptual instruments that were well within the province of popular culture—where vaudeville overlapped with novelty music and animated cartoons and whose most public practitioner during the 1950s was Spike Jones. His music on records and on his television show regularly involved water (such as Sousaphone spittle in the face and gargling songs) and his 1945 RCA recording was called "Drip, Drip, Drip (Sloppy Lagoon)." Brecht was a fan of Spike Jones, and so too was Fluxus if we follow George Maciunas's description of Fluxus as "the fusion of Spike Jones, Vaudeville, gag, children's games and Duchamp." Ernie Kovacs, the early television pioneer, also much admired by many artists, once put the music of Erik Satie to accompany the life of a drop of water and used many other water-related sight gags, among them a syncopated kitchen with a dripping faucet (similar to his syncopated office with its gurgling water cooler).

In painting, it was so hip to drip by the end of the 1950s that it eventually become annoying. In 1960, Andy Warhol showed the art dealer Ivan Karp his paintings in which Warhol reproduced cheap ads and cartoon characters (Dick Tracy, Popeye, Little Nancy) and splashed and dripped in the painterly gestures of the time. Warhol asked Karp if he had any reservations, and the conversation, paraphrased by Karp, went something like this:

Karp: Well some of the paintings here have all kind of drip marks.

Warhol: You have to do that. You must drip!

Karp: Why must you drip?

Warhol: It means that you're an artist if you drip.

Karp: ([as an aside] And, of course, paying homage to Pollock and all the great dripsters, you know?) You don't have to drip. Maybe you don't have to drip at all! Maybe, if you're going to deal with these kind of simple images, why don't you just deal with them, in God's name?

Warhol: That's just wonderful you should say that, because I don't think I wanna drip.[58]

In an even more deferential vein, Arshile Gorky once said of his stylistic derivations from Picasso, "When *he* drips, *I* drip."[59]

The precedents and genesis of Pollock's own dripping have been rehearsed too many times to do so again here. Even his contributions to the lesser known genitourological tradition in modernism have been detailed, whether it was when he urinated in Peggy Guggenheim's fireplace, the moral complaints served up by his critics, or the psychoanalytic explanations that posited that his paintings were compensation for his impotence or that they could be traced back to watching his father piss decoratively on a large flat rock. Tristan Tzara covered similar ground for the very different cause of antinationalism when he exclaimed, "we demand the right to piss in different colors," and in good dada fashion he also demanded

"No more urinary passages!"[60] Whether Brecht's dependence on *The Dada Painters and Poets* for writing his "Chance-Imagery" essay lead him to these passages by Tzara and, in turn, to his two events involving urination would be subsumed under a general fluidity.[61] We can, however, assume it was done dispassionately and cannot be immediately ascribed to the indelible effects of childhood development. After all, he was accustomed to working with bodily fluids while a chemist at Johnson & Johnson, where he was assigned, among other things, to the development of tampons.[62]

With regard to Zen, Brecht finished his section on Pollock in "Chance Imagery" with the rapturous proposition "that as art approaches chance-imagery, the artist enters a oneness with all of nature,"[63] and he supported this claim by following it with a lengthy quote from D. T. Suzuki. He was not alone in this respect; a year earlier Kaprow had also detected a "(perhaps) Zen quality" in Pollock's art.[64] Brecht began reading in Zen and related matters early in the 1950s and may have come across a passage on sound and koans in Suzuki's *Living by Zen* (1949), where dripping represents a "mutual fusion taking place between the different sense-functions" that itself "constitutes the content of satori":[65]

If you see with the ears
And hear with the eyes,
No doubts will you ever cherish:
How naturally falls
The rain dripping from the eaves![66]

Brecht systematically attempted to fuse the senses and align light and sound for the purposes of performance. The confluence of transparency and sound in *Drip Music* was such an attempt, just as the word *drip* functions as both noun and verb, object and action, when considered in isolation. Brecht was familiar with the Suzuki book, which included an example of enlightenment, when the question "What is the one drop of water that has come down from the Sokei source?" is answered by the statement "The one drop of water that has come down from the Sokei source."[67] There are numerous instances of dripping and water in the South and East Asian philosophical texts available to Brecht at that time, which may have moved him to muse about dripping in more general terms:

It's been remarked to me that out of all the people who heard water dripping, I'm the first person to make a score out of it, so in a way the score calls attention to the fact that water dripping can be very beautiful—many people find a dripping faucet very annoying, they get very nervous. It's nice to hear it in an appreciative way. But it's not important that I made it. I can imagine that in China and Japan people have been appreciating dripping water for centuries.[68]

This was certainly true in Japan during the nineteenth century, when people listened to the dripping of their *suikinkutsu*, a clay pot buried in the garden surrounded by stones into which water drains.[69] Brecht derived support for much of the singular focus of his work from the perplexing simplicity of *koans* and other elements from East Asian cultural practices. However, he was careful not to identify too heavily with them, even though he expressed his reluctance in a very Zen-like manner: "I wouldn't like it if someone tried to find a correspondence between what I do and Oriental thought. It wouldn't be appropriate. Because a glass of water is a glass of water."[70]

With regard to science, the sound of modern science had been wet at least since Helmholtz used dripping water in his acoustical studies to visualize sound waves,[71] and Brecht's job at Johnson & Johnson was a wet one day after day. Yet he was a chemist who felt that science had degenerated since the days of alchemy (a practice suffused with distillations, tinctures and dews, virgin's milk, water of life, and fountain's vinegar). Alchemy represented the ideal union of science with art, and this ideal, if not alchemy proper, underscored his own fusion of chemistry and art. This was very evident in the development of *Drip Music* detailed in the series of notebooks Brecht kept while attending Cage's class at the New School. The experimental focus of the class was hospitable to scientific experimentation, and many of the musical terms and concepts were derived from acoustical research, including Cage's visit to the anechoic chamber.

Cage's influence was particularly strong in the introductory phases of the class. In fact, on the second page of Brecht's first *Notebook* he jotted down the germ of his notion of *events* in a comment made by Cage: "'Events in sound-space.' (J.C.)."[72] By the late 1950s, the meaning of *events* for Cage could entail the discrete moments of sound and the elements of performance (both would eventually apply to *Drip Music*), whereas the defining moment for *sound space* for Cage was his visit to the anechoic chamber. The logic of withholding performative sounds in the space of the concert hall in *4' 33"* may have lead to the larger space of all outdoors, but the completely sealed-off indoors of the anechoic chamber certified that there are always sonic events everywhere in space. Moreover, the anechoic chamber episode signaled the crucial shift in Cage's thought where questions of noise were once and for all displaced onto those of audibility and small sounds. These considerations were not lost on Brecht, since he wrote an account of Cage's anechoic chamber anecdote on the very first day of class, and the first mention of dripping water occurred about three weeks later in a list he had written of different ways to make small sounds.[73]

Toward the end of April 1959, Brecht wrote down ideas for two performance pieces that incorporated dripping: *A Piece for Beaters*, which included a percussion rack fitted with eye-droppers to drip water into glasses, soon gave way to *Burette Music*, a burette being a piece of graduated glassware with a stopcock commonly used in chemistry laboratories.[74] *Burette Music* went through several versions, each one getting more complicated than the next in an attempt to introduce chance.[75] It eventually became a performed installation where nine to eleven small burettes in independent stands were to be randomly positioned in the classroom according to a grid of numbered floor tiles, the lights shut off, the burettes filled to any level and "set to drip *very* slowly."[76] This grid of dripping would eventually be simplified to the singular *Drip Music*, and, similar to Cage's extrapolation of the anechoic chamber experience, the clinical trappings derived from the chemistry lab would fall away to embrace quotidian instances of dripping: "It depends whether you shut it off or whether you let the water run out. If you're using the piece I built with the glass vessel, you could just let it run till it stops. But the *Drip Music* in the bathroom that we're hearing now, that will end when the reservoir fills. I can't hear it so well now because the refrigerator's running."[77]

The laboratory techniques through which *Drip Music* developed provided a means to isolate a single gesture from gesture painting, a single drop from the material and performative admixture of Pollock's dripping, and a *sound-in-itself* from all the competing sounds in a Cage composition.[78] They also guaranteed a lack of conscious control (Pollock) to displace the operations of chance in the artist's performance fully into a physical event of fluidity. However, the simplicity involved in the techniques of isolation ran counter to the techniques for generating chance.

Brecht depended on multiple elements and complicating factors to implement and demonstrate chance, as evident in the developmental versions of *Burette Music,* but these would be the very things eliminated by a process of simplification. Apparently, then, as the phenomenon of chance itself is isolated and emphasized, the means for achieving it outright become increasingly limited.

Drip Music resorted to the same fluidity he used in "Chance Imagery" to override Pollock's denial that his method involved accident. Instead of the tiny turbulence of "commingling pools" it was the chaotic aspect involved in the fluid mechanics of dripping itself, as evident in either the kitchen sink or chaos theory. A similar unpredictability was activated by Brecht in his events that used *incidental* processes and explored borderline states.[79] In addition, the open-ended simplicity of *Drip Music,* the lack of direction in the instructions, would do the work of chance by shifting the formation of the work off the artist and onto the performer, which in turn would be compounded by the range of interpretations provoked by its quotidian nature. The multiplicity that had been in the service of chance on the side of the artist/composer was given over to interpretation and reception.

These techniques enjoyed wider application in Brecht's word scores, such as those found in *Water Yam.* Known for their disarming simplicity and indecipherable enigma, they could be realized in the form of performance, object, or concept, and the interpretations involved all around would involve an incalculable variability. Brecht began sending these word scores to friends and acquaintances through the mail in a way reminiscent of his description, in "Chance Imagery," of Pollock's paints having "flowed into each other after application, resulting in a commingling completely out of the artist's hands." Instead of a diffusion through a physical medium, it occurs instead in a spatial and social one he would equate with experience. It was within this sense of circulation, in fact, that Brecht in 1959 made an early mention of "ecological processes": "Shouldn't scores be simply published in the newspaper, or available on printed cards or sheets of paper, to be sent to anyone?"[80]

The understated poetics of events would become a hallmark of Fluxus, distinguishing it from the compounded actions and elements used in Happenings. Although George Maciunas made decisions about the content of Fluxus performances and publications based along these lines, Brecht said he was not aware of any difference until after the "Happening and Fluxus" exhibition at the Koelnischen Kunstverein (1970–1971), and even then he thought the main difference was the aggressiveness displayed by happenings.[81] Wolf Vostell would seem to confirmed his suspicion when he wrote that "in the famous work by George Brecht, *Drip Music*, the water keeps its original form, and the glass into which he throws the water remains the same. The difference with me is that I break the glass."[82] Carolee Schneemann, like Vostell and several other artists, drifted in and out of the ranks of different groups, including Fluxus, but was excluded by Maciunas (and later, by curators and critics) from participation in the Fluxus milieu. For Schneemann, the simplicity characteristic of the "neat boys on the boat of Fluxus" could produce such exclusion through authoritarian reasons of sanitation.[83] In this respect, Maciunas at the helm forgot the boat had a bilge pump, given the dictionary meaning of *flux* he included in his *Manifesto* (1963). Citing Webster (while imagining Heraclitus), it read: "A flowing or fluid discharge from the bowels or other part: esp., an excessive and morbid discharge: as, the floddy *flux*, or dysentery. . . . Act of flowing: a continuous moving on or passing by, as of a flowing stream. . . . A stream: copious flow; flood; outflow. . . . The setting in of the tide toward the shore."[84]

The aqueous aspects of *Drip Music* would be explored in a number of works by Brecht and by an increasing number of artists, including those associated with Fluxus and Happenings. The incidence of so much water demonstrates the departure from the dryness of the arts up to midcentury. Brecht literalized the tradition of wet percussion in a version of the piece "For a drummer" (1966)—"Drum on something you have never drummed on before./Drum with something you have never drummed with before."—in which the "Performer drums with 2 slightly leaking water hoses over a real drum splashing the leaking water all around during the performance. If water hoses are not available bottles may be used. They should be stopped with cork having a small hole, so water will be splashed out in small quantities. Bottles should be held with necks downward."[85] He wrote a number of water-related works, perhaps the most distilled being *Three Aqueous Events* (1961):

ice
water
steam

Yoko Ono was even less complicated:

WATER PIECE
Water.   1964 spring

Instructions for water sound in the word scores of Ono's collection *Grape-fruit* include "Listen to the sound of the underground water" (*Water Piece*, 1963 spring); "Walk in the footsteps of the person in front . . . in water. Try not to make sounds" (*Walking Piece*, 1964 spring); and *Wink Talk* told us that the intensity of a wink was, among other things, "A water drop from a loose faucet."[86] The one that relates most directly to *Drip Music* is her *Waterdrop Painting*:

Let water drop.
Place a stone under it.
The painting ends when a hole is drilled
in the stone with the drops,
You may change the frequency of the waterdrop to your taste,
You may use beer, wine, ink, blood, etc.
instead of water.
You may use typewriter, shoes, dress, etc.
instead of stone.
1961 autumn[87]

Joe Jones realized a version of Brecht's *Drip Music* in which an amplified drip was displayed in his shopfront window on Moore Street in New York. The presentation was part of a week-long event organized by John Lennon and Yoko Ono entitled *Weight & Water* and *Fluxfaucet*, which in turn was part of over two months of Fluxfest Presentations of Lennon and Ono in 1971.

Mieko Shiomi likewise had several works involving water. Her *Water Music* (1964) reads

1. Give the water still form.
2. Let the water lose its still form.

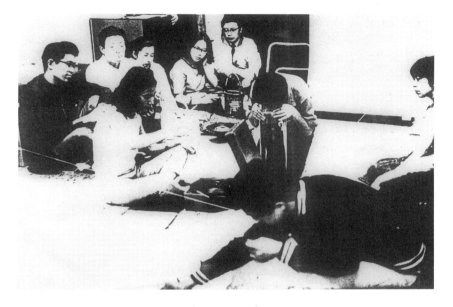

| **Figure 10.1** |
Mieko Shiomi performing her "Water Music" at the Crystal Gallery, Tokyo (8 September 1965)
Photo credit: Teruo Nishiyama

One of the most interesting derivations of dripping can be found in "record variation" of the same work, in which "A record is covered with any water soluble material, such as clay or water soluble glue etc. Play the record on a record player and drop a small amount of water over the record. The needle will pick up music from spots dissolved by water. Adjust quantity and location of water to obtain desired pattern of music and nonmusic."[88] The drops are neither sounds in themselves (dripping would be drowned out by the stylus raking loudly across a foreign surface) nor notation with the transparency of a whole note. The piece presents the physical release of music from the recording by the drops of water, as though the water contained the music and adhered irregularly on the surface in order to be heard (see figure 10.1).

Water continued to pour from many different quarters—in Robert Whitman's *Water* (1963), in a number of other happenings, in Max Neuhaus's *Water Whistle* (1971) performed underwater at a swimming pool, and in Emmett Williams's *Waterworks* (1976), with its long list of sound events also performed at a swimming pool.[89] Kaprow's penchant for immersion would reach acoustic saturation in the highly amplified work of La Monte Young and the Theatre of Eternal Music, with John Perreault unable to avoid the association when he described a Young concert as "walking into a room full of brine and discovering that surprisingly enough it was still possible to breathe," and in another instance when the customary electronic drone was replaced with the sound of the Atlantic Ocean while Marian Zazeela and Young sang.[90] This, as we see in chapter 8, is one of the main features of being *inside a sound*, when the sound itself defines the space. The composer Philip Corner used the sounds of water for his composition accompanying the Lucinda Child's dance *Pastime* (1962): "The music for *Pastime* turned out to be prophetic. My Korean name means 'Contemplating Waterfall,' and it was given to me by my calligraphy teacher. I have realized that I have a very passionate feeling for water. I've since done many water pieces."[91] Annea Lockwood began recording rivers around 1966 and, with the contributions of many others, has built The River Archive with the intent of recording every river in the world. The project has resulted in a series of installation and outdoor works, including *Walking on Water* (1973–1974), *Play the Ganges Backwards, One More Time, Sam* (1979), and culminated in *A Sound Map of the Hudson River* (1982), in which recordings from twenty-six sites along the river from source to the ocean, plus recordings of people who lived along its length, formed the basis for an installation.[92]

Since the early 1960s, innumerable artists have combined sound, fluidity, and water in every way imaginable, and they have done so concurrently with the rise of environmentalism, which politicized the naturalism and poetics of materiality already practiced within the arts, and the unfettering of the body. Many of these practices have become infused with sonic flows of semiosis that acknowledge that water is no longer an inert element. However, there is nothing intrinsically positive about the flows and dissolutions of the 1950s, for it could apply just as well to the increased flows of information and military communications, the pumping of petroleum economies, the profusive exchanges of commodity culture, among other systems. A glass of water is not a glass of water.

Meat Voices

Speak of the voice per se and one necessarily speaks of the body, yet the voice inhabits bodies differently. Modern Western culture typically locates the dominant operations of the embodied voice above the collarbone, attracted toward the head by the pull of the fusion of thought with speech and by an unconscious that serves as a proxy for the rest of the body. Within this restricted frame of reference, traveling the distance from the brain to the mouth could be understood, among the ranks of the avant-garde, as a radical departure in favor of the body. Tristan Tzara, for instance, undercut those people who would purify poetry and prepare it for an hygienic future, by revealing "the great secret: *Thought is made in the mouth.*"[1] The mouth, in other words, spoke unhygienically for the rest of the body and defended poetry from refinement by a social elite. Roland Barthes attempted to find a basis from which to make a distinction between two male singers of Western art music by descending to the throat and elevating the genitals, as though an Adam's apple found itself suddenly draped in trousers. In his famous essay, "The Grain of the Voice," he places the larynx over the lungs in a hierarchy of organs because the lung, "a stupid organ . . . swells but gets no erection; it is in the throat, place where the phonic metal hardens and is segmented."[2] For Barthes, every rake of the wind across the larynx superseded the *pneuma* of the breath and soul with a *jouissance* of the body. It is remarkable to consider, especially when compared to the understandings of the body by many singers, that this antisoul music could get caught in the throat. Other cultures place the operations of the voice throughout the body, and some place them primarily below the collarbone and symbolize the voice through an array of objects, economies, and forces both inside the body and well outside it.[3]

The three individuals examined in the chapters on *meat voices* likewise distribute the voice throughout the body: William Burroughs at the microbial and cellular levels, Michael McClure at the muscular, and Antonin Artaud throughout different sites in a phantasmatic body pinned around the axis of the spine. These voices are not limited to a privileged orifice or organ but instead use the whole body, which in turn embodies an array of influences and sophisticated processes. Burroughs's idea of *language as a virus* developed from organismic theories in which the human body was protoplasm, meat inscribed by and within a culture of recording and conditioned by the privatized struggle for survival in an increasingly pathogenic situation. Artaud's screaming developed from the exigencies of theater, Eastern body practices, and the torment of his own pain and eventually withdrew to vibrate within the spinal column as the meat was shed gnostically and scatalogically off the bones. McClure's *beast language* developed from complementary Eastern and Western body practices and, in contrast to the isolating effects of the imagined bodies of Burroughs and Artaud, sought interdependence within a context of mammalian identification and ecological politics. All three of these individuals' voices and bodies have remained quite influential, in the celebration by Gilles Deleuze and Felix Guattari of Artaud's *body without organs*, in Burroughs's viral tropes, and in McClure's participation in the culture of environmentalism. They demonstrate that the voice can say much more and, when it *speaks the body*, cannot help but speak of other things.

Burroughs's auditive affinities may not be immediately apparent, but this certainly would not have been through any fault of his own. Indeed, it could be argued that among the postwar arts only Cage was on par with Burroughs in the sophistication of his ideas about sound. Many artists have found in Burroughs's writings and audiophonic experiments the possibility of maintaining the types of associative links discouraged in Cagean musicalization and have found the combustible point at which experimentation in sound meets literature, electronic media, and tactics of political resistance. While there have been gallons of ink spilled over the virus, as if in a process of slide preparation, a negligible amount has been devoted to his ideas about sound or the genesis of the virus. An essay by Robin Lydenberg on Burroughs's audiotape experiments broke the scholarly ice on the topic of sound and voice,[4] but there appears to be no adequate account of the genesis of the virus. While not paying much attention to his actual audiophonic experiments, I hope to demonstrate that sounds reside at the center of development of one of the most pervasive of postmodern tropes.

TWO SOUNDS OF THE VIRUS:
WILLIAM BURROUGHS'S PURE MEAT METHOD

Abandoning past theories may do damage to treasured beliefs and one's nostalgic love of the old school tie, but a fact is a fact.

L. Ron Hubbard[1]

A Culture for Growing Viruses

"A battalion of rampant bores prowls the streets and hotel lobbies in search of victims. An intellectual avant-gardist—'Of course the only writing worth considering now is to be found in scientific reports and periodicals'—has given someone a bulbocapnine injection and is preparing to read him a bulletin on 'the use of neohemoglobin in the control of multiple degenerative granuloma.' (Of course, the reports are all gibberish he has concocted and printed up.)"[2] William Burroughs was only half joking when he wrote this self-parody. His own work was deeply informed by a variety of scientific and quasi-scientific theories—by an obsession with *fact*, as he was quick to say. It was within this culture of fact that his notion of the virus grew and subsequently became well known among a broad range of people, especially the Beat and beyond literati, heady punks, and other subcultured individuals, cybertypes, and urban degenerate renegades. Burroughs's influence has been rejuvenated at various times by Laurie Anderson's pop praise song declaiming that "language is a virus, oooooo," by David Cronenberg's film version of *Naked Lunch*, by the availability of *Re/Search* publications, and by a spate of collaborations with the likes of The Disposable Heroes of Hiphoprisy and Kurt Cobain. His work and ideas are firmly ensconced among several generations, and his presence, no matter how pallid was his countenance or how absent his vital signs now, shows no sign of fading.

Viral tropes likewise show no sign of backing off. They have proven as pervasive and contagious within culture as actual viruses among their host populations, no doubt because they can chose among any number of hospitable cultures. Of course, nobody has needed Burroughs to instruct them on virology or related genetic matters. This can be achieved just as well by the legacies of atomic and nuclear radiation, Agent Orange, and other environmental mutagens; the biological and cultural spread of HIV, ebola, and other virulent rain forest viruses; the telematic contagion of computer viruses, reproductive technologies, and genetic algorithms; genetic engineering and the genome project; the memetics of a mutating Darwinism; and other signs of the epidemic spread of epidemia. The cumulative weight of these conditions has nevertheless grounded Burroughs's ideas and made them seem prescient, moving some individuals to spuriously hail him as an eerie prophet of the HIV and AIDS epidemic, usually by referring to a passage in a 1957 letter to Allen Ginsberg:

Briefly, the novel [*Naked Lunch*] concerns addiction and an addicting virus that is passed from one person to another in sexual contacts. The virus only passes from man to man or woman to woman, which is why Benway is turning out homosexuals on assembly-line basis. Real theme of the novel is Desecration of the Human Image by the control addicts who are putting out the virus.[3]

The culture of fact within which Burroughs's notion of the virus grew was constituted in large part through his enthusiasm for three organismic theories, which in turn were associated with two fairly distinct phases of the virus. Indeed, it is important to note that he rarely expressed similar enthusiasm for other thinkers. The first two thinkers, the General Semantics of Count Alfred Korzybski and the orgone theory of Wilhelm Reich, were associated with the first phase of development of the virus, which lasted well into the auspicious year 1959, the year *Naked Lunch* was published. They thus informed *Junky, Queer, Interzone,* as well as the observations and images contained in his letters during the same period. This phase one virus was itself accompanied by two closely related bodies that at various times it inhabited, mimicked, animated, and subsumed.

The first body was the largely undifferentiated gelatinous body derived from the colloidal, protoplasmic, and amebic figures found in the theories of Korzybski and Reich. In these theories, discrete materiality and boundaries between and among inorganic and organic matter, between sites of physiological and psychological functioning, a body and its cellular constituents, bodies and their environment, were diminished by the pervasive flow and exchange of energies and the consequent prioritization of function over location. The term *protoplasm* could easily mean the entire human body, with colloids and energies being the bridge to every other aspect of the world. Thus, the first body of the initial virus could just as easily exist at the subperceptual cellular site of viral functioning or be amplified to the corporeal and societal levels.

The second body associated with the first virus was derived predominantly from Burroughs's own experience, one animated by the hungers and desires of junk and sex as represented in his writings; the functional energies of the organism, in other words, driven purely by need. These two bodies, the protoplasmic body and Burroughs's own depicted body, were fused and found a common host in the idea of *schlupping* bodies, the total osmotic ingestion or fusion of one body by another, first posited imagistically within the sphere of homosexual love—"to become the other person"—but then quickly pathologized to forms of predation, violence, and destruction. The virus behaved in the same undifferentiated manner as these two bodies combined and these two bodies combining, with a pronounced capacity to incorporate other phenomena in their entirety, taking over an organism or social formation through unspecified means. The first virus, the phase one virus, can be identified through its predominant functioning, and I therefore use the term the *usurper*.

Toward the end of 1959 the usurper virus underwent a major mutation; from its generally undifferentiated state and mode of functioning it quickly became highly differentiated, technically determinant, increasingly virulent, and widespread. It operated through particular actions; its transmission could be produced articulately through the contagion of actual communication, not just ingestion. Its usurpative functions ceased to mimic schlupping bodies and instead were deployed at the microbial scale that was the proper site of the virus all along. The mutation was similar to the one Donna Haraway characterized amid "the biomedical production of bodies" over the course of the last 100 years as being a shift from *organism* to *biotic component code*—that is, if we keep in mind that for Burroughs the "organism" belonged to organismic theories that attempted to explain so much within the physical, psychophysiological, and social realms.[4] Also, although Burroughs's virus was not generated at this time from a model of genetic code, the idea of inscriptive processes and language occurring at the cellular level was amply expressed through other means.

The second virus, known here loosely as the *mutated virus*, can be found in Burroughs's writings after *Naked Lunch*, including those from the same manuscript base as the cut-up trilogy: *The Soft Machine, The Ticket That Exploded,* and *Nova Express.* There is a shift from the sex and junk associations of the usurper virus to the language-based proclivities of the mutated virus, which happens to parallel Burroughs's own shift from uncertain standing as a writer prior to the fame created by *Naked Lunch*, to a new-found dedication to literary professionalism. The mutation of the virus also occurred after Burroughs encountered yet another organismic theory, that of L. Ron Hubbard's *Dianetics.* The manner in which Hubbard had taken earlier organismic theories, including most notably the theory of Korzybski himself, and reworked them to extend their pathogenic scope (thus generating a larger market for his therapeutic services) became a fortuitous expression of Burroughs's own penchant for pathography. On this newly broadened basis of disease Burroughs's virus began to function through specific means, returning to operate at its appropriate miniature scale and developing the capacity for language, one lodged securely within a relationship with communications technologies. Most important, whereas the usurper virus could render another entity nonexistent by ingestion into one body or circumvent otherness altogether by reproducing external replicants, the mutated virus existed parasitically as another body inside the organism, primarily in the form of Burroughs's well-known figure of the Other Half undetectably controlling a person's thoughts, words, and deeds. This internal phantom was less a personification or corporealization of the unconscious or homunculus written into the genetics of every cell or the congruent kinaesthetic body that makes its appearance after amputations than it was a literary manifestation of Hubbard's ideas of the "reactive mind" (the pathogenic unification of accumulated trauma recorded at the cellular level) and the "Dianetic demon" (a surrogate self speaking with words previously recorded by the reactive mind).

Burroughs's viral influence cannot be separated from a whole host of technological attachments. Despite the fact he was the old man of the largely atechnological Beats, he seemingly grows more youthful as tales of his psychotechnical use of drugs, Reich's orgone box, Scientology's

E-meter, and Gysin's *dream machine*, tape recorders, and radios have been told and retold over the years against an increasingly pervasive incidence of technological rhetoric. Accordingly, the development and mutation of Burroughs's virus was accompanied by various technologies, including those associated with the organismic theories to which he subscribed. The mutation in particular took place against a backdrop of background radiation from atomic and nuclear detonation, especially as it combined with Reich's orgone energy and with radiophonic transmissions in the earth's atmosphere. Most notably, radiation was directed to illuminate the cytological scene of the second virus's early moments of mutation and then as a specific means to transmute the inscriptions of language and computer code, presaging so much within present-day cyber rhetoric. Technology was sunk into the body and sent out signals—once the sole function of the psyche and voice—from any cell of the body. It constituted a technological shift from mechanics, with its modernist surface-rendered cuts and wounds and sutures, to a mechanistic genetics and all it can grow, engineer, communicate, or infect. The degree of its sophistication is found in a passage from *Nova Express* (1964), "Technical Deposition of the Virus Power," written with the assistance of Ian Sommerville, describing the habitat of computer code "developed by the information theorists" containing "our own image":

It was found that the binary information could be written at the molecular level. . . . However, it was found that these information molecules were not dead matter but exhibited a capacity for life which is found elsewhere in the form of virus.[5]

Preventing this mathematical virus from endlessly replicating the same exact image was achieved by "radiating the virus material with high energy rays from cyclotrons," creating a variety that would have "scientists busy for ever exploring the 'richness of nature.'"[6]

Thus, over thirty years ago Burroughs had developed viral tropes of genetic mutation, genetic algorithms, artificial life, binary code as genetic information of the human organism, and computer viruses. That his viral tropes had been developing for about two decades before *Nova Express* is some indication of their scope and complexity. To do justice to these rogue viruses would easily require a book-length treatment. Instead, I contain my comments to two main viruses—the usurper and mutated viruses—and to their sounds. Both viruses made sounds and were made of sounds. For the usurper virus, the sound was *schlupp;* for the mutated virus, the sound was the irrepressible speech of the Dianetic demon. These were the two sounds of the virus.

Schlupping

The body that Burroughs's virus first inhabited was a gelatinous body, not a body a virus might infect but the body of viral functioning itself. A representation of the virus appropriate to its own microbial scale would appear with any regularity only with the mutation, whereas the first usurpative viral functions were given human corporeal scale to operate interpersonally and socially. The first gelatinous bodies were associated not with any diseased or dilapidated condition but with the love Burroughs had for Allen Ginsberg toward the end of 1953 and, in particular, with the term *schlupping.* According to Ginsberg, "Schlupp for him was originally a very tender emotional direction, a desire to merge with a love, and as such, pretty vulnerable, tenderhearted and open on Burroughs's part."[7] The word made its way into Burroughs's *routines,* the performative stories that produced much of the raw material for Burroughs's writing, as the figure for a generalized desire for erotic fusion. The novel *Queer* contains a passage where Lee (pseud. for Burroughs) and Eugene Allerton (pseud. for Lewis Marker) are in a darkened movie theater to watch Jean Cocteau's *Orpheus,* with its penetrable mirrors and glycerine-filled passageways: "Lee could feel his body pull towards Allerton, an amoeboid protoplasmic projection, straining with a blind worm hunger to enter the other's body, to breathe with his lungs, see with his eyes, learn the feel of his viscera and genitals."[8] Erotic heterosexual union may create a two-backed beast; here Burroughs's homosexual desire produced an image of the cohabitation of one body since "It's a crucial factor in homosexual relationships," according to Burroughs, "to be the other person."[9] As he said in conversation in 1980:

In homosexual sex you know exactly what the other person is feeling, so you are identifying with the other person completely. In heterosexual sex you have no idea what the other person is feeling. . . . you can identify with them to the extent that you become them, which of course is quite impossible with heterosexual sex because you're not a woman therefore you cannot feel or know what a woman feels.[10]

In another scene from *Queer* Lee tells how a "wise old queen" named Bobo met his demise. It is a scene familiar to all those who know the legend of Isadora Duncan's death, only here the long flowing scarf was replaced by enormously distended hemorrhoids: "He was riding in the Duc de Ventre's Hispano-Suiza when his falling piles blew out of the car and wrapped around the rear wheel. He was completely gutted, leaving an empty shell sitting there on the giraffe-skin upholstery. Even the eyes and the brain went, with a horrible schlupping sound. The Duc says he will carry that ghastly schlup with him to his mausoleum."[11] The "protoplasmic projection" of desire of the earlier scene in *Queer* is mapped on junk and combines with the onomatopoeia of soft innards being sucked out to lead to the best known *schlupping* scene, the one in *Naked Lunch*. The narcotics agent Bradley the Buyer has trouble delineating the bounds of his profession and develops a special need to rub against junkies for a fix. A boy describes the experience as the "most distasteful thing I ever stand still for. . . . Some way he make himself all soft like a blob of jelly and surround me so nasty. Then he gets wet all over like with green slime."[12] When called into the District Supervisor's office for reprimand, Bradley the Buyer schlupps his boss:

His body begins to dip like a dowser's wand. He flows forward. . . .
"No! No!" screams the D.S.
"Schlup . . . schlup schlup." An hour later they find the Buyer on the nod in the D.S.'s chair. The D.S. has disappeared without a trace.
The Judge: "Everything indicates that you have, in some unspeakable manner uh . . . assimilated the District Supervisor.[13]

The word *schlupp* itself, because of its onomatopoeia, defies the arbitrary character of language that separates a word from some natural element or order of the world. Such acts of motivated speech may not be congruent with the things to which they refer, but at least a link has been made through which various associations and intensities can be played on. However, when the onomatopoeia refers to bodily sounds associated with

speech itself, then another order of association occurs. The very act of saying the word *schlupp* may indeed affectionately simulate Yiddish, close at
hand for Ginsberg, as if *schtup* got carried away by *schlep*. Even if it were
tongue in cheek, it would still require what Michel Leiris called "mouth
water" to pronounce. To really say schlupp is to moistly slur with an organ
of speech that is also "the orifice of respiration, the den where the pact of
a kiss is sealed . . . an oily factory of mastication." The mouth transmits
intelligence as well as being the "bottom rung of the organic ladder," spit-
ting just like ejaculating "in broad daylight."[14] According to Leiris, at this
rung humans join "those primitive animals that, possessing only a single
opening for all their needs and being therefore exempt from that elemen-
tary separation of the organ of nutrition from that of excretion to which
would correspond the differentiation of noble from ignoble."[15] A conflation of orifices in Burroughs's writings extends not only to a basis of varied
orificial exchange during sex, especially that predominantly associated
with but not limited to gay sexual activity, but also to the point where all
surface becomes orifice. Therefore, schlupp belongs to an act of motivated
speech that requires spit, "the very symbol of *formlessness*."[16] We can only
specify in Burroughs's case that formlessness does not mean an absence of
form but the lack of discrete or determinate form in the face of rampant
function.

The sound of the word *schlupp* is the word made flesh, the sound of
soft organs, a protoplasmic sound, a formlessness spoken with a wet wind
that inflates and vitalizes the gelatinous body, an unstructured cellular generalization bereft of bones and often the skin that might pose an obstacle
to osmosis. Schlupp has a cartoon-like onomatopoetic relationship to
sounds of saliva, "a great big sluppy kiss,"[17] sweat, semen, and other sexual
fluids that accompany the ingestion of penises and fingers and tongues, the
full-stop plosive *p* being a vacuum created and released by plunging. For
instance, just as Burroughs's famous "talking asshole" in *Naked Lunch* took
over the mouth's multiple functions, the sexual sound of Bobo's dilapidated
anus could be heard echoed in his total disembowelment. Skeletal clatter
would be too mechanical to incorporate the smooth sounds of multiple
functions of the body. Schlupp also bears an onomatopoetic relationship
to the sounds of eating and digestion, which, with the exception of teeth,
are sounds that have no bones. When one hears the sound of teeth against
one another, it is time to swallow, take another bite, or go on to another

activity besides ingestion. Yet, at the point of advanced schlupping, Bradley the Buyer has no teeth: "He kisses the D.S.'s hand thrusting his fingers into his mouth (the D.S. must feel his toothless gums)."[18] Schlupp, the word and what it describes, licks its chops and becomes the most pronounced moment of all ingestion. It is an appropriate sound for the unhewn hungers of junk or sex, for it is the body's interior making its needs conspicuously known within the world—all organs, all-organism finding itself in speech.

Through their respective propagation these two hungers call up a motivated speech and form a rhetorical motive on which viral tropes will emerge. Junk is an inorganic substance that comes from the outside to create hunger in order to replicate itself (as Burroughs says, replacing "the user cell by cell until he *is* junk") and thereby transforms the entire body into nothing but an organism of cellular existence.[19] Sexual desire, on the other hand, arises from within the body to fuse within another entity outside itself and, moreover, within an environment of pathography, will return as repression. Junk is an alien body, whereas sex alienates the body. They both commit the organism to external pursuits and in the process dissolve the bounds between the cellular, corporeal, and social. In this sense, the body itself is either an osmotic interface pinned between cellular needs and social satisfactions or one that usurps both as it mediates a zone of exchange. These hungers would by their simple functioning already have produced schlupped bodies were it not for an established practice among the species of channeling functions through certain orifices.

Exchange across dissolute bounds also imbues actions with the attributes of their objects. Cells take on psychosocial characteristics to fulfill their needs in the world, which itself is reduced to operating through the debased behavior of animal/organic or chemical/inorganic requirements. The body situated by its base needs, therefore, begs the fall of itself and the fall of society, especially given Burroughs's interest in Oswald Spengler's *Decline of the West*. One might expect a Christian influence descending from Burroughs's maternal grandfather, a Bible thumper from Georgia, but any Edenic eviction scenario would have to also include the behavioral capacity for protoplasm to sin or, rather, the capacity not to sin. Nevertheless, the Fall does occur within *Naked Lunch* cast in religious terms with regards to an "Arabian untouchable caste. . . . What is origin of untouchable? Perhaps a fallen priest caste."[20] The Fall is clearly evident in the procession of schlupping and schlupped bodies: what started out with his love for Ginsberg moved quickly through his routines to the raw lust of an "amoeboid protoplasmic projection" for Eugene Allerton, then degenerated as Bobo's innards were sucked out, and finally took on full usurpative characteristics with Bradley the Buyer schlupping the District Supervisor.

There was nothing necessarily pathogenic in the love for Ginsberg or the lust for Allerton. On the other hand, ostensibly an accident, the destructiveness of schlupp associated with Bobo was a disciplinary action against the grotesque, pegged to the "wise old queen's" body aging away from sexual desirability toward dilapidation and death. With Bradley the Buyer the schlupping sound and body became linked inextricably to junk. Indeed, the dead, inorganic, chemical nature of junk is the driving force behind the complete pathologization of drives and the quick fall of the schlupp, and through its personification as a junkie spans the dead-live, inorganic-organic divide that is the most salient feature of the virus. The word *cadaver* itself comes from the Latin *cadere*, to fall. The junkie is a fallen body doing nothing. When necessary, it comes alive to find a fix or a host, but it does not live in life. The junkie preys on its host society only to produce the immediate conditions for its own survival, just as junk lives within the junkie, just as a virus comes to life only with a host. That is why they are not just any parasite, for most parasites go from life to life. Unlike the Biblical expulsion, which was into life, Burroughs's Fall is not an expulsion from life into death but, worse, in between. It is the horror of an uncompleted fall, a falling into a viral interregnum:

It is thought that the virus is a degeneration from more complex life form. It may at one time have been capable of independent life. Now has fallen to the borderline between living and dead matter. It can exhibit living qualities only in a host, by using the life of another—the renunciation of life itself, a *falling* towards inorganic, inflexible machine, towards dead matter.[21]

The schlupped body is therefore laid out for inhabitation by the pathographic exploits of the virus, which in turn, as we shall see, models itself in its first phase on the usurpative function that motivates schlupping. It is a virus whose contagiousness is an act of ingestion, a virus that functions for the immediate needs of a body, not an intellect. It fixes and eats and copulates. It doesn't have language and has yet to become a writer.

On Goo Behavior

That Burroughs would elevate the gelatinous figure of single-celled organisms to represent the entire human body can be traced, first of all, to the organismic doctrine described in Count Alfred Korzybski's *Science and Sanity: An Introduction to Non-Aristotelian Systems and General Semantics* (1933) and, in particular, to his idea of "colloidal behaviour," to which an entire chapter is devoted.[22] Burroughs had an early and long-lasting respect for Korzybski's thought. In 1939 he traveled to Chicago to attend lectures at Korzybski's Institute of General Semantics;[23] a decade later he pleaded with Allen Ginsberg to "please do me one favor. Get Korzybski's *Science and Sanity* and read it. Every young man should get the principles of Semantics clear in his mind *before* he goes to college (or anywhere else for that matter)."[24] And then the following year: "You could do with a refresher course in Semantics."[25] Ginsberg himself remembered *Science and Sanity* as one of the gems in Burroughs library, "like a preliminary western version of the later oriental teaching of the difference between concept and suchness."[26] Burroughs would continue to cite Korzybski for years to come. The affinities between Burroughs and Korzybski are fairly obvious: both men promoted psychophysiological explanations against ones that isolated the psyche; both described a pernicious determinant of human affairs so pervasive and ingrained in the daily conduct of life as to be undetectable, whether it was Aristotelian thought or addictive behavior and social control; and both mounted ambitious, all-embracing theories to combat the threat: Korzybski's General Semantics and Burroughs's General Theory of Addiction.

Most important are the roles, imagistic and functional, afforded to protoplasm and colloids. When speaking of the human body, in all its multifariousness, Korzybski would often simply use the term *protoplasm*. Because protoplasm was itself a type of colloid, human beings were subject to being understood through the exigencies of inorganic structuring. There was no great divide between the organic and inorganic; indeed, protoplasm and colloids were not known for their contiguity but for their commonality and continuity. Likewise, they did not simply overlap but were in important respects congruent. No aspect of human body behavior, including the operations of psyche and sociality, could be isolated from colloidal behavior, which, as Korzybski writes, alone "formed the most important known link between the inorganic and organic. This fact also suggests entirely new fields for the study of the living cells and of the *optimum conditions for their development, sanity included.*"[27] Korzybski felt that it was only for matters of expediency that humans were first if not foremost psychophysiological, for they could not be fully understood apart from all other life forms and their structurally and electrical overlappings with inorganic matter.

The overarching figure of colloidal matter, with its attendant images of emulsions and gelatins, created an operational field of equivalencies wherein the surfaces that described boundaries were broken down and exchange between and among all entities increased. Moreover, all this goo provided the lubricant whereby imagistic slippages could also take place among Burroughs's protoplasmic bodies. We have already described the class of bodies with its completely malleable, osmotic surface typified by Dr. Benway's query, "Why not one all-purpose blob?"[28] As an expression of hunger and desire the "blob" was a body given over to being orificial. Indeed, bodily surfaces displayed orifices that were mobile and otherwise self-motivated in their pursuit to satisfy need. In *Naked Lunch* the Vigilante's body in "the tentative ectoplasmic flesh of junk kick"[29] transforms into a surface where "mouth and eyes are one organ that leaps forward to snap with transparent teeth . . . but no organ is constant as regards either function or position . . . sex organs sprout anywhere . . . rectums open, defecate and close . . . the entire organism changes color and consistency in split-second adjustments."[30] Needle holes turn into open sores, vaginas, and mouths permanently ready and asking for junk: "She seized a safety pin caked with blood and rust, gouged a great hole in her leg which seemed to hang open like an obscene, festering mouth waiting for unspeakable congress with the dropper which she now plunged out of sight into the gaping wound."[31] It is a scene echoed from Burroughs's experience: "From taking so many shots I have an open sore where I can slide the needle right into a vein. The sore stays open like a red, festering mouth, swollen and obscene."[32] Novel means for supplying a fix are devised, such as the galvanic Osmosis Recharge, as was done to discretely administer a high to the president (the first in 1956 corresponding to Eisenhower and his puffy lids): "erect penises brought into contact . . . but contact points wear out like veins. Now I sometimes have to slip my penis under his left eyelid."[32] The surface also takes on an internally driven agency, as when a vein becomes a suckling baby—"I kissed the vein, calling it 'my sweet little needle sucker,' and talked baby talk to it"[34]—when Burroughs remembered the shooting of his wife as though "the brain *drew* the bullet toward it,"[35] or when the talking asshole takes on a personality and seals over competing orifices with a gelatinous ooze. Even the jacketing of architecture can come to be comprised of rooms "made of plastic cement that bulges to accommodate people, but when too many crowd into one room there is a soft plop and someone squeezes through the wall right into the next house."[36] Korzybski's thought could be used as well to describe a body in any state of immateriality and dissolution because colloids exist not just as emulsions and gelatins but "also when solid particles are dispersed in a gaseous medium (smokes), or liquid droplets in gaseous media (mists)."[37] Burroughs's schlupped bodies exhibited such characteristics: before Bradley the Buyer schlupped someone, he would emit a "narcotic effluvium, a dank green mist that anesthetizes his victims and renders them helpless in his enveloping presence."[38] Similarly, hunger could slide into pleasure as the junky's "face dissolved. His mouth undulated forward on a long tube and sucked in the black fuzz, vibrating in supersonic peristalsis disappeared in a silent, pink explosion."[39]

For Korzybski the boundaries within bodies, between a body and other bodies, and between body and environment are blurred due to the sensitivity of the protoplasmic surface and the quickness with which a stimulus is relayed through protoplasm. To speak of a protoplasmic surface as a *surface* in the normal sense, however, is misleading. The distinction between interior and exterior becomes meaningless for colloids in general because they are in fact a *hypertrophied state of surface*, where surface is in effect miniaturized, multiplied, enveloped, and distributed evenly throughout the organism or environment. In the constitution of the colloidal body, in other words, the surface has become pervasive through internalization, through autoingestion. Although the usurper virus functions in the form of a body, given the importance of the surface to modernist techniques such as montage (in the engineering figure of assembling), this hypertrophied surface would provide Burroughs, at the historical interstices with postmodernism (or hypertrophied modernism, or however it might be characterized), the means through which techniques would later be cannibalized and installed at the cellular level, in the same way engineering would extend from mechanics to genetics.

According to Korzybski, the consciousness of the colloidal body responded at the speed of instinct due to the transmission of electrical impulses: "The ratio of *surface exposed to volume of material* is very large. . . . under such *structural* conditions the *surface forces* become important and play a prominent role in colloidal behaviour."[40] Surfaces are sites of electrical charges and thus, there occurs an accelerated transmission through a unified field of primed surfaces, diminishing the importance of physical space while at the same time establishing a body of energetic equivalencies, fusing such things as cellular activity with drives and cognition.[41] For Korzybski, "Psychogalvanic experiments show clearly that every 'emotion' or 'thought' is always connected with some electrical currents and that electricity seems fundamental in colloidal behaviour, and, therefore, for physical symptoms and the behaviour of the organism."[42] The electrical action of protoplasm can be found in Burroughs's scene of the Osmosis Recharge, the galvanic junk hit "which corresponds to a skin shot" of the president, when the fix is inadequate and he experiences "silent protoplasmic agonies, bone frenzies. . . . Tensions build up, pure energy without emotional content finally tears through the body, throwing him about like a man in contact with high-tension wires."[43] If cut off entirely, he "falls into such violent, electric convulsions that his bones shake loose, and he dies with the skeleton straining to climb out of his unendurable flesh."[44] Korzybski's "psychogalvanic experiments" would later be transformed into treatment technologies by the E-meters of Scientology.

External stimuli produced by physical, mechanical, chemical, and biological (which itself includes, as we read in *Science and Sanity*, "microbes, parasites and spermatozoa") factors have, according to Korzybski, quick access to consciousness and other parts of psychophysiological functioning. In turn, "*semantic relations*" themselves act as stimuli and can, if not complementary to free-flowing processes and organismic energy, cause illness.[45] This is not a simple statement of psychosomatics, for in his version philosophy can make you sick. Aristotelian thought, in particular—with its dualisms and identifications—can create *semantogenic blockages* resulting in disease, poor business practice, or an absolutist state. Despite the dominance of this philosophical malady within Western culture, Korzybski was not driven by the exaggerated rhetoric of pervasive pathology and therapeutics that would later characterize Burroughs, especially after his encounter with Dianetics. Korzybski's protoplasmic body was not intrinsically or intransigently pathogenic but was just a place where illness happens. Even blockages can be treated fairly easily by learning how they work and might be prevented to a large degree by developing social practices underscored by a new, non-Aristotelian philosophy.

The Cancer Virus

The second organismic theory to which Burroughs subscribed could be found among the writings of Wilhelm Reich, in particular *The Cancer Biopathy* (1948). Like Korzybski Reich trafficked in protoplasm and electricity but differed by directing them squarely into sex, a phenomenon close to the Burroughs's heart, and out into the earth's atmosphere where they literally took on global significance. Also, the site of pathology, being fairly dispersed and nondescript in Korzybski's thought, became located at an explicitly microbial level in the figures of Reich's cancerous cells and at the microscopic scene of inorganic matter coming to life once charged by the blue spark of orgone energy. Pathogenics, therefore, became situated at a protoplasmic and colloidal scale appropriate to actual viruses. In other words, Reichian cancer pathologized the usurpative functioning of Korzybskian protoplasm and colloidal behavior and thereby fortified the already existing ability for cancer to usurp the very being of individuals and societies through acts of metaphoricity. Moreover, during the 1950s it was common to simply confuse cancer with the contagious action of viruses, and indeed, Burroughs collapses the two into one another, aided by a notion of cancer as protoplasm gone awry, an attack of nondifferentiation overwhelmed by rampant reproduction.

Burroughs was as devoted to Reich's thought as he was to that of Korzybski, and, at the time, no other author produced similar enthusiasm. In 1949 he wrote to Jack Kerouac: "I have just done reading Wilhelm Reich's latest book *The Cancer Biopathy*. I tell you Jack, he is the only man in the analysis line who is *on that beam*. After reading the book I built an orgone accumulator, and the gimmick really works. The man is not crazy, he's a fucking genius."[46] About a year later Burroughs sternly reprimanded Ginsberg's incredulity about Reich and instructed him to take yet another refresher course in General Semantics.[47] *Junkie* contained a substantial section on Reich before it was edited out, and for at least another fifteen years his writing contained Reich-inspired material. Moreover, it was by integrating Reich's findings in proximity with the immense, totalizing scope of General Semantics that Burroughs developed his General Theory of Addiction, which, in its therapeutic applications, held "the key to addiction, cancer, and schizophrenia" [48]—*"On medical subjects I am seldom if ever wrong."* [49]

Reich's biopsychiatric theory is rife with colloids, protoplasm, protozoa, and amoebae, which are philosophically similar to Korzybskian goo in the way they are pitted against mechanistic thought: "Protoplasm functions on the basis of characteristics not possessed by machines. It functions *without being structured.*" [50] However, although Reich acknowledged that "the organism undoubtedly contains electricity in the form of electrically charged colloid particles and ions," [51] he was unwilling to extend its charge as far as Korzybski. Instead, he established an additional class of bionic energy at play between inorganic and organic states, inside and outside the organism, and he understood this energy in primarily sexual terms. Consequently, whereas Korzybski needed the fluctuating needle of a galvanometric reading to prove the electrical basis of psychosomatic responses, for Reich the sweep of an erection was demonstration enough. Both did agree that the inhibition of their respective energies lead to illness. For Reich, the repression of sexual and orgone energies caused, among other things, cancer.

Sexuality and the energetics of protoplasm can be found in the *Interzone* writing entitled "Word," the commonly acclaimed beginning of the style made famous in *Naked Lunch*. [52] It starts off with a pastiche, a sound salad heard on a radio receiver that was ejaculating:

The Word is divided into units which be all in one piece and should be so taken, but the pieces can be had in any order being tied up back and forth in and out fore and aft like an innaresting sex arrangement. This book spill off the page in all directions, kaleidoscope of vistas, medley of tunes and street noises, farts and riot yipes and the slamming steel shutters of commerce, screams of pain and pathos and screams plain pathic, copulating cats and outraged squawk of the displaced Bull-head, prophetic mutterings of *brujo* in nutmeg trance, snapping necks and screaming mandrakes, sigh of orgasm, heroin silent as the dawn in thirsty cells, Radio Cairo screaming like a beserk tobacco auction, and flutes of Ramadan fanning the sick junky like a gentle lush worker in the gray subway dawn, feeling with delicate fingers for the green folding crackle.

This is Revelation and Prophecy of what I can pick up without FM on my 1920 crystal set with antennae of jissom.[53]

Not only is the world and the future technologically conducted through semen as protoplasmic emulsion, ejaculation itself within Burroughs own experience links junk and Reichian energy. The only two ways he achieved spontaneous orgasm was with the hair-trigger masturbation resulting as a by-product of kicking a habit and within an orgone box: "The orgones produce a prickling sensation frequently associated with erotic stimulation and spontaneous orgasm."[54] "Now a spontaneous, waking orgasm is a rare occurrence even in adolescence. Only one I ever experienced was in the orgone accumulator I made in Texas."[55] For Reich orgasmic energy was at play between inorganic and organic states, sparking and tingling inside and outside the organism, and, most important, it was distributed throughout the earth's atmosphere. The orgone box was designed to receive and concentrate this energy and to pass it on to the individual seated inside; the principles for its construction were presented in *The Cancer Biopathy.* The dissipation and accumulation of orgonotic energy between the individual and the atmosphere was the fundamental, global exchange of life energies, a way of situating the seated.

Although Reich had invented the accumulator before 1945, by the time Burroughs began soaking up orgone energy it was set against the background of another radiation: the bombs the United States clinically exploded on the unsuspecting citizens of Hiroshima and Nagasaki and tested above ground during the postwar years. The atmosphere was now radiant with orgone energy *and* fallout, not to mention saturated with the transmissions of the consciousness industry in the form of radio and television. In 1950 Joan Burroughs had convinced her husband that atomic fallout was not merely degenerative physiologically but was also involved in psychic control.[56] Five years later the effects of above-ground nuclear tests conducted by "these life-hating, character armadillos" (Burroughs's Reichian slang for severely repressed individuals) were very much on his mind: "Thirty more explosions and we've had it, and nobody shows any indication of curtailing their precious experiments."[57] In 1957 Burroughs read the "most sinister news bulletin that reported that the only forms of life that mutate favorably under radiation are the smallest, namely the viruses. Flash. Centipedes a hundred feet long eaten by viruses big as bed bugs under a gray sky of fallout."[58] He thought that a virus in Tangier that purportedly suppressed the sex drive might be one such mutation: "God knows how many atypical virus strains may follow in the wake of atomic experiments."[59] In *Interzone* the imagery of atomic mutations combined with the radiation technology of the orgone accumulator to produce the variety of mutants in the famed "Spare Ass Annie" section. Instead of the organic material used in an orgone box, priests "built boxes from the moist, fresh bones of healthy youths" who had been hanged, inducing simultaneous death and orgasm, and then "Pregnant women were placed in the boxes and left on the peak for a period of three hours. Often the women died, but those who survived usually produced monsters."[60]

Reich's bioenergetic processes consisted of a pervasive *tension-charge* function expressed in such acts as the "total contraction of an amoeba [or] the orgastic contraction of a multicellular organism."[61] Its most important emblem was, of course, the orgasm: "There seems to exist *one* basic law that governs the total organism, in addition to governing its autonomic organs. . . . *The orgasm formula . . . emerges as the life formula itself.*"[62] There were three major ways in which such *orgonotic fusion* could take place: "The copulative act the male organ penetrates the female . . . in many hermaphroditic molluscs (snails, worms) penetration is mutual but restricted to the genitals . . . [and] the union of two gametes to form a zygote . . . is a perfect example of total interpenetration and fusion of substance."[63] This tripartite classification could also be broken down along the lines of heterosexual union, male homosexual union, and schlupping. Because Burroughs considered sexual urge as a "primitive back brain" affair and so much of life as the account of falling and the fallen, it would make sense to follow multicellular humans down the evolutionary if not ontogenetic scale to gametes, to the pure protoplasmic usurpation of zygotic sexuality. Also, because Reich also refused to distinguish between copulating and eating at a primitive biological state, the sexual ingestion of Burroughs's "amoeboid protoplasmic projection" could be traced to protozoan feeding habits.[64]

Similarly, cancer appeared to Reich to be "nothing but protozoa."[65] Thus, in the transfer to Burroughs's viral menagerie, a glorified amoeba driven by hunger for sex or junk could take on a pathogenic character schlupping its undifferentiated mass toward a destructive ingestion of its object of desire. In keeping with such amoebic lack of differentiation, the quite pronounced microbial exchange of identity among protoplasm, protozoa, cancer, and virus within Burroughs's initial schema of usurpation, even as it becomes generalized to the societal level, was best exemplified in the "Ordinary Men and Women" section in *Naked Lunch* where stem cell goo, cancer, virus, and viral metaphoricity all coexist. Within his discourse on the talking asshole, Dr. Benway describes how the asshole sealed off the mouth with a "transparent jelly . . . what the scientists call un-D.T., Undifferentiated Tissue, which can grow into any kind of flesh on the human body. He would tear it off his mouth and the pieces would stick to his hands like burning gasoline jelly and grow there, grow anywhere on him a glob of it fell."[66] It quickly becomes sexualized and produces multiple and mobile orifices: "globs of that un-D.T. . . . fall anywhere and grow into some degenerate cancerous life-form, reproducing a hideous random image. Some would be entirely made of penis-like erectile tissue, others viscera barely covered over with skin, clusters of 3 and 4 eyes together, crisscross of mouth and assholes, human parts shaken around and poured out any way they fell."[67] Cancer is then equated with a virus and both are fed into a description of bureaucracy:

The end result of complete cellular representation is cancer. Democracy is cancerous, and bureaus are its cancer. A bureau takes root anywhere in the state, turns malignant like the Narcotic Bureau, and grows and grows, always reproducing more of its own kind, until it chokes the host if not controlled or excised. Bureaus cannot live without a host, being true parasitic organisms. . . . Bureaucracy is wrong as a cancer, a turning away from the human evolutionary direction of infinite potentials and differentiation and independent spontaneous action, to the complete parasitism of a virus.[68]

This is the generalized character of the virus grown in the culture of the protoplasmic body, taking on the parasitic procedures of metaphor and usurping through its carcinogenic lack of differentiation even such large beasts as bureaucracy. This was the virus to 1959, the year that *Naked Lunch* was published. The schlupping body rendered pathogenic would soon cease being the primary culture in which the virus grew and would become just one among others, with the function of the virus becoming increasingly differentiated through a complex of other influences. This was because 1959 was also the year that Burroughs read L. Ron Hubbard's *Dianetics*, conducted his first tape recorder experiments with Brion Gysin, and met Ian Sommerville.

Cellular Phones

By the time Burroughs read *Dianetics* by L. Ron Hubbard, the founder of the Church of Scientology, it must have seemed very familiar, for here was not only the third in a sequence of influential organismic theories but one obviously influenced by Korzybski.[69] In addition, it was a theory whose pathological sphere was practically limitless, eagerly ascribing a distinctly causal and evil agency to all those areas Korzybski once granted benign existence. For Korzybski, disease was the exception; for Hubbard it was the norm. For Burroughs this was highly conducive to the (fallen) personifications that constituted his character studies; for Hubbard an expanded pathogenics meant the heroics of a correspondingly expanded therapeutic regime and formed the cornerstone of both his pretentiousness and popularity. For the Burroughs virus, it meant mutation into a newly pervasive and virulent role.

In terms of organismic theories, Hubbard's version must have seemed even more familiar to Burroughs because of a common American culture. Compared to the continental reasoning found in Korzybski and Reich, Hubbard's persistent appeal to a crude if-it-works pragmatism, his empiricism and persistent aversion of speculation, let alone the patently asocial, individualistic focus, must have seemed positively homegrown. Burroughs would seem to naturally favor Hubbard's definitively stated central presumption—"Man is motivated *only* by survival"—over the abstractions of non-Aristotelianism or the tension-charge principle.[70] Hubbard spent many years living in the naval town of Bremerton, Washington, where the ever-present gray steel of the fleet (mimicked by perpetually overcast skies) would have provided constant military legitimization for a theory of life based on survival, just as the American-style gun culture captivating Burroughs throughout his entire life butted up to his own words on the matter: "I am primarily concerned with the question of survival."[71] Hubbard too was famous for writing novels.

Brion Gysin encountered Scientology as early as 1955 or 1956, when a friend told him of "fascinating things about a billion buck scam he was onto called Scientology," an inviting option since Gysin's restaurant in

Tangier was in financial difficulty.[72] Burroughs had met and duly ignored Gysin while in Tangier, but they befriended one another in Paris beginning in 1958, after Burroughs had moved into what came to be known as the Beat Hotel. Beginning in October 1959, Burroughs wrote once again to Allen Ginsberg to champion his infatuation with yet another organismic theory: "Remembering has many levels. We remember our operations under anesthesia according to *L. Ron Hubbard—DIANETICS*—went on to *Scientology*, which you would do well to look into. A run in time, you know. Remember I gave you a tip said the Waiter. . . . Pick up on the action, pops, and don't forget to give Hubbard a run for his money. He thinks you should and so does/Your Reporter/William Seward Burroughs/'Hello—Yes—Hello.'"[73] The sign off of "Hello—Yes—Hello," itself part of the Dianetic regimen, would continue to crop up in Burroughs's vernacular for years to come. Later that same October Burroughs wrote once more to Ginsberg, "The method of directed recall is the method of Scientology. You will recall I wrote urging you to contact local chapter and find an auditor," and then he cautions Ginsberg: "Last call to dinner."[74] His championing and subsequent criticism of Hubbard are well known, but it is important to keep in mind that even during at his most critical, Burroughs fostered a distaste for Hubbard's handling of secrecy, institutional authoritarianism, and business footing and his transmutation to religiosity, he but continued to uphold the basic therapeutic validity found in Dianetics.[75]

The basic pathogenic building block in the system of Dianetics was the evil agent known as the *engram*—most simply, an injurious or otherwise painful moment literally recorded by the body. This recording should not be confused with memory that takes place within the brain, and it should not be assumed that a person even needs to be conscious to record an injurious experience. Instead, the recording occurs anywhere in the body at the cellular level as a "definite and permanent trace left by a stimulus on the protoplasm of a tissue . . . *a cellular trace of recordings impinged deeply into the very structure of the body itself.*"[76] These engrams contain absolutely everything and would be very much "like phonograph records or motion pictures, if these contained all perceptions of sight, sound, smell, taste, organic sensation, etc."[77] If these engrams stay in place and are not *discharged* through therapeutic means, they will predispose the individual to psychosomatic illnesses (which for Hubbard includes all the familiar diseases), mental disorders, and always something less than complete psychophysiological sanity. The therapeutic process basically entails discovering these recordings and playing them back over and over again until they lose their power, become boring, and are shifted out of what Hubbard calls the *reactive mind*, where the cumulative engrams act in a nefariously coordinated manner, and into the benign region of the regular memory banks, where they will do no harm. That was what Burroughs meant in his letter to Ginsberg when he said all that was required was to "simply run the tape back and forth until the trauma is wiped off. It works."[78]

Hubbard borrowed the term *engram* from Richard Wolfgang Semon's idea of the *mneme*, developed early this century.[79] His *mnemic principle* belonged to a larger sphere of reproductive phenomena including habit and heredity (an inclusion that drew the most criticism), as well as memory, and is based on how stimuli produce a "permanent record . . . written or engraved on the irritable substance"—that is, on cellular material energistically predisposed to such inscription.[80] The resulting *mnemic trace* (or engram) can be revivified when an element resembling a component of the original complex of stimuli is encountered. Thus, Semon recounts how the smell of Italian cooking oil invoked "most vividly the optic engram of Capri" from a trip years before.[81] It did not invoke "the melody of the barrel-organ, the heat of the sun, the discomfort of the boots," which were equally part of the original engram complex, but this does not rule out that sometime in the future a pair of tight boots might revivify Capri. The complete engram complex of the entire organism is thereby effectively reproducible from small units anywhere throughout the organism. Cut-up planaria, hydra, stentors, and begonias provided ample evidence for mnemic dispersal and regeneration from pieces approaching the size of *germ-cells*. But Semon ran into difficulty when confronted with the evidence for cortical localization of memory in vertebrates, for how could it be reconciled with a capacity for cellular recording and reproduction of stimuli throughout the organism?

Semon found evidence in the way that different parts of the body relate to each other involuntarily, such as "reflex spasms, co-movements, sensory radiations," to infer distribution of "engraphic influence" throughout the "whole irritable substance of the organism."[82] He also took inventive recourse to that well-known mnemonic device, the phonograph, a veritable mneme machine, to explain the uneven distribution and revivification of engrams. Here, each phonograph represents a primary site of excitation that privileges its immediate vicinity yet nevertheless contains fainter impressions of the entire orchestra, the organism. Thus, *tight shoes* might invoke walking to Capri, but another stimulus, such as the smell of cooking, would be weaker:

Let us imagine that in an opera house of the usual construction a great number of very similar phonographic recording machines are distributed in different parts of the building, among the boxes, the stalls, the dress and upper circles, on and behind the stage, and also in the orchestra between the seats of the players. In the separate reproductions of the various records made during the playing of the orchestra it will be found that no two of the records are alike, despite the similarities of the machines. According to the location of the machines, it will be possible to distinguish differences of clearness and power in the reproduction of the music. Among the instruments distributed in the orchestra itself, those in the vicinity of the basses will reproduce the renderings of the bass parts out of all proportion to the designed effect of the total production. The phonographs placed between the 'cellos will in their reproduction give us the impression that during the performance the 'cellos played the leading part, and that the rest of the instruments provided merely a pianissimo accompaniment. So, with the records made by the other machines, there would be differences of emphasis according to their position.[83]

Although Semon explicitly warned against following this model too closely because the relationship of an engram to a phonogram was the same as "a horse pulling a carriage to a locomotive propelling one,"[84] his qualification was based on the complete sensory register of the engram—"photic, thermal, and electric influences, that is, with stimuli belonging to all possible kinds of energies,"[85]—whereas the phonograph was capable only of recording events sonically. In other words, he would have been perfectly happy to compare his engram with some more advanced multisensory technology; recording technology or its prosthetic applicability to the *organism* did not bother him. Hubbard took repeated recourse to similar technological tropes.

Hubbard transformed what Semon considered functionally neutral in engramic activity into something intrinsically pathogenic, just as he had done to Korzybski's ideas. Whereas Semon understood engramic recording to be of a quotidian character, Hubbard's engram was first and foremost inscribed as an ostensibly exceptional record of trauma. The argument put forth in *Dianetics* indeed would seem to be at first isolated to only very exceptional cases of pain and injury, the most unadulterated being those instances where the individual/organism is abused while in an unconscious state resulting from accident, anesthesia, or some other means. The *analytic mind*, the beneficent agent of the conscious self that normally would be recording absolutely everything into the safety of the standard memory banks would, under anesthesia, be shut down purely for survival reasons. With the good *analytic mind* absent from its recording duties, the evil *reactive mind* takes over as it feeds on its newly recorded store of engrams. However, if engrams were created only by the exceptional traumatic events Hubbard initially describes, then few people would have need for therapy. He therefore retains the unconsciousness accompanying severe trauma for rhetorical clout while extending the functional capacity for engram formation to any degree of reduced consciousness whatsoever. In other words, any shortfall of complete, lucid consciousness on part of the analytic mind will be met with a proportionate degree of *unconsciousness* and with it a recording of engrams. In the end, engrams are generated by anything ranging from brutal surgical procedures performed while the person is in an extended coma due to a terrible car crash to feeling a bit vague. In fact, much of Hubbard's *Dianetics* is concerned with describing means by which engrams proliferate. For example, we are perversely alerted to the fact that fetuses are busy accumulating engrams not just by the underestimated frequency of attempted abortions (apparently, we are told, not as exceptional as one might suspect) but seemingly by any little bump or jostle. As an extension of such abuse, motherly love itself turns out to be nothing but a cruel hoax. The act of leaving that prenatal hell of a womb creates another slew of engrams as a result of the mother's labor pains and the rude exposure of the baby to the cruel world. The baby's cries then remind the mother of her labor pains, long after the birthday has passed, revivifying and entrenching the engrams further into the motherly protoplasm, and this in turn finds its way back to the baby as the mother *dramatizes* her engram-inscribed self to the baby, endowing her child with another set of engrams, and so forth in a truly vicious cycle. Since "zygote, embryo, foetus, infant, child, adult: these are all the same person" there will never be a shortage of therapy required.[86]

The accumulated bank of recorded and stored engrams produce the *combined cellular intelligence* constituting the *reactive mind,* the mind of a coalesced trauma body, an evil phantom double to the *analytic mind,* the intrinsically good and perfectly running calculating machine that is always recording everything as a matter of consciousness and storing it in the *standard memory banks.*[87] Assuming that anything short of epiphany has a dose of dim-wittedness about it, then it is clear that the reactive mind is likely to be ever present, causing problems for the analytic mind and for the health of the entire organism. The evil phantom that is the reactive mind underscores the *Other Half* in the oft-quoted passage from *The Ticket That Exploded* (1962) used to exemplify Burroughs's notion that *language is a virus:*

The "Other Half" is the word. The "Other Half" is an organism. Word is an organism. The presence of the "Other Half" a separate organism attached to your nervous system on an air line of words can now be demonstrated experimentally. One of the most common "hallucinations" of subjects during sense withdrawal is the feeling of another body sprawled through the subject's body at an angle ... yes quite an angle it is the "Other Half" worked quite some years on a symbiotic basis. From symbiosis to parasitism is a short step. The word is now a virus. The flu virus may once have been a healthy lung cell. It is now a parasitic organism that invades and damages the lungs. The word may once have been a healthy neural cell. It is now a parasitic organism that invades and damages the central nervous system. Modern man has lost the option of silence. Try halting your sub-vocal speech. Try to achieve even ten seconds of inner silence. You will encounter a resisting organism that forces you to talk. That organism is the word.[88]

The Other Half could, of course, be language itself as an entity that is acquired through contagious processes during youth long before any prophylactic possibility of critical self-consciousness and that dictates its own conditions on how the world might be understood and acted on. Most persuasively, language is a virus in that both are dead until they find life within a human host: "the evilest of them all are the virus. ... So bone lazy they aren't even hardly alive yet. Fuckin' transitional bastards."[89] The Other Half could also be the hallucinated body set askew during sensory deprivation, the kinaesthetic body, the astral body, the phantom body that makes its appearance felt when limbs are amputated, but none of these bodies have language and none have the agency, let alone a subaltern one, that could work the line between symbiosis and parasitism. None have the capability of effectively supplanting the host. On the other hand, the reactive mind has both a concrete corporeal existence and language. It also acts like the Other Half in the way that it exists submerged, in the modulations of consciousness and unconsciousness. The reactive mind builds itself up within its host during the absence of the agency of the host, the analytic mind, and thus is an oddly ephemeral parasite. But it can function just as well, as we shall see, on its own accord, animating the individual without announcing its own role, making it speak. In this way, the reactive mind can move well past parasitism.

The reactive mind meets the virus in Hubbard's assertion that "it is fairly well accepted in these times that life in all forms evolved from the basic building blocks: the virus and the cell."[90] Viruses may in fact have played a part in the electrical and cognitive functioning of an individual because "even neurons exist in embryo in the zygote, and neurons do not themselves divide but are like organisms (and may have the virus as their basic building block)."[91] Burroughs's version simply reverses the order; neurons do not have a virus in their collective past, but instead the healthy neural cell mutates into the virus that is language. The evolutionary development toward language proposed by Burroughs was aided by Hubbard in at least two ways: first, the reactive mind was already equipped with its own voice engramically recorded and played back, what Hubbard calls the *Dianetic demon*, to which a chapter in *Dianetics* is devoted, and second, there was a radio station available to transmit the recordings.

Hubbard derived his demon by pathologizing the comparatively benign figure of the Socratic dæmon, the independent internal voice that Socrates consulted when he had to make an important decision, effectively an oracle vented inside his head. It had his best interests in mind, whereas the Dianetic demon had only the interests of the reactive mind in mind. The Dianetic demon has fallen from Socratic utility and has become a demon "who gives thoughts voice or echoes the spoken word interiorly or who gives all sorts of complicated advice like a real, live voice exteriorly." It should not, he emphasized, be confused with psychotic voices: "People who hear voices have exterior vocal demons—circuits have tied up their imagination circuits."[92] Hubbard equates its form and function: "*A Dianetic demon is a parasitic circuit.* It has an action in the mind which approximates another entity than self. And it is derived entirely from words contained in engrams."[93] This other-entity-than-self is wired in between an individual's analytical consciousness and the standard data banks of memory. When the consciousness asks for data pure and simple, an exchange that usually transpires in silence, it is given some other data by a voice. That voice eventually insinuates itself more and more until it effectively takes over, leaving the "'I' on a tiny and forlorn shelf."[94]

This is not a hydraulic condition caused by what Korzybski would call a "semantogenic blockage"; instead it is an electronic flow redirected within circuitry fed with a countermanding engramic voice. Hubbard provided wiring instructions (the "analyzer" here belongs to the analytical mind of consciousness and self-identification and "got to listen to me, by God" are words, in this case, inscribed as an engram):

An electronics engineer can set up demons in a radio circuit to his heart's content. In human terms, it is as if one ran a line from the standard banks toward the analyzer but before it got there he put in a speaker and a microphone and then continued the line to the plane of consciousness. Between the speaker and the microphone would be a section of the analyzer which was an ordinary, working section but compartmented off from the remainder of the analyzer. "I" on a conscious plane wants data. It should come straight from the standard bank, compute on a sublevel and arrive just as data. Not spoken data. Just data. With the portion of the analyzer compartmented off and the speaker-microphone installation and the engram containing the above words "got to listen to me, by God" in chronic restimulation, another thing happens. The "I" in the upper-level attention units wants data. He starts to scan the standard banks with a sublevel. The data comes to him *spoken.* Like a voice inside his head.[95]

It might sound a bit disconcerting (although you know where to get help) that something as commonplace as inner speech might constitute an aberration caused by *other voices* interceding on the self-contained self, yet "It is a safe assumption that almost every aberree contains a demon circuit. . . . A Clear does not have any 'mental voices'! He does not think vocally. He thinks without articulation of his thoughts and his thoughts are not in voice terms."[96] Of course, this inner biologic is what Burroughs describes above in his rhetorical imperative to "Try halting your sub-vocal speech. Try to achieve even ten seconds of inner silence. You will encounter a re- sisting organism that forces you to talk."[97] Burroughs was declared to be a Clear at a certain point in the course of therapy, and, ostensibly, the Dia- netic demon was banished and the inner voice silenced. However, within the literary sphere of his pathogenics viruses continued to reproduce, pro- liferate, and become increasingly sophisticated both tactically and tech- nologically. Within his personal pathogenics, he feared this very state of silence among his peers using Buddhist techniques to quell the inner voice. Such techniques could create the type of *cured writer* mentioned in *Naked Lunch*, and a cured writer ceases to be a writer.[98] But when it came to actual practice, it was all a matter of priorities:

When Huxley got Buddhism, he stopped writing novels and wrote Buddhist tracts. Meditation, astral travel, telepathy, are all means to an end for the novel- ist. I even got copy out of scientology. It's a question of emphasis. Any writer who does not consider his writing the most important thing he does, who does not consider writing his only salvation, I—"I trust him little in the commerce of the soul."[99]

In other words, from the perspective of his writing there was little reason to resist the resisting organism—the virus, word, language—for it too sim- ply heeds the call for *survival*, the same one that for Hubbard is no less than the *Goal of Man* and for Burroughs, "I am primarily concerned with the question of survival—with Nova conspiracies, Nova criminals, and Nova police. A new mythology is possible in the Space Age."[100] The re- sisting organism, too, obviously has had a future and still does, surviving against therapies with the acumen of the mutated virus, not calling unto- ward attention to itself, not destroying its host.

The degree to which Burroughs adopted Hubbard's theory of record- ing and fused it with the virus, and the degree with which a new mythology of the space age was infused with both, was repeatedly demonstrated in his writings. For example, "The Beginning Is Also the End" (1963):

The entire human film was prerecorded. I will explain briefly how this is done. Take a simple virus illness like hepatitis. This illness has an incubation period of two weeks. So I know when the virus is in (and I do because I put it there).

I know how you will look two weeks from now: yellow. To put it another way: I take a picture or rather a series of pictures of you with hepatitis. Now I put my virus negatives into your liver to develop. Not far to reach: remember I live in your body. The whole hepatitis film is prerecorded two weeks before the opening scene when you notice your eyes are a little yellower than usual.

It should now be obvious that what you call "reality" is a function of these precisely predictable because prerecorded human activities. Now what could louse up a prerecorded biologic film?[101]

The mutated virus took on a "hands-on" quality as it entered a highly elaborate set of audiotape strategies and tactics within the biologic control game, since Gysin introduced Burroughs to audiotape cut-in experiments in 1959, the same year as he began reading Hubbard. He also met Ian Sommerville around the same time; they soon became lovers and collaborators and worked on numerous tape recorder experiments. Sommerville was a technological and mathematical wiz kid who assisted Burroughs in extending the virus's power for speech and reproduction through technically sophisticated means of differentiation, as was evident in the cyclotron-induced variation of computer code in "Technical Deposition of the Virus Power" cited above. At this point, the privileged trajectory of generating organic life from inorganic material within Burroughs's favored organismic theories, was unambiguously reversed. The focus had switched to the generation of the semblance of life born from lodging communication technologies at the cellular level. The Other Half had become all others, they had become all, and the *theys* were not necessarily biotic. Organism had shifted the rise of the inorganic to the fall of the inorganic, all on the wings of the life and death struggle of the virus, the internecine being of the virus, fuckin' transitional bastard.

CRUELTY AND THE BEAST:
ANTONIN ARTAUD AND MICHAEL MCCLURE

For Michael McClure meat is gene expression. The muscularity and mammalianism connecting humans with other species is meat expression, and the bounty of life's forces surge through traditions of revelatory poetics and mysticism. For Antonin Artaud meat is something to shed. Damaged by illness during childhood, later abused by various substances and nervous illnesses, made more decrepit from institutionalized starvation, torment, and electroshock, his body did not recommend itself to an exultation of other bodies. Why, then, place the two together? This is not the first time. In 1964, Carolee Schneemann sent a prospectus for her performance piece *Meat Joy* to Jean-Jacques Lebel in Paris:

There are now several works moving in mindseye. . . . *Meat Joy* shifting now, relating to Artaud, McClure, and French butcher shops—carcass as paint (it dripped right through Soutine's floor) . . . flesh jubilation . . . extremes of this sense. . . . Smell, feel of meat . . . chickens, fish, sausages?[1]

That Artaud and McClure had met in meat decades ago was itself because McClure was one of Artaud's earliest and most ardent of supporters in the United States. We could easily trace a diffusion of Artaud in America through McClure, through his poetry and plays beginning in the 1950s, through his cultural connections outside literature proper—a close friend and mentor of the poet and singer Jim Morrison, collaborator with the Italian painter Francesco Clemente, with keyboardist Ray Manzarek, also with The Doors—into his present-day status as a poet and environmentalist. As Gary Snyder has written, "I'm a close reader of Michael McClure's poetry, for his long, careful, intense dedication to developing a specific biological/wild/unconscious/fairytale/new/scientific/imagination form. Maybe he's closer to Blake than anybody else writing."[2] But the present chapter is not about McClure specifically or even about all the places Artaud and McClure intersect. I am instead most interested in the sound of meat—specifically, the distinct types of vocalization with which they are associated (Artaud with screaming and McClure with beast language) and in the respective links, so to speak, between meat and voice, situated around conceptions of the body, the body's relationship with other natural and cosmic forces, body practices and disciplines, and animality.

Why bother? Their ideas of meat are very different from one another, or, rather, McClure's ideas of meat are quite different than the meat implicit in many contemporary accounts and theoretical byproducts of Artaud. For many, Artaud's body has become a marker of anomie rooted in a self-concentrated attempt to evacuate and shed the body, generating a politics whereby the body acts as a lightning rod for the manifestations of a greater social sadism and as an accompanying set of metaphysical conditions. McClure's body, on the other hand, is animated by an organismic poetics under the auspices of biology, genetics, ecology, and mammalianism, rooted in a bioself concomitant with other creatures and elaborated in an *antipolitics* of biological activism.[3] With regard to contemporary concerns, there are no indications that anomie is subsiding, but there are many indications that the ecological disaster is accelerating and will reach a point where anomie will be the least of people's worries. If we can assume that the political-economic forces and cultural assumptions driving this global degradation are populated by ideas of bodies, that is motivation enough.

However, in what may be somewhat a surprise, we can detect a moment of ecological thinking—not just of poetic naturalism but a precisely directed political indictment—within Artaud's work itself. How this and other aspects of Artaud's writings might have played into the first flush of McClure's encounter with them as he roamed the Bay Area bohemian ranks of the San Francisco Renaissance and proto-Beat scene is part of the focus here. We will not limit ourselves to how McClure may or may not have been influenced by Artaud. At a certain point, I turn the chronological tables and ask how we might understand Artaud through McClure—in particular, how might Artaud's screaming be understood in light of the genesis of McClure's beast language and the bodies that come with it. But before talking about the influence of Artaud on anyone in America, we have to decide on *which* Artaud.

With respect to Beat meat, Burroughs was the old man of the Beats, and McClure the baby of the Beats. Although very different from one another, each elaborated complex ideas developed from organismic theories. In both cases, *meat* is not the body posed as a passive puppet for the individual or social intellect, not the old or new detritus of Cartesianism or cyberphilia. Burroughs's *pure meat method*, as Ginsberg called it, consisted of an accretion of a voice and an intellect of an other (the Other Half) from a dispersal throughout a body of traumatized meat. His meat was the by-product of a progressive pathologization, whereas for McClure voices emanated from muscles and meat of humans and other mammals across the full range of instinct and affect. While McClure's *meat science* may not have the postmodern or subcultural caché of Burroughs's viral trope, its pertinence lies in an imperative to supersede the destructive consequences of philosophies centered on a sociality isolated from biology and ecology.

Artaud in America

Voyage to the Land of the 50% Less Cruel. Although Artaud never traveled to the United States, he did visit the Americas and learned enough of the Tarahumara people to side with them, in his radio production *To Have Done with the Judgment of God*, against the entrepreneurial and militaristic mob north of the border. This is not to say that he hated all things American; avant-garde theater in Europe often found sources of inspiration in the vitality of American culture. The type of physical humor in Marx Brothers movies, for instance, was very interesting to him, as long as the humor itself was removed to access the core of its physicality. Yet on trans-atlantic balance whatever he made of the United States, artists in the United States would in due time make much more of him.

Beginning in the late 1940s American artists borrowed from him in every manner conceivable and regularly came up short of the deification or delectation more typical of his European reception. True, some conti-nental-style connoisseurship exists today, where romances and metaphysics of his evacuated organs are distilled with little nose for pain or politics. This came fairly late in the game, however, after Artaud had been filtered through French poststructuralism, whereon it became difficult to deter-mine where a theorist left off and an Artaud began, especially during a colec-tomy. The Artaud of an earlier reception arrived in America unaccompanied by other authorities; his texts were more readily raided, misread, and then tossed into the blender with other sources. Very few of them had a working image of Artaud during his famous performance at the *Vieux-Colombier* theater on 13 January 1947, where his shriveled countenance was indelibly etched into the consciousness of so many French intellectuals. In the United States during the 1950s and 1960s there was less an image of him than of his ideas, and it proved just as easy to recast his ideas as it did to rehydrate his image. For American artists Artaud would serve variously as the promoter of a new technical theater, of a new communal theater, a champion of shutting up and shouting out, the textbook example of the romantic artist and the purveyor of *no more masterpieces*, the barely sobered madman railing against psychiatric institutions and psychiatrists, critic of postwar politics or peddler of apolitical rites, the traveler in search of reve-latory hallucinations, renderer of complacency, mender of art and life.

Artaud in America? The most common scenario begins with M. C. Richards's translation, *The Theater and Its Double*, published by Grove Press in 1958, through which Artaud's ideas were then taken up for a significant but brief stint by experimental theater, most notably by The Living The-ater. Richards had in fact sent Julian Beck and Judith Malina, the founders of The Living Theater, a prepublication manuscript in 1958, but it was not until 1963 with the production of *The Brig* that they openly incorporated Artaud's ideas into their work.[4] As a consequence, Artaud becomes associ-ated with theater of a distinctly cathartic and Dionysian cast, shouting out in the existential void of a crowded room. He also becomes identified with the 1960s. There are several problems with this scenario. First, because he was used and dropped in the 1960s by theater, his artistic provocation is seen to have been exhausted, when in fact there were any number of artists at the time who incorporated his ideas and neither publicly nor privately discarded him, just as there remain today many Artauds to construct and use. Second, there were other influential texts by Artaud translated prior to Richard's translation of *The Theater and Its Double*, and among these texts could be counted about half of the same manuscript as it was published in 1953. Third, it was the 1950s not the 1960s where the earliest embrace of Artaud took place, in two places conspicuously *outside* theater: the new music ranks of David Tudor and John Cage and the literature of the Beat writers Carl Solomon, Allen Ginsberg, and Michael McClure. Tudor used Artaud to play the piano better, Cage used him in a very noncathartic form of composition and performance, the Beats were more interested in Artaud the political poet, and McClure and others were to mount an Artaud-inspired theater several years before The Living Theater. Artaud was a whole host of Artauds.

Musical Artauds: Tudor and Cage

Artaud's American presence began in force when the translation "Van Gogh: A Man Suicided by Society" appeared in *The Tiger's Eye* 7 (March 1949),[5] a journal with overlapping concerns of Surrealism, existentialism, the imagism of William Carlos Williams, and Abstract Expressionism. This proved to be fortuitous timing for underscoring the romance of Jackson Pollock just as he was reaching his stride pacing back and forth above his canvases. Indeed, throughout 1950s art world vernacular the name of Pollock would often accompany the name of Artaud: tortured by art, struggling with the body, signifying with gesture, under the influence of substance and psyche, dead early. Nevertheless, it was John Cage, with his well-known antipathy toward Pollock and all ego-driven artistic pursuits, who was to produce one of the earliest manifestations of Artaud's influence. His introduction to Artaud, however, was through the pianist David Tudor, who had incorporated Artaudian ideas of violence and physicality into his performance. Moreover, this proved to be the gateway through which M. C. Richards would be introduced to *Le Théâtre et son double* and decide to undertake her famous translation in the first place.

During the spring of 1949, John Cage and Merce Cunningham visited Europe. Cage, at the urging of Virgil Thomson, introduced himself to

Pierre Boulez, and they went on to become transatlantic allies over the next five years in the cause of new music. Cage returned to the United States with a number of Boulez compositions under his arm, including the notoriously difficult *Second Piano Sonata* (1948), which he took on himself to get performed. When his first choice did not work out, he gave the score to Tudor. They had met during autumn 1949 through the dancer Jean Erdman, whose husband was the noted mythologist Joseph Campbell (whose own collaboration with Cage was in the offing). Tudor, an unknown at the time, was very confident of his skills, but the *Second Sonata* proved to be beyond his prowess. With a dedication for which he would later become known, he taught himself French to read Boulez's writings to find a key to the piece. The key was in an article entitled "Propositions" in which Boulez wrote, "Finally, I have a personal reason for giving such an important place to the phenomenon of rhythm. I think that music should be collective hysteria and magic, violently modern—along the lines of Antonin Artaud and not in the sense of a simple ethnographic reconstruction in the image of civilizations more or less remote from us."[6]

Tudor went to Gotham Book Mart in New York City and left with a text of *Le Théâtre et son double* (1938). According to the primary authority on Tudor, John Holzaepfel, Tudor found a passage in Artaud's book that corresponded directly to Boulez's enthusiasm, where the *collective hysteria and magic* took tangible form in the practices of trances and music cures heard audibly on ethnographic recordings:

I propose then a theater in which physical images crush and hypnotize the sensibility of the spectator seized by the theater as by a whirlwind of higher forces. . . . A theater which, abandoning psychology, recounts the extraordinary, stages natural conflicts, natural and subtle forces, and presents itself first of all as an exceptional power of redirection. A theater that induces trance, as the dances of Dervishes induce trance, and that addresses itself to the organism by precise instruments, by the same means as those of certain tribal music cures which we admire on records but are incapable of originating among ourselves.[7]

Tudor took this as an encouragement to a performative violence, one with a temporal immediacy contrary to the types of duration involved in trance but not contrary to the immediacy produced by a trance-like abandon.

What he was abandoning were the conventions of musical time and continuity that stood between him and Boulez's *Second Piano Sonata*. Simply put, then, Artaud provided the violence and physicality needed to enter another type of time: "I recall how my mind had to change in order to be able to do it. . . . All of a sudden I saw that there was a different way of looking at musical continuity, having to deal with what Artaud called the affective athleticism. It has to do with the disciplines that an actor goes through. It was a real breakthrough for me, because my musical consciousness in the meantime changed completely. . . . I had to put my mind in a state of noncontinuity—not remembering—so that each moment is alive."[8]

For our purposes here, the crucial feature of Tudor's embrace of Artaud has to do with the role that Tudor himself played in the formation of American avant-garde music in the second half of the century, a role described convincingly by Holzaepfel. Because of Tudor's abilities as a performer of often daunting new music, he became closely associated with Cage, Earle Brown, Morton Feldman, and Christian Wolff. This was definitely not a service role, since they in turn felt compelled to compose at a level of difficulty and innovation to meet the challenge of Tudor's virtuosity. As Brown put it: "I think we all felt that about David—that we were *boring* him. 'What can we do next that he *can't* do?' I think we all felt he had a low threshold of boredom; he just breezed through these pieces, then seemed to ask, 'What next? Give me something *really* to do.'"[9] Artaud's writings contributed to Tudor's virtuosity, Tudor's virtuosity propelled the course of the New York School of composition and the Cagean aesthetic, and these in turn influenced the direction of a number of arts in the second half of the century. In this way alone one could find Artaudian traces throughout the 1950s and beyond.

Tudor's role has been underplayed no doubt due to his reticence at self-promotion and even social interaction, despite being a performer of great intensity. Cage, on the other hand, was a public person in so many ways. After being encouraged by Tudor to read *Le Théâtre et son double*, it was Cage who most energetically encouraged others to take notice of Artaud. Already fluent in French, he began to read Artaud in earnest at what proved to be a very auspicious time in his career. As he wrote to Boulez (22 May 1951), "I have been reading a great deal of Artaud. (This because of you and through Tudor who read Artaud because of you.) . . . I hope I have made a little clear to you what I am doing. *I have the feeling of just beginning to compose for the first time.* I will soon send you a copy of the first part of the piano piece. The essential underlying idea is that each thing is itself, that its relations with other things spring up naturally rather than being imposed by any abstraction on an 'artist's' part. (see Artaud on an objective synthesis)." [10] I have emphasized the one sentence to point out an assertion of a new confidence and resolve from someone already known for having an abundance of both. Indeed, the years 1951 and 1952 were exceedingly important in Cage's career, as evinced in a number of break-through compositions: *Music of Changes* (which used the *I Ching*), *Imaginary Landscape No. 4* (for twelve radios), *4' 33"*, *Water Music* (Cage's first theater piece), and *Williams Mix* (the audiotape piece that departed from the compositional tactics of *musique concrète*).

It was also in 1952 that Cage—inspired by a triangulation of the Huang Po Doctrine of Universal Mind, Marcel Duchamp's aesthetics of indifference, and Artaud—produced a performance piece at Black Mountain College. The event itself called on the participation if not the talents of Charles Olson, M. C. Richards, Robert Rauschenberg, David Tudor, Merce Cunningham, and others, and what might have happened exactly depends on which of various accounts from the participants and observers you read. [11] It would become commonly known later in the 1950s as both the *Black Mountain event* and, rightly or wrongly, as the first happening. One of Cage's accounts went like this: "At one end of the rectangular hall, the long end, was a movie and at the other end were slides. I was up on a ladder delivering a lecture which included silences and there was another ladder which M. C. Richards and Charles Olson went up at different times. . . . Robert Rauschenberg was playing an old-fashioned phonograph that had a horn and a dog on the side listening, and David Tudor was playing the piano, and Merce Cunningham and other dancers were moving through the audience and around the audience. Rauschenberg's [white] paintings were suspended above the audience." [12]

Cage's fascination with Artaud may seem odd. After all, by the early 1950s he had set himself against the heated, gestural assertions of the abstract expressionists in favor of a cool invocation of immaterial worldliness, and despite being lovers with a dancer his own comportment was guarded and seemingly out of touch with Artaudian corporeality. Cage's bodily restraint did not, however, contradict the specific attention within *The Theater and Its Double* given to the technical considerations of constituting theater from various artistic forms: "We got the idea from Artaud that theater could take place free of a text, that if a text were in it, that it needn't determine other actions, that sounds, that activities, and so forth, could all be free rather than tied together; so that rather than the dance expressing the music or the music expressing the dance, that the two could go together independently, neither one controlling the other. And this was extended on this occasion not only to music and dance, but to poetry and painting, and so forth, and to the audience. So that the audience was not focused in one particular direction."[13] Artaud's stance against the dominance of speech must have been especially attractive to Cage, since it was consistent with his own diminution of "literal" meaning through the musicalization of sounds (even though musicalization was just as ready to remove the affective body from performance). Cage's technical disposition toward Artaud was evident in his lesser motivations as well—for example, because Artaud had "made lists that could give ideas about what goes into theatre. And one should search constantly to see if something that could take place in theatre has escaped one's notice."[14] In contrast to Tudor who, equally attracted to the technical implications of Artaud, fused them in performance with an impassioned corporeality and metaphysics of violence, Cage was interested in the more patently formal attributes in service of a theater of things and events.

While in residence at Black Mountain College, Cage and Tudor brought Artaud's *Le Théâtre et son double* to the attention of M. C. Richards, who decided to translate the work into English. As her translation progressed, she gave readings to small groups of individuals; in attendance during one of these sessions was Barney Rossett, who decided to publish the translation with his fledgling Grove Press, although the publication would not appear until 1958. Around the same time as her readings (circa 1953), a number of her translations appeared in the journal *Origin: A Quarterly for the Creative*, and other parts of her manuscript circulated privately prior to publication.[15] Allen Ginsberg also cited her translation of "The Theater and the Plague" (a chapter not published in *Origin*) in his journal in April 1956:

Theater & Its Double—Antonin Artaud/M. C. Richards Translation/"our nervous system after a certain period absorbs the vibrations of the subtlest music and in a sense is modified by it in a lasting way."/Example of ignuschizoid perception.[16]

Artaud's presence was also felt among the ranks of happenings. Indeed, most of Cage's comments on Artaud were occasioned by discussions about happenings. Allan Kaprow, the key figure in their development, was positioned between the romance of Pollock and the disinterestedness of Cage. His work had developed first within the fervent milieu of Harold Rosenberg's *action* and the kinesthetic and hallucinatory *delirium*, if not *collective hysteria and magic*, of Pollock's paintings. His first happening was produced while attending Cage's class at the New School for Social Research, after hearing about the Black Mountain event from Cage. Although, as his essay "The Legacy of Jackson Pollock" demonstrated,[17] Kaprow could easily disentangle the valuable artistic provocations of Pollock from the prevailing romantic figure of Pollock, this did not prevent a group of dead artist phantoms from being marshaled against him by others in the early 1960s: "According to the myth, modern artists are archetypal victims who are 'suicided by society' (Artaud). In the present sequel, they are entirely responsible for their own life and death; there are no clear villains anymore. There are only cultured reactionaries, sensitive and respected older radicals, rising up in indignation to remind us that Rembrandt, van Gogh, and Pollock died on the cross (while we've 'sold out')."[18] Kaprow wanted the art-and-life nexus from Artaud but refused to suffer the suffering. Other *happeners* sported their own attitudes toward Artaud and, however conflicted these might have been, Michael Kirby could inventory the field in his 1965 book *Happenings* and propose that "Some Happenings are the best examples of Artaud's Theatre of Cruelty that have yet been produced."[19]

Beats Language

The other early sphere of influence occurred among the Beat writers, first with Carl Solomon and Allen Ginsberg and then more passionately with Michael McClure. Unlike the Cage–Tudor Artaud, who was the apolitical, pre-Rodez man of theater, the Beat Artaud began primarily with the post-Rodez, antipsychiatric, anti-American poet. The Beat Artaud first made his way around one psychiatric institution in particular on the East Coast and then was introduced to the West Coast at the famous Six Gallery reading in San Francisco (13 October 1955), famous for being where Ginsberg first read *Howl*, for unwittingly being the official launch of the Beat Generation, and, as more recently recognized, for inaugurating ecological poetry in the United States (or, as McClure has said, "the Beat Generation will be remembered as the literary wing of the environmental movement").[20]

Ginsberg's own encounter with Artaud's texts and the figure of Artaud started when Ginsberg checked into the Columbia Presbyterian Psychiatric Institute (PI) in June 1949, whereon he met fellow resident Carl Solomon—an avid fan of Artaud. Ginsberg's *Howl* was, of course, dedicated *for Carl Solomon*, and their first meeting at the PI became so legendary it pestered Solomon like a bad rash for years.[21] Right after the war, Solomon joined the U.S. Maritime Service and in 1947 jumped ship in France. He soon found himself circulating among avant-garde circles where he happened to witness Artaud's three-hour performance at the *Vieux-Colombier:* "Artaud was being described by a small circle of Paris admirers, some in very high places in the arts, as being a genius who had extended Rimbaud's vision of the poet seer. His name was even described by one admirer, known as 'the Alchemist', as Arthur Rimbaud without the HUR in Arthur and without the RIMB in Rimbaud."[22] Of course, Artaud had a particular relevance for Solomon once he was, as they say, institutionalized, and especially after he was subjected to a ruthless series of insulin shock treatments "forcibly administered in the dead of night by white-clad, impersonal creatures who tear the subject from his bed, carry him screaming into an elevator, strap him to another bed on another floor."[23] An entire range of intellectual pursuits were tolerated: "Yes, in mental hospitals patients still dance and dream hazily about the nurses. Others discuss anything from Artaud to Schweitzer and Oleg Cassini and some still wave their rumps."[24] All was tolerated, all except readings relevant to the operations of the institution itself, an activity that necessarily took on a clandestine character. Solomon read a book on shock therapy cloaked in the cover of Anna Balakian's *Literary Origins of Surrealism*.[25] The Artaud text most relevant to Solomon's situation, from the very beginning of his term in mental institutions, was "Van Gogh: A Man Suicided by Society,"[26] which in the *The Tiger's Eye* translation he passed onto Ginsberg.

Artaud's Van Gogh essay was one of texts that fed into *Howl*, the most salient feature shared by the two texts being a vehemence against psychiatry. Artaud castigates Van Gogh's "improvised psychiatrist" Dr. Gachet in the same way he publicly vilified Dr. Gaston Ferdière, the director of Rodez, during the *Vieux-Colombier* performance, and this antipsychiatric attitude was channeled through Solomon in the PI into Ginsberg's best-known poem. Moreover, the proposition within Artaud's Van Gogh text— "There is in every lunatic a misunderstood genius who was frightened by the idea that gleamed in his head and who could find an outlet only in delirium for the stranglings life had prepared him."[27]—seems to animate *Howl* from the very first line: "I saw the best minds of my generation destroyed by madness, starving / hysterical naked." Confirmation comes from Ginsberg himself when he noted candidly that "Van Gogh: A Man Suicided by Society" was one of the main texts informing *Howl*.[28]

Another Artaud text known to Ginsberg in the early 1950s figured into *Howl*, albeit a bit more obliquely. Citing the influence of Artaud's Van Gogh text, Ginsberg wrote that "Artaud's physical breath has inevitable propulsion toward specific inviolable insight on 'Moloch whose name is Mind!'"[29] While high on peyote (October 1954) he looked out the window from his apartment on Nob Hill in San Francisco and saw Moloch, the figure that went on to dominate part 2 of *Howl*,[30] in the looming specter of the Sir Francis Drake Hotel. The simple fact that Ginsberg was high on peyote at the time can also be traced to Artaud, specifically, another text given to him by Solomon: "by 1952 we already had the experience of peyote partly as a result of translations of Artaud's *Voyage au Pays des Tarahumaras*, which appeared in *Transition* magazine in the 40s, and Huxley's *Doors of Perception*."[31]

While Ginsberg recited *Howl* at the Six Gallery, Michael McClure was listening after having read his own poems earlier in the evening. Years later, he remembered sitting there *wondering* whether *Howl* was a "bourgeois Artaudism," a *flattened out* Artaud in a long poem style of *To Have Done with the Judgment of God* and Shelley's *Queen Mab*.[32] It is unlikely that Ginsberg had a working knowledge of *To Have Done with the Judgment of God*, Artaud's censored radio piece from 1948. McClure was referring to the script, not the recording, which circulated around San Francisco's bohemian locus of North Beach in the mid-1950s. It had been translated by Guy Wernham who, well known for his 1943 New Directions translation of Lautréamont's *Les Chants de Maldoror*, had fallen from grace a bit by the mid-1950s and was working as a bartender in North Beach. A frequent visitor to Ginsberg's apartment, Wernham was included in the roster of the first draft of

Howl as the person "who rapidly translated the Songs of Maldoror and threw himself / on the mercy of Alcoholics Anonymous." Despite his personal acquaintance with Wernham, Ginsberg did not place *To Have Done with the Judgment of God* on his reading list until December 1955, about six weeks after the Six Gallery reading. It is even less likely that it contributed to the writing of *Howl*, considering the bulk of the poem was written months before the reading.[33] McClure may have heard Artaud in *Howl* and may have heard a political post-Rodez poet, but what he was hearing was the antipsychiatric Artaud of "Van Gogh: The Man Suicided by Society." Besides, Ginsberg had a habit of generously crediting his sources; at a later date he would praise *To Have Done with the Judgment of God* for its critique of American militarism and commodity culture (diary note dated 13 April 1961):

You are me, God-
Artaud alone made accusation
against America.[34]

Another reason McClure remembered hearing Artaud in Ginsberg's *Howl* was because, more than any other Beat, he had an ear out for Artaud, experiencing such kinship that he felt he could have been Artaud's younger brother. Hadn't he been born on the same day of the year as Rimbaud?

The most complex and thoroughgoing response to Artaud's provocation was undoubtedly undertaken during the time by McClure. His first encounter with Artaud's writings had been in 1952 or 1953 while, as a university student in Arizona, he was searching the library for material on peyote. He moved to San Francisco in 1953 with the intention of studying with Clifford Still, not to learn painting but to learn how he might incorporate a gestural impulse into his poetry, to get the body onto the page, a desire naturally aligned to Artaud's work as well. Artaud had already attained mythic status in San Francisco, so McClure had little trouble in being exposed to a number of texts and, not knowing French, in seeking assistance from others for translation: the poet Philip Lamantia, had strong links to the Surrealists since the 1940s; Kenneth Rexroth, patriarch of the San Francisco Renaissance, was translating Artaud at the time; and Joanne McClure, his wife, translated a small portion of *Voyage au Pays des Tarahumaras* for Wallace Berman's little mag *Semina*.[35] Most significantly, Guy

Wernham gave McClure his translation of *To Have Done with the Judg* *of God* prior to the Six Gallery reading.[36] With this familiarity Mc could hear the text in *Howl*, and, perhaps more surprisingly, Artaud ⌣⌣⌣⌣ be heard in McClure's own environmentalist poems at the reading.

McClure grew up as a Dust Bowl baby, storms of top soil settling down vengefully on cars and homes. He moved as a young boy to the evergreens of the Pacific Northwest, the inland salt water of the Puget Sound resting between the Olympic and Cascade Mountain Ranges and then back to the plains of Kansas and desert scrub of Arizona for college stints. His youthful experience of rummaging around in various natural environs lent to the fact that when he entered San Francisco, he was as deeply interested in biology and naturalism as in poetry. The countryside surrounding the Bay Area supported his continued interest, as did the encouragement of Rex-roth, who was himself an amateur naturalist, and of other poets at the Six Gallery reading, including Gary Snyder and Phillip Whalen. At the read-ing McClure read poems formed by his politicized brand of naturalism that he would come to know in two years time as *ecology* or *environmen-talism*.[37] "The Mystery of the Hunt" was about his early discovery of as-pects of nature in the Bay Area, the scent of lemon verbena in someone's garden, sea otter games in the surf, "small things / That when brought into vision become an inferno." "For the Death of 100 Whales" was a response to the machine-gunning of 100 killer whales by American sailors at a NATO base in Iceland. The third poem, "Point Lobos: Animism," was emblematic of the deepening experiential basis of his mammalianism and meat science: "I was overwhelmed by the sense of animism—and how ev-erything (breath, spot, rock, ripple in the tidepool, cloud, and stone) was alive and spirited. It was a frightening and joyous awareness of my under-soul. I say *undersoul* because I did not want to join Nature by my mind but by my viscera—my belly. The German language has two words, *Geist* for the soul of man and *Odem* for the spirit of beasts. *Odem* is the undersoul. I was becoming sharply aware of it."[38]

He has singled out this poem in particular as having been derived from his fascination with Artaud's writings. McClure did not need Artaud to be interested in animism or ecology; he seemed to be attached more precisely to an *undersoul* viscerality of Artaud's writing: "In their direct statement to my nerves, lines of Artaud's were creating physical tensions, and gave me ideas for entries into a new mode of verse."[39] There was also a mystical, revelatory component in "Point Lobos: Animism" of becoming inextricably situated among natural forces, derived from "one phrase of Artaud's [which] fascinated me: 'It is not possible that in the end the miracle will not occur.'"[40] However oblique this contribution of visceral writing and mystical optimism was to McClure's developing environmentalism, it was more significant that there was nothing in Artaud's thought that McClure perceived as being contrary to the direction he was taking. Perhaps, whatever contradictions he may have encountered, there were other aspects that overrode them. Indeed, if we go back to read Artaud ecologically, which is an approach not immediately suggested by his writing, there arises the possibility that Artaud could have very well acted as a legitimization for these early stages of ecological poetry in the United States. This possibility is increased if we look back at *To Have Done with the Judgment of God*, the text in McClure's possession at the time of the Six Gallery reading, for here we can find a contemporary animism where animality moves to spirit to microbes and atoms,[41] all the while being accompanied by a scathing attack of the United States as a society that is slave to the imperative, where

new fields of activity must be created,
where all the false manufactured products,
all the vile synthetic ersatzes will finally reign,
where glorious true nature will just have to withdraw,
and give up its place once and for all and shamefully to all the triumphant
    replacement products

. . . No more fruit, no more trees, no more vegetables, no more ordinary or
    pharmaceutical plants and consequently no more nourishment,
but synthetic products to repletion,
in vapors.[42]

McClure intensified his naturalist inclinations and apprised himself of new developments in the biological sciences. Meanwhile, within the discursive environment the specific notion of *ecology* began to embed itself in the public vernacular in the latter half of the 1950s, prior to Rachel Carson's call to arms in the early 1960s with her book *Silent Spring*. For McClure, ecology was not merely a politicized naturalism. It emerged through the detailed and sensuous observation of large ecological systems in operation, which acted to deflect human-centered politics and replace it with a *mammalian patriotism*, and through the spiritual understandings of a deep ecology (as communicated by Alan Watts on his radio program on KPFA in Berkeley as early as the mid-1950s), which remained very *humane* to humans. Any warnings about the environment, however, had to compete with scenarios of an instantaneous annihilation by nuclear holocaust, as opposed to "slow motion explosion" of ecological catastrophe, dynamized by a petroleum economy that was evidenced by a pervasive cinderization of the surface of the earth.[43]

The male body in the 1950s that had been ravaged by World War II and the Korean War, put into cold storage by homegrown Christian puritanism and unfulfilling jobs, and rendered self-conscious in the light of nuclear annihilation, took on another incarnation altogether with the likes of Jackson Pollock, who threw his entire body into the open act of his painting; Charles Olson, who wrote the breath into poetic line; Charlie Parker, who blew intellectual life into a legacy of improvisation; and Robert Duncan, the Beats, and other writers whose declaration of gay sexuality and culture closed the door on the closet behind them. That Artaud, someone generally perceived as wanting to get rid of his body, might become associated with these activities of the body was not without contradiction and certainly did not escape McClure, who, speaking of his fellow poets among the San Francisco renaissance and the Beats, stated that Artaud "was truly a great gnostic, anti-body poet. Although we were all body poets, we looked to Artaud as our immediate ancestor."[44] Although it might seem difficult to maintain such a paradox today, in the context of 1950s America any attention to the body was refreshing, and even though Artaud wished to shed his body, his incredibly prolonged discourse around the moment of this desire rendered the body ever-present, if not desirous itself.

Artaud's abdication of his body could also be understood as being complicit with the 1950s, as an elaborate form of the masochistic and sacrificial Christian body, channeled and denied, or a fragmentation of the body commensurate with the products of an exhilarated postwar commodity culture, or the concentrated attention on the human body alone concurrent with the trodding destruction of species and environments. Indeed, McClure looked on the Artaudian body as impassioned but asexual, whereas he himself called forth the intensities of eros, sex, and animality. McClure thought that Artaud invoked the body like Van Gogh, portioning parts of the body off from one another so that they might be dispensed with as easily as an ear—in effect, a scatological preoccupation that resulted in, as McClure puts it, "the meat falling off the bones as shit."[45] The result was a body that fell away from itself—from other bodies, other mammalian bodies—and inhabited a metaphysical zone that itself had fallen away from the earth. McClure refused to carve up his body as though it were meat for the montage or to isolate it from any other influences. He wanted to keep meat intact, the body hospitable to mammalian, worldly, and cosmic energies, forces, voices, and potentialities coursing their way through. McClure was not advocating a solipsistic incarnation of the world or a narcissistic focus on the body but a situation in which "one has to move *in* to move *out*"—that is, the more one discovers his or her own biological being, then the more value that person can be to other people and creatures.[46]

Beast Language

McClure was initially interested in Artaud the poet. However, during the late 1950s in response to *The Theater and Its Double*, he took Artaud's lead and became a playwright and eventually was well known for such plays as *Josephine the Mouse Singer*, *Gorf*, *Gargoyle Cartoons*, and especially *The Beard*, which gained notoriety through a fierce censorship battle. McClure moved to theater after he began to conceive of his poetry as being a transcribed voice easy to move off the page and onto the stage. These poems, which would eventually be collected in the pages of *The New Book / A Book of Torture* (1961), a book containing poems written to his body influences Pollock, Olson, and Artaud: "I was convinced by Artaud that texts were needed for the theater and that it would be the poets who would write these texts. I was inflamed with his idea of theater, and the theater of cruelty. . . . But on reading Artaud, I looked at the poems that I was writing and I thought that the poems were voice notations (These would be many of the poems *The New Book / A Book of Torture.*) I said, 'Ah, this voice notation can be adapted to theater!'"[47]

One of his earliest plays was called *!The Feast! for Ornette Coleman!* (1960) and was written alternating between recognizable poetic speech in English and a mammalian tongue McClure called *beast language*.[48] It is not an interspecies language but a mammalian communication based on a commonality of meat, with a voice that, as McClure says, "comes right out of my muscles."[49] It did not develop out of any linguistic preoccupation but was instead borne by two visions. The first vision gave him the idea for *The Feast:* it "went off like a light bulb over my head—like in the cartoons. Flash, flash, flash! And I saw the whole play and I started to write it down in beast language with thirteen characters drinking black wine and eating loaves of French bread."[50] The second vision came in late summer 1962, when he sensed a ball of silence in the lower head and thoracic area in which "there were swirling 99 poems in a language other than English,"[51] poems that came from a "swirling ball of silence that melds with outer sounds and thought."[52] Unlike the beast language dispersed among the thirteen characters of *!The Feast!*, these poems were much more personal, and the act of writing itself became a spiritual process that matured with each poem. Gathered under the title of *Ghost Tantras*, they were written "in kitchens and bedrooms and front rooms and airplanes and a couple in Mexico City."[53] No. 39 was written the day Marilyn Monroe died (6 August 1962), and the last one was being completed just as the filmmaker Stan Brakhage called on the phone, "So he would have been the first person to hear any of them because I didn't read any of them to anybody while I was still writing them."[54] This is what Brakhage would have heard over the phone:

99

IN TRANQUILITY THY GRAHRR AYOHH
ROOHOOERING
GRAHAYAOR GAHARRR GRAHHR GAHHR
THEOWSH NARR GAHROOOOOOOOH GAHRR
GRAH GAHRRR! GRAYHEEOARR GRAHRGM
THAHRR NEEOWSH DYE YEOR GAHRR
grah grooom gahhr nowrt thowtooom obleeomosh.
AHH THEEAHH! GAHR GRAH NAYEEROOOO
GAHROOOOOM GRHH GARAHHRR OH THY
NOOOSHEORRTOMESH GREEEEGRAHARRR
OH THOU HERE, HERE, HERE IN MY FLESH

RAISING THE CURTAIN
HAIEAYORR-REEEEHORRRR
in tranquility

LOVE
thy
!oh my oohblesh!

These poems were not just for human ears alone. There are two remarkable recordings (sound recording and film) of McClure reading *ghost
tantras* to lions at the San Francisco Zoo. He had originally gone to the
zoo early in the morning with Bruce Connor to record lions roaring for a
play he was working on, when Connor asked him, "Why don't you read
the lions a poem?"[55] He had a copy of *Ghost Tantras* in his back pocket and
very soon found himself trading a cadence of *Ghrahhrs!* from No. 49 with
four lions. Later, for a film for public television, he returned to the lion
house, and the same thing happened. Also, while the crew was setting up
the equipment for the shoot, McClure went over to the tree kangaroos: "I
decided beast language was not right for them, so I recited Chaucer. A
couple of them literally clamored down from the stumps they were on,
walked over to the edge of the moat and stood in a wobbly-wavy way looking at me."[56] Another episode at the zoo involved listening to a female snow
leopard, whom McClure had approached very closely. The leopard speaks
in the type of beast language that he understands "more clearly than any
other," and he hears it with his whole body, including at the source of his
own beast language:

She puts her face within an inch of the wire and SPEAKS to me. The growl
begins instantly and almost without musical attack. It begins gutturally. It
grows in volume and it expands till I can feel the interior of her body from
whence the energy of the growl extends itself as it gains full volume of fury. It
extends itself, vibrating and looping. Then, still with the full capacity of un-
tapped energy, the growl drops in volume and changes in pitch to a hiss. The
flecks of her saliva spatter my face. I feel not smirched but cleansed. Her eyes
are fixed on me. The growl without a freshly drawn breath, begins again. It is
a language that I understand more clearly than any other. I hear rage, anger,
anguish, warning, pain, even humor, fury—all bound into one statement. . . .

I am surrounded by the physicality of her speech. It is a real thing in the air. It absorbs me and I can hear and feel and see nothing else. Her face and features disappear, becoming one entity with her speech. The speech is the purest, most perfect music I have ever heard, and I know that I am touched by the divine, on my cheeks, and on my brow, and on the tympanums of my ears, and the vibrations on my chest, and on the inner organs of perception.[57]

Although beast language did not evolve directly from any linguistic practice, it was associated with two body practices McClure had undertaken at the time: Wilhelm Reich's orgone therapy as discussed in the book *Character Analysis* and Kundalini yoga as described in Sir John Woodroffe's *The Serpent Power*.[58] These practices were not taken up in the most disciplined manner and were also ill-advisedly attempted while McClure was ingesting various psychotropics, suffering from a serious bout of a dark night of the soul and, *pace* Reich, "masochism was me," resulting in nothing but "a fool on the floor of his beat pad, taking psychedelics at the same time and experiencing states that are profoundly non-normal."[59] Only the immediate support of his wife and daughter prevented him from succumbing to this admixture. Actually, this state of psychic affairs may have made him a candidate for orgone therapy but not to practice Kundalini, which requires a general well-being and a high degree of discipline already achieved and the dedicated assistance and a deep understanding of another set of cultural codes and which can be both psychologically and physiologically dangerous if not approached properly.

Reich's *Character Analysis* corresponded to beast language in several ways. First of all, McClure's mammalianism could only be legitimated by Reich's lionization of his own animal pride, even though Reich's organismic project was more concerned with situating human self-consciousness than extending to an environmental interconnectedness: "A general may be a 'dignified' person; we do not want to magnify or minimize him. But we are entitled to regard him as an animal which is armored in a certain way. I would not object if some scientist were to reduce my scientific curiosity to the biological function of a puppy sniffing at everything. I would be glad to be compared biologically, to an alive, friendly puppy, for I do not have the ambition to distinguish myself from the animal."[60] Second, Reich argued for a move away from the *word language* of the talking cure to a *biological language* expressed by the body, thereby paralleling both

McClure's muscle speech and Artaud's move away from psychologically driven dialogue in theater. Reich thought that reliance on the talking cure was insufficient because *"word language very often also functions as a defense: The word language obscures the expressive language of the biological core."*[61] Moreover, it also obscured the presence within the body of the derivation of life from the nonorganic and thus where *"cosmic energy functions in the living."*[62] For Reich the union of the carnal and cosmic was effected through the energetics of the orgasm, while the organism itself was animated by the orgasm reflex with the result that *"the living is nothing but a bit of pulsating nature."*[63] The orgasm reflex could not be contained simply to the orgasm proper; it pertained to how the entire body functioned, especially how energy flowed from one section of the body to the next.

For Reich the human body was segmented and pulsational, being comprised of seven somatic regions ringing the head, neck, and trunk that, when functioning at peak performance, traded energy freely in a peristaltic action. The operative segmentation and pulsation in the human organism could better be seen in simpler organisms such as the worm, whereas in "higher vertebrates, only the segmental structure of the spine which corresponds to the segments of the spinal cord and the spinal nerves, and the segmental arrangement of the autonomic ganglia, indicate the origin of the vertebrates from segmentally functioning primitive organisms."[64] The task of orgone therapy was to remove the obstacles, in the form of character armor built up in the muscles and organs, preventing energy flow from one segment to the next, starting from the head down to the pelvis, the hub of orgasmic energy.[65]

There were several ways in which orgone therapy overlapped with Kundalini yoga. The number of Reich's somatic regions corresponded closely to the chakras in Kundalini, and the pulsational energy that Reich likened to the worm's legacy in the segmentation of the spine and ganglia could be compared with the serpent's transit in the spine in Kundalini. However, as Reich worked from head to groin, Kundalini directed energy in the opposite direction, from the base of the trunk to the top of the head. Also, that orgasm could simultaneously invoke animality and cosmos in Reichian thought fell in line with the common misconception at the time that Kundalini was a means of gaining pure consciousness while copulating.[66]

McClure called "Kundalini the inspiring force, the inspiring element," for beast language, and although he was aware of the risk involved, he also thought that "danger itself creates an edge, a precipice which brings new things into being."[67] He learned about Kundalini yoga primarily through his reading of *The Serpent Power*, which, in its compass and detail, is a dense and difficult text. Basically, the practice entailed "raising the goddess through the seven chakras from the perineum to the top of the skull, raising from dimension state to dimension state," and as he wrote in the introduction to *Ghost Tantras*, "A goddess lies coiled at the base of man's body, and pure tantric sound might awaken her."[68] The sound of beast language does not function in this way; in fact, it may be the result of a certain malfunction of Tantrism.

The Goddess Shakti, a powerful energy coiled at rest at the base of the trunk, through various means employed by the yogi is awakened and begins the ascent, often intensely experienced as a molten flow of energy, up the spine through the chakras. Both the coiled, dormant energy and the spine itself when fused with the rising power are often symbolized as a snake.[69] As the serpent reaches and cleanses the chakra, various states are achieved and powers obtained, until it reaches the top of the head, where a fusion with pure consciousness occurs. McClure's vision of the silent ball of beast language took place near the Visuddha chakra, in which the sense of hearing is stimulated. This overlapping position at the lower half of the head, throat, and thorax is subtended by the breath, and the breath is the vehicle of sound in the form of speech or mantra. The breath alone is thus unmanifested sound. This may be the reason he *heard* that the poems in the *silent* ball were in beast language. It is also obvious that the sonority of the voice per se and an expanded sense of listening come into play as a sound that unites the world spiritually, as he states in his introduction to the *Ghost Tantras:*

To dim the senses and listen to inner energies a-roar is sometimes called the religious experience. It does not matter what it is called. Laughter as well as love is passion. The loveliness the nose snuffs in air may be translated to sound by interior perceptive organs. The touch of velvet on the fingertips may become a cry when time is stopped. Speed like calmness may become a pleasure or gentle muffled sound. A dahlia or fern might become pure speech in meditation. A woman's body might become the sound of worship. A goddess lies coiled at the base of man's body, and pure tantric sound might awaken her.[70]

Within the process of raising the goddess, the initial carnality of the first chakra (the animality of the serpent) is supposed to dissipate as she ascends in an increasingly rarefied form toward an absence of the body and the state of pure consciousness. If this dissipation does not occur, then it is believed by some that the power of carnality where consciousness alone should reside will have negative consequences as it is manifested in the world. However, any notion of a persisting carnality or evil at the level manifested in beast language needs to be tempered with the general Hindu proscription against animality in the chain of being that elevates humans as a whole over animals, and then certain types of humans over each other to levels of supremacy, whereas McClure's own creature cosmology would not submit to such a representational order.

The question arises of whether McClure's beast language—with its corporeal and cosmic energy, its Reichian *biological language*, and its animality—was derived in any part from Artaud's own emphasis on vocables and vocalizations, from Artaud's glossolalia or screaming. Notable instances of glossolalia had appeared in both the Van Gogh essay and *To Have Done with the Judgment of God*, and although it was incantatory and scatological McClure had no way of knowing it was actually, in his own words, *shriekalalia* or *copralalia* before listening to the recording of *To Have Done with the Judgment of God* several years later, after Jean-Jacques Lebel sent Ginsberg and him copies liberated from the vaults of the *RTF* in Paris during the events of May 1968. If what was at stake was a simple removal or diminishment of meaning, then McClure had long been aware of the sound poetry of Ball, Schwitters, and Arp since scouring old copies of *Transition* in used book stores in Lawrence, Kansas, before moving to San Francisco. In retrospect, McClure understood the tradition of sound poetry as the result of a European rationalism acted on by an equally European negativity. Although it was easier to sense the body at work in Artaud's glossolalia, and indeed some words allude to body parts and substances, there was a reliance on Latinate sounds and an overall religiosity that privileged a God who alone could understand.

McClure acknowledges his European roots; however, he considers beast language much more a product of the West Coast of the United

States looking toward Asia with its back toward Europe.[71] He did consider Artaud an exception, however, since unlike the sound poets McClure could look to Artaud and still look to Asia. It was not immaterial that Artaud himself sought sources of inspiration among many other cultures, including Asian cultures, but ultimately it was not crucial. In his short celebration of *To Have Done with the Judgment of God*, entitled "Artaud: Peace Chief" from *Meat Science Essays*, he wrote, "We, new creatures, must accept the admissions of Artaud and tantric Shakti texts such as *The Serpent Power* and all images of reality and body."[72] For McClure there was no surface similarity between Artaud and beast language but a common source announced by the position of both Artaud and beast language in proximity to Kundalini, body practices, and the body in general. Although McClure never examined this possibility in his own writing, I would now like to shift the focus on how Artaud might have influenced McClure and examine how, given the body practices underpinning the genesis of beast language, our understanding of McClure's experience might help to interpret screaming and other aspects in Artaud.

Affected and Afflicted Screaming

Screams when trafficked in culture in their powerful self-evidence, in their amplitude and affect, simultaneously assert themselves and elude meaning. They resemble noise in this respect. In their natural habitat screams are heard or experienced during momentous occasions: childbirth; life-threatening situations and those perceived as such; psychic or physiological torture, terror, and anguish; sex expressed as pleasure or pain; the fury of an argument; the persecution and slaughter of animals. Screams demand urgent or empathetic responses and thereby create a concentrated social space bounded by their audibility. That they are resolutely communicative and meant for others is demonstrated by the fact that people who have been in a life-threatening situation often must be told by others that they were screaming. Although screaming does not engage language, we are still attuned to its signals. A parent knows when a child's scream at play becomes a true call of alarm or when an infant's fever has taken a dangerous turn, and people regularly walk by the screams coming from white-knuckle rides at carnivals comfortable in the knowledge that they are not heartless.

How might art screams relate to screams in their natural habitat? Elaine Scarry in *The Body in Pain* suggests that the inability of knowing the experience of a person screaming produces an appropriate type of representation by default: "Even prolonged, agonized human screams, which press on the hearer's consciousness in something of the same way pain presses on the consciousness of the person hurt, convey only a limited dimension of the sufferer's experience. It may be for this reason that images of the human scream recur fairly often in the visual arts, which for the most part avoid depictions of auditory experience. The very failure to convey the sound makes these representations arresting and accurate."[73] There are some problems with this statement. Knowing any experience of another person beyond a *limited dimension*, not just a person screaming, poses the same problem, yet there is no general indication toward muteness. Besides, in many instances people *do* understand the scream; they may not reproduce the experience, but something else is repeated within oneself that brings one closer to it, more so than most other experiences. Instead of attempting to assign any intrinsic relationship between experienced screams and represented screams, it would be better to consider the historical nature of the means to represent the auditive characteristics of screams and to concentrate more directly on the play of meaning within art screams. While Peter Stastny has written about how Western culture's inheritance of screams has been conditioned by the powerlessness of text to convey their sonorous power, and the film music composer Bernard Herrmann has done what he could to notate the orchestral shower stall scream in Hitchcock's *Psycho*, the question remains of whether there would be proclamations about the accuracy of mute representations of screams if phonography had had a longer history.[74]

When we begin to locate specific invocations of screaming in modernist French literature, including those of Artaud, we find a particularly loud node concentrated on ideas of gender and animality. We have already heard the screaming within Lautréamont's *Les Chants de Maldoror*, and nowhere in the book do screams occur too far from animals, *homo sapiens* among them. The humans devoured by the lobster-like Creator were "bellowing like flayed elephants, brushing my scorched hair with their fiery wings,"[75] and elsewhere Lautréamont fosters a family of emphatic vocalizations consisting of howling dogs, the cry of a hungry child, a wounded cat, a woman in labor, a dying plague victim, or a "young girl singing a divine melody."[76] Throughout the cantos Lautréamont speaks of human conduct through the actions of animals, yet he does not merely do this. His animals also have enough autonomy to establish a sphere of natural forces apart from human actions, and this autonomy is not easily reconciled in moral chains of being or ideas of primitivism or cruelty—unless a shark or tiger would dig its teeth into a child's chest just to relish in its screams for hours on end, as does the protagonist with his fingernails, or one would deny the existence of cranes with a philosophical bent and howling dogs who yearn for the infinite.[77] Gaston Bachelard in his book on Lautréamont (1939) acknowledges the diversity of character in Lautréamont's bestiary, but it is always a characterological plenitude in the service of human beings and being. The main exception in Bachelard's analysis arrives at the very moment where humans and animals take on a common voice—the cry or scream—and it is here he runs into a problem since, on the one hand, "the cry is in the throat before being in the ear. It imitates nothing,"[78] and on the other it is shared with other species, both in instinctual immediacy and directness and in the sonorous event. Indeed, Bachelard goes through the meat voice of the human body to connect with the "biological mass" of the nonhuman *crowd* but then must assert a distinction on another level to keep humans distinct and elite:

Everything in the body is articulated when the cry, itself inarticulate but marvelously simple and unique, speaks the victory of power. All animals, even those least on the offensive, articulate their war cry. But all forces are parodied in Nature. And in the manifold animal life that Lautréamont lived out he heard warlike cries that were "droll chuckles." He heard cries that are born from within the biological mass. It is this same thought that Paul Valéry utters through Monsieur Teste: "The gentle were bleating, the bitter were caterwauling, the fat were bellowing, the thin were screaming." One must move up to the human to attain dominating cries.[79]

In Georges Bataille's "The Lugubrious Game" (1929) the imprisoned Marquis de Sade screams down a sewer pipe his response to howling dogs.[80] Around the same time, writing about the orifice of the scream (following Hegel's hierarchies of the senses in humans and animals), he explains that "The mouth is the beginning or, if one prefers, the prow of animals; in the most characteristic cases, it is the most living part, in other words, the most terrifying for neighboring animals," whereas corresponding prow on humans "is the eyes or the forehead that play the significatory role of an animal's jaws."[81] However, during certain exceptional situations the human prow descends to the same position as that on an animal: only when it *vents the spine with a scream:*

On important occasions human life is still bestially concentrated in the mouth: fury makes men grind their teeth, terror and atrocious suffering transform the mouth into an organ of rending screams. On this subject it is easy to observe that the overwhelmed individual throws back his head while frenetically stretching his neck so that the mouth becomes, as far as possible, a prolongation of the spinal column, *in other words, it assumes the position it normally occupies in the constitution of animals.* As if explosive impulses were to spurt directly out of the body through the mouth, the form of screams.[82]

Do these examples belong to the literature to which Jacques Rivière referred in his correspondence with Artaud, "which is the product of the immediate and, so to speak, animal functioning of the mind. . . . One can say that it is the most accurate and direct expression of that monster which every man carries within him but which he usually seeks instinctively to chain with the bonds of facts and experience."[83] As we shall see, Artaud did not trumpet his spine through the mouth. His screams were the product of a traversal of several locations amid an exchange of two bodies, where his spine finally vented itself between the vertebrae. And Artaud did not think of the guts and guttedness of these bodies as animalistic or instinctual; they were mainly theatrical and medical, whether played out across theatrical techniques and acupuncture or on a metaphysical staging of psychosis.

With or without animals, there can be no natural habitat for Artaudian screams. The mad screams we rightfully imagine occurring within psychiatric hospitals recur nowhere else except to fortify the rhetoric of screaming found in his work. Screaming is, after all, well suited to the movement away from dialogue and speech in theater toward a communication represented as a vibrational exchange among bodies, and away from the word toward gesture, away from general gratuitousness of theater toward an emphatic necessity of a theater of cruelty. The difficulty arises when his mad screams are mapped back to any point of his career and when their perceived authenticity silences more localized attention. The seduction is powerful for an argument can garner the force of necessity when punctuated with the blinding affect of a mad scream. There are, of course, instances where other people report on Artaud's screaming. Perhaps the best known is Anaïs Nin's report of his lecture on "The Theatre and the Plague" at the Sorbonne, where he gave up his notes to become a plague victim in screaming death throes: "Imperceptibly almost, he let go of the thread we were following and began to act out dying by plague. No one quite knew when it began. . . . His face was contorted with anguish, one could see the perspiration dampening his hair. His eyes dilated, his muscles became cramped, his fingers struggled to retain their flexibility. He made one feel the parched and burning throat, the pains, the fever, the fire in the guts. He was in agony. He was screaming. He was delirious. He was enacting his own death, his own crucifixion."[84] It would be easy to bolster this act of screaming by retrospectively infusing it with his institutionalized mad screams, which would enable him to more authentically conjure up the very being of a dying and delirious plague victim. Thus, he merely tapped a deep source of natural screams that could be distributed equitably to either a lecture or psychosis. It would also be easy to forget that many in the audience laughed and hissed and that most had left by the time Artaud finished. Afterward among friends, Artaud protested, "They always want to hear *about*; they want to hear an objective conference on 'The Theatre and the Plague,' and I want to give them the experience itself, the plague itself, so they will be terrified, and awaken. I want to awaken them. They do not realize *they are dead*."[85] Since the audience did not know they were dead, they would have forgotten what it was to have died, whereas Artaud only confused the performance with "the experience itself, the plague itself."

On the other hand, we can actually hear Artaud's screams, or at least a recording of them, in the production of *To Have Done with the Judgment of God*. These screams happened after Rodez so it would be reasonable to expect to hear an echo of his mad screams. Indeed, we can hear in his voice throughout the program a deep-seated, constricted trembling so penetrating that it could get under any thick hide and make it crawl. It would be easy to think that no amount of special techniques and rehearsal could inform this demeanor, and what we are hearing is fueled by the abrading remnants of the preceding years of madness. It is also easy to acknowledge that this voice and these screams arose from a script and were performed in a studio. In the first section the constricted affect of his voice is not just the charged sound of fettered nerves; it is also part of a sarcastic reportage of the pretense of authority, and his screams are tempered by technical exigencies as he steps back into a stairwell to add the space of a void and to avoid overmodulation. Most screams occur during the fourth interlude, just before the conclusion, and are high pitched—a male falsetto version of a scream, a feminized scream. Elsewhere in his writing "the scream of a frightened woman" is compared to the "bawling of a calf."[86] A lower-pitched scream would be closer to despair than to threat: the former retains a degree of volition and through that a male prerogative for aspirations of the highest magnitude lost, frustrated, or denied or an anguish over squandered greatness, whereas a feminized scream is the sound of subjugation, where little can be ventured outside incitement and motive. When a rare lower-pitched scream does occur in the radio production, it quickly threatens to trail off into song, to become discursive. We could probably assume that Artaud was often talking through his mad screams.

Perhaps we are hearing another source of his screams, a more deeply seated physiological and psychic pain, compounded from a time early enough to inform a career of screaming. This source can be found beginning with his childhood meningitis, carrying through his recurrent fatigues and maladies, with all the accompanying struggles for consciousness and against his body, through the anguished living and metaphysical heyday of frustration, and with all the therapeutic regimes both Eastern and Western and addictions in which he sought solace and self-medication. The complex of his afflictions produced elements interwoven with literary and performative ideas throughout his career. The screaming differed, however, when the cure ceased being one he sought through his own volition in Eastern practices and instead became one to which he was subjugated by his own sick culture in the form of confinement and electroshock, as we can tell on examining the theatrical scream manual that is "The Theater of the Seraphim" and the post-Rodez hallucinatory scene depicted in *Winches of Blood* from *Suppôts et supplications*.

Seraphic Screams and the Tortuous Blast

In "The Theater of the Seraphim" Artaud outlines a remarkable technique for screaming in theaters. He had tried unsuccessfully to include the essay as a chapter to *The Theater and Its Double*. It would have followed naturally from the chapter "An Affective Athleticism" with its concerns for breath and gendered principals (*masculine, feminine,* and *neuter*) deriving from the Kabalah, for the role of the fantasmatic body within acting: "To make use of his emotions as a wrestler makes use of his muscles, he has to see the human being as a Double, like the Ka of Egyptian mummies, like the perpetual specter from which the affective powers radiate."[87] The most tangible link between the two chapters can be found in the famous *nota bene* to "An Affective Athleticism" that begins, "No one in Europe knows how to scream any more."[88] For such a statement to be written in 1935 in Europe might have seemed like the crassest political insensitivity or a sign of remarkable insularity. It was, however, directed at techniques of the theater, as it concludes, "and particularly actors in trance no longer know how to cry out." "The Theater of the Seraphim" instructs them. It is not a physical training of the body but a training in how to imagine the body and the movement of breath and voids throughout the body.

The commonsensical approach to making screams, one that could be thought of as being informed by the masculine principal, might entail filling one's lungs with air and then aggressively forcing it out to produce a scream consisting of the dual presence of "the irruption of the lungs in the breath and of the breath in the lungs."[89] Artaud has a more complicated approach in mind. He first invokes the place between two breaths. This place is both the actual temporal and spatial location between two breaths and also the conceptual and kinesthetic figuration of this location. Indeed, throughout the several steps of this procedure he oscillates between the concept and reality as he would between two breaths. Where there is none, he installs necessity into the process by instructing one to hold or expel a breath to the limits to be driven by asphyxiation to the next stage by "the energetic will of the breath."[90] For Artaud the idea of *asphyxiation,* which he employed throughout his career, ran across breath, air, and social space as a means to mediate between life and death corporeality and the suffocating effects of society. Indeed, asphyxiation and the scream formed the parameters of the complex of this exchange—one a withholding of breath/air/space, the other its ultimate activation, both determined by total purpose. Internally, within the technique of the seraphic scream, asphyxiation sets off a series of events where the differences among actual breath, imagined breath, and the space of a void—all of them inflating, expanding, and moving within the body—become interchangeable and indistinguishable from one another. Yet, contrary to the masculine, he does not fill the lungs with breath or vice versa, disgorging both in sound, but empties the entire body of both sound and organs and methodically directs the breath/void in search of the source of the scream in weakness and subjugation, which he associates with the neuter and feminine. Once emptied he then adds to the spaces of breath and void the space of another body, one of the many doubles one finds dispersed throughout Artaud's writings. What was once the actual body has been left intact and rendered fantasmatic, reduced to a double that exports a few organs into the functioning, vacant body when called for. These organs no longer retain their normal functions but have been reduced to serving only as signposts to locate the movements of breath and void in the vacated, actual body.

The breath/void driven by necessity and inflated by asphyxiation travels down to the belly, is hurled up to the uppermost lungs where it carves out a greater void, and then continues in the same motion back to the lower back to a location (apparently an admixture of yogic and acupuncture influences) where "on the left it is a feminine cry, then on the right, at the point where Chinese acupuncture treats nervous fatigue, when this indicates a malfunctioning of the spleen or the viscera, when it reveals intoxication."[91] As he had pointed out in "An Affective Athleticism," "There are 380 points in Chinese acupuncture, with 73 principal ones which are used in current therapy. There are many fewer crude outlets for human affectivity."[92] It just so happens that the affective points for screaming reside in those areas and maladies for which Artaud himself sought treatment from his acupuncturist George Soulié de Morant. This is an important connection. It not only shows a predilection in Artaud for specifying locations fairly precisely within the body, as opposed to sporting a body without organs or organization, by pinpointing the location of the Eastern treatment of nervous fatigue. As the trigger for his theatrical scream this technique merges into a larger complex of Artaudian afflictions, therapies, appropriations, and theater interwoven throughout his career. Most notably, he not only sought to serve up screams for the theater but sought to treat theater by forgoing the talking cure in favor of a directly applied medicinal communiqué:

To know in advance what points of the body to touch is the key to throwing the spectator into magical trances. And it is this invaluable kind of science that poetry in the theater has been without for a long time.[93]

I propose to return through the theater to an idea of the physical knowledge of images and the means of inducing trances, as in Chinese medicine which knows, over the entire extent of the human anatomy, at what points to puncture in order to regulate the subtlest functions.[94]

After several more steps described in "The Theater of the Seraphim," the scream occurs. It should be noted, finally, that although the scream is generated from the neuter and feminine principals, it is manifested through the gendered personage of Artaud himself and results in two representative figures of screaming males: war wounded and a dog, the thunderous "baying of an incredible mastiff."[95]

Actors in trance, now knowing how to scream, search out a scream with acupunctural precision to induce trances in the spectator. These trances and screams belong to a vibrational scheme found throughout modernism, whereby communication occurs through the correspondence of internal and external vibrations, the sympathetic identifications of different vessels, often bridging different perceptual registers and always attempting to elude cultural mediation. The acoustic space of theater immersing actor and audience becomes a vibrational medium that extends to resonating souls that emanate and absorb. As he had said in "An Affective Athleticism," the soul operating in this theatrical space could be "physiologically reduced to a skein of vibrations," and just as the trigger point for the seraphic screaming indicated intoxication, this "soul-specter can be regarded as intoxicated with its own screams, something like the Hindu *mantras*—those consonances, those mysterious accents, in which the material secrets of the soul, tracked down to their lairs, speak out in broad daylight."[96] And this soul was, of course, yet another double, one imagined as a "perpetual spectre from which the affective powers radiate."[97] If the vibrations of the soul were aching for self-intoxication through screaming, as a surrogate if brutal mantra, then seraphic screaming would infuse the entire acoustic and vibrational space, placing actor and audience in an intoxicated trance that anesthetizes linguistic significance and cultural mediation and dopes up affective athleticism to new levels of performance. And this is why screams are so important to Artaud. Screams mimic, occupy, and activate the communicative process of vibrational space. Both are motivated by necessity and are comprised by an encompassing acoustic space that spills into a nonacoustic, embodied realm of ineluctable communication, soul to soul. A scream lends the force of its elusion of mediation the greater range of vibrational subtleties. In this way, the scream is the utterance cast to speak for the vibrational space of theater.

The unmediated vibrational space of the theater was also a social space, one that included other bodies than Artaud and his coterie of doubles. His madness, largely a solitary affair, locked in a social space constituted by the utterances of doctors, not actors, evoked a different acoustical and vibrational configuration, especially as the individuating forces of his longstanding afflictions flourished in the environs of confinement, starvation, and electroshock. In *Winches of Blood (Reality)*, a short hallucinatory text from the collection *Suppôts et supplications*, sounds and vibrations occupy a space carved out within his body as the body itself is suspended within a vast unpopulated space of abyss and eternity. The text begins with a dream in which "a man whom I knew well, spun around me with alcohols and repressed drug addictions in the middle of the spider web of facts."[98] Artaud soon realized that the "spider web was of cords, and that those cords, on the top of an abyss, at that moment, kept me from falling." Here the spider web/cords, riveted at numerous points by his ego, both restrained him and kept him from falling into screams.[99] Struggling to free himself he frees himself only from dream to awaken "in the true light of the three windows of the dormitory of the asylum of Rodez." Here, he also awakens to a space in which the social middle ground has fallen away, leaving only a fusion of individual and cosmos, a space enveloped in the "placenta of the ego proper that one calls eternity: conscious of the subconscious and subconsciousness of the unconscious, outside space, but within time."[100]

He may be tied down with the actual restraints employed at Rodez or the restraints of his own resistance to a dissociation with the terrestrial fact of his body. But any and all facts, the spider web of facts, were contested by the voice of yet another double:

And he who had said "Who am I?" was in reality another, really and corporeally another, who in times past, had always wished to believe himself against my eternal and non-temporal self, a sort of adulterated imbecile who had always put all its consciousness into not wanting to agree with the facts, but to live as Buddha to their humdrum, syrupy contemplation. For et cetera et cetera, nirvana is, et cetera et cetera, more facts to compete with the facts, and no less, et cetera et cetera.[101]

With the cords tethering a webbed suspension above the abyss, holding down the dissociation of his body with rivets of an ego opening out to eternity, they suddenly become vibrational and worm inside and out the spine, at once tying it down, fusing with the spinal cord such that the spinal column itself becomes a resonant body. The debate with his double generates a tension that, coursing through the vertical axis of his body, triggers a blast from the gut that is a scream, a fart, or a blast lacking a venting orifice, resulting in release from restraint and suspension:

I sensed all these cords on my hands and I sensed one at the summit of my vertebral column, one which made music on the earth which held it and which was another point on my vertebral column, nothing more.

That cord disengaged itself and sang alone.

A hollow noise with a circumstantial sonorous coating, of a gold and a blue which cramped me elsewhere; because they were not verities:

And the sound that a cord can make between one vertebra and another is not gold and liturgical blue, not euphonic or liturgical, but fecal, bloody and scabrous.

It is in this way that suddenly, by force of debating myself in the consciousness of my ego, there arouse from the remotest depths of my belly a blast, and that blast took the form of beings who threw themselves like maniacs on my bonds.

And cut them.[102]

The whole process reminds Artaud of abject monks in Tibet who use various means of restraint and brutal devices to enchain "all the consciousnesses of men who wish to escape their particularist notion of man, on the physical plane as well as on the metaphysic, organic, intellectual, neurotic and sensorial plane."[103] Of course, the rack of reverie in Artaud's vision most resembles the way in which the spine is strapped down along the table in preparation for electroshock, the spine that contorts to make final contact with earth before the body is left behind cold to form a union with pure consciousness (in this case, a coma), while the blast from the gut calls forth the alimentary necessity of a mad scream, conflating torment and the torment of torture masquerading as therapy.

There are a number of parallels between the images generated in *Winches of Blood* and a drawing from the same period *La Projection du véritable corps* (The projection of the true body, circa. 1947).[104] The apparent body on the left, tormented by the radiating blasts of a soldier's rifle, is shackled at the ankles and shackled at the wrists by blue cords. There are also tormented faces located at the knees that appear to provide yet another point of restraint. The blue cords connect the apparent body to its double on the right, a skeletal structure whose meat has fallen off and been replaced by a vibratory figure, whose circularity of ribs creates a hollow body tilting stiffly along the verticality of the spine. The cords flow outward from the manacled wrists of the apparent body but originate from a field of blue that extends up from the shirt to outline the head in a type of aura, as though the energies of the ego were being gathered up and channeled to his eternal self. The cords turn vibratory as soon as they reach the True Body, but contrary to *Winches of Blood* in which "the sound that a cord can make between one vertebra and another is not gold and liturgical blue," the cords, sounds, and vibrations remain blue and gold. There are traces of blood red only within the two blasts emanating from the True Body— one from the gut and one from the head. The blast from the gut is similar to the one in *Winches of Blood*. Indeed, the faces at the knees of the apparent body also appear to be blasting out with traces of red and, thus, may relate to "that blast [which] took the form of beings who threw themselves like maniacs on my bonds." The blast from the head, which lacks the violent delineation in black and radiates more brightly with red, blue, and gold, may be the expression of the ego as eternal and atemporal or the yogic release of energy at the point of fusion with pure consciousness.

There are within *Winches of Blood* themes and images that may be found throughout Artaud's writings prior to his confinement within psychiatric institutions. For instance, the cord "at the summit of my vertebral column . . . which made music on the earth which held it," resembles a passage from *The Theater and Its Double* in which he explains how the vibrational space within theatrical communication functions in the manner of snake charming. The snake in this sense is a solitary spine in contact at all points along the earth, differing from the prostrate madman or electro-shock victim only by lack of restraint: "If music affects snakes it is not on account of the spiritual notions it offers them, but because snakes are long and coil their length upon the earth, because their bodies touch the earth at almost every point; and because the musical vibrations which are communicated to the earth affect them like a very subtle, very long massage; and I propose to treat the spectators like the snakecharmer's subjects and conduct them *by means of their organisms* to an apprehension of the subtlest notions."[105]

We can track Artaud's spine further back through a recurrent series of afflictions. They are described in detail in letters to his acupuncturist, especially where his famous nervous fatigue expresses itself in tandem with the self-same "summit of my vertebral column" mentioned in *Winches of Blood* and his childhood meningitis. Moreover, one specific passage extends the comparison with *Winches of Blood* further by situating the spine in a prostrate position in contact with its ground, anchoring a cosmic, spatial dissociation:

This sensation of monstrous, horrible fatigue, this vast, extraordinary pressure at the top of the skull and the back of the neck, a pressure whose force and whose volume, seemingly, is so great that it feels like the weight of the world on one's shoulders, is accompanied by one knows not what cosmic emotion, is combined with the tactile sensitivity, the vast feel of interstellar space, and the proof of this is that when I am lying in bed the sensation, far from disappearing, grows worse, is transformed into an impression of painful emptiness, operating magnetically, which presses on the limbs and the whole length of the spinal column and surrounds the pelvis.[106]

Artaud had a destructive childhood bout with meningitis, a condition marked by a rigidified and torsional spine clouded with diseased fluid, releasing pain at the neck into the head, inflaming the three membranes that negotiate the space between the brain and the spinal cord: one soft mother, one hard mother (*pia mater, dura mater*), and a spider web (the *arachnoid* membrane). Moreover, given a likelihood that his meningitis at age four contributed to his stuttering between ages of six and eight, the disease was latent in his recurrent stammering later on in life and at the root of his afflictions and malaise (including the side-effects from palliative intake of opiates and other drugs). For Artaud, his stuttering was associated with an ingrained inability to move thought or rather too many thoughts (either as wildly proliferating insight, association, or incoherence) onto the tongue. When he attempted to do so, a contraction would occur "that shuts off my thought from within, makes it rigid as in a spasm."[107] If we take Artaud's well-known difficulty in speaking, especially when it came to acting, as one reason among many that he would find a theater that moves away from a dependency on speech a sensible thing to do, then it appears that there exists a physiological continuity whereby his spine, with its serpentine generation of theater, could after Rodez contain the vibrations and sounds from which a theater might have once emanated.

In "The Theater of the Seraphim" Artaud directed breath and void around a fantasmatic body toward the location where acupuncture directs the energies of the body. Through a technical emulation of certain mystical and Asian body practices, he hoped to produce a "scream in an armature of bone,"[108] a scream to lead the way in a supercession of the theatrical effects of gratuitious culture. He was not in direct control of the direction of internal bodily energies but instead sought to direct an appropriation of traditions that were in control to a degree of great subtlety. When he had lost virtually all control, he was reduced to elaborating a vibrational economy in the confines of his own body and cosmos and to becoming the product of a culture that had impetuously elevated, in the highest reaches of its own medicine, the barbaric practice of electroshock, of imposing extreme internal chaos with a gross omnidirectional discharge of external energy. Indeed, electroshock is the titrated scream of a culture that knows so little about directing energies in the body. The same is true for insulin shock for a society so unschooled in its own animality—as Carl Solomon explained after his treatment: "There can be no hierarchization of different levels of transcendency when they are induced by an intravenously-injected animal secretion."[109] The way this culture directs energies outside the body, in its own theater of operations, becomes equally suspect. What is the electroshock of telecommunications, the insulin shock of evolutionary biology and genetics? Their acupuncture, Kundalini?

Notes

Introduction

1. The term *generation* is used for its inseparable sense of old and new. Examining the generation of techniques, tropes, and practices has many advantages, especially in the way that contributing factors can be observed before becoming too obscured by further elaboration. Of course, we can never be present at the birth, and there can never be a fully adequate account of the origins, of an individual's ideas by anyone—whether by authors like myself, close friends of the individual, or the individual himself or herself—only a representation that takes a certain density of sources and maneuvers into account. No matter how inadequate in comparison to an individual's experience, emphasizing this type of density at least avoids the limiting myths of individual action by posing a greater range of plausibility within an array of social practices.

2. Rudolf Arnheim, *Radio* (London: Faber & Faber, 1936), 226. While writing the book in the mid-1930s Arnheim thought the topic of radio itself was retrograde, since television was surely just around the corner. See the preface to the American edition (New York: Da Capo Press, 1972), 7.

3. Certain sounds may indeed express the inexpressible, but are they incapable of "expressing" other things at the same time, despite who might be listening and how they might be listening? And why would the inexpressible demand such superb isolation? Historically, the inexpressible has been defended by thinking of certain sounds as *mundane*. The word derives from *mundus*, meaning "world," and its pejorative sense has religious roots in the rejection of pagan attachments with the world in favor of a transcendence from the world. The scholarly disciplines and artistic practices that continue to rely on such a notion, whatever productive role such discrimination may have locally, will necessarily indulge in a deracination of these *worldly* sounds by denying them their subtleties and intensities in the terrestrial sphere of culture.

4. A contemporary parallel can be found in virtual reality where debates, theories, symposia, and publications sprang up long before artists even touched the equipment, let alone generated an artistic practice, and where the major provocation in the field was William Gibson's novel *Neuromancer*, which was written on a typewriter. The response in the late nineteenth and early twentieth centuries was spread out over a longer period of time than the lag between virtual reality promise and practice and was largely disorganized. The laggard development of auditive technologies and institutions, as we shall see, did not diminish the energetic trade in the arts of aurality.

5. The Creator appears to be the excremental Satan of Dante and Bosch, relating to cantos 18 and 32 of Dante's *Inferno* and to Bosch's picture of the devil sitting on the toilet, still known in the vernacular as a throne.

6. Comte de Lautréamont, *Les Chants de Maldoror* (1868), trans. Guy Wernham (New York: New Directions, 1965), 76. I am using Wernham's translation here with respect to his role in chapter 12.

7. Ibid.

8. Ibid., 77.

9. Ibid., 78.

10. See chapter 6, "The Voice That Keeps Silence," in Jacques Derrida, *Speech and Phenomena*, trans. David Allison (Evanston: Northwestern University Press, 1973), 70–87.

11. Voice is attached to thinking in various ways, from a Socratic *dæmon* to the persecuting voices of a psychosis. While I am assuming here the garden-variety "inner speech" and its manifestation when (following Tristan Tzara's phrase about poetry) thought is made in the mouth, this does not preclude that one's own voice might not be fully identified as one's own and thus can and does undercut self-presence. How this subversion might relate to the relationship of writing and speech is another

question altogether. For our purposes the question is directed less toward the tensions in an individual's experience of hearing one's own voice or imagining alien versions thereof (although this is discussed in chapter 11) and more toward the alienation of one's own voice in the sonorous realm. On the contrast between Derrida's and Lacan's notions of voice and *hearing oneself speaking*, see Slavoj Zizek, "Prolegomena to a Future Answer to Dr. Butler," special issue of an exchange between Rex Butler and Zizek, *Agenda: Australian Contemporary Art* (June 1995): 49–51.

12. There will also be a bit of *grain of the voice*, the marker of the body in the voice that Roland Barthes described in his essay of the same name. The erectile tissue (with which Barthes might be describing his own desires) that produces the body in the ears of others is but an emulation of the bones removed from selfsame speech once heard by others. Roland Barthes, "The Grain of the Voice," in *Image, Music, Text*, trans. Stephen Heath (New York: Hill and Wang, 1977). See part 5 of the present text for examples of a more elaborate investment of the body in the voice.

13. Marcel Duchamp, "The Box of 1914," in *The Writings of Marcel Duchamp*, ed. Michel Sanouillet and Elmer Peterson (New York: Oxford University Press, 1973), 23.

14. A measure these abilities could be found in the radio contests where audiences were asked to identify very short fragments of several songs strung together. These were not merely small timbral moments. Each one was also linked to social content as well, to which the redundancy making them audible in the first place attested. A similar capability is practiced daily with remote-control channel surfing.

15. Alan Nadel, *Containment Culture: American Narratives, Postmodernism and the Atomic Age* (Durham: Duke University Press, 1995).

16. Interview with the author, Berkeley, California (5 April 1995). It is interesting to note that both William Burroughs and John Cage in the years just before they died registered their fears about overpopulation.

17. Stein—like James Joyce or Samuel Beckett, who are also absent from this book—would require a dedicated study. Some exclusions are truly regrettable. For instance, Carolee Schneemann's work and the sounds of *Meat Joy* would have been integral to part 5. As the present manuscript was being prepared, however, a new book appeared that makes an important contribution to the area, *Sound States: Innovative Poetics and Acoustical Technologies*, ed. Adalaide Morris (Chapel Hill: University of North Carolina, 1997). Of special note with regard to women and modernism is Morris's own essay on H.D. [Hilda Doolittle].

18. Douglas Kahn, "Histories of Sound Once Removed," introduction to *Wireless Imagination: Sound, Radio and the Avant-garde*, ed. Douglas Kahn and Gregory Whitehead (Cambridge: MIT Press, 1992).

19. Two were by composers: John Cage's *Silence* (Middletown: Wesleyan University, 1961) and R. Murray Schafer's *The Tuning of the World: Toward a Theory of Soundscape Design* (New York: Knopf, 1977). Whereas Cage's ideas are addressed throughout the book, Schafer is mentioned only in passing, since artistic activities influenced by his approach fall outside the historical timeframe of the book. There were also materials associated with intermedia, Fluxus, text-sound, *poésie sonore*, soundscapes and acoustic ecology, electroacoustic music and other *new music* activities, *Das neue Hörspiel*, and the like. Again, most of these were by artists themselves. A brief list of relevant publications would include *Neues Hörspiel: Texte Partituren*, ed. Klaus Schöning (Frankfurt: Suhrkamp Verlag, 1969); Mark Ensign Cory, *The Emergence of an Acoustic Art Form: An Analysis of the German Experimental Hörspiel of the 1960s* (Lincoln: University of Nebraska, 1974); Michael Nyman, *Experimental Music: Cage and Beyond* (New York: Schirmer Books, 1974), as well as his magazine articles during the same period; Henri Chopin, *Poesie Sonore Internationale* (Paris: Jean-Michel Place Éditeur, 1979) and his review *Ou*; Germano Celant, *The Record as Artwork: From Futurism to Conceptual Art*, exhibition catalog (Fort Worth: Fort Worth Art Museum, 1977); René Block et al., *Für Augen und Ohren* (Berlin: Akademie der Künste, 1980); Ursula Block and Michael Glasmeier, *Broken Music: Artists' Recordworks* (Berlin: DAAD and gelbe Musik, 1989), Nicholas Zurbrugg's journal *Stereo Headphones*. People such as Amirkhanian and Schöning also published *acoustically* over the radio—the former at KPFA-FM in Berkeley, the latter at the WDR-Köln.

20. See *Cinema/Sound*, special issue of *Yale French Studies* 60 (1980); Tom Levin, "The Acoustic Dimension," *Screen* 25, no. 3 (May-June 1984): 55–68; *Film Sound: Theory and Practice*, ed. Elisabeth Weis and John Belton (New York: Columbia University Press, 1985); Kaja Silverman, *The Acoustic Mirror: The Female Voice in Psychoanalysis and Cinema* (Bloomington: Indiana University Press, 1988); Michel Chion, *Audio-Vision: Sound on Screen* (New York: Columbia University Press, 1994); Rick Altman, *Sound Theory, Sound Practice* (New York: Routledge, 1992); and Margaret Morse, "Talk, Talk, Talk," *Screen* 26, no. 2 (March-April, 1985); 2–15.

21. To my knowledge, the Canadian audio artist Dan Lander first coined the term in the mid-1980s. It spread quickly throughout Canada and the United States, although the general concept seems to have developed

independently around the same time in Australia among individuals associated with the audio arts at the Australian Broadcasting Corporation and with students and staff at the University of Technology, Sydney. On the basis of Lander's suggestion, I presented a paper entitled "The Sound of Music" at *Der freie Klang* symposium at the 1987 Ars Electronica festival, ed. Gottfried Hattinger et al. (Linz: Ars Electronica, 1987), 33–51. Individuals who favored the critique surprisingly found themselves accused of hating everything musical and of not appreciating the complexity of meanings and politics attendant on music. In fact, they were merely concerned with inhibitions within certain traditions of music (those that impinged on notions of worldly sound as discursive foil and actual material and promised response to changing social conditions of aurality and to create others) and with reading politics through such inhibitions. Still, the implications for music itself were much more consequential than standing Hanslick on his head. In keeping with the thinking of the day, those involved in sound were clearly intent on not repeating the type of demarcative procedures they criticized in others.

22. Among publications in Australia have been *Earshot*, ed. Shelly Cox et al., special issue of *3rd Degree*, no. 4 (1988); special issue on sound, ed. Martin Harrison et al., *Art & Text*, no. 31 (December-February 1989); special issue on sound, ed. Frances Dyson, *New Music Articles*, no. 8 (1990); *Sound Cultures*, ed. Colin Hood, special issue of *West*, no. 5 (192); the journal *Essays in Sound* (since 1992); and Paul Carter, *The Sound Inbetween* (Kensington: University of New South Wales, 1992); *Lyre's Island*, special section on Australian sound art and new music, ed. Douglas Kahn, *Leonardo Music Journal*, no. 6 (1996). Among publications in Canada have been the influential *Sound by Artists*, ed. Dan Lander and Micah Lexier (Toronto: Art Metropole, 1990); special issue on sound, *Public*, nos. 4–5 (1990); *Radio-phonics and Other-phonies*, special issue ed. Dan Lander of *Musicworks*, no. 53 (Summer 1992); *Radio Rethink*, ed. Daina Augaitis and Dan Lander (Banff: Walter Phillips Gallery, 1994). Among publications in the United States have been *Wireless Imagination* (1992); *Radiotext(e)*, ed. Neil Strauss (New York: Semiotext(e), 1993); Allen S. Weiss, *Phantasmatic Radio* (Durham: Duke University Press, 1995); *Experimental Sound and Radio*, ed. Allen Weiss, special issue of *TDR* 40, no. 3 (Fall 1996); and other relevant publications, including a special issue on the voice of *Notebooks in Cultural Analysis*, ed. Norman Cantor and Nathalia King (Durham: Duke University Press, 1986); *Voice-Over: On Technology*, ed. Laurence Rickels, special issue of *Substance 61*, 19, no. 1 (1990); and *October*, no. 55 (1991). For a very few European publications: the catalog

for the 1987 Ars Electronica Festival mentioned above, the book associated with the Sonambiente festival, *Klangkunst,* ed. Christian Kneisel et al. for the Akademie der Künste, Berlin (Munich: Prestel-Verlag, 1996); see also *Oor/Ear,* special issue of *Mediamatic* 6, no. 4 (1992), and various special issues of *Positionen* (Berlin). In Japan there have been the special issue on sound of *Music Today,* no. 19 (1993); *Tuning Forks: Technologies of Sound and Music,* special issue of *InterCommunication,* no. 9 (1994), and the activities dedicated to sound and new music of Xebec in Kobe, including their newsletter *Sound Arts.*

Chapter 1

1. Michel Serres, "Platonic Dialogue," in *Hermes: Literature, Science, Philosopher,* ed. and trans. Josué V. Harari and David F. Bell (Baltimore: Johns Hopkins University Press, 1982), 65–70.
2. Ibid., 70.
3. Ibid.
4. Walter Benjamin, "On the Mimetic Faculty," in *Reflections* (New York: Harcourt Brace Jovanovich, 1978), 335. The passage continues: "It may be supposed that the mimetic process that expresses itself in this way in the activity of the writer was, in the very distant times in which script originated, of utmost importance for writing. Script has become, like language, an archive of nonsensuous similarities, of nonsensuous correspondences" (334).
5. Ibid., 336. See also the first, similar version of this essay, "Doctrine of the Similar," trans. Knut Tarnowsky with prefatory article by Anson Rabinbach, *New German Critique* No. 17, 6, no. 2 (Spring 1979): 60–69.
6. Benjamin, "One Way Street," in *Reflections,* 68.
7. Naum Gabo and Anton Prevsner, "The Realistic Manifesto", in *Russian Art of the Avant-garde: Theory and Criticism, 1902–1934,* ed. and trans. John E. Bowlt (New York: Viking Press, 1976), 208–14.
8. Charles Baudelaire, *Artificial Paradise,* trans. Ellen Fox (New York: Herder and Herder, 1971), 77. Compare with Rainer Maria Rilke's "tall tree in the ear" in *Sonnets to Orpheus,* part 1, sonnet 1.
9. Ibid., 21.
10. Michel Leiris, "Persephone," in *Rules of the Game, I, Scratches,* trans. Lydia Davis (New York: Paragon House, 1991), 70.
11. Benjamin, "One Way Street," 68.
12. Ibid. Please refer to Michael Taussig as he puts this passage through its paces in *Mimesis and Alterity* (New York: Routledge, 1993), 38ff.
13. Benjamin, "Marseilles," *Reflections,* 132.

14. Friedrich Nietzsche, *The Gay Science*, trans. Walter Kaufmann (New York: Vintage, 1974), 123–24.

15. Ibid., 123.

16. Rüdiger Campe, "The *Rauschen* of the Waves: On the Margins of Literature," *SubStance 61*, 19, no. 1 (1990): 21–38.

17. Nietzsche, *The Gay Science*, 124.

18. Of section 60 of *The Gay Science* Jacques Derrida in "The Question of Style" says: "*'Women, and their action at a distance*. Do I still have ears? Am I all ears and nothing else?' All of Nietzsche's questions, those on woman in particular, are coiled up in the labyrinth of an ear." *The New Nietzsche*, ed. David B. Allison (Cambridge: MIT Press, 1985), 176–89. The project regarding the question of woman in Nietzsche for Derrida, as well as for Sarah Kofman, which is comprised primarily of establishing the proliferation of positions and undecidability over the corpus of his writings, does not grant a commensurate proliferation and undecidability for women. Such attempts to temper generalizations about Nietzsche's misogyny appear spurious in the face of so many statements of contempt.

19. Nietzsche, *The Gay Science*, 124.

20. Salvador Dalí, "L'Ane pourri," from *Le Surréalisme au Service de la Révolution*, translated as "The Stinking Ass," *Surrealists on Art*, ed. Lucy R. Lippard (Englewood Cliffs, N.J.: Prentice-Hall, 1970), 97–100. See also chapter 4 of Dawn Ades, *Dalí and Surrealism* (New York: Harper and Row, 1982).

21. Antonin Artaud, "The Mountain of Signs," from *A Voyage to the Land of the Tarahumara*, in Antonin Artaud, *Selected Writings*, ed. Susan Sontag, trans. Helen Weaver (Berkeley: University of California Press, 1988), 379–82.

22. Ibid., 380.

23. Ibid., 381.

24. Max Ernst, "Comment forcer l'inspiration" (1933), in *The Autobiography of Surrealism*, ed. Marcel Jean (New York: Viking Press, 1980), 270–72.

25. Other Surrealist techniques of provoking images from fields of visual noise included Wolfgang Paalen's *fumage*, where a sooty candle or lamp leaves its billowy traces on a primed canvas or paper, and Oscar Dominguez's *decalcomania*, where a surface is pressed on another surface covered in inks or paints and then peeled away, producing a rippling, tributary effect of fractal shading (George Sand called them *dendrites*). There were also the marbling effects of *écrémage*, the scrapings of *grattage*, the pre-Pollock drippings of *coulage*, among others.

26. André Breton, "Surrealism and Painting," in *What Is Surrealism?* (New York: Haskell House, 1974), 9–10.

27. Ibid.

28. Ibid.

29. Leonardo da Vinci, *Treatise on Painting*, trans. A. Philip McMahon (Princeton: Princeton University Press, 1956), 50.

30. It has been said that the bells triggered epileptic seizures causing auditory "hallucinations" of angelic voices. William Booth, "Joan of Arc Had Epilepsy?" *San Francisco Chronicle*, 3 May 1990, sec. B, pp. 3, 7.

31. See E. P. Thompson, "Rough Music," *Customs in Common* (London: Penguin Books, 1991), 467–538. The character of voices heard in bells can be as variable as the acoustics. Baudelaire transcribed a woman's description of what she heard in bells themselves. Immobilized by hashish, she imagined how "brilliant tropical birds flew over my head; and, as my hearing perceived the distant sound of little bells about the necks of horses who were proceeding, far away, along the highway, the two senses blended their impressions into a single idea, and I attributed the mysterious, tinkling song to the birds, imagining that they sang with metal throats. Evidently, they were speaking about me, rejoicing in my captivity." Baudelaire, *Artificial Paradise*, 60.

32. André Breton, "Silence Is Golden," trans. Louise Varèse, *Modern Music*, 21, no. 3 (March–April 1944); reprinted in Minna Lederman, *The Life and Death of a Small Magazine (Modern Music, 1924–1946)* (New York: Institute for Studies in American Music, 1983), 85–87.

33. Ibid.

34. Ibid.

35. Ibid.

36. André Breton, *Anthologie de l'humour noir*, cited in L. C. Breunig, "The Laughter of Apollinaire," in *Yale French Studies*, no. 31 (May 1964): 66–73. The same would be true for the person described in the following: "His voice was like the thunder that ascends from watering cans when the evening sun shines on them." Alexis (pseud.), "A Visit to the Cabaret Dada," in *Dada Performance*, ed. Mel Gordon (New York: PAJ, 1987), 83–85.

37. Vicente Huidobro in *Altazor* (1919–1931), *The Selected Poetry of Vicente Huidobro*, ed. David Guss (New York: New Directions, 1981), 84.

38. Ibid.

39. Jack Kerouac, *Big Sur* (London: Flamingo, 1993), 30. Kerouac was referring to the Proteus episode of *Ulysses*, itself evincing the word fusion that would become intensified in *Finnegans Wake*. "Listen: a fourworded

wavespeech: seesoo, hrss, rsseeiss, ooos. Vehement breath of waters amid seasnakes, rearing horses, rocks. In cups of rocks if slops: flop, slop, slap: bounded in barrels. And, spent, its speech ceases. It flows purling, widely flowing, floating foampool, flower unfurling." James Joyce, *Ulysses* (New York: Vintage, 1990), 49.

40. Appendix to Kerouac, *Big Sur*, 167–88. Compare with the more conventional onomatopoeic device in a Louis Zukovsky poem:

A Sea
the
foam
claws

cloys
close

Zukovsky was not required to sit by the sea to make this expert evocation of the sound and sight of a small wave breaking, flowing, and ebbing. The sounds correspond to the field of water noise; they are not culled from it.

41. Cited in Alan Watts, *The Way of Zen* (New York: Pantheon, 1957), 187.

42. Kerouac, *Big Sur*, 20.

43. Jarry's allegory of the dangers of nonalcoholism, "The Habits and Behaviour of the Drowned," describes the immersion of all those who, on the water wagon that has spilled over into a river, form an entirely separate species. In *Atlas Anthology No. 3*, ed. Alastair Brotchie and Malcolm Green (London: Atlas Press, 1985), 41–42. Kerouac's drunken speech seemed to help with the slurred sounds of his "Sea":

Helen Hinkle: Oh, God. What poetry. It was beautiful to hear it spoken.

Al Hinkle: Even drunk, it was.

Helen Hinkle: May it was even more so. It was absolutely lovely. The sounds of the sea.

Barry Gifford and Lawrence Lee, *Jack's Book: An Oral Biography of Jack Kerouac* (New York: St. Martin's Press, 1978), 292.

44. See Plato in the *Timaeus:* "We may in general assume sound to be a blow which passes through the ears, and is transmitted by means of the air, the brains and the blood, to the soul; and that hearing is the vibration of

this blow, which begins in the head and ends in the region of the liver." Cited in Frederick Vinton Hunt, *Origins in Acoustics* (New Haven: Yale University Press, 1978), 19.

45. Kerouac, *Big Sur*, 153.

46. Ibid., 154.

47. Ibid., 161.

48. Ibid., 161.

49. Allen Ginsberg, *Allen Verbatim: Lectures on Poetry, Politics, Consciousness*, ed. Gordon Ball (New York: McGraw-Hill, 1974), 160.

50. Jack Kerouac, "Essentials of Spontaneous Prose," in *Good Blonde and Others* (San Francisco: Grey Fox Press, 1993), 69–71.

51. Louis Zukovsky, *Complete Short Poetry* (Baltimore: Johns Hopkins University Press, 1991), 242.

52. Robert Creeley, "Preface," ibid., xii.

53. Statement made at Bard College (2 November 1972), cited in Michele J. Leggot, *Reading Zukovsky's 80 Flowers* (Baltimore: Johns Hopkins University Press, 1989), 50. This was, of course, a moment of self-depreciation; Zukovsky was a polyglot growing up in the capital of American polylingualism, New York City. "As a child he memorized large chunks of Longfellow's *Hiawatha* in Yiddish, a fact that delighted his neighbors, the Italian bullies, who would plague him as he went to do errands and not stop till he'd recited enough to satisfy them." Creeley, ibid.

54. Walter Benjamin, "Hashish in Marseilles," in *One Way Street and Other Writings*, trans. Edmund Jephcott and Kingsley Shorter (London: New Left Books, 1979), 222.

55. This movement toward foreignness, toward noise within language, can lead to the incapacitation of aphasia or the powerful nonsense of incantation. For Velimir Khlebnikov, the power exerted by the unintelligible phonemes of magical and religious charms and incantations demonstrated the right of *zaum*, transrational or beyonsense language, to "exist alongside the language of reason. But there does in fact exist a way to make beyonsense language intelligible to reason," and this provided Khlebnikov with a basis for his system of Word Creation—neology culled from nonsense. Velimir Khlebnikov, "Our Fundamentals," in *Collected Works of Velimir Khlebnikov*, Vol. 1, trans. Paul Schmidt (Cambridge: Harvard University Press, 1989), 383.

56. René Daumal, "A Fundamental Experiment" (1944), trans. Roger Shattuck, *The Drug User: Documents 1840–1960*, ed. John Strausbaugh and Donald Blaise (New York: Blast Books, 1991), 63.

57. I am referring here to accounts in the medical literature and to my own experience.

58. Benjamin, "The Writer's Technique in Thirteen Theses," in *One-Way Street and Other Writings*, 65.

59. Jean Cocteau, *Cocteau's World: An Anthology of Writings by Jean Cocteau*, ed. Margaret Crosland (New York: Dodd, Mead, 1973), 406.

60. Baudelaire, *Artificial Paradise*, 54.

61. Ibid.

62. Walter Benjamin, *Charles Baudelaire: A Lyric Poet in the Era of High Capitalism*. (London: New Left Books, 1976), 49.

63. George Simmel, *Soziologie* (Berlin, 1958), 486, cited in ibid., 37–38. The condition of big-city travel may be somewhat different with the proliferation of personal audiocassette and compact disc units. And then there is Allen Ginsberg, not so much traveling to work as working while traveling: "Yeah. Like if you're talking aloud, if you're talking—composing aloud or talking aloud to yourself. Actually I was in the back of the bus, talking to myself, except with a tape recorder. So every time I said something interesting to myself I put it on tape." Allen Ginsberg, *Composed on the Tongue: Literary Conversations, 1967–1977* (San Francisco: Grey Fox Press, 1980), 29.

64. Leonardo da Vinci, *Treatise on Painting*, trans. A. Philip McMahon (Princeton, NJ: Princeton University Press, 1956), 59.

Chapter 2

1. Richard Huelsenbeck, introduction to *The Dada Almanac*, ed. Richard Huelsenbeck (1920), English edition by Malcolm Green (London: Atlas Press, 1993), 10.

2. Tristan Tzara, "Zurich Chronicle," ibid., 21.

3. Richard Huelsenbeck, "Plane," ibid., 20.

4. Richard Huelsenbeck, "Collective Dada Manifesto" (1920), in *The Dada and Painters and Poets: An Anthology*, ed. Robert Motherwell (New York: Hall, 1981), 245.

5. Richard Huelsenbeck, "En Avant Dada" (1920), ibid., 25.

6. Ibid., 26.

7. Richard Huelsenbeck, *Memoirs of a Dada Drummer* (New York: Viking Press, 1969), 8–9.

8. Ibid.

9. Ibid. That he would concoct poems from another language in the first place is reminiscent of the spontaneous knowledge of language claimed by the Russian Futurist Aleksei Kruchenykh in his *Explodity* (1913): "On

April 27 at 3 o'clock in the afternoon I instantaneously mastered to perfection all languages Such is the poet of the current era I am here reporting my verses in Japanese Spanish and Hebrew:

iké mina ni
sinu ksi
iamakh alik
　zel
　GO OSNEG KAID
　M R BATUL'BA
　VINU AE KSEL
　VER TUM DAKH
　　GIZ
　　SHISH

Kruchenykh's language acquisition was not performed as noise but was instead enacted, in this respect at least, under the guise of a universal language. Aleksei Kruchenykh, "From *Explodity*," in *Russian Futurism through Its Manifestoes, 1912–1928*, ed. Anna Lawton and Herbert Eagle (Ithaca: Cornell University Press, 1988), 65–66. Vladimir Markov in his standard text, *Russian Futurism: A History* (Berkeley: University of California, 1968), noted that "much of the Russian *zaum*," or the transrational verse of which Kruchenykh was the most radical practitioner, was "written to imitate the sound of foreign tongues" (20). The Italian Futurists also imitated foreign languages, including African ones that no doubt reminded them of their colonial exploits.

10. Rudolf E. Kuenzli, "Hugo Ball: Verse without Words," *Dada/Surrealism*, no. 8 (1978): 30–35.
11. Francis M. Naumann, "Janco/Dada: An Interview with Marcel Janco," *Arts Magazine* 57, no. 3 (November 1982): 80–86.
12. The poem is reproduced in *Dada Performance*, ed. Mel Gordon (New York: PAJ, 1987), 38–39.
13. Hugo Ball, *Flight out of Time: A Dada Diary* (New York: Viking Press, 1974), 57.
14. Ibid., 4.
15. Ibid.
16. Ball (24 June 1916), ibid., 71. All six sound poems are reprinted in Harold B. Segel, *Turn-of-the-Century Cabaret* (New York: Columbia University Press, 1987), 337–339. For a good introduction to the performative practices of the Cabaret Voltaire, see Segel's chapter on Zurich Dada

(321–65) and Annabelle Melzer, *Latest Rage the Big Drum: Dada and Surrealist Performance* (Ann Arbor: UMI Research Press, 1980).

17. See *Dada Performance*, 40.

18. Ball, *Flight out of Time*, 68.

19. (3 June 1916), ibid., 65. There was a tradition of noise making in the Christian church. For the three days prior to Easter when bells were banned, rattles were used in their place to signal certain events, within processionals, and as ritual devices.

20. (23 June 1916), ibid., 71. Ball knew he was not the first modern artist to give up the word. He was well aware of Christian Morgenstern's *Songs of the Gallows* (1905) and, through Kandinsky, the *zaum* poetry of Aleksei Kruchenykh, Velimir Khlebnikov (although his version of it was not really comparable), and others in Russia. Ball was probably most directly influenced by Kandinsky himself, both because of their personal contact and because of the spiritual basis for Kandinsky's own artworks. About a year after the sound poems Ball gave a lecture on Kandinsky in which he said that in his *Der gelbe Klang* (The Yellow Sound) Kandinsky was "the first to discover and apply the most abstract expression of sound in language, consisting of harmonized vowels and consonants." ("Kandinsky" [7 April 1917], in *Flight out of Time*, 324.) The script for Kandinsky's *son et lumière* was printed in *Der Blaue Reiter Almanac* in 1912, the same year as the publication of *Concerning the Spiritual in Art* and the same year Ball met Kandinsky. In *Der gelbe Klang* intelligible words were kept at a bare minimum, and there were plenty of voices *ohne Worte*. Just as darkness fell on the end of Ball's recitation, at the end of scene 3, "Suddenly, one hears from behind the stage a shrill tenor voice filled with fear, shouting entirely indistinguishable words very quickly (one hears frequently [the letter] *a:* e.g., "Kalasimunafakola!"). Pause. For a moment it becomes dark." Wassily Kandinsky, *Complete Writings on Art*, vol. 1, ed. Kenneth C. Lindsay and Peter Vergo (Boston: G. K. Hall & Co., 1982), 278.

21. Richard Sheppard, "Dada and Mysticism: Influences and Affinities," in *Dada Spectrum: The Dialectics of Revolt*, ed. Stephen C. Foster and Rudolf E. Kuenzli (Madison: Coda Press, 1979), 92–113.

22. Blaise Cendrars, "Crépitements," in *Selected Writings of Blaise Cendrars*, (New York: New Directions, 1966), 72.

23. Huelsenbeck, *En Avant Dada*, 35.

24. Ibid., 36.

25. Ibid.

26. Richard Huelsenbeck, "Collective Dada Manifesto" (1920), in *The Dada and Painters and Poets*, 244. We are reminded of Satie's question, "Which do you prefer, music or pork butchery?" Christopher Schiff, "Banging on a Windowpane," in *Wireless Imagination: Sound, Radio and the Avant-garde*, ed. Douglas Kahn and Gregory Whitehead (Cambridge: MIT Press, 1992), 159.

27. Hans Richter, *Dada Art and Anti-Art* (New York: McGraw-Hill, 1965), 77.

28. F. T. Marinetti, *Stung by Salt and War: Creative Texts of the Italian Avant-Gardist F. T. Marinetti*, translated in Richard J. Pioli (New York: Lang, 1987), 48.

29. Guillaume Apollinaire, "Through the Salon des Independents," in *Apollinaire on Art*, ed. Leroy Breunig (New York: Da Capo Press, 1972), 286–293.

30. Robert Delaunay, *The New Art of Color: The Writings of Robert and Sonia Delaunay*, trans. David Shapiro and Arthur A. Cohen (New York: Viking Press, 1978), 116 (emphasis in the original).

31. For many artists the Eiffel Tower was the emblematic oracle of simultaneism, technologically gathering up and distributing France's cosmopolitanism from the reach of its wireless transmissions and receptions—"I AM THE QUEEN OF THE DAWN OF THE POLES" (Vicente Huidobro); "It was the Queen of Paris. Now it's the handmaiden of the telegraph" (Jean Cocteau); and providing the internationalism of the proletarian sort championed by Mayakovsky, "Come to Moscow! . . . It's not for you—model genius of machines—here to pine away from Apollinairic verse." Apollinaire himself rebuilt the tower in his monumental graphic poem *Lettre-Océan*. See Vicente Huidobro, "Tour Eiffel" (Geoffrey O'Brien, trans.), in *The Selected Poetry of Vicente Huidobro*, ed. David Guss (New York: New Directions, 1981), 19–21; Jean Cocteau, "Les mariés de la Tour Eiffel," (1921), in *Modern French Theatre*, ed. and trans. Michael Benedikt and George Wellwarth (New York: Dutton, 1966). See also chapters 1 and 6 in Marjorie Perloff, *The Futurist Moment: Avant-Garde, Avant-Guerre, and the Language of Rupture* (Chicago: University of Chicago Press, 1986); Vladimir Mayakovsky, "Paris" (1923), in *Mayakovsky*, trans. Herbert Marshall (New York: Hill and Wang, 1965).

32. Blaise Cendrars, *Dan Yack [Le Plan de l'aiguille]* (1927), trans. Nina Rootes (New York: Kesend, 1987), 25.

33. Ibid., 34.

34. Ibid., 36.

35. Compare with Vicente Huidobro's poem "Sale la Luna" (1918): "This afternoon I saw/The latest phonographic presses/It was a maze of screams/And songs as varied/As in foreign ports." *The Selected Poetry of Vicente Huidobro*, trans. David M. Guss (New York: New Directions, 1981), 37–43.

36. Franz Fanon, "This Is the Voice of Algeria," in *A Dying Colonialism* (1959), trans. Haakon Chevalier Chevalier (New York: Grove Press, 1965), 71. "It also gives him the feeling that colonial society is a living and palpitating reality, with its festivities, its traditions eager to establish themselves, its progress, its taking root. But especially, in the hinterland, in the so-called colonization centers, it is the only link with the cities, with Algiers, with the metropolis, with the world of the civilized."

37. Arthur W. J. G. Ord-Hume, *Clockwork Music* (New York: Crown, 1973), 281–82.

38. Tristan Tzara, "Dada Manifesto 1918," in *The Dada Painters and Poets*, ed. Robert Motherwell (New York: Wittenborn, 1951), 81.

39. Luigi Russolo, "The Art of Noises Futurist Manifesto" (1913), in *The Art of Noises* (1916), trans. Barclay Brown (New York: Pendragon Press, 1986), 25 (emphasis in original).

40. Appended to Rodney Johns Payton, "The Futurist Musicians: Francesco Balilla Pratella and Luigi Russolo" (Ph.D. diss., University of Chicago, 1974), 91–96.

41. "I must say that some affirmations, of a polemic and others of a theoretical nature, which one can read in my *Manifesto* refer to a rapport between music and machines. These were neither written nor even thought by me and often are in contrast to the rest of the ideas. These inventions were added by Marinetti arbitrarily and at the last moment. I was then astonished to read them over my signature, but the act was already done." Cited ibid., 15–16.

42. Russolo, *The Art of Noises*, 23.

43. Giovanni Lista, *L'Art des bruits* (Lausanne: Editions l'Age d'Homme, 1975), 18–19.

44. Russolo, *The Art of Noises*, 26.

45. Ibid.

46. Ibid., 27.

47. See Linda Landis, "Futurists at War," in *The Futurist Imagination* (New Haven: Yale University Art Gallery, 1983), 60–75.

48. Luigi Russolo, "The Futurist Intonarumori" (22 May 1913), trans. Victoria Nes Kirby, in Michael Kirby, *Futurist Performances* (New York: Dutton, 1971), 176.

49. For instance, on Marinetti's *free words*, Russolo wrote "since traditional poetry lacks suitable means for rendering the reality and the value of noises, modern war cannot be expressed lyrically without the noise instrumentation of futurist *free words*." Russolo, "Noises of War," in *The Art of Noises*, 49.

50. Jacques Attali in his book *Noise*, trans. Brian Massumi (Minneapolis: University of Minnesota Press, 1985), understands Russolo's *art of noises* to be a premonition of World War I: "It is not by coincidence that Russolo wrote his *Art of Noises* in 1913; that noise entered music and industry entered painting just before the outbursts and wars of the twentieth century, before the rise of social noise" (10). This belongs to Attali's general assertion that social organizations of music historically prefigure political economic systems. The critique he ranges against certain social formations should not mask the fact that he grants music itself a grandiloquence not enjoyed since the music of the spheres came crashing down to earth. The problem with his specific observation regarding Russolo is that the war noise involved occurred prior to the manifesto, in the battles covered by Marinetti. Music echoed war, not vice versa. The only premonition involved might only be that regional combat prefigured the Great War, but then there would be no special powers granted music. I have found another similar formulation from André Breton, although he chose not to historiographically elevate the observation. After quoting Apollinaire's account of Alberto Savinio compositional assaults on the piano, "after each piece the blood had to be wiped off the keys," Breton notes that "two months later, the war broke out." See André Breton, "Alberto Savinio," in *Alberto Savinio: Menschengemüse zum Tachtisch* (Munich, 1980), cited in *Broken Music*, ed. Ursula Block and Michael Glasmeier (Berlin: DAAD, 1989), 220. I can think of only one legitimate instance where music preceded militarism, and that was when Bob Burns, the hillbilly comedian Spike Jones backed up on radio during the 1940s, invented an instrument out of a gas pipe and whisky funnel and called it a *bazooka*, and then the U.S. Army took the name for their new over-the-shoulder rocket launcher. Bob "Bazooka" Burns now awaits a theory of history in his image.

51. F. T. Marinetti, "The Founding and Manifesto of Futurism," trans. R. W. Flint, in *Futurist Manifestos*, ed. Umbro Apollonio (New York: Viking Press, 1973), 22.

52. Although these *parole in libertà* would not appear in publication until the 1914 collection *ZANG–TUMB-TUMB*, Marinetti had already been performing portions them in Rome and Berlin a month before the issuance

of Russolo's manifesto on 11 March 1913. In any case, the style of military onomatopoeia had already been established in 1912 with his first example of *parole in libertà*, "Battle (Weight+Stink)." See Marinetti, *Stung by Salt and War*, 41–43. The artistic form of *parole in libertà* themselves was itself patently "born on two battlefields Tripoli and Adrianople." "From the Café Bulgaria in Sofia to the Courage of the Italians in the Balkans and the Military Spirit of Désarrois," *Marinetti: Selected Writings*, ed. R. W. Flint (New York: Farrar, Straus and Giroux, 1972), 332. Marinetti reported combat action first in October 1911 during the Italo-Turkish War in Libya, which he covered as a correspondent for *L'Intransigeant* of Paris and then, about a year later, during the Balkan War at Adrianople.

53. *Marinetti: Selected Writings*, 332–33. For other sounds of horses on the battlefield, see Erich Maria Remarque, *All Quiet on the Western Front* (1929) (London: Picador Classics, 1993), 46.

54. *Marinetti: Selected Writings*, 332–33.

55. Velimir Khlebnikov, Letter to Filippo Marinetti (2 February 1914), in *Collected Works of Velimir Khlebnikov*, vol. 1, trans. Paul Schmidt (Cambridge: Harvard University Press, 1987), 87–88.

56. Kruchenykh, "New Ways of the Word (the Language of the Future, Death to Symbolism)," in *Russian Futurism through Its Manifestoes*, 76.

57. Rudolf Leonhard, "Marinetti in Berlin, 1913," in *The Era of German Expressionism*, ed. Paul Raabe (London: Calder, 1980), 115–18.

58. C. R. W. Nevinson, *Paint and Prejudice* (1937), 57, cited in James Joll, *Three Intellectuals in Politics* (New York: Pantheon Books, 1960), 152.

59. Harold Monro (December 1913), cited in Alan Young, *Dada and After: Extremist Modernism and English Literature* (Manchester: Manchester University Press, 1981), 72. This was an impression gained from a previous visit to London.

60. Cited in Caroline Tisdall and Angelo Bozzolla, *Futurism* (London: Thames and Hudson, 1977), 104.

61. Wyndham Lewis, *Blasting and Bombardiering* (1937) (Berkeley: University of California Press, 1967), 33. The last sentence suggests a Parisian review of the first performance of the intonarumori at the Teatro dal Verme in Milan (21 April 1914) with its outbreak of fisticuffs: "An impressive simultaneity of bloody faces and noisy enharmonics in an infernal din. The battle of *Ernani* was a matter of insignificance beside this riot." Cited in Luigi Russolo, "Polemics, Battles, and the First Performances of the Noise Instruments," in *The Art of Noises*, 34.

62. F. T. Marinetti, "Dynamic and Synoptic Declamation" (11 March 1916), in *Marinetti: Selected Writings*, 147.

63. In "Destruction of Syntax—Wireless Imagination—Words in Freedom" (*Lacerba*, 11 May and 15 June 1913), Marinetti wrote the following:

> Those who use the telephone today, the telegraph, the phonograph, the train, bicycle or automobile, the ocean liner, dirigible or airplane, the cinema or a great daily newspaper (the synthesis of a day in the whole world) do not dream that these diverse forms of communication, transportation and information exert such a decisive influence upon their psyches.

Marinetti, *Stung by Salt and War*, 45.

64. See "Technical Manifesto of Futurist Literature" (May 1912), in *Marinetti: Selected Writings*, 84–89. See also Linda Landis, "Futurists at War," in *The Futurist Imagination*, 60–75.

65. A reproduction of the poem can be found in *Futurismo and Futurismi*, ed. Pontus Hulten (Milan: Bompiani, 1986), 604.

66. Marinetti, "Battle (Weight + Stink)," in *Stung by Salt and War*, 47–48.

67. Russolo, *The Art of Noises*, 36.

68. Diary entry on 19 October 1915, cited in Tisdall and Bozzolla, *Futurism*, 180.

69. F. T. Marinetti, "Manifesto of the Futurist Dance," in *Marinetti: Selected Writings*, 137–41.

70. Ibid., 139.

71. Russolo, "Noises of War," in *The Art of Noises*, 49.

72. Ibid., 50.

73. "Shrapnels do not explode on contact but are timed by a fuse that is automatically ignited at the moment of firing and continues to burn during the flight of the shell, thus setting off the explosive while the shrapnel is still some meters from the target. In these shells the whistling is violently interrupted by a furious *meow*, simultaneous with the explosion itself. No matter how short, this *meow* produces a rapid enharmonic passage, descending more than an octave. . . . I remember that soldiers remarked of the first shrapnels that there must have been a cat inside!" Ibid., 51.

74. Remarque, *All Quiet on the Western Front*, 40–41. The original German and the English translation were both 1929.

75. "Human multitudes, gases, electrical forces were hurled into the open country, high-frequency currents coursed through the landscape, new

constellations rose in the sky, aerial space and ocean depths thundered with propellers, and everywhere sacrificial shafts were dug in Mother Earth." Walter Benjamin, "One-Way Street," in *Reflections*, trans. Edmund Jephcott (New York: Harcourt Brace Jovanovich, 1978), 93.

76. As Apollinaire reported in his poem "Guerre": "Contact by sound/We're firing toward noises that were heard." Guillaume Apollinarie, *Calligrammes*, trans. Anne Hyde Greet (Berkeley: University of California, 1980), 160–63. For a history of sounds within tactical communications, see chapter 8, "Signaling by Sound," of David L. Woods, *A History of Tactical Communication Techniques* (New York: Arno Press, 1974), 131–48.

77. Remarque, *All Quiet on the Western Front*, 88. Also: "We sharpen their ears to the malicious, hardly audible buzz of the smaller shells that are not easily distinguishable. They must pick them out from the general din by their insect-like hum—we explain to them that these are far more dangerous than the big ones that can be heard long beforehand" (90–91).

78. Ibid., 85.

79. Ibid., 86.

80. Ibid., 142.

81. Ibid., 147.

82. Ibid., 148.

83. Russolo, *The Art of Noises*, 28.

84. Russol, "The Noise Instruments," in *The Art of Noises*, 78.

85. Marinetti, "Let's Murder the Moonshine," in *Marinetti: Selected Writings*, 46.

86. Georges Ribemont-Dessaignes, "History of Dada," in *The Dada Painters and Poets*, 117.

87. George Antheil, "The Negro on the Spiral," in *Negro: An Anthology* (1934), ed. Nancy Cunard (New York: Ungar, 1970), 218.

88. Walter Benjamin, "Theories of German Fascism: On the Collection of Essays *War and Warrior*, ed. Ernst Jünger," *New German Critique*, no. 17 (Spring 1979): 120–28.

89. Russolo, "The Noises of War," in *The Art of Noises*, 49.

90. Luigi Russolo, "The Art of Noises Futurist Manifesto," ibid., 26.

Part II

1. Gershwin cited in *A Dictionary of Musical Quotations*, ed. Ian Crofton and Donald Fraser (New York: Schirmer Books, 1985), 79; James Joyce, *Ulysses* (New York: Vintage Books, 1990), 282; DeMarinis cited from program literature for Sound Cultures San Francisco, Spring 1996.

Chapter 3

1. Kathi Meyer-Baer, *Music of the Spheres and the Dance of Death* (Princeton: Princeton University Press, 1970), 12–15.

2. For a brief overview of the role of figure of vibration, through which neo-Pythagoreanism primarily manifests itself within modernism, in relation to figures of inscription and transmission, see my introduction to *Wireless Imagination: Sound, Radio and the Avant-Garde*, ed. Douglas Kahn and Gregory Whitehead (Cambridge: MIT Press, 1992), 14–26.

3. See "An Epilogue on Romanticism," in John Neubauer, *The Emancipation of Music from Language* (New Haven: Yale University Press, 1986), 193–210. The evolution of synesthetic systems varies with locale and individual, but Pythagoreanism usually found the most direct route through metaphysical and occultist connections and through Platonic thought. It was also buttressed by scientist ideas relating light and sound vibrations proportionally through frequency and with the ongoing connection of mathematics and music. In the sphere of language can be found what Gérard Genette has called the tradition of mimologics, usually known as the Cratylian tradition of motivated speech, which itself was interlaced with Pythagoreanism, especially beginning in the late eighteenth century.

4. Noise was in effect eliminated with respect to the experiences of actual synesthetes. For a brief demonstration of the variation from one system to the next, see the side bars in Mel Gordon, "Songs from the Museum of the Future: Russian Sound Creation" (1910–1930), *Wireless Imagination*, 198–243. Moreover, the image realm of other synesthetic experiences were much more richly constituted than just color and tone. See, for example, A. R. Luria, *The Mind of a Mnemonist* (Cambridge: Harvard University Press, 1987), 22–24. The irony of an artistic enterprise deferring to the *ratio*nality of Pythagoreanism can be explained by the appeals synesthetic systems made variously to interiority and individuality, spiritism, and the occult and the comprehension of different perceptual registers. Any inertia of the rationality of the various systems was, of course, muted by the way it was put to use by specific artists, no more so than the Russian poet Velimir Khlebnikov, who appropriated Pythagoreanism at the very core of its precepts, replacing its foundation on space with time, as is evident in his Tables of Destiny.

5. One of the earliest recorded appeals to water for understanding was made by the Stoic philosopher Chrysippus (ca. 280–207 B.C.): "Hearing occurs when the air between that which sounds and that which hears is

struck, thus undulating spherically and falling upon the ears, as the water in a reservoir undulates in circles from a stone thrown into it." Cited in Frederick Vinton Hunt, *Origins in Acoustics* (New Haven: Yale University Press, 1978), 23–24.

6. A working distinction used within Thomas L. Hankins and Robert J. Silverman, *Instruments and the Imagination* (Princeton: Princeton University Press, 1995).

7. Ibid., 135.

8. Alfred Jarry, *Exploits and Opinions of Doctor Faustroll Pataphysician* (1911), in *Selected Works of Alfred Jarry*, ed. Roger Shattuck and Simon Watson Taylor (New York: Grove Press, 1965), 244.

9. Ibid., 245.

10. Ibid.

11. This observation was made by Linda Dalrymple Henderson, *The Fourth Dimension and Non-Euclidean Geometry in Modern Art* (Princeton: Princeton University Press, 1983), 48–49.

12. Sir William Thomson, *Popular Lectures and Addresses*, vol. 1, *Constitution of Matter* (London: MacMillan, 1891), 271.

13. Ibid., 297.

14. Ibid., 282–83.

15. Ibid., 284.

16. Ibid., 278–79.

17. Ibid., 460.

18. Ibid., 282.

19. Ibid., 282–83.

20. Ibid., 281–84. Also: "all that can be represented by a whole page or two pages of orchestral score, as the specification of the sound to be produced in, say ten seconds of time, is shown to the eye with perfect clearness by a single curve on a riband of paper a hundred inches long" (284).

21. Hermann Helmholtz, *On the Sensations of Tone as a Physiological Basis for the Theory of Music* (1877; New York: Dover Publications, 1954), 8.

22. Ibid., 8–9.

23. Luigi Russolo, "Physical Principles and Practical Possibilities," *The Art of Noises* (1916), trans. Barclay Brown (New York: Pendragon Press, 1986), 37.

24. Ibid.

25. Ibid., 39.

26. Ibid.

27. Ibid., 37–40. Elsewhere, in the chapter "The Noises of Nature and Life," he points out that "water represents in nature the most frequent, most

varied, and richest source of noises" and as only one example points to the "fundamental pitch with its fifth, tenth, and the minor seventh of the second octave," of Fingal's Cave—the Scottish cave itself, not the Mendelssohn composition (42).

28. Russolo, "New Acoustical Pleasures," ibid., 87.

29. The connection with the world was primarily elaborated through four avenues: (1) an expansion of timbral effects to a point of rejection within existing conventions of Western art music, signaling a breach to the outside; (2) the surrounding discourse of manifestos, declamations, and texts rife with extramusical rationale and images of the world; (3) a shift from purity to plenitude; and (4) the introduction of the intonarumori, the instruments specifically designed to play Russolo's music, which in many ways repeated organologically the process by which noises were introduced semiologically.

30. Russolo, "The Art of Noises, Futurist Manifesto," ibid., 30.

31. Henry Cowell, "The Joys of Noise," *The New Republic* (31 July 1929): 287–88. This article will be included in a collection presently in preparation by Dick Higgins, *First Gleanings: Selected Writings of Henry Cowell* [working title].

32. Ibid., 287.

33. Ibid.

34. Ibid., 288.

35. Ibid., 287.

36. Sergei Yutkevich, "Eccentrism" (1922), in *The Film Factory: Russian and Soviet Cinema in Documents, 1896–1939*, ed. Richard Taylor and Ian Christie (Cambridge: Harvard University Press, 1988), 62.

37. Sirens almost found their way into Diaghilev's unfinished ballet *Liturgie* (1914) and were in Cocteau's early plans for *Parade* (1917) but were dropped because of "material difficulties." This concurrence moved Christopher Schiff to observe, "The siren is something that Cocteau had included in his very first draft of the Little American Girl [dancer in *Parade*], and thus it is likely that it was a meeting of minds between Diaghilev and Cocteau that finally brought the noise element into *Parade*." Christopher Schiff, "The Three Parades: The Ballets Russes, and the Beginnings of Surrealism" (Master's thesis, Wesleyan University, 1988), 161.

38. Francis Bacon, *New Atlantis* (Oxford: Clarendon Press, 1924), 42–43.

39. Ferruccio Busoni, "Insufficiency of the Means for Musical Expression" (1893), in *The Essence of Music and Other Papers*, trans. Rosamond Ley (London: Salisbury Square, 1957), 38–39.

40. Ferruccio Busoni, *Sketch of a New Esthetic of Music* (1911), published in full in *Three Classics in the Aesthetics of Music* (New York: Dover, 1962), 89.

41. For Varèse's use of glissandi, see Anne Florence Parks, "Freedom, Form, and Process in Varèse" (Ph.D. diss., Cornell University 1974), 270–72.

42. Cited in Louise Varèse, *Varèse: A Looking Glass Diary*, vol. 1 (New York: Norton, 1972), 42. Helmholtz's *Physiology of Music* was published in English as *On the Sensations of Tone as a Physiological Basis for the Theory of Music*.

43. Fernand Ouellette, *Edgard Varèse* (London: Calder & Boyars, 1973), 35.

44. Edgard Varèse, "Que la musique sonne" *391*, no. 5 (June 1917), cited in ibid., 39.

45. Louise Varèse, *Varèse*, 105; Frederic Grunfield, "The Well-Tempered Ionizer," *High Fidelity Magazine* (September 1954): 39–41, 104, 106–8.

46. Varèse's position on Russolo's music was formed in the first instance against the reputation of Russolo's art of noises and the semantic standing of noise itself, whereas later in Paris they would become friends. In fact, Russolo signed a copy of his manifesto: "To my dear and great friend Edgar Varèse, my soul still filled with the passionate enthusiasm aroused in me by his magnificent *Amériques*. May 29, 1929." Ibid., 101.

47. Ibid., 150.

48. Cited in Peter Garland, "Americas," the "Ives, Ruggles, Varèse" special issue of *Soundings* (Spring 1974): 115.

49. Luigi Russolo, "The Conquest of Enharmonicism," in *The Art of Noises*, 63.

50. Henry Cowell, *New Musical Resources* (New York: Something Else Press, 1969), 5, 18. The book was written 1919 and first published in 1929.

51. Ibid., 19–20.

52. Ibid., 20.

53. Percy Grainger, Letter to Olin Downes (10 September 1942), quoted from *A Musical Genius from Australia: Selected Writings by and about Percy Grainger*, ed. Teresa Balough (Nedlands, W. Aust.: Department of Music, University of Western Australia, 1982), 141.

54. Percy Grainger, "Free Music" (December 6, 1938), appended to John Bird, *Percy Grainger* (London: Faber and Faber, 1982), 283–84.

55. Grainger, Letter to Olin Downes, 141.

56. Grainger, "Free Music," 284.

57. For the four main types of instrumental experiments, see my introduction to *Lyre's Island*, a special section on Australian sound art and new music in the 1996 issue of *Leonardo Music Journal*. Also included with the

issue is a compact disc with examples of Grainger and Cross's *Free Music* experiments. For a selection of materials in the Grainger Museum's holdings and a bibliography relevant to Free Music, see *Percy Grainger's Paradoxical Quest for "World Music": Free Music and Free Music Machines*, ed. Elinor Wrobel (Melbourne: Grainger Museum, University of Melbourne, 1994). For further information, see *The Percy Grainger Companion*, ed. Lewis Foreman (London: Thames, 1981); Burnett Cross, "Grainger Free Music Machine," *Recorded Sound: Journal of the British Institute of Recorded Sound*, nos. 45–46 (January-April 1972): 17–21, reprinted in *The Grainger Society Journal* 8, no. 1 (Spring 1986) 72–75; John Bird, *Percy Grainger*, chap. 18; and Richard Franko Goldman, "Percy Grainger's 'Free Music'," *Juilliard Review II* (Fall 1955), reprinted in *A Musical Genius from Australia*, 145–54, and in *The Grainger Society Journal*. Finally, see Andrew McLennan's interview with Burnett Cross for a program produced for *The Listening Room*, ABC Classic FM (Sydney).

58. Bird, *Percy Grainger*, 232.
59. For example, one experiment, the *Oscillator-Playing Tone-Tool 1st Experiment* (October 1951), was constructed with a Singer sewing machine driving a hand drill that in turn operated a Codemaster, a small oscillator for practicing Morse code equipped with knobs for controlling pitch and amplitude.
60. "Graphic Phonetics," report on paper originally published in *La Nature*, *Scientific American* (17 November 1877): 307.
61. Alfred M. Mayer, "On Edison's Talking-Machine," *Popular Science Monthly* (April 1878): 722–23.
62. Roland Gelatt, *The Fabulous Phonograph: The Story of the Gramophone from Tin Foil to High Fidelity* (London: Cassel, 1956), 28.
63. László Moholy-Nagy, "Production-Reproduction (1922)," in Krisztina Passuth, *Moholy-Nagy* (New York: Thames and Hudson, 1985), 289–90.
64. Moholy-Nagy, "New Film Experiments" (1933), ibid., 322.
65. Sibyl Moholy-Nagy, *Moholy-Nagy: Experiment in Totality* (New York: Harper, 1950), 68, 97. The similarly inspired technique of Brazilian composer Heitor Villa-Lobos of transcribing landscapes and skyscraper silhouettes to generate melodic lines found such extensive application that a photograph of the family scene at the breakfast nook of the Nicholas Slonimsky household offered up its own melody. However, as Slonimsky wrote, "The melody is not very attractive, but Villa-Lobos could not help it. He did his best with the material at hand." Nicholas Slonimsky, *The Road to Music* (New York: Dodd, Mead, 1966), 81.

66. W. K. L. Dickson and Antonia Dickson, *History of the Kinetograph, Kinetoscope, and Kineto-Phonograph* (1895; reprint, New York: Arno Press, 1970), 4.
67. Ibid., 8–9.
68. Rainer Maria Rilke, "Primal Sound" (1919), in *Rodin and Other Prose Pieces* (London: Quartet Books, 1986), 126–32.
69. Ibid., 129–30.
70. Ibid., 130.
71. As an inscriptive subsumption, the potency of the wave form itself became evident through the arithmetical and graphical means of harmonic analysis beginning with Lord Kelvin's tide predictor (1876) and then through an application to the study of "acoustics, . . . electricity, optics and mathematics. . . . In meteorology it is applied to the study of hourly or daily temperature changes, barometric changes, etc., In astronomy the periodicity of sun spots, magnetic storms, variable stars, etc. . . . In mechanical engineering, valve motions and other mechanical movements. The method is also used in geophysics, in naval architecture, and the study of statistics." Dayton Clarence Miller, *The Science of Musical Sounds* (1916; New York: MacMillan, 1934), 133.
72. Ibid.
73. Ibid., 22.
74. Ibid., 23–24.
75. Ibid., 25.
76. Ibid., 119.
77. Ibid., 120.
78. Ibid.
79. John Cage, "The Future of Music: Credo" (1937), in *Silence* (Middletown: Wesleyan University Press, 1961), 3–6. D. C. Miller's book was known among American new music circles at large, as evidenced by its citation within the movement's key text at the time, Henry Cowell's *New Musical Resources*. Cage, Cowell's student and friend, was no doubt familiar with Miller's book. This was a time when Cage was particularly enamored with the musical possibilities of new technology, especially as they were expressed in Carlos Chavez's book *Toward a New Music: Music and Electricity*, published the same year as "The Future of Music: Credo." In the mid-1930s, Cage had met the filmmaker Oskar Fischinger, who had already begun experimenting with synthetic music using drawn sound film, and although I have seen no indication that Fischinger employed the specific technique of line drawing, his efforts no doubt either buoyed Cage's hopes or underscored his parody.

80. Ibid., 4.

81. John Cage, "Forerunners of Modern Music," *Silence.*, 65.

82. For Cage's campaign against Beethoven, see David Wayne Patterson, "Appraising the Catchwords, C. 1942–1959: John Cage's Asian-Derived Rhetoric and the Historical Reference of Black Mountain College" (Ph.D. diss., Columbia University, 1996), 208–9.

83. Henri Michaux, *Miserable Miracle* (1956), trans. Louise Varèse (San Francisco: City Lights Books, 1963), chap. 5.

84. Ibid.

Chapter 4

1. Edgard Varèse, "The Music of To-morrow," *Evening News* (New York), 14 June 1924, reproduced in Timothy Day, "The Organized Sound of Edgard Varèse," in *Recorded Sound: The Journal of the British Library National Sound Archive*, no. 85 (January 1984).

2. Phillippe Soupault, "Traces Which Last," *Yale French Studies*, no. 31 (May 1964): 21. "Surrealism was unable to exercise any influence: and this helps explain the decadence of the French school of music before Messiaen."

3. John Cage in conversation with Peter Gena, "After Antiquity," in *A John Cage Reader*, ed. Peter Gena and Jonathan Brent (New York: Peters, 1982), 169.

4. Félix Guattari, "Towards a Micro-Politics of Desire," in *Molecular Revolution: Psychiatry and Politics* (London: Penguin Books, 1984), 106–7.

5. Gabrielle Buffet-Picabia, "Some Memories of Pre-Dada: Picabia and Duchamp" (1949), in *The Dadas and Painter and Poets: An Anthology*, ed. Robert Motherwell (New York: Hall, 1981), 256.

6. Wassily Kandinsky, "Whither the "New" Art?" (1911), in *Complete Writings on Art*, vol. 1, ed. Kenneth C. Lindsay and Peter Vergo (Boston: Hall, 1982), 101. In *On the Spiritual in Art*, Kandinsky also writes that Wagner's "famous use of *leitmotiv* is likewise an attempt to characterize the hero not by theatrical props, makeup, and lighting, but by a certain, precise motif—that is, by purely musical means. This motif is a kind of musically expressed spiritual ethos proceeding from the hero, which thus emanates from him at a distance" (148). That sound would have a scent falls into Kandinsky's own synesthetic tendencies: "The expression 'the scent of colors' is common usage." *On the Spiritual in Art*, ibid., 159.

7. Kandinsky, "On Stage Composition," ibid., 261.

8. Ibid.

9. Kandinsky, *On the Spiritual in Art*, 155.

10. Ibid.
11. "Cologne Lecture" (1914), ibid., 400.
12. Piet Mondrian, "The Manifestation of Neo-Plasticism in Music and the Italian Futurists' *Bruiteurs*" (1921), *The New Art—The New Life: The Collected Writings of Piet Mondrian*, ed. and trans. Harry Holtzman and Martin S. James (Boston: Hall, 1986), 153.
13. Ibid.
14. Ibid., 155. Mondrian supported this impression by pointing to the names of the instruments themselves—screechers, growlers, cracklers, graters, howlers, buzzers, cluckers, gluggers poppers, hissers, croakers, and rustlers. In other words, he was criticizing the sound of Russolo's discursive formation and not the sound of the instruments.
15. "Neo-Plasticism: Its Realization in Music and in Future Theater," ibid., 163.
16. "The Manifestation of Neo-Plasticism in Music and the Italian Futurists' *Bruiteurs*," ibid., 153.
17. Ibid.
18. Piet Mondrian, letter to Carel Mondrian, October 28, 1938, reproduced in Els Hoek, "Mondrian in Disneyland," *Art in America* 77, no. 2 (February 1989): 136–43, 181.
19. Roger Scruton, *The Aesthetic Understanding* (New York: Methuen, 1983), 72.
20. Ibid.
21. John Diliberto, "Pierre Schaeffer and Pierre Henry: Pioneers in Sampling," *Electronic Musician* (December 1986): 54–59, 72. See also Pierre Schaeffer, *Traité des Objets Musicaux* (Paris: Éditions du Seuil, 1966).
22. Ibid., 56.
23. Pierre Schaefer interviewed by Tim Hodgkinson, *Re Records Quarterly Magazine* 2, no. 1 (March 1987): 8.
24. Ibid., 5.
25. This took place at the home of Alvin Lucier, when Cage was in town for the Cage at Wesleyan Symposium, Middletown, Connecticut, February 1988.
26. Schaefer interviewed by Hodgkinson, *Re Records Quarterly Magazine*, 7.
27. Claude Lévi-Strauss, *The Raw and the Cooked*, trans. J. and D. Weightman (New York: Harper and Row, 1969), 22–23.
28. Stanley Diamond, "The Inauthenticity of Anthropology," in *In Search of the Primitive: A Critique of Civilization* (New Brunswick: Transaction Books, 1981), 298.
29. Lévi-Strauss, *The Raw and the Cooked*, 14.

30. See Carol Flinn, "The 'Problem' of Femininity in Theories of Film Music," *Screen* 27, no. 6 (November-December 1986): 58. "While the feminisation of music operates only implicitly in Freud's work, Claude Lévi-Strauss . . . openly displays an obsession with castration and lack."

31. And, as Stanley Diamond points out, a neo-Pythagorean and Leibnizian mathemusic reasserts itself: "The supreme mystery essentialized in music is the ultimate, inescapable anthropological problem. Lévi-Strauss is obviously referring to a final principle of order underlying all cognition and communication, a principle, one would add, that he believes may one day be reducible to mathematical formulation." Diamond, *In Search of the Primitive*, 300.

32. Karlheinz Stockhausen, "Electronic and Instrumental Music," *Die Reihe* 5 (1961): 59–67.

33. Cited in Trevor Wishart, *On Sonic Art* (York: Imagineering Press, 1985), 70.

34. "Art Must Reflect Reality," *Music Journal* 20 (September 1962): 20–21, 77, 83.

35. Gilles Deleuze and Félix Guattari, *A Thousand Plateaus: Capitalism and Schizophrenia*, trans. Brian Massumi (Minneapolis: University of Minnesota Press, 1987), 343. The reference is to Varèse's statement: "Personally, for my conceptions, I need an entirely new medium of expression: *a sound-producing* machine (not a sound-*reproducing* one)." Edgar Varèse, "Music as an Art-Science" (1939), in *Contemporary Composers on Contemporary Music*, ed. Elliott Schwartz and Barney Childs (New York: Holt, Rinehart, and Winston, 1967).

36. Ibid., 343.

37. Ibid., 344.

38. Lest this tendency toward demarcation be confused as a conservatism belonging to the past alone, the British musician and musicologist Chris Cutler, in his capacity as editor of *Re Records Quarterly Magazine*, was nevertheless determined to reassert a sanctity of music, semantic and otherwise. After reviewing an article on the history of live electronic music, he felt compelled to "resist the unquestioning inclusion of a randomly derived, aleatory and raw environmental sound in what we understand when we use the work *music*." Pitted specifically against the threat posed by Cage, he argued:

If, suddenly, *all sound* is "music," then by definition, there can be no such thing as sound that is *not* music. The word *music* becomes meaningless, or rather it means "sound." But *sound* already means that. And when the word *music* has been long minted and nurtured to refer to a *particular* activity in respect to sound—namely, its conscious and deliberate organization within a definite aesthetic and tradition—I can see no convincing argument at this late stage for throwing these useful limitations into the dustbin.

Chris Cutler, "Editorial Afterword," *Re Records Quarterly Magazine* 2, no. 3 (1988): 46–47. Cutler tried to fend off the totalizations of Cagean thought, at a time when so much Cagean thought had been benignly internalized, by rhetorically positing music *as we know it* and politically marginalizing the other through common sense. The problems with Cage's notion that all sound is music, which do not revolve around a music/not-music distinction, will be taken up in chapter 6.

39. Caroline Bayard and Graham Knight, "Vivisecting the Nineties: An Interview with Jean Baudrillard, Part 1," *CTHEORY* 18, nos. 1–2 (August 1995): art. 24a.

40. For Newton's clearest statement on the relationship of sound to light, see his "Letter to Mr. Oldenburgh" (1675), in Humphrey Jennings, *Pandæmonium, 1660–1886* (New York: Free Press, 1985), 17.

41. Charles Baudelaire, "Correspondences," in *Les Fleurs du Mal,* trans. Richard Howard (New York: Harvester Press, 1982), 15.

42. Emanuel Swedenborg, *The Universal Human,* trans. George F. Dole (New York: Paulist Press, 1984), 151.

43. Ibid., 152.

44. Ibid., 152–53.

45. The most notable exception to vowel devotion within a synesthetic system was from the Russian Futurist poet Velimir Khlebnikov, who felt that vowels were too euphonious. His synesthetic system was highly complex, informed by contemporary mathematics, linguistics, and astronomy and associated with a new Pythagoreanism mapped along the temporal coordinates of history.

46. Arthur Rimbaud, "A Season in Hell," in *A Season in Hell and The Drunken Boat,* trans. Louise Varèse (New York: New Directions, 1961), 51.

47. Pierre Petitfils, *Rimbaud,* trans. Alan Sheridan (Charlottesville: University Press of Virginia, 1987), 119–20. In summation Petitfils writes, "Thus all those who have tried to elucidate *Voyelles* in the light of metaphysics, psychoanalysis, sexuality, etc., have fallen into a trap."

48. Wassily Kandinsky, *On the Spiritual in Art,* collected in *Complete Writings on Art,* vol. 1, ed. Kenneth C. Lindsay and Peter Vergo (Boston: Hall, 1982), 158.

49. H. F. Ellenberger, *Discovery of the Unconscious* (New York: Basic Books, 1970), 122.

50. Anaïs Nin, *The Diary of Anaïs Nin, 1947–1955*, vol. 5, cited in *Drug User: Documents 1840–1960*, ed. John Strausbaugh and Donald Blaise (New York: Blast Books, 1991), 143.

51. J. K. Huysmanns, *A Rebours* (1884), translated as *Against the Grain* (New York: Dover Press, 1969), 44–46.

52. Roland Barthes, "Reading Brillat-Savarin," in *The Rustle of Language* (New York: Hill and Wang, 1986), 250.

53. Charles Baudelaire, "On Wine and Hashish," in *Artificial Paradise* (New York: Herder and Herder, 1971), 4–5.

54. A. R. Luria, *The Mind of a Mnemonist* (Cambridge: Harvard University Press, 1987), 24.

55. Ibid.

56. Ibid., 22–23.

57. Kandinsky, *On the Spiritual in Art*, 159.

58. Cited in Richard C. Cytowic, *Synesthesia: A Union of the Senses* (New York: Springer-Verlag, 1989), 263–69.

Chapter 5

1. Donald Friede, *The Mechanical Angel* (New York: Knopf, 1948), 61 and the chapter "Flop *Mécanique*."

2. Vladimir Kirillov, "We," trans. Arthur Jacobsen, in *Russian Literature of the 1920s: An Anthology*, ed. Carl R. Proffer et al. (Ann Arbor: Ardis, 1987), 457–58.

3. Arseni Avraamov, "The Symphony of Sirens" (1923), trans. Mel Gordon, in *Wireless Imagination: Sound, Radio and the Avant-Garde*, ed. Douglas Kahn and Gregory Whitehead (Cambridge: MIT Press, 1992), 246–52. See also Mel Gordon, "Songs from the Museum of the Future: Russian Sound Creation" (1910–1930), in the same volume (198–243).

4. Ibid., 246. Not all Russian sirens were attached to factories. Grigori Alexandrov, while discussing the sound experimentation in the opening nature sequence of his film *Romance Sentimentale* to the film critic Harry Potamkin, explained how, "instead of recording the *slope* up to and down from highest pitch of a siren's whistle, [he] cut the sound into ascending and descending steps, a much more exciting method." Harry Potamkin, "Playing with Sound," in *The Compound Cinema: The Film Writings of Harry Alan Potamkin* (New York: Columbia University, 1977), 87.

5. George Antheil, *Bad Boy of Music* (Garden City, N.Y.: Doubleday, Doran, 1945), 139–40.

6. Interview circa 1925. Cited in Wyndham Lewis, *Time and Western Man* (1927) (Boston: Beacon Hill, 1957), 41–42. Lewis used the occasion of this statement to "repudiate any association" with Pound and to wonder out loud how Pound, after opposing Marinetti, could participate in a similarly "ridiculous gospel."

7. Cited in Linda Whitesitt, *The Life and Music of George Antheil: 1900–1959* (Ann Arbor: UMI Research Press, 1983), 111.

8. George Antheil, letter to Ezra Pound concerning Cyclops (1923–1924?). Beinecke Rare Book and Manuscript Library, Yale University. Quoted with kind permission of Charles Amirkhanian, former Executor of the Antheil Estate.

9. Nikolai Kulbin, "Free Music," *The* Blaue Reiter *Almanac* (New York: Viking Press, 1974), 146.

10. Cited in Susan C. Cook, *Opera for a New Republic: The Zeitopern of Krenek, Weill, and Hindemith* (Ann Arbor: UMI Research Press, 1988), 139.

11. Made-for-phonograph-record music is here the translation of *Original-schallplattenmusik*. Heinrich Burkhard, "Anmerkungen zu den 'Lehr-stücken' und zur Schallplattenmusik," *Melos* 9 (May-June 1930), cited in Thomas Y. Levin, "For the Record: Adorno on Music in the Age of Its Technological Reproducibility," *October* 55 (Winter 1990): 23–47.

12. László Moholy-Nagy, "New Film Experiments" (1933), in Krisztina Passuth, *Moholy-Nagy* (New York: Thames and Hudson, 1985), 322.

13. Henry Cowell, "Music of and for the Records" (1931), *Modern Music* 8, no. 3 (March-April 1931), 32–34.

14. Ibid.

15. Most phonographic techniques were employed during the earliest acoustical and musical experiments with the phonograph. To give one example: Edison remembered how he "used to reverse some tunes we had upon the records and the results were surprising. We played them backwards and some of the reversed tunes were far more interesting and charming than the originals." Cited in Ronald W. Clark, *Edison: The Man Who Made the Future* (New York: Putnam's, 1977), 168. Prior to Edison, we find Lewis Carroll listening to music boxes played backward (might he have, like Fluxus artist Joe Jones, broken teeth off to form another tune?). Speech too ran backward; in 1878, the year after Edison launched the phonograph, the topic of reversible speech was being investigated:

> An attempt has been made to obtain speech from the phonograph by taking the words registered inversely to their true direction. In this way the sounds obtained were necessarily quite unlike the words uttered; yet Messrs. Fleeming Jenkin and

Ewing have observed that not only are the vowels unchanged by this inverse action, but consonants, syllables, and even whole words may be reproduced with the accent they would have if spoken backward.

Count du Moncel, *The Telephone, The Microphone and the Phonograph* (New York: Harper, 1879), 244.

16. Richard Schmidt James, "Expansion of Sound Resources in France, 1913–1940, and Its Relationship to Electronic Music" (Ph.D. diss., University of Michigan, 1981), 203–4.

17. Interview with Arthur Hoérée by Richard Schmidt James, ibid., 204–16.

18. Among the sound-effects organs and machines used in theater were "the Noiseograph, the Dramagraph, the Kinematophone, the Soundograph or the Excelsior Sound Effect Cabinet . . . from whose keyboards and associated equipment came galloping horses, railroad whistles and bells, rooster crows, hen cackles, cow bawls, canary chirps, mockingbird calls, tugboat whistles, auto horns, cowbells, anvil strikes, marching feet, gun shots, tom-toms, thunder, temple bells, castanets, frog croaks, slide whistles, tambourines, telephone bells, glass crashes, auto chugs, water splashes, and the blowing of noses." Raymond Fielding, "The Technological Antecedents of the Coming of Sound: An Introduction," in *Sound and the Cinema: The Coming of Sound to American Film*, ed. Evan William Cameron (Pleasantville, N.Y.: Redgrave, 1980), 4.

19. Eugene Deslaw, "Cinema and Robots," *Close Up* 7, no. 6 (1930): 422–24.

20. Eugene Deslaw, "My First Sound Film," *Close Up* 8, no. 1 (1931): 61–62.

21. Carol-Bérard, "Recorded Noises: Tomorrow's Instrumentation," *Modern Music* 6, no. 2 (January-February 1929): 26–29 (27). Carol-Bérard composition cited in Fred Prieberg, *Musik ex Machina* (Berlin: Verlag Ullstein, 1960), 84, and in the "sound effects" entry written by Hugh Davies in *The New Grove Dictionary of Musical Instruments*, vol. 3, ed. Stanley Sadie (New York: Macmillan, 1984), 423–27. I was unable to locate satisfactory information on Carol-Bérard, whose pseudonym used for writing poetry was Olivier Realtor. Davies lists a publication *Instrumentation par le système des bruits enregistrés* (Paris, circa 1925), which I was unable to locate.

22. Carol-Bérard, "Recorded Noises," 28.

23. Ibid., 26–29.

24. Ibid., 29.

25. László Moholy-Nagy, "Problems of the Modern Film" (1930), in *Moholy-Nagy*, 311–15.

26. Raymond Lyon, quoted in "Le Phonograph d'avant-garde," *La Joie musicale* 3 (1930), 34, cited in James, "Expansion of Sound Resources in France," 258–60.

27. Hans Richter, "Experiments with Celluloid," *Penguin Film Review* 9 (1949): 114. See also Mark E. Cory, "Soundplay: The Polyphonous Tradition of German Radio Art," in *Wireless Imagination*, 331–71.

28. Cowell, "Music of and for the Records," 32–34.

29. Rudolf Arnheim, *Radio: An Art of Sound* (1936), trans. Margaret Ludwig and Herbert Read (New York: Da Capo Press, 1972), 122–25.

30. Ibid., 226.

31. See Barry A. Fulks, "Film Culture and Kulturfilm: Walter Ruttmann, the Avant-Garde Film, and the Kulturfilm in Weimar Germany and the Third Reich" (Ph.D. diss., University of Wisconsin–Madison, 1982).

32. Carlos Chavez, *Toward a New Music: Music and Electricity* (New York: Norton, 1937), 170.

33. Ibid., 111.

34. Ibid., 119.

35. Ibid., 99.

36. John Cage, "The Future of Music: Credo," in *Silence* (Middletown: Wesleyan University Press, 1961), 3–6.

37. Ibid. The noise of percussion would act as the intermediary between the old and the new, between the temperament of "keyboard-influenced music to the all-sound music of the future" rooted in the new phonographic and electronic media (5–6).

38. Ibid., 57.

39. Letter (17 September 1940, addressed 228 17th Avenue, San Francisco) in possession of Antheil's son, Chris Beaumont. Quoted with kind permission Mr. Beaumont. Cage's letter to Antheil was also a good five years before Cage reviewed *Bad Boy of Music* noting its "empty, cheap and gaudy quality." John Cage, "The Dreams and Dedications of George Antheil" (1946), in *John Cage*, ed. Richard Kostelanetz (New York: Praeger, 1970), 73.

40. Script available in Kenneth Patchen, *Patchen's Lost Plays*, ed. Richard G. Morgan (Santa Barbara: Capra Press, 1977). Background information provided during interview with Miriam Patchen, Palo Alto, California (April 1989). For all the effort the play was performed only once on a Sunday night (31 May 1942). Kenneth and Miriam Patchen listened to the broadcast with Burl Ives on his boat in New York.

41. John Cage, *Conversing with Cage*, ed. Richard Kostelanetz (New York: Limelight Editions, 1988), 158–59. Cage moved to Chicago after being invited by Moholy-Nagy to teach a class at the School of Design.

42. Ibid., 158.

43. Cage interviewed by Peter Gena, in *A John Cage Reader*, 168.

44. Pierre Schaefer interviewed by Tim Hodgkinson, *Re Records Quarterly Magazine* 2, no. 1 (March 1987): 4–10.

45. Despite the widespread notoriety and influence of Russolo through the 1920s, his reputation had lapsed sufficiently over the span of fifteen years that Cage was able to write in 1946 that "The Italian 'Art of Noise' established by Luigi Russolo has totally disappeared; in memory it is mistakenly associated with Marinetti," and although he was speaking about Virgil Thomson in particular (Thomson wrote that Cage's "work attaches itself to . . . the percussive experiments begun by Marinetti's Futurist noisemakers and continued in the music of Edgard Varèse, Henry Cowell, and George Antheil"), the mistake was a common one. See John Cage, "The Dreams and Dedications of George Antheil" (1946), and Virgil Thomson, "Expressive Percussion" (1945), in *John Cage*, 71–73.

46. From interview by Richard Schmidt James, "Expansion of Sound Resources in France," 218.

47. The manifestos were regularly published in Russia soon after their appearance in Italy, with two collections published in Moscow in 1914, and a number of artists including Nikolai Kulbin and Vadim Shershenevich actively promoted Italian Futurist doctrines and work. See Anna Lawton, "Vadim Shershenevich: A Futurist Westernizer," *Russian Literature Triquarterly*, no. 12 (Spring 1975): 327–44. Moreover, Marinetti's visit of 1914 to Moscow and St. Petersburg received good coverage from the press and an attentive and energetically antagonistic reception from a number of artists. For a translation of documents relating to Marinetti's visit, see Wiktor Woroszylski, *The Life of Mayakovsky* (New York: Orion Press, 1970). See also the chapter "Russian and Italian Futurism" in Vahan D. Barooshian, *Russian Cubo-Futurism, 1910–30* (The Hague: Mouton, 1974), and Benedikt Livshits, *The One and a Half-Eyed Archer*, trans. John E. Bowlt (Newtonville, Mass.: Oriental Research Partners, 1977), chap. 7.

48. Edward J. Brown, *Mayakovsky: A Poet in the Revolution* (Princeton: Princeton University Press, 1973), 89–90. Translated as "Little Noises, Noises, Booms" (1913), in Vladimir Mayakovsky, *Electric Iron*, trans. Jack Hirschman and Victor Erlich (Berkeley: Maya, 1971), n.p.:

The city's echoes the real carriers of noise
in the soles' whispers in the wheels' clatter
with humanity and horses up as the jockeys
running after the distant swishings of scythes.

Little girls walk by with their tiny noiselings,
the truck careening with its carton of rumbles,
a stallion rippling musically in perforated tunic,
trolley shearing the foam of thunder.

All swim toward the square through by-way arcades
and canals of intricately crisscrossing thoughts
and there all smeary with soot the gargoyle of
Noise is crowned King of the deafening markets.

49. Dziga Vertov, "On Mayakovsky," in *Kino-Eye: The Writings of Dziga Vertov*, ed. Annette Michelson (Berkeley: University of California Press, 1984), 180. Sergei Prokofiev, after returning from a trip where he was introduced to the Italian Futurists through Diaghilev, wrote about the *intonarumori* in his article "The Musical Instruments of the Futurists" in the magazine *Muzyka* (8 April 1915).

50. Ibid., 40.

51. Seth R. Feldman, *Evolution of Style in the Early Work of Dziga Vertov* (New York: Arno Press, 1977), 12–15.

52. Vertov, Speech of 5 April 1935, ibid., 13.

53. Vertov, "The Birth of Kino-Eye," in *Kino-Eye*, 40.

54. Ibid., 56. Alexander Rodchenko was connected with radio, remarking in *Novyi Lef*, no. 6 (1927) that since photography was 90 percent art, to balance it out he was "also working with radio—for discipline's sake" because "radio doesn't have more than 10% art." See *The Avant-Garde in Russia: 1910–1930*, ed. Stephanie Barron and Maurice Tuchman (Cambridge: MIT Press, 1980), 237. Rodchenko was Vertov's ally in the Lef circles and worked with him on his Kinopravda. See Feldman, *Evolution of Style*, 81–84.

55. Vertov, "From the History of the Kinoks" (1929), in *Kino-Eye*, 98.

56. Vertov, "Let's Discuss Ukrainfilm's First Sound Film: *Symphony of the Donbas*," ibid., 111.

57. Vertov, "Replies to Questions," ibid., 105–6.

58. Lucy Fischer, *"Enthusiasm:* From Kino-Eye to Radio-Eye," in *Film Sound: Theory and Practice*, ed. Elisabeth Weis and John Belton (New York: Columbia University Press, 1985), 247–64.

59. His request to use sound on *Man with the Movie Camera* had been rejected. See Feldman, *Evolution of Style*, 166. For the musical treatment of the film, see Yuri Tsivian, "Dziga Vertov's Frozen Music: Cue Sheets and a Music Scenario for *The Man with the Movie Camera*," *Griffithiana*, no. 54 (October 1995): 93–111.

60. Vertov, "First Steps," in *Kino-Eye*, 112 n.

61. Cited in Herbert Marshall, *Masters of Soviet Cinema* (Boston: Routledge & Kegan Paul, 1983), 81.

62. Vertov, "First Steps," in *Kino-Eye*, 114.

63. Vertov, "Let's Discuss Ukrainfilm's First Sound Film: Symphony of the Donbas," in *Kino-Eye*, 109.

64. Ibid. (emphasis in original).

65. Dziga Vertov, "Speech to the First All-Union Conference on Sound Cinema" (1930), in *The Film Factory: Russian and Soviet Cinema in Documents, 1896–1939*, ed. Richard Taylor and Ian Christie (Cambridge: Harvard University Press, 1988), 301ff.

66. Ibid., 304–5. "But it is not adequate if we are talking about location shooting in the broad sense of the word, on the level of the 'Radio-Eye's' general prospects, and we shall have to orientate ourselves beyond the mobile film unit to the sound-recoring and sound-reproducing radio station."

67. Jay Leyda, *Kino: A History of the Russian and Soviet Film* (New York: Collier Books, 1960), 176–77.

68. Cf. Vertov, "Sound March," in *Kino-Eye*, 289–293; Annette Michelson's comments, ibid., 327.

69. Vertov, "From Notebooks, Diaries," in *Kino-Eye*, 170.

70. Vladimir Mayakovsky, "The Relationship between Contemporary Theatre and Cinema and Art," in *The Film Factory*, 37.

71. Ibid., 37. See also "The Destruction of 'Theatre' by Cinema as a Sign of the Resurrection of Theatrical Art," ibid., 34–35.

72. Sergei Eisenstein and Sergei Yutkevich, "The Eighth Art: On Expressionism, America and, of Course, Chaplin," in *S. M. Eisenstein: Selected Works*, vol. 1, *Writings, 1922–34*, ed. and trans. Richard Taylor (London: BFI, 1988), 29.

73. Ibid.

74. Ibid., 30.

75. Leyda, *Kino*, 269.

76. Sergei Eisenstein, Vsevolod Pudovkin and Grigori Alexandrov, "Statement on Sound," in *The Film Factory*, 234–35.

77. Jay Leyda and Zina Voynow, *Eisenstein at Work* (New York: Panthem Books and the Museum of Modern Art, 1982), 38.

78. Ibid., 39.

79. Leonard Maltin, *Of Mice and Magic: A History of American Animated Cartoons* (New York: New American Library, 1987), 35.

80. Ibid.

81. John Grierson, "Pudovkin on Sound," *Cinema Quarterly*, 2, no. 2 (Winter 1933–1934): 106–8.

82. Mary Ann Doane, "The Voice in the Cinema: The Articulation of Body and Space," in *Film Sound*, 162.

83. Maltin, *Of Mice and Magic*, 32–33.

84. Sergei Eisenstein, *Eisenstein on Disney*, ed. Jay Leyda, trans. Alan Upchurch (London: Methuen, 1988), 12ff.

85. Ibid., 69.

86. Ibid., 21.

87. Ibid., 24–33, 44–47.

88. Ibid., 41. He arrives finally at Heraclitus, Hegel on Heraclitus, and Lenin on Hegel on Heraclitus.

89. Sergei Eisenstein, *Nonindifferent Nature*, trans. Herbert Marshall (Cambridge: Cambridge University Press, 1987), 389.

90. Ibid., 391.

91. Leyda and Voynow, *Eisenstein at Work*, 39.

92. Ibid., 40.

93. Marie Seton, *Sergei M. Eisenstein* (New York: Grove Press, 1960), 158, 160.

94. *S. M. Eisenstein: Selected Works*, vol. 4, *Beyond the Stars: The Memoirs of Sergei Eisenstein*, ed. Richard Taylor, trans. William Powell (London: BFI, 1995), 201–3; Seton, *Sergei M. Eisenstein*, 139, 141; Grigori Alexandrov, "Working with Eisenstein," in *Cinema in Revolution*, ed. Luda Schnitzer, et al. (New York: Da Capo Press, 1973), 58. Luis Buñuel wrote that "Eisenstein's friends have tried to blame Alexandrov for the debacle of the dreadful and shoddy production of *Romance Sentimentale*. But I saw Eisenstein making it with my own eyes, since he was shooting it on the stage next to me when I was making *L'Age d'or*." Cited in Francisco Aranda, *Luis Buñuel: A Critical Biography* (New York: Da Capo, 1976), 87.

95. Sergei Eisenstein, "The Dynamic Square (1930)," in *S. M. Eisenstein: Selected Works*, vol. 1, *Writings, 1922–34*, ed. and trans. Richard Taylor (London: BFI, 1988), 218.

96. Letter dated (12 September 1930), Léon Moussinac, *Sergei Eisenstein* (New York: Crown, 1970), 53–54.

97. Harry Potamkin, "Playing with Sound," in *The Compound Cinema*, 86–88.

98. Ibid., 9.

99. See Hugh Davies, "Drawn Sound" entry, in *The New Grove Dictionary of Musical Instruments*, vol. 3, 596–99. *The Plan for Great Works* culled footage from many other films including Vertov's *The Eleventh Year.*

100. See, for example, Eisenstein, "Beyond the Shot" (1929), in *Selected Works*, vol. 1, 138–50.

101. Eisenstein, "An Unexpected Juncture" (1928), ibid., 115–22 (119).

102. Ibid., 117.

103. Eisenstein, "Beyond the Shot," ibid., 149.

104. Eisenstein, "Unexpected Juncture," ibid., 118.

105. Ibid.

106. Ibid., 119.

107. Ibid.

Chapter 6

1. Ananda K. Coomaraswamy, *The Transformation of Nature in Art* (1934; New York: Dover, 1956), 67.

2. Michael Zwerin, "A Lethal Measurement," in *John Cage*, ed. Richard Kostelanetz (New York: Praeger, 1970), 166.

3. Only a limited number of compositions may have overtly incorporated sounds in this way, but all of his music after the mid-1930s was discursively and philosophically dependent on this strategy. This general strategy within avant-garde music presents difficulties for musicology, for it requires new notions and analyses of musical materiality, including the establishment of a vantage point outside music, the source of the new materiality, in order to gain some type of critical distance. This would require an interdisciplinary approach with corresponding transformation of the object of study and would ideally then contribute toward a transformation of artistic practice.

4. John Cage, "Composition as Process" (1958), in *Silence* (Middletown: Wesleyan University Press, 1961), 41. It is helpful to hear Cage read excerpts from this text in Dick Fontaine's 1967 film *Sound??* (New York:

Rhapsody Films, 1988, videocassette) to detect the degree of castigation in his questions and realize that the affable Cage of later years had not yet fully emerged.

5. John Cage, "Edgard Varèse" (1958), in *Silence*, 83–84. The way imagination impaired hearing was not restricted to Varèse: "Composers are spoken of as having ears for music which generally means that nothing presented to their ears can be heard by them. Their ears are walled in with sounds of their own imagination." John Cage, "45′ for a Speaker" (1954), ibid., 155. Cage's criticism of Beethoven, Varèse, and composers in general has implications for the question of structure and continuity in music. For his comments on Beethoven in this respect, see "Defense of Satie." Regarding Varèse, he suggested a corrective measure that "discontinuity has the effect of divorcing sounds from the burden of psychological intentions." Cage, "Edgard Varèse," 84.

6. Zwerin, "A Lethal Measurement," 161–67.

7. In this respect, he has not effected the historical rupture credited to him but instead exudes a loyalty to the mission of *absolute music* in the nineteenth century, with its roots in the neo-Pythagoreanism of the sixteenth and seventeenth centuries. See John Neubauer, *The Emancipation of Music from Language* (New Haven: Yale University Press, 1986), 45ff. and epilogue.

8. The year 1952 was a good one for nothing to happen. Following Rauschenberg's white and black paintings of the year before, and his erasure of the drawing by Willem de Kooning a year after, there was Beckett's *Waiting for Godot* (1952), with its not-so-pregnant pauses scattered throughout a larger nonevent. If *Godot* was a play "where nothing happens twice," then *4′33″*, with its three movements, was a composition where nothing happens thrice. In 1952 also appeared the final version of Guy Debord's film *Hurlements en faveur de Sade*, which consisted of black and white imageless screens with a pared-down sound track of people speaking. Debord used another form of withholding in his 1961 address to the Group for Research on Everyday Life by not participating in the everyday life of the conference and, instead, delivering his speech using a tape recorder: "These words are being communicated by way of a tape recorder, not, of course, in order to illustrate the integration of technology into this everyday life on the margin of the technological world, but in order to seize the simplest opportunity to break with the appearance of pseudocollaboration, of artificial dialogue, established between the lecturer 'in person' and his spectators." Guy Debord, "Perspectives for Conscious Alterations in Everyday Life," in *Situationist International An-*

thology, ed. and trans. Ken Knabb (Berkeley: Bureau of Public Secrets, 1981), 68–75. For an account of reductionism within the arts of this period, see Edward Strickland, *Minimalism: Origins* (Bloomington: Indiana University Press, 1993). The true anthem to nothing, of course, was sung by the Fugs.

9. The piece was initially made up of three fixed lengths of silence (30″, 2′23″, 1′40″) arrived at by using chance operations and then underwent modification when it was published in 1960. It may be played on other instruments besides the piano, and involve more than one performer.

10. For the historical nature of silence among audiences, see James H. Johnson, *Listening in Paris: A Cultural History* (Berkeley: University of California Press, 1995).

11. Remy Charlip was one of Merce Cunningham's dancers and the lover of Lou Harrison, who also had music performed the same evening. See Judith Malina, *The Diaries of Judith Malina, 1947–1957* (New York: Grove Press, 1984), 163.

12. *John Cage*, ed. Kostelanetz, 12. On the question of whether it was or was not "his piece," he could go either way: "I think perhaps my own best piece, at least the one I like the most, is the silent piece." John Cage, *Conversing with Cage*, ed. Richard Kostelanetz (New York: Limelight Editions, 1988), 65.

13. John Cage in conversation with Peter Gena, "After Antiquity," in *A John Cage Reader*, ed. Peter Gena and Jonathan Brent (New York: Peters, 1982), 169–70.

14. Stephen Montague, "John Cage at Seventy: An Interview," *American Music* (Summer 1985): 213.

15. Michael Kirby and Richard Schechner, "An Interview with John Cage," *Tulane Drama Review* 10, no. 2 (Winter 1965): 53, reprinted in *Happenings and Other Acts*, ed. Mariellen R. Sandford (London: Routledge, 1995), 53; Irwin Kremen, e-mail message to Larry Solomon (17 June 1997), posted to the *Silence List*. One of the other interesting, if fanciful, reasons that have been entertained is based on the observation that 273, the number of seconds in four minutes and thirty-three seconds, is the positive value of absolute zero (minus 273 degrees Centigrade).

16. John Cage, Roger Shattuck, and Alan Gillmor, "Erik Satie: A Conversation," *Contact*, no. 25 (Autumn 1982): 22.

17. Montague, "John Cage at Seventy," 213. James Pritchett cites the lecture in connection with *4′33″* but then steers clear of the social implications within the text itself and states instead, "Thus the silent piece's origins lie not in Cage's works of the 1950s and 60s, but rather in the aesthetic

milieu we are considering here: the late 1940s, the *String Quartet in Four Parts*, and the 'Lecture on Nothing.'" James Pritchett, *The Music of John Cage* (Cambridge: Cambridge University Press, 1993), 59.

18. *Musik Texte*, nos. 40–41 (Cologne, August 1991) and *Musicworks*, no. 52 (Toronto, Spring 1992). Subsequent citations to "A Composer's Confessions" will be to the *Musicworks* publication. Calvin Tomkins apparently had access to this text, perhaps from a publication of which I am unaware, when he wrote his portrait of Cage for *The New Yorker*, but he did not mention information relevant to the genesis of *4' 33"*. See Calvin Tomkins, *The Bride and the Bachelors* (New York: Penguin Books, 1976), 69–144.

19. Cage did not make matters easier by selling off portions of his library, including many of his Asian books, during some financially difficult times.

20. David Wayne Patterson, "Appraising the Catchwords, C. 1942–1959: John Cage's Asian-Derived Rhetoric and the Historical Reference of Black Mountain College" (Ph.D. diss., Columbia University, 1996), 129. The inclusion of Meister Eckhart and other Christian mystics within the period of South Asian influence is explained by the chapter on Eckhart appearing in Coomaraswamy's *The Transformation of Nature in Art*.

21. Coomaraswamy, *The Transformation of Nature in Art* (1934); Ananda K. Coomaraswamy, *The Dance of Shiva* (Bombay: Asia Publishing House, 1948); Mahendranath Gupta, *The Gospel of Sri Ramakrishna* (New York: Ramakrishna-Vivekananda Center, 1942).

22. Carl Jung, *The Integration of the Personality*, trans. Stanley M. Dell (London: Kegan Paul, Trency, Trubner, 1940); Aldous Huxley, *The Perennial Philosophy* (London: Chatto and Windus, 1946).

23. Coomaraswamy's *The Transformation of Nature in Art* contains much Chinese, medieval Christian material, most significantly Meister Eckhart, and some Zen sources. *The Dance of Shiva*, more consistently Indian, contains chapters of "Intellectual Fraternity" and Nietzsche. The Huxley and Jung texts are based entirely on cross-cultural comparisons and contain explicit references to East Asian sources. In 1923 Jung also wrote about Meister Eckhart in *Psychological Types* (Princeton: Princeton University Press, 1971).

24. See Patterson, "Appraising the Catchwords," 72–73. In the same respect, his reliance on Jung should temper his well known rejection of psychoanalysis as well as place him closer to the abstract expressionists, to whom he was supposedly diametrically opposed.

25. Ibid., 95–99.

26. Jung, *The Integration of the Personality*, 11.

27. This is the point around which could pivot a fruitful comparison of avant-garde and modernist musics with that other postwar impulse of lounge, easy-listening, novelty, and exotica musics—what Ken Sitz has called Deep 50s music.

28. Cage, "A Composer's Confessions," 13. Henry Cowell advised the OWI "on serious works, American pieces, and music especially selected to go out to particular districts. . . . We used art music, old and new from all countries, and found that pieces by modern Americans whose style is not too complex were well received." Henry Cowell, "Shaping Music for Total War," *Modern Music* 22, no. 4 (May-June, 1945): 223–26.

29. Jung, *The Integration of the Personality*, 30–31.

30. John Cage and Daniel Charles, *For the Birds* (Boston: Marion Boyars, 1981), 105.

31. Jung, *The Integration of the Personality*, 31–32.

32. The last paragraph of his book states it explicitly: "When all is said and done, the hero, the leader, and saviour is also the one who discovers a new way to greater certainty. Everything could be left as it was if this new way did not absolutely demand to be discovered and did not visit humanity with all the plagues of Egypt until it is found. The undiscovered way in us is like something of the psyche that is alive. The classic Chinese philosophy calls it 'Tao,' and compares it to a watercourse that resistlessly moves towards its goal. To be in Tao means fulfillment, wholeness, a vocation performed, beginning and end and complete realization of the meaning of existence innate in things. Personality is Tao." Ibid., 304–5.

33. Ibid., 4.

34. Ibid., 15.

35. Ibid., 26.

36. Cage, "A Composer's Confessions," 13.

37. The question of how spiritual matters relate to the workaday world of occupations runs throughout all the readings, which move closer to one another in discussions of "vocations," or callings. Coomaraswamy expands the field of what Westerners might think as artists by listing more than eighteen professional arts, the sixty-four avocational arts in India, embracing "every kind of skilled activity, from music, painting, and weaving to horsemanship, cookery, and the practice of magic, without distinction of rank, all being equally of angelic origin." *The Transformation of Nature in Art*, 9. See also Patterson, "Appraising the Catchwords," 73–75.

38. Cage, "A Composer's Confessions," 13–14. In "Defense of Satie," a lecture given at Black Mountain College the summer after the Vassar lecture, Cage repeated the link between Jung and music: "Music then is a problem parallel to that of the integration of the personality: which in terms of modern psychology is the co-being of the conscious and the unconscious mind, Law and Freedom, in a random world situation. Good music can act as a guide to good living." *John Cage*, ed. Kostelanetz, 84.

39. Patterson, "Appraising the Catchwords," 86–92. There is a temptation to identify Cage's disinterestedness with Duchamp's indifference, but his engagement with Duchamp's ideas would come later.

40. *The Transformation of Nature in Art*, 28.

41. Cage, "A Composer's Confessions" 14.

42. Ibid.

43. Huxley, *The Perennial Philosophy*, 143.

44. Ibid., 115, 134.

45. In "Lecture on Nothing" (1950), Cage extended his idea of disinterestedness by associating it with a lack of interest in possessing things ("a piece of string or a sunset," "one's own home") or in possessing moments in time ("We need not destroy the past: it is gone") and specified it by setting it against the conventional forms of continuity within Western art music ("themes and secondary themes; their struggle, their development; the climax; the recapitulation"). *Silence*, 110–11.

46. Cage, *Conversing with Cage*, 231.

47. Cage, "A Composer's Confessions," 15.

48. Ibid.

49. Among them were the members of Spike Jones's band, who chose to satirize Petrillo openly, following his every command as though given by military top brass. Cage had no apparent interest in Spike Jones, although the band would be celebrated in the post-Cagean ranks of Fluxus. See Jordan R. Young, *Spike Jones and His City Slickers* (Berkeley: Disharmony Books, 1984), 36, 77. See also Russel Sanjek, *American Popular Music and Its Business* (New York: Oxford University Press, 1988), 3:229–30, 286. The big companies also had a new technology on their side: the same month as Cage's talk, ABC Radio Network announced it was going "all-tape" for nighttime programming, using the latest improvements on the German Magnetophone that had been discovered by American troops.

50. Cage, "A Composer's Confessions," 15. What critics wrote was also a *literary* matter, in accord with other instances of Cage's use of the term,

because they were interested almost entirely in the playing of the literature—the repertoire—and not new music.

51. Two years later in "Lecture on Nothing" (1950) he stated, "Record collections, that is not music. The phonograph is a thing, not a musical instrument. A thing leads to other things, whereas a musical instrument leads to nothing." *Silence*, 125. The idea of an instrument literally leading to nothing that is music is, of course, the foundation of *4' 33"*.

52. John Cage, "Other People Think" (1927), in *John Cage*, ed. Kostelanetz, 48.

53. Ibid.

54. Cage, "A Composer's Confessions," 13.

55. Ibid., 15.

56. Ibid.

57. Yvonne Rainer, "Looking Myself in the Mouth," *October*, no. 17 (Summer 1981): 65–76.

58. Ibid. The last two sentences are less enigmatic when taken as rhetorical devices. In this capacity, there is no synesthetic shift away from in/audibility. The *idea* is to be made seductive as a means (short of interrupting his lecture with several minutes of standing quietly at the podium) to induce his Vassar audience into imagining what it might be like to actually *listen* to "silence" for such a length of time and not immediately understand it as a withholding of utterance. And in lieu of the type of markers of time or development that might provide an anticipation of an end, the end approaches imperceptibly and, thereby, approaches imperceptibility. He had, after all, associated disinterestedness with his own brand of continuity in music two years later in his "Lecture on Nothing," and it would be understandable that, within the realm of all the ends of disinterestedness, imperceptibility would lie near the end of the trajectory from quietness to silence.

59. Busoni, *Sketch of a New Esthetic of Music*, included in *Three Classics in the Aesthetic of Music* (New York: Dover, 1962), 89 (emphasis in the original).

60. Translated by Victoria Kirby in Michael Kirby, *Futurist Performance* (New York: Dutton, 1971), 293.

61. See Patterson, "Appraising the Catchwords," 204, 232. Patterson interviewed W. P. Jennerjahn, who places the invention of "happenings" not with Cage's *Black Mountain Piece* (1952) but with these cabin performances in 1948: "The music of Satie, played on two pianos inside the open window of one of the cottages on campus while the audience sat on the ground outside, or strolled about."

62. Rollo H. Myers, *Erik Satie* (1948; New York: Dover, 1968); Pierre-Daniel Templier, *Erik Satie* (Paris: Les Éditions Rieder, 1932); and Constant Lambert, *Music Ho! A Study of Music in Decline* (London: Faber and Faber, 1934). Cage was fluent in French by the time of his study of Satie.

63. Myers, *Erik Satie*, 60.

64. Templier, *Erik Satie*, 46, and cited in Alan M. Gillmor, *Erik Satie* (New York: Norton, 1988), 232.

65. "It took a Satie and a Webern to rediscover this musical truth, which, by means of musicology, we learn was evident to some musicians in our Middle Ages, and to all musicians at all times (except those whom we are currently in the process of spoiling) in the Orient." Also: "There can be no right making of music that does not structure itself from the very roots of sound and silence—lengths of time. In India, rhythmic structure is called Tala. With us, unfortunately, it is called a new idea." Cage, "Defense of Satie," in *John Cage*, ed. Kostelanetz, 81.

66. Ibid., 78–79.

67. Ibid., 81.

68. Ibid., 83.

69. Huxley, *The Perennial Philosophy*, 249–50. Jung's *The Integration of the Personality*, 10, contains a similar passage: "The enormous increase of technical facilities only serves to occupy the mind with all sorts of sensations and impressions that lure the attention and interest from the inner world. The relentless flood of newspapers, radio programs, and movies may widen or fill the external mind, while at the same time, and in the same measure, consciousness of the inner world becomes darkened and may eventually disappear altogether. But 'forgetting' is not identical with 'getting rid of.'"

70. While a student at Pomona College: "One day the history lecturer gave us an assignment, which was to go to the library and read a certain number of pages in a book. The idea of everybody reading the exact same information just revolted me. I made an experiment. I went to the library and read other things that had nothing to do with the assignment, and approached the exam with that sort of preparation. I got an A." Tomkins, *The Bride and the Bachelors*, 78.

71. Cage, "A Composer's Confessions," 15.

72. Ibid.

73. In the interviews with Daniel Charles circa 1968, Cage defined Muzak to include the daily bill of fare for radio: "Music for factory workers, or for chickens to force them to lay eggs. The miscellaneous music played

throughout the day by most radio stations." Cage and Charles, *For the Birds*, 137.

74. Quoted in "Percussionist," *Time* (22 February 1943): 70; cited in Patterson, "Appraising the Catchwords," 108–9.

75. "Lecture on Nothing," *Silence*, 125–26.

76. Ibid., 117.

77. Cage, "A Composer's Confessions," 13. *Credo in Us* (1942), a percussion quartet piece with piano that included among its instruments a radio or phonograph, was composed and first performed during wartime. Instructions for the piece include this statement: "If radio is used, avoid news programs during national or international emergencies." In an 1965 interview, Cage recalled that "when the Second World War came along, I talked to myself, what do I think of the Second World War? Well, I think it's lousy. So I wrote a piece, *Imaginary Landscape No. 3*, which is perfectly hideous." *Conversing with Cage*, 59.

78. Cage, "A Composer's Confessions," 13.

79. Ibid.

80. "Composition as Process" (1958), in *Silence*, 30–31.

81. John Cage and Roger Reynolds, "A Conversation," *Musical Quarterly* 65, no. 4 (October 1979): 578.

82. John Cage, interview with Roger Reynolds, *John Cage* (New York: Henmar, 1962), 46.

83. Cage and Reynolds, "A Conversation," 578:

> *Reynolds:* When [in 1961] I asked you about sounds that had been distasteful to you, such as Beethoven and the vibraphone, you mentioned Muzak. I especially admire the impulse to seek resistant materials, and wonder in this connection if there are any sounds you have recently come to find distasteful.
>
> *Cage:* The only problem that I am aware of in terms of sounds themselves . . . it's still the vibraphone for me.

84. Cage, Shattuck, and Gillmor, "Erik Satie: A Conversation," 22.

85. Huxley, *The Perennial Philosophy*, 325.

86. Ibid., 249–50.

87. "The thing that makes Muzak tolerable is its very narrow dynamic range. It has such a narrow dynamic range that you can hear many other things at the same time as you hear Muzak. And if you pay attention carefully enough, I think you can put up with the Muzak—if you pay attention, I mean, to the things that are not Muzak." *Conversing with Cage*, 231.

88. Montague, "John Cage at Seventy," 205. In another interview Cage elaborated on the technique: "I translate the sounds into images, and so my dreams aren't disturbed. It just fuses. There was a burglar alarm one night and I was amazed because the pitch went on for two hours, was quite loud. It seemed to me to be going slightly up and slightly down. So what it became in my dreams was a Brancusi-like shape, you know, a subtle curve. And I wasn't annoyed at all." Sears (1981), *Conversing with Cage*, 26.

89. Cage and Reynolds, "A Conversation" (1977), 577.

90. During the question period of his Norton lectures he said, "When I wrote *4'33"* I was in the process of writing the *Music of Changes*. That was done in an elaborate way. There are many tables for pitches, for durations, for amplitudes, all the work was done with chance operations. In the case of *4'33"*, I actually used the same method of working and I built up the silence of each movement, and the three movements add up to *4'33"*. I built up each movement by means of short silences put together." John Cage, *I–VI* (Cambridge: Harvard University Press, 1990), 20–21.

91. Huxley, *The Perennial Philosophy*, 327.

92. Ibid., 327.

93. John Cage, *A Year from Monday* (Middletown: Wesleyan University Press, 1967), 134.

94. John Cage, "Experimental Music" (1957), in *Silence*, 8.

95. John Cage, "Composition as Process," ibid., 22–23.

96. Ibid., 23.

97. Erik Satie, "Memoirs of an Amnesiac," in *The Writings of Erik Satie*, ed. and trans. Nigel Wilkins (London: Eulenburg Books, 1980), 58.

98. R. Raven-Hart, "Composing for Radio," *Musical Quarterly* 16, no. 4 (October 1930): 138.

99. Advertisement in the *Village Voice* for the U.S. premiere (9 November 1958) of Varèse's *Poème électronique* in New York, reproduced in George Brecht, *Notebook* (Cologne: Verlag der Buchhandlung Walther König, 1991), 2:86.

100. "Future of Music Credo," in *Silence*, 6.

101. Robert Dumm, "Sound Stuff," *Newsweek* (Jan. 11, 1954): 76.

102. Cage, *John Cage*, 144.

103. *Conversing with Cage*, 69–70.

104. From a 1965 interview with Cage by Lars Gunnar Bodin and Bengt Emil Johnson, *Conversing with Cage*, 70.

105. From a 1970 interview with Nax Nyffeler, *Conversing with Cage*, 74. For a discussion of *Variations VII*, see Pritchett, *The Music of John Cage*, 153.

106. In a 1966 interview, Cage remarked, "We are living in a period when our nervous systems are being exteriorized by electronics, so that the whole glow [*sic*] is happening at once." Zwerin, "A Lethal Measurement," 163. On the inaudibilities and disappearances in transmission and reception of "media that have reached their levels of saturation," see Friedrich Kittler, "Observations on Public Reception," in *Radio Rethink*, ed. Daina Augaitis and Dan Lander (Banff, Canada: Walter Phillips Gallery, 1994), 75–85.

107. Cage, *A Year from Monday*, 34.

108. Kirby and Schechner, "An Interview with John Cage," 54.

109. R. Murray Schafer, *The Tuning of the World* (Philadelphia: University of Pennsylvania Press, 1977), 5 (emphasis in original).

110. *Conversing with Cage*, 106.

111. Ibid.

112. Ibid., 70.

113. Cage and Charles, *For the Birds*, 220–21. He states the same thing in "The Future of Music" (1974), in *Empty Words* (Middletown: Wesleyan University Press, 1979), 179. "Within each object, of course, a lively molecular process is in operation. But if we are to hear it, we must isolate the object in a special chamber."

114. Cage and Charles, *For the Birds*, 73–74. Also: "[Oskar Fischinger] spoke to me about what he called the spirit inherent in materials and he claimed that a sound made from wood had a different spirit than one made from glass. The next day I began writing music which was to be played on percussion instruments." Cage, "A Composer's Confessions," 9.

115. In 1948 Cage described a wider notion of percussion: "It is used in a loose sense to refer to sound inclusive of noise as opposed to musical or accepted tones." Cage, "A Composer's Confessions," Ibid.

116. Richard Huelsenbeck, "En Avant Dada: A History of Dadaism" (1920), in *The Dada Painters and Poets*, ed. Robert Motherwell (1951; New York: Hall, 1981), 26.

117. F. T. Marinetti and Pino Masnata, "La Radia" (1933), trans. Stephen Sartarelli, in *Wireless Imagination: Sound, Radio and the Avant-garde*, ed. Douglas Kahn and Gregory Whitehead (Cambridge: MIT Press, 1992), 265–68.

118. Dane Rudhyar wrote the following on Varèse's music: "Every tone . . . is a molecule of music, and as such can be dissociated into component

sonal atoms and electrons, which ultimately may be shown to be waves of the all-pervading *sonal energy* irradiating throughout the universe, like the recently discovered cosmic rays which Dr. Millikan calls interestingly enough 'the *birth-cries* of the simple elements: helium, oxygen, silicon, iron.'" Cited in Henry Miller, "With Edgar Varèse in the Gobi Desert," in *The Air-Conditioned Nightmare* (New York: New Directions, 1945), 170–71.

119. George Sand, *Les Sept cordes de la lyre* (1839; Paris: Flammarion, 1973), 111, cited in Joscelyn Godwin, *Music, Mysticism and Magic* (New York: Arkana, 1987), 229.

120. Cage and Charles, *For the Birds*, 221.

121. *Conversing with Cage*, 230.

122. John Cage, "The Future of Music" (1974), in *Empty Words*, 179.

Chapter 7

1. Stephen Handel, *Listening* (Cambridge: MIT Press, 1989), 64.

2. Aristotle, *De Caelo*, book 2.9, 290b, lines 16–32, as cited in Frederick Vinton Hunt, *Origins in Acoustics* (New Haven: Yale University Press, 1978), 12.

3. Ibid.

4. Virgil, *The Aeneid* (book 4, lines 174–88), trans. C. Day Lewis (Oxford: Oxford University Press, 1986), 96–97.

5. Ovid, *Metamorphoses* (xii, 42ff), trans. A. D. Melville (Oxford: Oxford University Press, 1986), 275–76.

6. Ibid. It continues:

Inside, no peace, no silence anywhere,
And yet no noise, but muted murmurings
Like waves one hears of some far-distant sea,
Or like a last late rumbling thunder-roll,
When Jupiter has made the rain-clouds crash.
Crowds throng its halls, a lightweight populace
That comes and goes, and rumours everywhere,
Thousands, false mixed with true, roam to and fro,
And words flit by and phrases all confused.
Some pour their tattle into idle ears,
Some pass on what they've gathered, and as each
Gossip adds something new the story grows.
Here is Credulity, here reckless Error,

Groundless Delight, Whispers of unknown source,
Sudden Sedition, overwhelming Fears.
All that goes on in heaven or sea or land
Rumour observes and scours the whole wide world.

7. Plutarch, *Moralia* (I, 421), trans. Frank Cole Babbit (London: Loeb Classical Library, 1927).

8. The "frozen sounds" scene is from François Rabelais, *Gargantua and Pantagruel* (1532), book 4, chaps. 55 and 56, trans. Burton Raffel (New York: Norton, 1990).

9. Ibid.

10. Michael B. Kline, *Rabelais and the Age of Printing*, tome 4 of *Études Rabelaisiennes* (Geneva: Librairie Droz, 1963), 154.

11. Rabelais alluded to Baldesar Castiglione's book in Book 3, so he was quite familiar with the version in *The Book of the Courtier*. See translation by George Bull (Baltimore: Penguin Books, 1967), 164–65. For Addison's version see, *The Tatler*, vol. 3, ed. Donald F. Bond (Oxford: Clarendon Press, 1987), 288–92, and for an account of precedents see appendix D. *Frozen Words*, in Richmond P. Bond, *The Tatler: The Making of a Literary Journal* (Cambridge: Harvard University Press, 1971), 227–28. Another affinity that could account for the roots of the tale in antiquity can be found in the mnemotechnics, or what Francis Yates calls the art of memory, from the time of Simonides, Cicero, and the *Ad Herennium* to the seventeenth century, in which everything from oratories to cosmologies were remembered by investing words in the images of objects and aspects architecturally deployed, which would then be "sounded" when the mnemonist took a mental walk through the space. It was as though the stasis of objects was but a form of freezing and the whole world a potential record of things more transient. That memory called for such impressive measures was itself inscribed in the word *mnemonic*, for Mnemon was the servant whom Achilles killed because he forgot to tell him not to kill any child of Apollo. Frances Yates, *The Art of Memory* (Chicago: University of Chicago, 1966).

12. On the twelfth-century incursion of air, see Kathi Meyer-Baer, *Music of the Spheres and the Dance of Death* (Princeton: Princeton University Press, 1970), 279–81.

13. Cited in Frederick Vinton Hunt, *Origins in Acoustics* (New Haven: Yale University Press, 1978), 23–24.

14. Vitruvius, book 5, chap. 3, *The Ten Books of Architecture*, trans. Morris Hicky Morgan (New York: Dover, 1960), 138–139.

15. On Chaucer's acoustic influences, see J. A. W. Bennett, *Chaucer's Book of Fame* (Oxford: Clarendon Press, 1968), 78–80.

16. Geoffrey Chaucer, "The House of Fame," in *The Complete Poetical Works of Geoffrey Chaucer*, trans. John Tatlock and Percy MacKaye (New York: Macmillan, 1938), 527.

17. Ibid., 531.

18. Ibid., 535.

19. Ibid., 538–39.

20. Ibid., 541.

21. Ibid., 539.

22. Ibid., 543.

23. Ibid., 544.

24. Ibid., 545.

25. Leonora Carrington, "The House of Fear," in *The House of Fear* (New York: Dutton, 1988), 27–32.

26. Charles Babbage, *The Ninth Bridgewater Treatise* (1837), (London: Cass, 1967), 108–10. For background on the *Treatise*, see chapter 10 in Anthony Hyman, *Charles Babbage: Pioneer of the Computer* (Princeton: Princeton University Press, 1982), 136–42.

27. Ibid., 111–12.

28. Ibid., 118–19.

29. Charles Dickens, "Speech given at the Birmingham and Midland Institute: Annual Inaugural Meeting" (27 September 1869), in *The Speeches of Charles Dickens*, ed. K. J. Fielding (London: Humanities Press, 1988), 399.

30. Florence McLandburgh, "The Automaton Ear," in *The Automaton Ear and Other Sketches* (Chicago: Jansen, McClurg, 1876), 18.

31. Ibid., 19. Of course, if one is looking for a few important words in Judeo-Christian culture, then there is a natural gravitation toward the Word or the voice of Jesus. Although Chaucer found in the House of Fame "Josephus, who told of Jewish history; and upon his lofty shoulders he bore up the fame of Jewry" (536), much more was expected from new technology, no matter how ancient. When the simplicity of the materials and mechanism of the phonograph was realized, there came the lament that it had not been invented in time to record the Sermon on the Mount.

32. Francis Jehl, *Menlo Park Reminiscences* (Dearborn, Mich.: Edison Institute, 1937), 181.

33. *The Diary and Sundry Observations of Thomas Alva Edison*, ed. Dagobert D. Runes (New York: Philosophical Library, 1948), 241.

34. Ibid.

35. Ibid., 221.

36. For background on Broca's discovery, see chapter 10, "A Manner of Not Speaking," in Francis Schiller, *Paul Broca* (Berkeley: University of California, 1979).

37. Edison, *The Diary and Sundry Observations*, 210.

38. Shaw Desmond, "Edison 'Spirit Finder' Seeks Great Secret: Electric Wizard Discusses Life Beyond," *San Francisco Chronicle*, 27 August 1922, sec. F, p. 5.

39. Edison, *The Diary and Sundry Observations*, 214.

40. Ibid., 226.

41. Ibid., 213.

42. Ibid., 221.

43. Ibid., 240.

44. Jehl, *Menlo Park Reminiscences*, 140.

45. Wyn Wachhorst, *Thomas Alva Edison: An American Myth* (Cambridge: MIT Press, 1981), 122.

46. Edison, *The Diary and Sundry Observations*, 239–40.

47. As one appeal went:

    Mothers, sisters, wives and sweethearts who have lost their beloved in the war, find their souls hungering for them. . . . You, it becomes known, are investigating the problem, the question whether personality persists after so-called "body-death." . . . People everywhere are anxiously awaiting word from you.

    A. D. Rothman, "Mr. Edison's 'Life Units': Hundred Trillion in Human Body May Scatter after Death—Machine to Register Them," *New York Times*, 23 January 1921, sec. 7, p. 1.

48. For my earlier discussion on death and phonography, see "Death in Light of the Phonograph: Raymond Roussel's *Locus Solus*," in *Wireless Imagination: Sound, Radio and the Avant-Garde*, ed. Douglas Kahn and Gregory Whitehead (Cambridge: MIT Press, 1992), 69–103.

49. Edison, *The Diary and Sundry Observations*, 240–41.

50. Ferruccio Busoni, "A Fairy-Like Invention," in *The Essence of Music and Other Papers*, trans. Rosamond Ley (London: Salisbury Square, 1957), 190–93.

51. Ibid., 190–91.

52. Ibid., 192.

53. Ibid., 193.

54. Konstantin Raudive, *Breakthrough: An Amazing Experiment in Electronic Communication with the Dead*, trans. Nadia Fowler (New York: Taplinger, 1971), 23. See also Peter Bander, *Voices from the Tapes* (New York: Drake, 1973).

55. Raudive, ibid., 22.

56. Ibid.

57. William Burroughs, "It Belongs to the Cucumbers," in *The Adding Machine* (New York: Seaver Books, 1986), 59.

58. Ibid., 59–60.

59. Ibid., 60. This relates to his notion of the way that "the future leaks out" in his cut-up texts. See *The Job: Interviews with William S. Burroughs*, ed. Daniel Odier (New York: Penguin Books, 1989), 28.

60. Cited in Stuart Hood, "Brecht on Radio," *Screen* vol. 20, nos. 3–4 (Winter 1979–1980): 18.

61. Wiktor Woroszylski, *The Life of Mayakovsky*, trans. Boleslaw Taborski. (New York: Orion Press, 1970), 380.

62. Tristan Tzara, "Seeds and Bran" (1935), in *Approximate Man and Other Writings*, trans. Mary Ann Caws (Detroit: Wayne State University, 1973), 215.

63. Tristan Tzara, "Maturity," trans. Michael Benedikt, in *The Poetry of Surrealism: An Anthology*, ed. Michael Benedikt (Boston: Little, Brown, 1974), 102–3.

64. Luigi Russolo, "The Noises of War," in *The Art of Noises* (1916), trans. Barclay Brown (New York: Pendragon Books, 1986), 50.

65. Jonathan Cott, *Stockhausen, Conversations with the Composer* (New York: Simon and Schuster, 1973), 80–81.

66. J. G. Ballard, "The Sound Sweep," in *The Voice of Time and Other Stories* (New York: Berkley, 1962), 38–71.

Chapter 8

1. Some of the issues addressed in this chapter were introduced in my "The Latest: Fluxus and Music," in *In the Spirit of Fluxus*, ed. Elizabeth Armstrong and Joan Rothfuss (Minneapolis: Walker Art Center, 1993), 101–20.

2. James Tenney, interview with the author, March 21, 1991.

3. Stan Brakhage, "Letter to P. Adams Sitney" (11 March 1962), in *Film Culture Reader*, ed. P. Adams Sitney (New York: Praeger, 1970), 242–43.

4. Tenney, interview with author.

5. George Brecht, *Notebooks I* (Cologne: Verlag der Buchhandlung Walther König, 1991), 3, 17, entries for the 24 June 1958 and 3 June 1958 sessions of Cage's experimental composition class at the New School for Social Research.

6. Dick Higgins, interview by the author (February 1994), Columbus, Ohio.

7. Ibid. Higgins continued: "I had a staggered head stereophonic tape machine—not a very good one, but for that kind of thing it didn't really matter—so my piece was in stereo. Because the sounds would actually split and cause very coarse sounds as well as rather readily pitched ones—it sounded like square waves, actually—I was able to make quite a variety of sounds and quite a variety of patterns. And because there were only two sounds at a time, plus whatever interference sounds were made as an aggregate, I was able to have simple enough patterns so you would have a sense of the movement of the speakers and the microphone passages too." Hugh Davies puts the duration as twenty minutes. Hugh Davies, *International Electronic Music Catalog* (Cambridge: MIT Press, 1968), 215. In a number of works Cage would later call for amplified sounds produced without feedback, while he called for the simple production of feedback in *Solo for Voice 41 and 42* from *Song Books* (1970).

8. John Perreault, *Village Voice* (22 February 1968), describing Young's performance of *Map*, cited in Edward Strickland, *Minimalism: Origins* (Bloomington: Indiana University Press, 1993), 160.

9. Henry Flynt, "La Monte Young in New York, 1960–62," in *Sound and Light: La Monte Young and Marian Zazeela*, ed. William Duckworth and Richard Fleming (Lewisburg: Bucknell University Press, 1996), 51.

10. La Monte Young, "Lecture 1960," *Tulane Drama Review* 10, no. 2 (Winter 1965): 75, reprinted in *Happenings and Other Acts*, ed. Mariellen R. Sandford (London: Routledge, 1995), 79.

11. Ibid.

12. Tony Conrad, liner notes to *Four Violins* (1964), audio compact disc (Table of the Elements, #17 [chlorine], 1996), n.p.

13. John Cage, Interview with Roger Reynolds, *John Cage* (New York: Henmar Press, 1962), 59.

14. Conrad, *Four Violins*.

15. Ibid.

16. Ibid.

17. Tony Conrad, "Inside The Dream Syndicate," *Film Culture*, no. 41 (Summer 1966): 5–8.

18. Conrad, *Four Violins.*

19. James Tenney would later argue for the harmonic provocations of Cage in his "John Cage and the Theory of Harmony," *The Music of James Tenney*, special issue, *Soundings 13* (1984): 55–83.

20. Cage, Interview with Roger Reynolds.

21. Flynt, "La Monte Young in New York, 1960–62," 52.

22. These features were elaborated on in "drone" and intricately pitched harmonic pieces where phasing and beating patterns compounded and diversified the intrinsic complexity. Young's repetition piece also demonstrated that true repetition was itself impossible: factors of performing the task, of the physics of the instrument, the acoustics of the setting, the vicissitudes of listening, and the resonant complexity of the chosen sound in the environment forbid it.

23. John Cage, "Indeterminacy" (1958–1959), in *Silence* (Middletown: Wesleyan University Press, 1961), 262.

24. John Gruen, *The New Bohemia* (New York: Shorecrest, 1966), 123–24.

25. Interview with La Monte Young, *Flash Art* vol. 25, no. 167 (November–December 1992): 54.

26. John Cage, "The Future of Music," in *Empty Words: Writings '73–'78* (Middletown: Wesleyan University Press, 1979), 177.

27. Cage, *Conversing with Cage*, 231. Helen Keller gauged audience response with her toes and the deaf dance in discos.

28. John Cage, "Afterword," in *A Year from Monday* (Middletown: Wesleyan University Press, 1967), 165.

29. Jean-Jacques Nattiez, *Music and Discourse: Toward a Semiology of Music*, trans. Carolyn Abbate (Princeton, N.J.: Princeton University Press, 1990), 43.

30. La Monte Young, "Lecture 1960," 75.

31. Ibid., 76.

32. Ibid., 74.

33. Yoko Ono, *Grapefruit* (New York: Simon and Schuster, 1970), unpaginated.

34. Daisetiz T. Suzuki, *Living by Zen* (Tokyo: Sanseido, 1949), 183. Some of her other word scores have similarity to specific Zen writings.

35. Ono, *Grapefruit.*

36. Yoko Ono, "To the Wesleyan People," in *Yoko Ono: to see the skies*, ed. Jon Hendricks (Milan: Mazzotta, 1990), 13.

Part IV

1. Michael Kirby and Richard Schechner, "An Interview with John Cage," *Tulane Drama Review* 10, no. 2 (Winter 1965): 60, reprinted in *Happenings and Other Acts*, ed. Mariellen R. Sandford (London: Routledge, 1995), same pagination throughout.
2. Ibid., 61.
3. Ibid., 60.
4. William Benson Fetterman, "John Cage's Theatre Pieces: Notations and Performances" (Ph.D. dissertation, New York University, 1992), 95.

Chapter 9

1. Written on an invitation to Slonimsky, cited in David Revill, *Roaring Silence* (New York: Arcade, 1992), 160.
2. Kirby and Schechner, 51. Perhaps Cage was following Kierkegaard's entrancement in fluids as a way to escape boredom: "The first words in my diary, *How to Improve the World*. It says, 'Continue; I'll discover where you sweat (Kierkegaard).' Do you remember that remark? What it refers to is the fact that Kierkegaard was listening to an incessant talker who was very boring. Kierkegaard noticed that perspiration was running down the nose of this boring person, and he became interested. So do whatever you like: I will find in what you do, the circumstance that is liberating. Even if I'm the only one who notices it." John Cage in conversation with Peter Gena, "After Antiquity," in *A John Cage Reader*, ed. Peter Gena and Jonathan Brent (New York: Peters, 1982), 179–80. Regarding the existence of the subterranean pool sitting among the brass section, I am reminded of the remarkable trombone playing of Stuart Dempster, who taps this source to great effect.
3. "Open Letter to the Workers" (1918), cited in Anatolii Strigalev, "The Art of the Constructivists: From Exhibition to Exhibition, 1914–1932," *Art into Life: Russian Constructivism, 1914–1932* (New York: Rizzoli, 1990), 27.
4. I have in mind works by Alvin Lucier, Ellen Fullman, Paul Panhuysen, and a number of people who, like Thoreau, have taken to the aeolian stylings of telegraphic and other long lines. Mayakovsky's long-stringed instrument could itself be thought of as a euphemism for the transatlantic cable.
5. Cited in Carl Dalhaus, *The Idea of Absolute Music*, trans. Roger Lustig (Chicago: University of Chicago Press, 1989), 23–24.

6. For a few of these, see chapter 4, "An Epilogue on Romanticism," in John Neubauer, *The Emancipation of Music from Language* (New Haven: Yale University Press, 1986), 193–210.

7. Luigi Russolo, "The Noises of Nature and Life," in *The Art of Noises* (1916), trans. Barclay Brown (New York: Pendragon Press, 1986), 42.

8. Franceso Cangiullo, *Le serate futuriste* (Napoli: Edizioni Tirrena, 1930), cited in Raffaele Carrieri, *Futurism* (Milano: Edizioni del Milione, 1963), 143.

9. *Pall Mall Gazette* (London), 18 November 1913, cited by Brown in his introduction to Russolo, "The Noises of Nature and Life," 35.

10. Rodney Johns Payton, "The Futurist Musicians: Francesco Balilla Pratella and Luigi Russolo" (Ph.D. diss., University of Chicago, 1974), 71. This type of comment belongs to a rich tradition of insult in music. See Nicolas Slonimsky, *Lexicon of Musical Invective* (Seattle: University of Washington, 1965). For instance, Bartok's Fourth String Quartet was described once as "the singular alarmed noise of poultry being worried to death by a Scotch terrier." Slonimsky engages in some of his own after describing a fight that broke out after in Milan after a performance of Russolo's *Network of Noises* and noting that for all the excitement, futurist music came ultimately to naught. He says, "The Italian Futurists seem to have a brilliant future behind them" (19). A London paper in 1914 had a similarly styled comment: "The audience seemed to be of the opinion that Futurist music had better be kept for the future. At all events they show an earnest desire not to have a present." William C. Wees, *Vorticism and the English Avant-Garde* (Toronto: University of Toronto Press, 1972), 106.

11. Luigi Russolo, "Psofarmoni: New Musical Instruments," *The Little Review* 11, no. 2 (Winter 1926): 51–52.

12. Satie's use of the boutelliphone in *Parade* occurred not only within a context of the well-known contraptual sources but also with "squishy puddles" (*flaques sonores*), produced by sponge-tipped sticks on cymbals. See Alan M. Gillmor, *Erik Satie* (New York: Norton, 1988), 200. Also within *Parade* was a huge programmatic wave that washed over the crippled Titanic. See Robert Orledge, *Satie the Composer* (Cambridge: Cambridge University Press, 1990), 128–31. In *Parade* Satie may have moved into actual water use; some accounts have a glass of water being splashed at the end of the Little American Girl's dance, but this may have been stage instructions and not musical ones. I am indebted to Christopher Schiff for this qualification. The boutelliphone was also used in Arthur Honegger's *Le Dit des jeux du monde* of the same year.

13. Satie's French "La section des gaz de batterie" comes from "section de batterie" (drum section) and "section des gaz de batterie" (section of poison gas artillery). This is primarily a reference to the huge percussion section called for in Stravinsky's *Sacre du printemps*, which had premiered 29 May 1913. It may also be a reference to the Italian Futurists' use of military imagery or Russolo's *Art of Noises* as is suggested by Ornella Volta (294). Erik Satie, "Musique sur l'eau" was first published in *La Revue Musicale S.I.M.*, vol. 10, 15 April 1914, under the pseudonym "L'Homme à la contrebasse." It is reprinted in Erik Satie, *Écrits, réunis, établis et présentés par Ornella Volta, nouvelle édition revue et augmenté* (Paris: Éditions Champ Libre, 1981), 140–41, (translation and notes by Christopher Schiff).

14. Henry Cowell, *Ostinato Pianissimo (For Percussion Band)* (1934), New Music Edition, 1953. "Other sorts of bowls may be substituted." Although not directed in the score, certain modifications of the pitch and other more complex embellishments can be produced by bringing the striking instrument, traditionally a bamboo stick with a cork or felt tip, into contact with the water. Similar instruments exist in Turkey and Central Asia, and in Japan the *Orugori* is still found in Buddhist temples and in *kabuki* music.

15. Henry Cowell, "Current Chronicle: New York," *Musical Quarterly* 38, no. 1 (January 1952): 124.

16. See the water heading in Gardner Read, *Thesaurus of Orchestral Devices* (New York: Pitman, 1953), and Rita Mead, *Henry Cowell's New Music, 1925–1936* (Ann Arbor: UMI Research Press, 1981), 335–39.

17. Lou Harrison, phone interview with author, May 1993. Cowell has described a percussion concert at Mills in 1939 of the music of Cage, Harrison, and William Russell where the instruments included a wash tub, various bowls, and a conch shell. Henry Cowell, "Drums along the Pacific," *Modern Music* (November-December 1940): 46–49.

18. "I think my very first step in music composition was the accompaniment for a water ballet. I used percussion instruments and when the people swam below the water they couldn't hear the instruments. So it occurred to me to put a gong in the water and then it could be heard either below the surface of the water or above. And it worked perfectly. And that's the beginning of the water gong. Of course, the people above heard one pitch and the people below heard a different one but that made no difference. What was important was the time." From Peter Greenaway, *4 American Composers: John Cage* (VHS tape) (New York: Mystic Fire Video, 1989). See also *Conversing with Cage*, ed. Richard Kostelanetz

(New York: Limelight Editions, 1988), 9, and John Cage, *Silence* (Middletown: Wesleyan University Press, 1961), 86.

19. *Conversing with Cage*, 60–61.

20. John Cage, "The Future of Music Credo" (1937), *Silence*, 3. "Wherever we are, what we hear is mostly noise. When we ignore it, it disturbs us. When we listen to it, we find it fascinating. The sound of a truck at fifty miles per hour. Static between the stations. Rain. We want to capture and control these sounds and use them not as sound effects but as musical instruments." As an indication of Cage's own cognizance of his inheritance of noise, he once took Cowell to task for attributing noise to Marinetti and not Russolo.

21. The properties, instruments, and instructions in *Water Music* relevant to water include the following:

    • three whistles: water warbler, duck whistle (plastic) and siren
    • a bowl of water
    • two receptacles for receiving and pouring water
    • duck whistle in bowl of water
    • duck whistle gradually into water
    • pour water from one receptacle to another and back again

22. Properties and instruments in *Water Walk* relevant to water include the following:

    1 Bath tub 3/4 filled with water
    1 Toy Fish (automative in water . . .) [fish vibrates strings of piano . . . then goes in bathtub]
    1 Pressure Cooker with hot water having removable cap or valve at center of lid
    1 Supply of Ice Cubes and means for containing them (Ice Bucket or Insulated Paper Bag)
    1 Ordinary Drinking Glass . . .
    1 Pitcher . . .
    1 Toy Rubber Duck which sounds when squeezed
    1 Garden Sprinkling Tin Can with handle and water
    1 Chinese Gong
    1 Bottle of Campari
    1 Soda Syphon
    etc.

23. Cited in Michael Nyman, *Experimental Music* (New York: Schirmer Books, 1974), 78.

24. Raymond Roussel, *Impressions of Africa*, trans. Lindy Foord and Rayner Heppenstall (New York: Riverrun Press, 1983), 271–72, see also 54–59 and chap. 16.

25. Ibid., 273.

26. For a detailed description of Le Caine's *Dripsody*, see Gayle Young, *The Sackbutt Blues: Hugh Le Caine, Pioneer in Electronic Music* (Ottawa: National Museum of Science and Technology, 1989), 89–91, 97. See also "Water," in Toru Takemitsu, *Confronting Silence: Selected Writings*, trans. Yoshiko Kakudo and Glenn Glasow (Berkeley: Fallen Leaf Press, 1995), 132–33. The language of the recording studio itself contained wet sound and dry sound, and mike fright was known as drying up because of the parched throat it caused.

27. Young, *The Sackbutt Blues*, 90.

28. Aldous Huxley, "Water Music" (1920), in *On the Margin* (London: Chatto and Windus, 1923), 39–44.

29. Kurt Schwitters, "Merz," in *The Dada Painters and Poets*, ed. Robert Motherwell (New York: Wittenborn, 1951), 62–63.

30. Plumbing sounds occur at the beginning of the auditive avant-garde with Russolo in his *Art of Noises* manifesto inviting readers to "wander through a great modern city with our ears more attentive than eyes . . . and distinguish the sounds of water, air, or gas in metal pipes" (Russolo, *The Art of Noises*, 23), while one of Marinetti's radio pieces, *The Construction of a Silence*, read, "Construct a floor with a rumbling of water in pipes (half-minute)." *Gazzetta del Popolo*, Turin (22 September 1933), 3.

31. Marcel Duchamp, *The Writings of Marcel Duchamp*, ed. Michel Sanouillet and Elmer Peterson. (New York: Oxford University Press, 1973), 50. The mixture of glycerine and water recalls the white worm's heavy water in Roussel's *Impressions of Africa*, whereas the addition of spangles to the mixture recalls the *aqua micans* in Roussel's *Locus Solus*.

32. In *Zyklus*, one of the best known pieces associated with Fluxus, water is poured from one container (often bottles) to the next as arrayed in a circle (as in the *cycle* of *zyklus*), until no water remains. It had another coarse precedent from the same period when on stage in the Picabia production of *Relâche* a fireman repeatedly pours water from one bucket to another and back again.

33. In Duchamp's own time, there was Benjamin Péret's urinal in "Death to the Pigs and the Field of Battle" (c. 1922–1923) at which one would stand once the national anthem began to play, but not necessarily in that order.

Dear Friend,

Believe me that I was sincerely afflicted when I learned of the loss you suffered: a steam-powered urinal is not easily replaced. Yours, which had, among other precious peculiarities, the ability to sing the *Marseillaise* when in use, was certainly worthy of the esteem you bestowed upon it.

Benjamin Péret, *Death to the Pigs and Other Writings*, trans. Rachel Stella et al. (Lincoln: University of Nebraska Press, 1988), 103.

34. "Parmi nos articles de quincarillerie paresseuse, nous recommandons un robinet qui s'arrête de couler quand on ne l'écoute pas." Duchamp, *The Writings of Marcel Duchamp*, 106. The saying also appears in an etching of a urinal entitled "An Original Revolutionary Faucet: 'Mirrorical Return?'" Ibid.

35. Louis Aragon, *Le Paysan de Paris* (1926), trans. Frederick Brown as *Nightwalker* (Englewood Cliffs: Prentice-Hall, 1970), 16–17.

36. André Breton, "Soluble Fish" (1924), in *Manifestoes of Surrealism*, trans. Richard Seaver and Helen R. Lane (Ann Arbor: University of Michigan Press, 1974), 88.

37. Raymond Roussel, *Locus Solus*, trans. Rupert Copeland Cuningham (New York: Riverrun Press, 1983), 51–52.

38. Anaïs Nin, *The Diary of Anaïs Nin, 1947–1955*, vol. 5, cited in *The Drug User, Documents: 1840–1960*, ed. John Strausbaugh and Donald Blaise (New York: Blast Books, 1991), 142–43.

39. Ibid., 145.

40. Robert J. Belton, "Androgyny: Interview with Meret Oppenheim," *Dada/Surrealism*, no. 18 (1990): 72.

41. For instance, see Renée Riese Hubert, *Surrealism and the Book* (Berkeley: University of California, 1988), 76–78.

42. Sibyl Marcuse, *A Survey of Musical Instruments* (New York: Harper and Row, 1975), 111–14.

43. Charles Baudelaire wrote on how the entrancement of water might be compounded with another type of intoxication and thereby open oneself to a soul snatching by a water-sprite:

It is . . . to this essentially voluptuous and sensual stage that one must attribute the love for any clear water, whether running or still, that develops so astoundingly in the intoxicated brains of certain artists. Mirrors become a make-shift for such preoccupation, which resembles a sort of thirsting of the mind, and is conjoined with the throat-parching thirst I spoke of earlier; onrushing water, sportive plays of water, melodious cascades, the blue immensity of the sea—all are there, rilling, singing, sleeping with an inexpressible charm. Water displays itself as a true enchantress; and although I do not much believe in the uncontrollable crazes said to be caused by hashish, I would not take it on oath that contemplation of a limpid pool was totally without danger for a mind enamored of space and crystal clarity; nor would I swear that the old story of the Water-sprite could not become a tragic reality for some enraptured soul.

Artificial Paradise, trans. Ellen Fox (New York: Herder and Herder, 1971), 69–70.

44. Georges Bataille, "The Solar Anus," *Visions of Excess: Selected Writings, 1927–1939* (Minneapolis: University of Minnesota Press, 1985), 5–9.

45. Klaus Theweleit, *Male Fantasies*, Vol. 1, *Women, Floods, Bodies, History*, trans. Stephen Conway (Cambridge: Polity Press, 1987), 284. He continues:

The various forms of "devotion" to women have passed themselves off as philo-gynous, yet the attitude they adopt seems in essence to be a secular offshoot of the Catholic cult of the Virgin. It extends even as far as to Henry Miller, who, on the one hand, is one of its frankest critics, but, on the other, introduces dissat-isfaction into even the most liberated lovemaking by fixing men's hopes on the arrival of some woman in whose vagina the oceans of the world quite literally flow and by saddling women with corresponding expectations of performance. There is still more of transcendence in the "juices" he writes of than the real wetness of the women who have made love to him. (Ibid., 284–85)

According to Theweleit, even those male writers who had "little time for misogyny" nevertheless still "retained a certain ignorance of the reality of women, often in spite of numerous relationships with females. Since their notion of emancipation was predicated on the dissolution of wom-en's boundaries—depersonalization, that is—they lost sight of the in-equality that stamped their relations with women. Their desire for women did not arise in relation to actual women, but as a part of their search for a territory of desire. Hence, their desire remained oppressive." Ibid., 380–81.

46. Sanford Kwinter, "Soft Systems," in *Culture Lab*, ed. Brian Boigon (Princeton: Princeton Architectural Press, 1993), 207–28.

47. Louis Aragon, *Treatise on Style* (1928), trans. Alyson Waters (Lincoln: University of Nebraska, 1991), 104.

48. Antonin Artaud, "Draft of a Letter to the Director of the Alliance Fran-çaise" (1935), in *Selected Writings*, ed. Susan Sontag, trans. Helen Weaver (Berkeley: University of California, 1988), 348.

Chapter 10

1. Claes Oldenburg, "I am for an Art . . ." (1961), in *Art in Theory: 1900–1990*, ed. Charles Harrison and Paul Wood (Oxford: Blackwell, 1992), 727–30.
2. David Revill, *The Roaring Silence: John Cage* (New York: Arcade, 1992), 141.
3. Jackson Pollock, "Interview with William Wright," in *Art in Theory*, 583.
4. The performative qualities of these works arose in part from Cage's work with Merce Cunningham, particularly *Sixteen Dances* (1951), a key tran-sitional work in Cage's development of chance operations, within which a chart of a "fixed gamut of noises, tones, intervals, and aggregates" is established while "systematic moving upon this chart determined the succession of events." Program notes from the Edition Peters catalog, *John Cage* (New York: Henmar Press, 1962), 28. Also, as is discussed in chapter 12, it was at this time that Cage engaged the ideas of Antonin Artaud, the Black Mountain event being an outcome of this engagement.
5. Henry Cowell, "Current Chronicle: New York," *Musical Quarterly* 38, no. 1 (January 1952): 123–36.
6. Harold Rosenberg, "American Action Painters" (1952), in *Art in Theory: 1900–1990*, 581–84.
7. Ibid., 583.
8. Jackson Pollock, "My Painting," *Possibilities 1* (Winter 1947–1948): 78–83, cited in Claude Cernuschi, *Jackson Pollock: Meaning and Significance* (New York: HarperCollins, 1992), 105–7. For the context of Pollock's rhetorical use of sand painting, see W. Jackson Rushing, "Ritual and Myth: Native American Culture and Abstract Expressionism," in *The Spiritual in Art: Abstract Painting 1890–1985*, ed. Maurice Tuchman (New York: Abbeville Press, 1987), 273–95.
9. Pollock, "My Painting," 105–7.
10. John Cage, "Forerunners of Modern Music," in *Silence* (Middletown: Wesleyan University Press, 1961), 65.
11. Irving Sandler, *Abstract Expressionism: The Triumph of American Painting* (n.p.), (New York: Praeger, 1970), 213. Numerous attempts by myself and others to locate this text have failed.
12. Cage, "Forerunners of Modern Music," 65 (punctuation in original).

13. John Cage, "Interview with Irving Sandler" (1966), in *Conversing with Cage*, ed. Richard Kostelanetz (New York: Limelight Editions, 1988), 216.

14. Cage, "Forerunners of Modern Music," 65.

15. Ibid.

16. Ibid.

17. He had earlier championed the use of recorded sound in music and employed test-tone recordings on variable speed turntables in performance as glissandi generators in *Imaginary Landscape No. 1* (1939), but *Williams Mix* was his first entrance into the territory opened up by *musique concrète* in 1948. He later considered the recording of chance operations to be a contradiction in terms, an imposition of stasis onto variability, to be resolved through the operations of indeterminacy. Recording need not be technologically defined, since he criticized his 1951 composition *Music of Changes* on the same grounds. See James Pritchett, *The Music of John Cage* (Cambridge: Cambridge University Press, 1993), 109 and chapter 4, "Indeterminacy (1957–1961)."

18. Caroline A. Jones, "Finishing School: John Cage and the Abstract Expressionist Ego," *Critical Inquiry* 19 (Summer 1993): 628–65.

19. Gay aesthetics in music is not my topic here, nor am I capable at this point of addressing the issues involved. The matter is made more complicated because, unlike Burroughs and other Beats, Cage was not as forthcoming about his sexuality to a larger public, and music was less conducive than literature to dealing with sexuality. With respect to the former, the memory of his friend Henry Cowell being imprisoned would have introduced a cautionary mode. In my discussions with artists who were active in the 1950s and early 1960s, some matters have been emphasized: (1) there needs to be an understanding of how sexualities were negotiated within the different arts scenes in New York, (2) the differences between bohemia and the larger society need to be appreciated, and (3) caution should be taken when mapping back present-day understandings.

20. Jones, "Finishing School," 638. The individuals included happen to be amenable to a market-driven discourse within art history and journalism, the same one that historically excluded Fluxus, intermedia artists, and the international scene to which the activity in New York belonged. Kaprow would be included because of the predominance of visual artists in Happenings, versus the musical, performative, or literary base of Fluxus and other intermedia arts. Jones also explains in a footnote her exclusion of women: "That these are all male artists may follow from the particular

kind of space opened by Cage; the fact is also a function of the historical period (the 1960s), since women did not emerge with any force in the New York art world until the generalized climate of a feminist critique (in the 1970s) empowered them do so." Ibid., 638. In fact, women did emerge in the late 1950s and early 1960s and populated the 1960s with a force unique up to that time in the history of avant-garde and modernist arts (with the possible exception of the Russian and Soviet avant-gardes), with such artists as Alison Knowles, Carolee Schneemann, Yoko Ono, Mieko Shiomi, Charlotte Moorman, and many others. Many were strongly influenced by Cage, but with regard to our topic here, others were influenced by both Cage and Pollock.

21. Dick Higgins, "Something Else about Fluxus," *Art and Artists* 7, no. 7 (October 1972): 16–21.

22. Bruce Altshuler, "The Cage Class," in *FluxAttitudes*, ed. Cornelia Lauf and Susan Hapgood (Gent: Imschoot Uitgevers, 1991), 17–23.

23. Allan Kaprow, *Assemblage, Environments and Happenings* (New York: Abrams, 1966), 165. See also Allan Kaprow, "The Legacy of Jackson Pollock," in *Essays on the Blurring of Art and Life*, ed. Jeff Kelley (Berkeley: University of California Press, 1993), 4.

24. Jean-Jacques Lebel, "Interview with Saul Gottlieb," *Boss* (Spring 1967): 7.

25. Jackson Pollock interview with B. H. Friedman, cited in Cernuschi, *Jackson Pollock: Meaning and Significance*, 135.

26. William Shakespeare, *The Tempest* (London: Penguin Books, 1968), 78. These titles were suggested by Pollock's professionally literate neighbors, Ralph and Mary Mannheim. See Steven Naifeh and Gregory White Smith, *Jackson Pollock: An American Saga* (New York: Potter, 1989), 553.

27. An early instance of alcoholic immersion in the avant-garde is Alfred Jarry's "The Habits and Behaviour of the Drowned"; dry in wit alone, it is a natural history of dipsomania that might help explain the dripsomaniac. In *Atlas Anthology III*, ed. Alastair Brotchie and Malcolm Green (London: Atlas Press, 1985), 41–42.

28. Willem de Kooning, Interview with James T. Valliere, *Partisan Review* (Fall 1967): 114–15.

29. B. H. Friedman, *Jackson Pollock: Energy Made Visible* (New York: McGraw-Hill), 228.

30. Naifeh and Smith, *Jackson Pollock: An American Saga*, 756–57. See also Jeffrey Potter, *To a Violent Grave: An Oral Biography of Jackson Pollock*

(New York: Putnam, 1985), 185–86, and Friedman, *Jackson Pollock: Energy Made Visible*, 226.

31. "I have a definite feeling for the West: the vast horizontality of the land, for instance; here only the Atlantic Ocean gives you that." Jackson Pollock, "Answers to a Questionnaire," *Art in Theory: 1900–1990*, 560–61.

32. Kaprow, "The Legacy of Jackson Pollock," 5.

33. Ibid.

34. Allan Kaprow, "Impurity," in *Essays on the Blurring of Art and Life*, 38.

35. Kaprow, "The Legacy of Jackson Pollock," 6.

36. Richard Kostelanetz, "Interview with Allan Kaprow," in *The Theatre of Mixed Means* (New York: Dial Press, 1968), 104.

37. Ibid., 107–8.

38. Allan Kaprow, "In Response," a letter published in *Tulane Drama Review* 10, no. 4 (T32), reprinted in *Happenings and Other Acts*, ed. Mariellen R. Sandford (New York: Routledge, 1995), 219–20. This was true for numerous of artists working the line from action painting to performance, such as Georges Mathieu, Yves Klein, Viennese Actionism, the Gutai Group, and Nam June Paik with his action music.

39. Unpublished audiotape interview by Ellen Zweig with Kaprow, circa 1984, regarding his participation in Cage's New School class. Ms. Zweig was generous far beyond the call of duty in sharing with me her interviews with participants in the class.

40. Ibid. This is but one influence acting on spatial extension for Kaprow. Trained as an art historian in the postwar years, the idea of extension itself as a sign of historical development was supported by any number of other late-modernist representations, even if they led the other direction to reduction, as with Greenberg's historical trajectories. Having written a M.A. thesis on Mondrian, Kaprow could have had prior knowledge of the immersive environs of Mondrian's neoplasticist disco. In any case, his interest in Mondrian, "a painter who used painting to destroy painting," was not dissimilar to his interest in Pollock, although Kaprow thought that Mondrian was, like Duchamp, a philosophical artist whereas Pollock was, more like himself, an experiential artist. See Kostelanetz, "Interview with Allan Kaprow," 105.

41. Lebel, "Interview with Saul Gottlieb," 7.

42. Zweig, "Interview with Allan Kaprow," audiotape.

43. Allan Kaprow, "18 Happenings in 6 Parts/the script," in *Happenings*, ed. Michael Kirby (New York: Dutton, 1965), 53–66.

44. Kaprow, "The Legacy of Jackson Pollock," 7–9.

45. Allan Kaprow, *Echo-logy* (New York: D'Arc Press, 1975).

46. As with most Fluxus word scores great latitude was left for interpretation. In one a performer on a tall ladder poured water from a pitcher or pail down the bell of a french horn or tuba held by a second performer. *FLUXUS etc./Addenda 1: The Gilbert and Lila Silverman Collection*, ed. Jon Hendricks (New York: Ink &, 1983), 164. Fluxus events can also be performed simultaneously or in conjunction with other pieces. *Drip Music* could segue into Robert Watts *f/h Trace: Solo for French Horn*, where "The same performer with the horn in the previous piece empties his horn of the water (behind stage and fills it instead with small balls (ball bearings or plastic beads etc.). He then enters the stage and takes a deep bow, tipping the bell in such a way that all the small balls cascade our and roll out towards the audience." In turn, in other versions of *f/h Trace* a horn can be filled with mud or water and then the performer takes a bow.

47. Henry Martin, *An Introduction to George Brecht's Book of the Tumbler on Fire* (Milano: Multipha Edizioni, 1978), 83.

48. Ibid.

49. He continued to be a student of Duchamp's work, so we can assume a later familiarity with the chance music. He would later say that by the end of the 1950s he had breathed all of Duchamp's gas and water. George Brecht, "Notes on the Inevitable Relationship GB:MD (If There Is One)," in *Marcel Duchamp*, ed. Anne d'Harnoncourt and Kynaston Mc-Shine (New York: Museum of Modern Art, 1973), 185–86.

50. George Brecht, "Chance Imagery," in Martin, *An Introduction to George Brecht's Book of the Tumbler on Fire*, 148.

51. Ibid., 135.

52. Ibid., 135–36.

53. Ibid., 136. "His paintings seem much less manifestations of one of a group of techniques for releasing the unconscious . . . than they do of a single, integrated use of chance as a means of unlocking the deepest possible grasp of nature in its broadest sense." Ibid., 135.

54. "An Interview with George Brecht by Michael Nyman," in Martin, *An Introduction to George Brecht's Book of the Tumbler on Fire*, 106. Brecht's chance paintings relate better to the paintings Pollock did after the drip paintings, when he applied thinned paint onto raw canvas, a technique taken up in 1952 by Helen Frankenthaler, who said that "My paint was becoming thinner and more fluid and cried out to be soaked." Cited in Cernuschi, *Jackson Pollock: Meaning and Significance*, 278.

55. Brecht, "Chance Imagery," 148.

56. Brecht's notebooks, written while he was a student in John Cage's class at the New School for Social Research, are characterized by a shift beginning during the first months of 1959 into a mode of categorizing things of a more general nature. This occurs as a result of sitting in on classes by Eugene Gadol on Ernst Cassirer and Giorgio Tagliacozzo "on problems of unity of knowledge, general education, history of economics and science." It is in specific response to the second class that Brecht's self-categorization of the tripartite "Expression of Man's Needs" as "Zen, Science, and Art" occurs. George Brecht, *Notebooks* (3 vols.) ed. Dieter Daniels (Cologne: Verlag der Buchhandlung Walther König, 1991), 2:121.

57. Brecht, "Chance Imagery," 134–35.

58. Recording of Ivan Karp on *Andy Warhol: uh yes uh no,* audio compact disc 10072–8 (New York: Sooj Records, 1996). See also Michael Duncan, "Painterly Pop," *Art in America* (July 1993): 86–89, 117.

59. Dore Ashton, *The New York School* (Berkeley: University of California Press, 1992), 61.

60. Tristan Tzara, "Zurich Chronicle" (1915–1919), in *The Dada Painters and Poets,* ed. Robert Motherwell (New York: Wittenborn, 1951), 98, 236.

61. One event from 1962 appears in *Water Yam* and simply reads

- raining
- pissing

The other, entitled *THREE DANCES* (Spring 1961), reads

1.
Saliva

2.
Pause.
Urination.
Pause.

3.
Perspiration

Cited in Jon Hendricks, *Fluxus Codex* (New York: Abrams, 1988), 219. The best known Fluxus pissing piece is by Nam June Paik. He concurs with Tzara's antinationalism when he placed urination near the center of his musical aesthetic by citing *Fluxus Champion Contest* (1962) as an example of his PHYSICAL MUSIC: "Performers gather around a large tub or bucket on stage. All piss into the bucket. As each pisses, he sings his national anthem. When any contestant stops pissing, he stops singing. The last performer left singing is the champion." *FLuxus cc fiVe ThRee*, June 1964, reprinted in *In the Spirit of Fluxus*, ed., Elizabeth Armstrong and Joan Rothfuss (Minneapolis: Walker Art Center, 1993), 166. The first champion was "F. Trowbridge. U.S.A. 59.7 seconds." Larry Miller urinates on an egg in *Patina* (1968), and the brand name American Standard that is found on many toilet fixtures may have prompted the pomp and circumstance in Robert Watts's *Washroom* (1962), where "local national anthem or another appropriate tune is sung or played in the washroom under the supervision of a uniformed attendant." Yoko Ono lets the plumbing itself resound in her *Toilette Piece* (1971). Outside Fluxus, the best-known works involving pissing were by Warhol.

62. Martin, *An Introduction to George Brecht's Book of the Tumbler on Fire*, 95.

63. Brecht, "Chance Imagery," 137.

64. Kaprow, "The Legacy of Jackson Pollock," 7. Pollock's library included *Zen in the Art of Archery*; *Bhagavad Gita*; Lao-Tze, *The Way of Life*; Witler Byrner, *The Way of Life According to Lao-Tze*, and other books of Asian philosophy.

65. Daisetiz T. Suzuki, *Living by Zen* (Tokyo: Sanseido, 1949), 184. Suzuki says that the inverse functions of the senses "means transcending the world of sense and intellect, entering into the state of things prior to the differentiation of light and darkness, good and bad, God and his creation." The "naturally" in the poem, Daito's "Thirty-One Syllables," is to be understood in the deepest spiritual sense and not in any natural sense.

66. Ibid.

67. Suzuki's discussion of the *Kegon Sutra*. D. T. Suzuki, *Studies in Zen* (New York: Philosophical Library, 1955), 97, 100. Another version appears in *Zen Buddhism: Selected Writings of D. T. Suzuki*, ed. William Barrett (New York: Doubleday Anchor, 1956), 126; this is the Suzuki book cited by Brecht in "Chance-Imagery."

68. "An Interview with George Brecht by Michael Nyman," in Martin, *An Introduction to George Brecht's Book of the Tumbler on Fire*, 110–1.

69. Yu Wakao, "On the Suikinkutsu: A Traditional Japanese Sound Installation" (unpublished paper, n.d.). Recently, the artist Keiko Torigoe worked with an architect to build a small pavilion that contained a sui-

kinkutsu. The pavilion also happened to be in the noisiest urban setting imaginable, a place where the gentle dripping sounds of a suikinkutsu could never be heard. It was placed there as a gauge of the noise. Torigoe's art work employs a strategy of purposeful failure in a politics of perception. People could hear the piece only when noise-abatement policies had secured a sufficient degree of silence.

70. Martin, *An Introduction to George Brecht's Book of the Tumbler on Fire*, 82.
71. Hermann Helmholtz, *On the Sensations of Tone* (1877; New York: Dover, 1954), 10.
72. Brecht, *Notebooks* 1:4.
73. Ibid., 1:40 (15 July 1958).

percussive (17) Water ~~squirted~~ from ketchup bottle onto (~~pie plate?~~) foil. *dripped*

A list of eighteen different small sounds originally included the rather large sound produced by squirting water from a plastic ketchup dispenser onto a pie plate, which was replaced by dripping on foil (the sound was classified as "percussive"). The sounds were developed for use in *3 Lights*, a piece performed in the class.

74. *A Piece for Beaters (Notebooks*, 3:13–21); *Burette Music (Notebooks*, 3:25, 45).
75. The first version has a burette dripping water onto a ball of crumpled foil set in a drinking glass. The second version drips onto contraptions of propeller-like strips of paper and foil with a pie plate beneath. A drop would make a sound when it hit the foil but not the paper, and the entire contraption would rotate and jostle under the momentum of the water. In other words, as his ideas ensued, the dripping became more complicated: from the eye-droppers, to the crumpled foil, to the foil and paper contraptions. The complication was apparently meant to generate chance, much the same way as when he crumpled up the sheets in his earlier paintings. Also, Cage had scolded him early on for exerting too much control in a performance. Brecht had already broken down events into their simple/single and compound/multiple forms in *The Nature of Events* tables and had listed the compound version of water dripping in foil as "Multiple units as above." These multiple units would become *Burette Music* and, in fact, the "single/multiple" designations first appearing in these tables would make their way into the final instructions for *Drip Music* itself.
76. Brecht, *Notebooks*, 3:45. The piece would last until all the burettes were empty, although he had rates calculated to last anywhere between

between seven and twenty minutes. Chemistry, dripping, and music connections were made explicit in *Chemistry Music*, a 1969 slide lecture at the Drury Lane Arts Lab, London.

77. Interview with Michael Nyman, in Martin, *An Introduction to George Brecht's Book of the Tumbler on Fire*, 115. Although the process of simplification is key here, it is also not simple. On a backdrop of short forms within mass media and popular culture, including advertising and sight gags, there were those forms arising from Brecht's immediate interests, including simplicity in Eastern philosophies, the Occam's Razor with which any scientist is urged to shave away the unnecessary, and long-standing traditions of minimalism and zero-sum endgames within the arts (including *4'33"*). As a unrepentant generalist, Brecht kept a wide variety of technical means at his artistic disposal to achieve "maximum meaning with a minimal image . . . multiple implications through simple, even austere means." Martin, *An Introduction to George Brecht's Book of the Tumbler on Fire*, 126–27. This had a Zen equivalent in how "the waves of the four great oceans could be made to flow into one pore of the skin." *Zen Buddhism: Selected Writings of D. T. Suzuki*, 45. Brecht also reacted against the complications of continental philosophy he encountered during another class at the New School, after which he began his concise plans for pieces like *Burette Music* and for the first set of events that survived into *Water Yam*. A subsequent prospectus for a class Brecht was hoping to teach called "Experimental Performance of Music" (*Notebooks*, 3:137) included Huang Po, Chuang Tze, D. T. Suzuki, and Alan Watts but failed to list one European philosopher.

78. It has been observed that the sounds of Cage's music organize themselves by default in the ear of the listener despite the fact that they are not subject to organizing principles in any conventional sense and thus detract from the focus implicit in a *sound in itself*. Thus, simplicity may have appeared as the obvious remedy. However, the compositional means by which Cage used to distance himself from the material were themselves not simple.

79. See Kahn, "The Latest: Fluxus and Music," in *In The Spirit of Fluxus*.

80. Brecht, *Notebooks*, 3:135.

81. Martin, *An Introduction to George Brecht's Book of the Tumbler on Fire*, 91.

82. Cited in Jean-Yves Bosseur, *Sound and the Visual Arts* (Paris: Dis Voir, 1993), 105.

83. See Ubi Fluxus ibi motus 1990–1962, ed. Gino Di Maggio, exhibition catalogue (Milan: Nuove edizioni Gabriele Mazzotta, 1990), 89.

84. *Fluxus Etc.: The Gilbert and Lila Silverman Collection*, ed. Jon Hendricks (Bloomfield Hills, Mich.: Cranbrook Academy of Art Museum, 1981), 7.

85. "Fluxus Performance Workbook," ed. Ken Friedman, special issue of *El Djarida 9* (1990): 17.

86. Yoko Ono, *Grapefruit* (London: Sphere Books, 1971), np.

87. Another painting is called "PAINTING TO BE WATERED" (1962 summer), with the instruction: "Water every day." See announcement for the exhibition *this is not here*, held at the Everson Museum, Syracuse (October 1971), in which the following request was framed by the outline of a bottle: "yoko ono wishes to invite you to participate in a water event (one of the events taking place in the show) by requesting you to produce with her a water sculpture, by submitting a water container or idea of one which would form half of the sculpture. yoko will supply the half—water. the sculpture will be credited as water sculpture by yoko ono and yourself." *In the Spirit of Fluxus*, 180. That water was everywhere in Ono's work was summed up in her song "We're All Water" (1972), based on her *Water Talk* (1967) word score.

88. See also Mieko (Chieko) Shiomi and Robert Watts "Flux Record Player" and "Flux Record," the latter being a record to be played under water, cited in Jon Hendricks, *Fluxus Codex* (New York: Abrams, 1988), 479, 484. Other notable Fluxus works include Tomas Schmit's *Zyklus* (1962), which reads: "Water pails or bottles are placed around the perimeter of a circle. Only one is filled with water. Performer inside the circle picks the filled vessel and pours it into the one on the right, then picks the one on the right and pours it into the next one on the right, etc., till all the water is spilled or evaporated." See Al Hansen, *A Primer of Happenings & Time/Space Art* (New York: Something Else Press, 1965), 73. George Maciunas codified water works in his *Duet for Full Bottle and Wine Glass* (1962) "shaking/slow dripping/fast dripping/small stream/pouring/splashing/opening corked bottle/roll bottle/drop bottle/strike bottle with glass/break glass/gargle/drink/sipping/rinsing mouth/spitting."

89. Michael Kirby, *Happenings* (New York: Dutton, 1965), 172–83. Max Neuhaus, "Water Whistle," *Source: Music of the Avant-Garde* 6, no. 1 (1972): 48–51. A well-known avant-garde percussionist at the time, Neuhaus had been living on a boat for a year when he decided to compose for a submerged audience. The twelve-hour concert consisted of water running through hoses with police whistles attached at the ends, while the audience swam underwater, relaxed back with their legs hooked over the edge of the pool or floated on inflatable rings. He has since, of

course, become one of the major artists working with sound. Emmett Williams, *My Life in Flux—And Vice Versa* (London: Thames and Hudson, 1992), 325–31.

90. John Perreault, *Village Voice* (22 February 1968), describing Young's performance of *Map*, cited in Edward Strickland, *Minimalism: Origins* (Bloomington: Indiana University Press, 1993), 160. The aborted Columbia Records release of Young and Zazeela singing along with the Atlantic is cited in Strickland, 170–71.

91. Sally Banes, *Democracy's Body: Judson Dance Theater, 1962–1964* (Ann Arbor: UMI Research Press, 1983), 99.

92. Lockwood's interest in water began with wet percussion in *Glass Concert*. See Anna Lockwood, *"Glass Concert 2," Source: Music of the Avant-Garde* 3, no. 1 (January 1969): 3–10; recorded as *Glass World of Anna Lockwood* (Tangent Records, TGS 104). See also Anna Lockwood, *"A Sound Map of the Hudson River," Ear Magazine* 8, nos. 1–2 (1983), np, recorded by Lovely Music (LCD 2081). And correspondence with the author (2 April 1994).

Part V

1. Tristan Tzara, "Seven Dada Manifestoes," in *The Dada Painters and Poets*, ed. Robert Motherwell (New York: Hall, 1981), 87.

2. Roland Barthes, "The Grain of the Voice," in *Image, Music, Text*, trans. Stephen Heath (New York: Hill and Wang, 1977), 183.

3. Geneviève Calame-Griaule, "Voice and the Dogon World," in *Notebooks in Cultural Analysis*, ed. Norman Cantor and Nathalia King (Durham: Duke University Press, 1986), 15–60. With their reliance on millet, the Dogon celebrate a different grain of the voice than Barthes.

4. Robin Lydenberg, "Sound Identity Fading Out: William Burroughs' Tape Experiments," in *Wireless Imagination: Sound, Radio and the Avant-Garde*, ed. Douglas Kahn and Gregory Whitehead (Cambridge: MIT Press, 1992), 409–33.

Chapter 11

1. L. Ron Hubbard, *Dianetics* (New York: Hermitage House, 1950), 103. The "pure meat method" in the chapter title derives from the first line of Allen Ginsberg's poem "On Burroughs' Work" (1954): "The method must be purest meat." In *The Portable Beat Reader*, ed. Ann Charters (New York: Viking Penguin, 1992), 101. See also the line "Gimme . . . a plate of pure meat" in Ginsberg's 1955 poem "Naked Lunch," Allen Ginsberg,

Journals, Mid-Fifties: 1954–1958, ed. Gordon Ball (New York: Viking Press, 1995), 187.

2. William S. Burroughs, *Naked Lunch* (New York: Grove Press, 1959), 38.

3. Letter of 28 August 1957, *The Letters of William S. Burroughs: 1945–1959,* ed. Oliver Harris (New York: Viking Penguin, 1993), 364 (cited hereafter as *Letters*).

4. Donna Haraway, "The Biopolitics of Postmodern Bodies: Determinations of Self in Immune System Discourse," *Differences* 1, no. 1 (1988): 3–43 (12).

5. William S. Burroughs, *Nova Express* (New York: Grove Press, 1964), 48–49.

6. Ibid.

7. Quoted in Barry Miles, *Ginsberg: A Biography* (London: Penguin Books, 1990), 155.

8. William S. Burroughs, *Queer* (New York: Viking Penguin, 1985), 36. *Queer* was written circa 1952.

9. Burroughs cited in a 1980 conversation in Victor Bockris, *A Report from the Bunker with William Burroughs* (London: Vermillion, 1982), 60. See also *Naked Lunch,* 166: "There are queer bars where shameless citizens openly consort with their replicas."

10. Bockris, *A Report from the Bunker with William Burroughs,* 60. In certain instances he begins to feel female—"I feel myself turning into a Negress, the black colour silently invading my flesh" (*Naked Lunch,* 109)—or heterosexual—"I feel myself change into a Negress complete with all the female facilities. Convulsions of lust accompanied by physical impotence. Now I am a Negro fucking a Negress. My legs take on a well rounded Polynesian substance. Everything stirs with a peculiar furtive writing life like a Van Gogh painting. Complete bisexuality is attained. You are man or woman alternately or at will." 8 July 1953, *Letters,* 180. This occurred under the influence of yage, which brings on "a tremendous sexual charge, but *heterosex.* This was not in any way unpleasant." 18 June 1953, *Letters,* 171. It is no coincidence that yage brought on raciality and racial difference as well: "The blood and substance of many races, Negro, Polynesian, Mountain Mongol, Desert Nomad, Polyglot Near East, Indian, races as yet unconceived and unborn, passes through the body." *Naked Lunch,* 109–10. How Burroughs might have negotiated the vicissitudes of the status of homosexuality in organismic theories, especially as expressed by the homophobic Hubbard, is beyond the scope of this chapter.

11. *Queer*, 40. In the *Naked Lunch* version of this story, Bobo becomes the neurologist Professor Fingerbottom of Vienna. *Naked Lunch*, 165.

12. *Naked Lunch*, 16.

13. Ibid., 17.

14. Michel Leiris, "Mouth Water," *Brisées: Broken Branches* (San Francisco: North Point Press, 1989), 34–35. See also *Encyclopædia Acephalica*, ed. Georges Bataille, reprint editor Alastair Brotchie (London: Atlas Press, 1995), 79–80, which includes Marcel Griaule's entry on "Spittle-Soul."

15. Ibid.

16. Ibid. Leiris's *formlessness* relates to Bataille's notion of the *informe*, with its own attendant spit, "affirming that the universe resembles nothing and is only *formless* amounts to saying that the universe is something like a spider or spit." See "Formless" (1929), in *Visions of Excess: Selected Writings 1927–1939* (Minneapolis: University of Minnesota Press, 1985), 31.

17. Letter to Allen Ginsberg (22 April 1952), *Letters*, 119.

18. *Naked Lunch*, 17.

19. William S. Burroughs, "Ginsberg Notes," in *Interzone* (New York: Viking Penguin, 1989), 123.

20. *Naked Lunch*, 118–19.

21. Ibid., 134 (emphasis in original).

22. Alfred Korzybski, *Science and Sanity* (1933) (Lakeville, Conn.: Institute of General Semantics, 1958).

23. The Institute had been established in 1938 for the purposes of "neuro-linguistic, neuro-epistemologic, scientific research and education" and for training individuals "how to use our nervous systems most efficiently." Ibid., xxvi.

24. Letter to Allen Ginsberg (18 March 1949), *Letters*, 44. Burroughs's comment was occasioned by Ginsberg's being "leery of [Wilhelm] Reich for no other reason than the general disrespect with which he is regarded."

25. Letter to Allen Ginsberg (1 May 1950), *Letters*, 67.

26. Allen Ginsberg, "The New Consciousness" (1975), interview with Yves Le Pellec, *Composed on the Tongue* (San Francisco: Grey Fox Press, 1980), 82.

27. Korzybski, *Science and Sanity*, 114.

28. *Naked Lunch*, 131.

29. Ibid., 8.

30. Ibid., 9.

31. Ibid.

32. Letter to Allen Ginsberg (16 June 1954), *Letters*, 215.

33. *Naked Lunch*, 67.

34. Letter to Allen Ginsberg (27 February 1956), *Letters*, 312.
35. Letter to Allen Ginsberg (7 February 1955), *Letters*, 263. See also the nurse whose vocation invites her own death: "During his first severe infection the boiling thermometer flashed a quicksilver bullet into the nurse's brain and she fell dead with a mangled scream." *Naked Lunch*, 70. See also Doc Scranton's prolapsed asshole (*Naked Lunch*, 126), which acted with the same blind worm hunger as the Allerton schlupp scene in *Queer*.
36. *Naked Lunch*, 178.
37. Korzybski, *Science and Sanity*, 112.
38. *Naked Lunch*, 18.
39. *Naked Lunch*, 52.
40. Korzybski, *Science and Sanity*, 112.
41. "Surface energies and electrical charges become of fundamental importance, as by necessity all surfaces are made up of electrical charges." Ibid., 113. "Because the inter-cellular films probably play the role of electrodes and so the entire protoplasm structurally represents the 'immediate vicinity' of the electrodes." Ibid., 115.
42. Ibid., 508.
43. Letter to Allen Ginsberg (26 February 1956), *Letters*, 309.
44. Ibid., 309–10.
45. Korzybski, *Science and Sanity*, 116.
46. Letter to Jack Kerouac (24 June 1949), *Letters*, 51.
47. Letter to Allen Ginsberg (1 May 1950), *Letters*, 67.
48. Letter to Allen Ginsberg (19 October 1957), *Letters*, 372.
49. Letter to Allen Ginsberg (8 October 1957), *Letters*, 370 (emphasis in the original).
50. Wilhelm Reich, *The Cancer Biopathy* (1948), trans. Andrew White et al. (New York: Farrar, Straus and Giroux, 1973), 49.
51. Ibid., 6.
52. William S. Burroughs, "Word," in *Interzone*, 123 (repeated in the "The Atrophied Preface" of *Naked Lunch*).
53. Burroughs, "Word," 135–36.
54. *Nova Express*, 136.
55. Letter to Allen Ginsberg (16 September 1956), *Letters*, 326.
56. Letter to Allen Ginsberg (1 May 1950), *Letters*, 70 and note 11.
57. Letter to Allen Ginsberg (9 January 1955), *Letters*, 254.
58. Letter to Allen Ginsberg (15 June 1957), *Letters*, 359.
59. Letter to Jack Kerouac (4 December 1957), *Letters*, 379.
60. *Interzone*, 102–3.

61. Reich, *Cancer Biopathy*, 4.
62. Ibid., 5.
63. Ibid., 44–45.
64. Ibid., 46.
65. Ibid., 53.
66. *Naked Lunch*, 133.
67. *Naked Lunch*, 133–34. See also Letter to Allen Ginsberg (7 February 1955), *Letters*, 259. Per this cancerous "hideous random image," Burroughs elsewhere describes the dissolution of someone's ego in alcohol as "leaving a mass of irritable and random protoplasm." Letter to Allen Ginsberg (May 1951), *Letters*, 88.
68. *Naked Lunch*, 134. See also Letter to Allen Ginsberg (7 February 1955), *Letters*, 259.
69. 7 October 1959 mention of *Dianetics* in *Letters*, 429. This edition was L. Ron Hubbard, *Dianetics* (New York: Hermitage House, 1950); see *Letters*, 432. Korzybski was one of the very few sources of Hubbard's ideas to retain any acknowledgment within the book. See Hubbard, *Dianetics*, 91.
70. Hubbard, *Dianetics*, 4.
71. Bockris, *A Report from the Bunker*, 2.
72. Brion Gysin, interviewed by Terry Wilson, *Here to Go: Planet R-101* (San Francisco: Re/Search Publications, 1982), 121.
73. Letter to Allen Ginsberg (7 October 1959), *Letters*, 429.
74. Letter to Allen Ginsberg (27 October 1959), *Letters*, 431–32. In a postscript he explains: "Movement now called '*Scientology*'; used more for manipulation than therapy. Known to Russians since long time. Everybody—I mean on top level—now picking up. Southern California camouflage seemingly necessary."
75. "I feel that I have benefited greatly from Scientology processing. In an earlier article in Mayfair I said that Scientology can do more in ten hours than psychoanalysis can do in ten years. For what it is worth I still think so. Scientology is incomparably more precise and efficient than any method of psychotherapy now in use." William S. Burroughs, *Ali's Smile, Naked Scientology* (Bonn: Expanded Media Editions, 1991), 72. For Burroughs's statements on Hubbard and Scientology, see, first of all, *Ali's Smile, Naked Scientology*, then *The Job* (New York: Viking Penguin, 1974), 38–48, and *Electronic Revolution* (Bonn: Expanded Media Editions, 1982), 42–52.
76. Hubbard, *Dianetics*, 87.

77. Ibid.
78. Letter to Allen Ginsberg (27 October 1959), *Letters*, 431.
79. Richard Semon, *The Mneme* (London: George Allen & Unwin, 1921).
80. Ibid., 24.
81. Ibid., 92.
82. Ibid., 123.
83. Ibid., 125.
84. Ibid., 124.
85. Ibid., 125.
86. Hubbard, *Dianetics*, 188.
87. Ibid., 185.
88. William S. Burroughs, *The Ticket That Exploded* (New York: Grove Press, 1962), 49–50. The body at an angle intersecting this passage was a reference to one of the results of John Lilly's experiments with sensory transformation in isolation tanks begun in the late 1950s. Elsewhere in *The Ticket That Exploded* Burroughs wonders what would happen if you put a marine (the subjects for these experiments) and his girlfriend together in a tank, implying that their kinaesthetic bodies might meld or intersect. In effect, then, an angled phantom marine body has intersected with the body of the reactive mind, unaware no doubt of L. Ron Hubbard's own boating interests.
89. Letter to Allen Ginsberg (13 October 1956), *Letters*, 335.
90. Hubbard, *Dianetics*, 73.
91. Ibid., 185.
92. Ibid., 126.
93. Ibid., 124.
94. Ibid., 125.
95. Ibid., 124–25.
96. Ibid., 125.
97. What looks like premonition of *language as a virus* by Burroughs in 1955—"It's almost like automatic writing produced by a hostile, independent entity who is saying in effect, 'I will write what I please,'" Letter to Allen Ginsberg (7 February 1955), *Letters*, 262—could be understood as a melding of traditional muse, Surrealist automatism and Socratic dæmon, for it is too beneficial for Burroughs, too insufficiently pathogenic, to be Dianetic and viral.
98. *Naked Lunch*, 138.
99. William S. Burroughs, "The Retreat Diaires," in *The Burroughs File* (San Francisco: City Lights Books, 1984), 189.

100. Bockris, *A Report from the Bunker*, 2.

101. William S. Burroughs, "The Beginning Is Also the End," (1963), in *The Burroughs File*, 62.

Chapter 12

1. Carolee Schneemann, letter to Jean-Jacques Lebel responding to an invitation to create a happening for his Festival of Free Expression, reprinted in *Happenings and Other Acts*, ed. Mariellen R. Sandford (London: Routledge, 1995), 255.

2. Gary Snyder, *The Real Work: Interviews and Talks 1964–1979* (New York: New Directions, 1980, 124.

3. The term *politics* denotes for McClure a priority of sociality and thus the primacy of *homo sapiens* among all other living creatures. If biology were to replace politics, the conduct of human affairs would be first of all directed at the well-being of all species, and not just humans, and would be addressed practically against the present state of pollution, overpopulation, ransacking of natural resources, habitat destruction, species extinction, and so on.

4. Pierre Biner, *The Living Theater* (New York: Horizon Press, 1972); John Tytell, *The Living Theater: Art, Exile and Outrage* (New York: Grove Press, 1995). The anarchist polymath Paul Goodman, an important ingredient in The Living Theater, situated Artaud in America in this manner: "In his *Theater of Violence*, Antonin Artaud declares that theater is precisely not communicating ideas but acting on the community, and he praises the Balinese village dance that works on dancers and audience until they fall down in a trance. (For that matter, the shrieking and wailing that was the specialty of Greek tragedy would among us cause a breach of the peace. The nearest we come are adolescent jazz sessions that create a public nuisance.)" Paul Goodman, "Pornography, Art and Censorship," originally published in *Commentary* (March 1961), included in *Format and Anxiety: Paul Goodman Critiques the Media*, ed. Taylor Stoehr (Brooklyn: Autonomedia, 1995), 81.

5. Antonin Artaud, "Van Gogh, the Man Suicided by Society," trans. Bernard Frechtman, *The Tiger's Eye* 7 (March 1949): 93–115, excerpted in the appendix of Ann Eden Gibson, *Issues in Abstract Expressionism: The Artist-Run Periodicals* (Ann Arbor: UMI Research Press, 1990), 181–204.

6. Originally published in *Polyphonie 2* (1948): 65–72, cited in John Holzaepfel, "David Tudor and the Performance of American Experimental Music, 1950–1959," (Ph.D. diss., City University of New York, 1994),

31–32. My information on Tudor is indebted to Holzaepfel's research. On Boulez and Artaud, see Peter F. Stacey, *Boulez and the Modern Concept* (Aldershot, Eng.: Scolar Press, 1987), 22–25.

7. Antonin Artaud, *The Theater and Its Double*, trans. M. C. Richards (New York: Grove Press, 1958), 22.

8. David Tudor interviewed by Austin Clarkson (1982), cited in Holzaepfel, "David Tudor," 33.

9. Brown interviewed by Holzaepfel (1992), ibid., 45.

10. John Cage, "Letter from John Cage to Pierre Boulez" (22 May 1951), *The Boulez-Cage Correspondence*, ed. Jean-Jacques Nattiez (Cambridge: Cambridge University Press, 1993), 96 (my emphasis).

11. See Martin Duberman, *Black Mountain: An Exploration in Community* (New York: Anchor Press, 1973), 368–79.

12. Michael Kirby and Richard Schechner, "An Interview with John Cage," *Tulane Drama Review* (T30) 10, no. 2 (Winter 1965): 53, reprinted in *Happenings and Other Acts*, 53.

13. Interview with Emma Harris (1974), cited in John Cage, *Conversing with Cage*, ed. Richard Kostelanetz (New York: Limelight Editions, 1988), 104.

14. Kirby and Schechner, "An Interview with John Cage," 54.

15. *Origin: A Quarterly for the Creative*, no. 11 (Autumn 1953), included the following sections: "Preface: The Theater and Culture," "Staging and Metaphysics," "On the Balinese Theater," "Let's Have Done with Masterpieces," "The Theater of Cruelty (First Manifesto)," "The Theater of Cruelty (Second Manifesto)."

16. Allen Ginsberg, *Journals, Mid-Fifties: 1954–1958*, ed. Gordon Ball (New York: Viking Press, 1995), 96. Those wishing to understand *ignuschizoid perception* are referred to Ginsberg's poem *Ignu* in *Collected Poems, 1947–1985* (London: Penguin Books, 1995), 203–5.

17. Allan Kaprow, "The Legacy of Jackson Pollock" (1958), in *Essays on the Blurring of Art and Life*, ed. Jeff Kelley (Berkeley: University of California Press, 1993), 1–9.

18. Kaprow, "The Artist as a Man of the World" (1964), ibid., 48–49.

19. Michael Kirby, *Happenings* (New York: Dutton, 1965), 35; the introduction is reprinted in *Happenings and Other Acts*. Other American happeners with Artaudian connections include Claus Oldenburg, see Barbara Rose, *Claus Oldenburg* (New York: Museum of Modern Art, 1969), 27; and Al Hansen—"My goal . . . is to involve the ideas of all my favorite people—Artaud and John Cage and Ray Johnson—in a total theater

project in which things which weren't possible before will be done." Al Hansen, *A Primer of Happenings and Time/Space Art* (New York: Something Else Press, 1965), 109.

20. Cited in Daniel Barth, "NY Beats 2," *Beat Scene*, no. 21 (1995), 5–6.

21. "Didn't Ginsberg and I go through all that nonsense about Dostoievsky some fifteen years ago and then it was about three hundred years old. What do you want me to say? Moo? Goo? Or moo goo guy pan??" From Carl Solomon, "Age: 36," in *Mishaps, Perhaps* (San Francisco: City Lights Books, 1966), 8.

22. Solomon, "Artaud," ibid., 13–14.

23. Ibid., 37.

24. Solomon, "Another Day, Another Dollar . . . After the Beat Generation," ibid., 12.

25. Solomon, "Report from the Asylum: Afterthoughts of a Shock Patient," ibid., 42.

26. In his "Letter to Governor Rockefeller" (25 February 1962), Solomon wrote: "I am content that I am the American Mayakovsky and have been all but suicided by the society (read Van Gogh 'The Man Suicided by Society' by Antonin Artaud)." Ibid., 27.

27. Antonin Artaud, "Van Gogh, the Man Suicided by Society," in *Selected Writings*, ed. Susan Sontag, trans. Helen Weaver (Berkeley: University of California, 1976), 189.

28. Allen Ginsberg, "Model Texts: Inspirations Precursors to HOWL," app. 4 in Allen Ginsberg, *HOWL: Original Draft Facsimile, Transcript and Variant Versions, Fully Annotated by Author, with Contemporaneous Correspondence, Account of First Public Reading, Legal Skirmishes Precursor Texts and Bibliography*, ed. Barry Miles (New York: Viking Penguin, 1987), 175.

29. Ibid., 175. In 1968 Ginsberg placed Artaud's "physical breath" and cries in the context of Charles Olson's idea of putting the breath in the poetic line. Cf. Allen Ginsberg, *Composed on the Tongue* (San Francisco: Grey Fox Press, 1980), 40.

30. Ginsberg, *Journals*, 61–62.

31. Ginsberg, *Composed on the Tongue*, 76. Ginsberg could not have known of Aldous Huxley's "The Doors of Perception" in 1952, since it was written about an experience in 1953 and not published until 1954.

32. Interview with the author, Berkeley, California (5 April 1995). This should not be construed as a sudden lack of generosity toward *Howl* on McClure's part. He has repeatedly praised the poem and recognized its status as an emblem of a new era: "Ginsberg read on to the end of the

poem, which left us standing in *wonder*, or cheering and *wondering*, but knowing at the deepest level that a barrier had been broken" (my emphasis). Michael McClure, *Scratching the Beat Surface* (New York: Penguin Books, 1982), 15.

33. Ginsberg, *Journals*, 215.

34. Ibid., 195. The same day he had also written "Artaud expresses himself/ like a can of spy-being,/exploded" (195–96). On this point McClure concurs: "If you look at *To Have Done with the Judgment of God* today, it's exactly about the cold war, exactly about the state of Europe and America in those days." Michael McClure, *Lighting the Corners* (Albuquerque: University of New Mexico, 1993), 168.

35. Antonin Artaud, "Seven Short Poems," trans. Kenneth Rexroth, *The Black Mountain Review* 1, no. 2 (Summer 1954): 8–11, reprinted in *Artaud Anthology*, ed. Jack Hirschman (San Francisco: City Lights Books, 1965), 208–11.

36. Wernham's translation was eventually published in *Northwest Review* 6, no. 4 (Fall 1963): 45–72. The university editor responsible for publishing the translation was fired. See Michael Schumacher, *Dharma Lion: A Biography of Allen Ginsberg* (New York: St. Martin's Press, 1992), 412.

37. See interview with Michael McClure, *The San Francisco Poets*, ed. David Meltzer (New York: Ballantine Books, 1971), 252. "I met Sterling Bunnell in 1957 and before that I thought in terms of biology or natural history or physiology or morphology. Sterling introduced the concept of ecology to me."

38. McClure, *Scratching the Beat Surface*, 26.

39. Ibid., 24.

40. Ibid. McClure here refers to the first line of a poem published in *Origin: A Quarterly for the Creative*, no. 11 (Autumn 1953): 131, the same issue in which a large portion of Richard's translation of *The Theater and Its Double* appeared.

41. See Antonin Artaud, *To Have Done with the Judgment of God*, trans. Clayton Eshleman, in *Wireless Imagination: Sound, Radio and the Avant-Garde*, ed. Douglas Kahn and Gregory Whitehead (Cambridge: MIT Press, 1992), 327.

42. Ibid., 311.

43. Michael McClure, interview with the author (April 1996), San Francisco.

44. McClure, *Lighting the Corners*, 168.

45. Interview with author.

46. McClure, *Lighting the Corners*, 11.

47. McClure, *The San Francisco Poets*, 254.

48. "!THE FEAST!, for Ornette Coleman." was first performed at the Batman Gallery in San Francisco (22 December 1960), first published as a *Floating Bear* pamphlet (1961), and reprinted in Michael McClure, *The Mammals* (Berkeley: Cranium Press, 1972).

49. Interview with author.

50. "Cartoon light bulb: a truly American *visionary* mode! We can only imagine what accompanied Edison's idea for the light bulb." McClure, *The San Francisco Poets*, 251–52.

51. Interview with author.

52. Michael McClure, "Introduction" (1964), in *Ghost Tantras* (San Francisco: Four Seasons Foundation, 1969), n.p.

53. Ibid.

54. Interview with the author.

55. Interview with the author.

56. Interview with the author.

57. McClure, "A Mammal Gallery," *Scratching the Beat Surface*, 155–56.

58. Wilhelm Reich, *Character Analysis*, trans. Theodore P. Wolfe (London: Vision Press, 1950). Sir John Woodroffe, *The Serpent Power* (1918), being the Satcakra-nirupana and Paduka-Pancaka, with a lengthy introduction by Woodroffe (Madras: Ganesh, 1995).

59. Interview with author.

60. Reich, *Character Analysis*, 379.

61. Ibid., 362.

62. Ibid., 393.

63. Ibid., 393.

64. Ibid., 370.

65. "Since the body of the patient is held back and since the goal of orgone therapy is that of reestablishing the plasmatic currents in the pelvis, it is necessary to start the dissolution of the armor in the regions farthest away from the pelvic. Thus, the work begins with the facial expression." Ibid., 370.

66. Another variation on Reich equated a clear mind with a proper quota of orgasms. In Jack Kerouac's "Essentials of Spontaneous Prose," under the last section entitled "Mental State," he urges the writer to "write excitedly, swiftly, with writing-or-typing-cramps, in accordance (as from center to periphery) with laws of orgasm, Reich's 'beclouding of consciousness.' *Come* from within, out—to relaxed and said." Jack Kerouac, *Good Blonde and Others* (San Francisco: Grey Fox Press, 1993), 69–71.

67. Interview with the author.

68. Interview with the author.

69. On McClure's idea of chakras, and their relationship to peyote, see *Lighting the Corners*, 141:

> [Peyote] acts directly on the sense centers of eyes, ears, touch, etc. It works on the syndromes of physical interior self-perception in throat and stomach and other areas of physical energy that are not centered in specific organs (as known by Kundalini Yogis).

70. McClure, Introduction, *Ghost Tantras*, n.p.

71. To this day McClure finds it odd and inappropriate that his *Ghost Tantras* have been placed by some in the context of European sound poetry. Artaud's glossolalia has suffered the same fate.

72. Michael McClure, "Artaud: Peace Chief," in *Meat Science Essays* (San Francisco: City Lights Books, 1966), 94–95.

73. Elaine Scarry, *The Body in Pain* (New York: Oxford University Press, 1985), 51–52.

74. Peter Stastny, "Piercing the Page," in *Notebooks in Cultural Analysis*, vol. 3 (Durham: Duke University Press, 1986), 168–98.

75. Comte de Lautréamont, *Les Chants de Maldoror*, trans. Guy Wernham (New York: New Directions, 1965), 78.

76. Ibid., 13.

77. Ibid., 2, 15.

78. Gaston Bachelard, *Lautréamont* (1939), trans. Robert S. Dupree (Dallas: Dallas Institute, 1986), 64.

79. Ibid., 66.

80. Georges Bataille, "The Lugubrious Game," from *Documents* 7 (December 1929), in *Visions of Excess: Selected Writings, 1927–1939*, ed. Allan Stoekl (Minneapolis: University of Minnesota, 1985), 28.

81. Georges Bataille, "Mouth," from *Critical Dictionary and Related Texts*, originally appearing in *Documents, 1929–1930*, ed. Georges Bataille, as included in *Encyclopædia Acephalica*, ed. Alaister Brotchie (London: Atlas Press, 1995), 62–64. G. W. F. Hegel, *Aesthetics*, trans. T. M. Knox (Oxford: Clarendon Press, 1975), 728–37.

82. Bataille, "Mouth," 62–64.

83. Artaud, *Selected Writings*, 40.

84. Anaïs Nin, *The Journals of Anaïs Nin, 1931–1934* (London: Owen, 1970), 191–92.

85. Ibid., 192.
86. Artaud, "The Marx Brothers," in *The Theater and Its Double*, 144.
87. Artaud, "An Affective Athleticism," ibid., 134.
88. Ibid., 141.
89. Artaud, "The Theater of the Seraphim," in *Selected Writings*, 273.
90. Ibid.
91. The location according to Chinese acupuncture is also described in "An Affective Athleticism" from *The Theater and Its Double*, 139:

> The man who lifts weights lifts them with his back; it is by a contortion of his back that he supports the fortified strength of his arms; and curiously enough he claims that inversely, when any feminine feeling hollows him out—sobbing, despair, spasmodic panting, dread—he realizes his emptiness in the small of his back, at the very place where Chinese acupuncture relieves congestion of the kidney. For Chinese medicine proceeds only by concepts of empty and full. Convex and concave. Tense and relaxed. *Yin* and *Yang*. Masculine and feminine.

> In Tantrism the Sasi, which is the Moon and feminine, is on the left side of the Meru, or spinal column. See Woodroffe, *The Serpent Power*, 320–21; and Artaud, "Theater of the Seraphim," in *Selected Writings*, 273.

92. Artaud, "An Affective Athleticism," in *The Theater and Its Double*, 140.
93. Ibid.
94. Artaud, "No More Masterpieces," in *The Theater and Its Double*, 80.
95. Artaud, "Theater of the Seraphim," in *Selected Writings*, 273–74.
96. Artaud, "An Affective Athleticism," in *The Theater and Its Double*, 135.
97. Ibid., 134.
98. Antonin Artaud, "Les Treuils du sang," from *Suppôts et supplications*, in *Oeuvres complètes*, vol. 14, pt. 1 (Paris: Editions Gallimard, 1978), 38–41, translation by Christopher Schiff. All subsequent citations are taken from this text.
99. The image here is reminiscent of a passage in one of Anaïs Nin's letters to Artaud: "You who have used the language of nerves and the perception of the nerves, who have known what it is to lie down and feel that it is not a body which is laying down, flesh, blood, muscles, but a hammock suspended in space swarming with hallucinations, may find here an answer to the constellations your words create, and the fragmentation of your feelings, an interweaving, a parallelism, an accompaniment, an echo, an equal speed in vertigoes, a resonance." Nin, *The Journals of Anaïs Nin*, 188.

100. Artaud, "Les Treuils du sang."
101. Ibid.
102. Ibid.
103. Organologically, sound from a spine is reminiscent of the Tibetan human-thighbone flute (*rkang gling*), while Vladimir Mayakovsky's *back-bone flute* topped off with a versifying mouth would be insufficiently wretched. The *rkang gling* of the Gcod tradition of Tibetan Buddhism. See Rinjing Dorje and Ter Ellingson, "Explanation of the Secret *Gcod Da Ma Ru:* An Explanation of Musical Instrument Symbolism," *Asian Music* 10, no. 2 (1979): 63–91.
104. For a reproduction of this drawing, see *Antonin Artaud: Works on Paper,* edited by Margit Rowell (New York: The Museum of Modern Art, 1996), 129.
105. Artaud, "No More Masterpieces," in *The Theater and Its Double,* 81.
106. Artaud, Letter to George Soulié de Morant (19 February 1932), *Selected Writings,* 291.
107. Artaud, Two letters to George Soulié de Morant (17 February and 19 February 1932), ibid., 288–89, 293.
108. See "The Theater of the Seraphim," ibid., 273–74.
109. Solomon, "Report from the Asylum: Afterthoughts of a Shock Patient," in *Mishaps, Perhaps,* 37.

Index